Convergence and divergence in Ibero-Romance across contact situations and beyond

Beihefte zur Zeitschrift für romanische Philologie

Herausgegeben von
Éva Buchi, Claudia Polzin-Haumann, Elton Prifti
und Wolfgang Schweickard

Band 457

Convergence and divergence in Ibero-Romance across contact situations and beyond

Edited by
Miriam Bouzouita, Renata Enghels,
and Clara Vanderschueren

DE GRUYTER

Published with the support of the Institut für Romanistik of the Humboldt-Universität zu Berlin

ISBN 978-3-11-127373-0
e-ISBN (PDF) 978-3-11-073625-0
e-ISBN (EPUB) 978-3-11-073631-1
ISSN 0084-5396

Library of Congress Control Number: 2021938653

Bibliographic information published by the Deutsche Nationalbibliothek
The Deutsche Nationalbibliothek lists this publication in the Deutsche Nationalbibliografie;
detailed bibliographic data are available on the Internet at http://dnb.dnb.de.

© 2023 Walter de Gruyter GmbH, Berlin/Boston
This volume is text- and page-identical with the hardback published in 2021.
Typesetting: Integra Software Services Pvt. Ltd.
Printing and binding: CPI books GmbH, Leck

www.degruyter.com

Contents

Miriam Bouzouita and Renata Enghels
Convergence and divergence in Ibero-Romance across contact situations and beyond. An introduction —— 1

Part 1: Convergence and divergence in contact situations in the Iberian Peninsula

Bruno Camus Bergareche and Sara Gómez Seibane
Gender loss in accusative clitics in Basque Spanish. A contact-induced convergence phenomenon —— 25

Sara Gómez Seibane
Exploring historical linguistic convergence between Basque and Spanish —— 55

Kim Schulte
Structural convergence of two Ibero-Romance varieties. The case of colloquial Valencian as the outcome of contact between Catalan and Spanish —— 87

Xosé A. Álvarez-Pérez
Language contact on the Spanish-Portuguese border. A contribution from the linguistic landscape perspective —— 115

Xosé Luís Regueira
Portuguese as a contact language in Galicia. Convergence, divergence, ideology and identity —— 147

Part 2: Convergence and divergence across Ibero-Romance varieties outside Europe

Johanna Wolf
Linguistic perceptions on Spanglish discourse settings. Processes of divergence in constructing identity —— 179

Eugenia Mangialavori Rasia
Building locations from directional prepositions. Divergent uses of *estar hasta* in Spanish varieties —— 209

Pedro Gras and María Sol Sansiñena
Discourse structure, constructions and regional variation. Non-embedded indicative *que*-clauses in three regional varieties of Spanish —— 245

Susana Afonso
Impersonal *se* constructions in the Portuguese of East Timor. Notes on the relation between language contact and second language acquisition —— 281

Index —— 307

Miriam Bouzouita and Renata Enghels
Convergence and divergence in Ibero-Romance across contact situations and beyond
An introduction

1 Introduction

As is the case with any other natural language, the Ibero-Romance languages have entered in contact with diverse languages, through particular historical, geographical and political situations. The colonialist and commercial endeavours that were undertaken in previous centuries, for example, have contributed to the emergence of various language contact situations over different continents, which have left their marks on the Ibero-Romance languages at different moments in their histories, and at different linguistic levels. Consequently, these contact situations have been an inexhaustible source for the emergence of interesting language phenomena that have caught linguists' attention. The resulting diversification is apparent at the intercontinental, international, national, and local level. Therefore, the Ibero-Romance languages, specifically as languages in contact and contrast with other languages, can be studied from various perspectives and within different approaches. In particular, this book focuses on convergence, divergence and related phenomena (e.g. linguistic stability) observed (i) in different languages spoken in the Iberian Peninsula, and (ii) across different varieties of one particular language outside Europe. The latter needs to be understood in a broad sense, as we also include languages with non-official status, as seen in the contact of English with different Spanish varieties in the United States and its resultant Spanglish.[1]

It should be pointed out that in this volume the notions of "convergence" and "divergence" refer both to a process and a result, which can, but need not, be the outcome of a language or dialect contact situation. On the one hand,

---

[1] We are aware of the controversy surrounding the term "Spanglish", but we will use it here for the sake of convenience. For more details on the discussion surrounding the use of this term, we refer the reader to the chapter by Wolf (in this volume).

Miriam Bouzouita, Humboldt-Universität zu Berlin
Renata Enghels, Ghent University

https://doi.org/10.1515/9783110736250-001

according to the most common definition, convergence and divergence denote processes of change which generate increasing or decreasing similarities between languages in contact situations (cf. Clyne 2003; Kühl/Braunmüller 2014, 14, among others). On the other hand, these notions are used in certain contributions to refer to the degree of (dis)similarity between intra-lingual varieties. As such, they are the result of their internal and external diachronic development, thus including, but not restricted to, language contact (cf. Harnisch 2010; Wright 2012). Indeed, through various case studies it is shown that not only standard varieties of languages, but also (supra)regional varieties, can converge or diverge with respect to a particular feature. Additionally, it should not be forgotten that other outcomes, besides convergence and divergence, are possible due to language contact. In fact, it might be more straightforward to conceive the various resulting situations as either convergence or non-convergence cases, whereby the latter is an umbrella term for instances in which no convergence is observed and which include, among others, divergence, but also linguistic stability, both of which also receive attention in this volume (see the contributions by Regueira in this volume; Schulte in this volume; Wolf in this volume; see Kaufman 2010 for more details on other non-convergence cases).

This book aims to provide a better understanding of the concepts of convergence and non-convergence cases, such as divergence, from different theoretical perspectives and unites contributions from different fields, such as contact linguistics and variational linguistics, which tend to rarely interact. Firstly, it sheds light on the different types of consequences and mechanisms involved in language contact within the Ibero-Romance world, a geographical space characterised by a high rate of multilingual speakers and settings. Concretely, while most studies on language contact focus solely on phenomena of convergence between languages and varieties, as this has long been assumed to be the default outcome of contact situations, much less attention has been paid to divergence as a possible outcome of linguistic contact, a phenomenon that has even been characterised as a "rare element" (Kaufmann 2010, 481). Various contributions not only deal with convergence (e.g., morpho-syntactic convergence: Camus Bergareche/Gómez Seibane in this volume), but also with (i) linguistic (structural) stability despite contact (e.g., Schulte in this volume) and (ii) the combination of convergence and divergence in its various senses (e.g., Regueira in this volume; Gras/Sansiñena in this volume; Mangialavori in this volume; Afonso in this volume), as for instance in studies on different varieties of the same language, as well as (iii) less studied aspects, such as the relation between language contact and second language acquisition (e.g., Afonso in this volume), the linguistic landscape perspective of language contact (e.g., Álvarez-Pérez in this volume) and divergence in linguistic identity construction (e.g., Regueira in this volume; Wolf in this volume). Various theoretical aspects of convergence and divergence phenomena are also highlighted and explored in detail. Further, this volume covers (i) a wide range of phenomena from different linguistic levels, ranging from morphosyntactic (e.g., Camus Bergareche/Gómez Seibane in this volume; Schulte in this volume), to discourse-pragmatic features (Gras/Sansiñena in this volume), and includes linguistic perceptions and language attitude (e.g., Wolf in this volume), as well as (ii) a wide range of European and non-European contact languages (e.g., Basque, Catalan, Portuguese, English, Tetun Deli, etc.).

The first part of the volume contains a number of empirical case studies that highlight possible outcomes as a result of different contact situations within the Iberian Peninsula. This part zooms in on convergence and divergence between the various main Ibero-Romance languages, i.e. Spanish, Portuguese, and Catalan, as well as their non-Indo-European adstrate/substrate Basque. These papers point out that both convergence and divergence occur quite regularly in contact situations, as a direct or an indirect outcome. The second part of the volume mainly looks into phenomena of convergent and divergent variation between standard and non-standard language varieties of Spanish and Portuguese outside of the Iberian Peninsula.

2 Convergence and divergence in contact situations in the Iberian Peninsula

The first set of articles in this book, described in this section, deals with (non-)convergence and divergence as observed in language contact settings in the Iberian Peninsula. The first paper, which is written by **Camus Bergareche and Gómez Seibane**, deals with a classic theme within Hispanic Linguistics, namely *leísmo*, i.e. the use of a dative clitic, *le* or *les*, instead of an accusative one, such as *lo/los/la/las*, for the direct object function. The originality of this paper lies in the fact that it focuses on feminine *leísmo*, i.e. the use of a dative clitic for a direct object with a feminine referent, a phenomenon which has received considerably less attention in the literature, presumably due to its more restricted use in comparison to its masculine counterpart (cf. Fernández-Ordóñez 1994; 1999; see also Gómez Seibane in this volume). This contribution provides an empirically rich account for the contact-induced explanation of feminine *leísmo* in Basque Spanish, which draws on a variety of sources, such as oral databases, like the *Corpus Oral y Sonoro del Español Rural* ('Audible Corpus of Spoken Rural Spanish', COSER), linguistic atlases, and historical corpora.

After giving a synchronic overview of the various types of *leísmo* found in northern Peninsular Spanish, the authors briefly sketch the historical presence of *leísmo* in Basque Spanish texts, where they observe, to a greater or lesser extent, increasing frequencies of use from the 16th to the 19th century (for a detailed historical account of this phenomenon in Basque Spanish in 18th and 19th century bilinguals, see Gómez Seibane's contribution in this volume). The authors further provide a synchronic sociolinguistic, geographic and semantic-syntactic characterisation of feminine *leísmo*.

As concerns the sociolinguistic use of feminine *leísmo*, it is a linguistic feature that is observed nowadays in the speech of a whole range of socio-economic groups, such as rural, uneducated speakers, but also semi-urban, highly educated ones. Interestingly, as concerns the urban and semi-urban areas, it is not only restricted to bilingual individuals, but also appears in monolingual speakers' utterances. Notwithstanding this, as the latter group employs this phenomenon less, Camus Bergareche and Gómez Seibane conclude that there are diastratic differences. As such, a positive correlation seems to exist between the use of feminine *leísmo* and the knowledge an informant possesses about the Basque language.

As for its geographic distribution, feminine *leísmo* is attested in the three Basque Country provinces, namely inland Bizkaia, Gipuzkoa and the northern part of Araba, as well as in the northwest of Navarre. Strictly speaking, its diatopic spread extends thus beyond the political boundaries of the Basque Country, although it coincides with areas with a historical strong contact between Basque and Spanish.

Regarding the semantic-syntactic characterisation of this type of *leísmo*, it appears most frequently with human referents, both in the speech of monolingual and bilingual Basque Spanish speakers, in urban and rural areas. Its use with non-human animate referents, on the contrary, is not common and appears to be restricted to the speech of uneducated, rural informants, as is also the case for its appearance with inanimate referents. While the lexical aspect of the verb does not seem to be a governing factor, certain syntactic contexts, such as clitic doubling and left-dislocation constructions, favour the appearance of feminine *leísmo*.

It is further posited that gender markers are at the bottom of the pronominal hierarchy scale, which makes them more prone to (convergent) change, thus explaining their loss in intense contact situations with a language that does not exhibit them. This contact-induced convergence hypothesis is then corroborated by several arguments.

Firstly, as has been observed by others (e.g., Fernández Ulloa 2002, among others), Basque grammar, unlike Spanish, does not contain pronominal clitics, but expresses this information through verbal morphemes, which agree with the arguments in number and person, but not in gender. As such, the parameters used for Basque verbal-argument agreement are reminiscent of those for Basque Spanish *leísmo*, which displays the same selection criteria. Said differently, the grammar of Spanish in the Basque Country appears to have converged towards that of Basque by removing formal gender markers in its pronominal paradigm, resulting as such in the appearance of feminine *leísmo* in Basque Spanish.

Secondly, there exist other Spanish contact varieties which exhibit similar (but not identical) gender loss phenomena and thus indirectly validate the convergence hypothesis: for instance, Ecuadorian Highland Spanish, on the one hand, and, on the other, Peruvian Highland, Bolivian Highland and north western Argentinian Spanish, all diatopic varieties in contact with Quechua and, to a lesser extent, Aymara, display *leísmo* and *loísmo*, i.e. the use of the accusative clitic *lo* for both feminine and masculine referents, respectively. Similar examples are discussed for Spanish varieties in contact with Guaraní and Mayan languages.

Subsequently, Camus Bergareche and Gómez Seibane adopt and apply to Basque Spanish the analysis developed by Palacios (2005) for Latin American Spanish, according to which, due to convergence pressures, the grammar of Spanish adopted linguistic features from the languages it entered in contact with, –in this case Basque–, resulting in the (partial) elimination of gender as one of the selection parameters in the pronominal paradigm of Basque Spanish. In other words, convergence has led in Basque Spanish to the loss of gender marking for the direct object function given that Spanish dative clitics, unlike the accusative ones, do not distinguish between masculine and feminine referents. This contrasts with the etymological pronominal system inherited from Latin, which can be found in other diatopic varieties of Spanish and is governed by three parameters: to wit, case, gender and number. This contribution demonstrates thus that contact-induced convergence processes can affect different varieties of a language in a similar way by reorganizing the selection criteria of pronominal paradigms, albeit with differences in the resulting pronoun systems.

The following contribution by **Gómez Seibane** also deals with feminine *leísmo* in Basque Spanish as a convergence phenomenon, but zooms in on the historical development of this phenomenon in the speech of bilinguals from the 18th and 19th century, the latter being a pivotal period for the progressive spread of bilingualism through the entire Basque Country (and not just in the original border regions with Spanish). This chapter also explores two other morpho-syntactic phenomena which are found more extensively in Basque Spanish due to linguistic convergence: to wit, the use of a null object instead of an accusative third person clitic and of the object-verb (OV) pattern.

After first sketching how the Basque-Spanish bilingualism came about historically in the Basque Country, the author sets out the theoretical background against which the qualitative and quantitative studies presented in this paper are conducted. The framework adopted has been developed by Palacios (2007; 2013) and Matras (2009): language contact scenarios are here viewed as complex situations in which contact-induced changes rise from the communication needs of bilingual speakers, who have in their repertoire a continuum of uses which are associated with the type of social activity and are regulated by the speech community's prescriptive attitudes. An important distinction between direct and indirect contact-induced changes is made: while linguistic material is incorporated from one language to another in the former, two languages converge in the latter and thus become more similar in certain aspects without sharing the actual linguistic forms. In other words, convergence is viewed as the bilinguals' syncretisation of processing strategies used in both languages (Matras/Sakel 2007).

The corpora used for Gómez Seibane's studies encompass, on the one hand, 19th-century letters written in Basque Spanish by three bilingual, rural farm managers and, on the other, 18th and 19th-century letters from monolingual Spanish speakers, which serve as a control corpus. Contrastive analyses are then carried out for the three phenomena and yield the following results.

The omission of accusative clitics, the so-called use of null objects, appears to be pervasive in the bilingual corpus as 30% (175/582) of all contexts exhibit such null objects, while in the monolingual letters its use amounts to a mere 1.5% (8/529). Moreover, the syntactic and semantic conditions under which the accusative clitics can be omitted are also shown to differ considerably between the bilingual Basque-Spanish and monolingual speakers. To illustrate, more than 30% (53/175) of the null object cases found in Basque Spanish have a referent in a preceding clause, whereas this was not observed at all in the speech of monolingual speakers. Gómez Seibane goes on to conclude that the Animacy Hierarchy appears to govern the use of null objects in Basque Spanish, given that those with inanimate referents occur substantially more frequently than animate and human ones. Moreover, the omission of accusative clitics is considered a convergence phenomenon as the use of null objects is structurally similar to Basque's lack of a pronominal system and its morphological encoding of the direct object on the verb.

The next convergence phenomenon discussed from a historical perspective is feminine *leísmo*, whereby case and gender are neutralised for the unstressed third person clitic pronouns (see also Camus Bergareche/Gómez Seibane in this volume). The letter corpus from the bilingual Basque Spanish speakers from the 19th century exposes a clear preference for the use of dative clitics for male humans, while for female human referents the accusative counterparts are more commonly found. In contrast, it is the etymological pronoun system that predominates in the letters of monolinguals, for both male and female human referents. Additionally, *leísmo* is significantly common in the speech of bilinguals and this both for male and female referents.

The relationship between *leísmo* and the forms of address system is then examined in order to investigate more closely the so-called *leísmo de cortesía* 'politeness *leísmo*', which has received hardly any attention from a historical perspective. For this part of the study, the different clitic forms used for human direct objects have been cross-tabulated with the different types of referents, i.e. the third and the second deferential forms. The results of this analysis show, once again, a clear difference between the bilingual and monolingual speakers, considering that *leísmo de cortesía* is the predominant type found in the latter corpus, whereas in the former the *leísmo* with third person referents prevails.

The spread of *leísmo* to female referents in Basque Spanish is interpreted by Gómez Seibane as an indirect contact-induced change, more specifically convergence, due to the fact that gender is not a grammatically relevant feature in the Basque language, which tends to gender-mark nouns lexically.

The third phenomenon that is scrutinised is the OV word order in Basque Spanish, which is due to the unmarked SOV ordering found in Basque. As is expected under the contact-induced change hypothesis, the bilingual data reveal a higher frequency of use of preverbal direct objects than in the monolingual corpus. Moreover, these preposed objects also have other pragmatic functions in Basque Spanish than in monolingual Spanish: while they function primarily as discourse links and sometimes as focalisations containing new information in the former, they are always discourse links which mainly contain given information in the latter. In other words, there is also a difference in information-structural status of the referent.

In sum, null objects, female *leísmo*, and OV word order in Basque Spanish appear to be due to contact-induced changes which result in linguistic convergence.

While the first two chapters examine different convergence cases in Basque Spanish, the contribution by **Schulte** is centred on the Catalan-Spanish contact found in the Valencian Community. A variety of phonological, lexical, phraseological, pragmatic and morpho-syntactic phenomena are qualitatively examined in order to illustrate the different linguistic effects of the contact between Spanish and Valencian Catalan, including observed convergence processes.

Once the external history of the linguistic situation in the Valencian Community has been sketched, the author details the complex diglossic situation between the two closely related languages, Spanish and Valencian Catalan, that are spoken by a more or less bilingual population, whereby Spanish is an adstrate, at times the prestigious H-language, but in recent times also the less prestigious L-variety considering that linguistic attitudes appear to be changing.

As concerns phonological convergence, the Spanish influence on Valencian Catalan is felt both in the stressed and unstressed vowel system (cf. Regueira in this volume for Spanish's phonological influences on Galician). For the former, the original seven-vowel arrangement, which distinguishes /i, e, ɛ, a, o, ɔ, u/, reduced to five members as open /ɛ/ and /ɔ/ have merged with closed /e/ and /o/, modelling as such the Spanish vowel system. Conversely, Spanish appears to be inhibiting a change observed in other Catalan varieties, where the five unstressed vowels (/i, e, a, o, u/) reduced to three (/i, ə, u/), as this change is not observed in Valencian Catalan, possibly due to the presence of the same set of unstressed vowels in Spanish. In other words, convergence can result in contact-induced change but can also inhibit (or slow down) change (cf. Enrique-Arias 2012 for change-inhibiting contact phenomena in Spanish due to Majorcan Catalan). Other phonological mergers due to Spanish include the palatal lateral /ʎ/ with the palatal approximant /j/ in favour of the latter, as well as the loss of voicing opposition between /z, ʒ, dʒ/ and /s, ʃ, tʃ/.

Structural convergence can be observed in the use of the *have*-perfect in Valencian Catalan: while gender and number agreement between the direct object and the past participle was already lost in Old Spanish (Rodríguez Molina 2010), Catalan retained this agreement pattern, unlike the Valencian variety, however, which appears to converge towards the Spanish system, thus giving rise to a structural simplification.

In the pronominal clitic system, both convergence and divergence processes can be observed. Historically, the pronominal object clitic placement system in Old Spanish converged syntactically towards Old Catalan favouring a preverbal distribution with finite verbs instead of one which also allowed postverbal clitics (cf. Bouzouita 2008; 2016; Bouzouita/Sentí in press). Additionally, the current Valencian Catalan pronominal paradigm converged to the Spanish one, as no allomorphs exist distinguishing between pro- and enclitics, unlike in other Catalan varieties. Nonetheless, historical evidence points to the existence of pronominal allomorphy in earlier stages in Valencian Catalan. Further morphological convergence in Valencian Catalan can be observed in (i) the creation of the indirect object pronoun *lis*, mimicking Spanish *les*, whereby a plural marker is added to the singular form *li*, replacing as such the opaque indirect form *els*, which is also syncretic with the masculine plural direct object, and (ii) the appearance of *leísmo*, not documented for other Catalan varieties, but widely used in Peninsular Spanish.

Contrarily to the pronominal object clitics, the adverbial counterparts do not seem subject to a convergence-driven simplification: the use of *hi* and *en*, absent from Spanish, remains present in Valencian Catalan and appears to be a case of linguistic stability (cf. Breitbarth et al. 2019). Moreover, it could be claimed that they are undergoing a process of divergence, whereby once relatively uniform, linguistic elements become more dissimilar (cf. Kaufman 2010), considering that their use is expanding to underline semantic differences. To illustrate, the Valencian verb *vore-hi* 'to be able to see (i.e. not to be blind)' with a pronominal adverbial is now used to differentiate it from *vore* 'to see'. Schulte suggests that the use of the adverbial pronouns might in fact act as a marker of linguistic distinctness and identity.

Taking stock of the various described phenomena, Schulte concludes that contact between Spanish and Valencian Catalan appears to favour the reduction of paradigm opacity, if a more transparent or less complex model is available in the H-language, although it is known that contact can also foster complexity. The contact situation in the Valencian Community is said to present some of the hallmarks typically associated with koineisation, which can lead to the emergence of a variety in which differences are evened out in favour of the simpler variant and iconic features of one of the contributing varieties are maintained (Tuten 2003).

The contribution by **Álvarez-Pérez** aims to answer, among others, the question whether the notions of convergence and non-convergence can also be extended to include national identities, whereby the former refers to different linguistic systems becoming similar due to the transfer of material of one language to another, and the latter to the lack of such a transfer despite language contact (Kaufmann 2010). Indeed, the intense contact typical of the borderland may have implications at different linguistic levels and could in theory lead to linguistic and sociolinguistic identity assimilation or differentiation. In order to reply to this question, Álvarez-Pérez studies the contact between Spanish and Portuguese in different border-crossing areas: (i) Verín (Spain)-Chaves (Portugal), which form a so-called *Eurocity*, i.e. a cross-border entity for which the medium-sized towns have signed an agreement to share infrastructures and organize joint activities, (ii) the rural villages Feces de Abaixo (Spain)-Vila Verde da Raia (Portugal), and (iii) the cross-border conurbation Fuentes de Oñoro (Spain)-Vilar Formoso (Portugal). The borderland seems apposite as study object for the verification of (non-)convergence in national identities due to its intense contact and, consequently, the potential existence of a strong feeling of belonging to a supranational community, despite the co-presence of state identities.

The linguistic landscape framework is adopted for this study and, as such, the author focuses on the written testimonies accessible in public spaces, which are said to have a twofold function: through their informative function, they define the territory in which a language is used, and their symbolic function is related to the status of a language or variety in the corresponding community. The choice of the linguistic code for a sign can thus reveal explicit and implicit language policies, both at the private and the public level. In view of this, the use of the linguistic landscape methodology is justified as an innovative contact approach as it links linguistic and cultural relationships. For this research, the degree of presence, the position within the sociolinguistic hierarchy and the spheres of use of each foreign language are examined for each individual text.

Special attention has been paid not only to the selection of the geographical areas, but also to the types of texts included in the corpus: only static items written in one or more non-official language(s) of the country in which the text was located and which are visible from public areas have been included. A distinction between items produced by an official organisation (top-down) and those written by individuals or private entities (bottom-up) is also made. Through a quantitative and qualitative analysis of a corpus of 306 items, collected during fieldwork in 2015, and balanced between Portugal and Spain, the author is able to provide a detailed description of the non-official languages represented in the linguistic landscapes of the examined border towns.

The results of the corpus analysis confirm the high degree of complexity of the linguistic landscapes at the borderland. Moreover, the situation in Spain and Portugal differ greatly in view of the greater presence of Portuguese in Spain than vice versa. It is also interesting to observe that Portuguese texts are predominantly multilingual, whereas in Spain a similar proportion of monolingual Portuguese and multilingual texts is observed. Additionally, in Spain, multilingual texts exhibit less internal diversity and fewer language combinations. Linguistic errors of Portuguese in Spanish texts are also far more frequent than the other way around.

This study also reveals the heterogeneity of such linguistic landscapes, which necessitates the distinction between close vs. distant-border contact. In situations of distant contact, there exists a complete ignorance of the neighbour's language; and worse, some instances even point to the strategy of making the neighbour's language invisible. This is the case for the cities Verín and Chaves: instead of using the neighbour's language, Spanish and Portuguese are replaced mainly by English in these border towns. Consequently, no convergence between the Spanish and Portuguese national identities appears to be taking place in the linguistic landscapes of Verín and Chaves. On the contrary, one could state that we are dealing with a non-convergence case (cf. Kaufman 2010), which appears ironic given the existence of a *Eurocity* agreement between these border towns and they thus supposedly form a cross-border entity.

The linguistic landscapes observed in close-border communities, on the contrary, are very different as they do tend to include the neighbour's language, as illustrated by those in the villages Feces de Abaixo and Vila Verde da Raia, and the conurbation Fuentes de Oñoro-Vilar Formoso. As for the top-down texts, on the Spanish side, Portuguese was present in the majority of items, while, in Portugal, Spanish was less present, albeit more visible than in Chaves. Similarly, Portuguese was used in most bottom-up texts in Spain, whereas in around half of the Portuguese texts Spanish was included and constituted the main foreign language in the area. These linguistic landscapes clearly differ from the ones encountered in Verín and Chaves. The author concludes his paper by observing that the vindication of national identity (as opposed to celebrating the neighbour's identity) is most vital in more distant cities, where the neighbour's language is replaced by tourism's major languages (e.g., English), whereas smaller villages and conurbations tend to display a more open (socio)linguistic attitude.

In the final chapter of the first part, **Regueira** examines the role of Portuguese as a contact language of Galician. He first explores their historical relationship, the linguistic similarities across the political border, the divergence between the standard languages, and the importance of Portuguese in the standardisation of Galician. Subsequently, the author analyses three public discourses from two Galician nationalist politicians whose linguistic ideology is "Reintegrationist" and wish to align Galician with Portuguese. Interestingly, their speech not only presents grammatical and lexical features proceeding from Portuguese, but also Spanish phonic features. Building further on studies of identity construction in linguistic interaction (Eckert 2012) and the concept of indexicality (Silverstein 2003), this article aims to show that these features are resources used by speakers to build and strengthen identities at different levels (social, ideological and political, amongst others).

Although Portuguese, unlike Spanish, is not generally regarded as one of the contact languages of Galician, both are closely related and share in fact a common written ancestor in the Middle Ages –Galician-Portuguese. However, at the end of the medieval period, this unity got ruptured due to Portuguese's development as a standard language which centred on the southern variety of Lisbon, as such diverging from the northern dialects. Galician, on the contrary, was less fortunate as it vanished as a written language from the 16th until the 19th c. Galicia, which remained under the rule of the Kingdom of Castile, became politically separated from Portuguese and language substitution also took place. Consequently, the degree of contact with Spanish is very high, especially in urban settings. Notwithstanding the previous, Galician is used by the regional and local administration, is present in education, cultural and political life. Due to the intense contact, the Galician variety employed in public life exhibits Spanish features, especially phonic ones, which is causing a discrepancy between 'public' Galician and the variety spoken by of 'traditional' speakers, which differs in many aspects from Spanish and is often closer to Portuguese, especially phonetically. In addition, the spread of standard Galician in the 20th c. is also causing the centuries-old linguistic continuum between Galician and the northern Portuguese varieties to crumble rapidly.

Although, with the recovery of Galician as a written language, Portuguese played a prominent role in Galician culture, its role in the standardisation process of Galician is marginal until the 1970s. Since then, the Galician standard has started converging towards Portuguese, as can be observed in its morphology and lexicon. So-called "Reintegrationist" groups support further convergence with Portuguese's spelling and grammar.

As concerns the framework used, in this study speakers are regarded as dynamic beings who use linguistic codes that can be analysed as objective entities external to themselves, but who take part in linguistic practises "in which speakers place themselves in the social landscape through stylistic practice" (Eckert 2012, 93–94). Identity is thus understood as "the product rather than the source of linguistic and other semiotic practices and therefore is a social and cultural rather than primarily internal psychological phenomenon" (Bucholtz/Hall 2005, 585). Through linguistic interaction, indexicality can produce identities and can act at different levels (Silverstein 2003): in view of this, a form which indicates geographical or social origin, can index ideological values, such as loyalty to a social group, a social or linguistic ideology, etc. (Silverstein 2014, 183).

The analysis of the speeches of deputy Lobeira reveal that he always uses, apart from lexical Lusisms, forms closest to Portuguese, such as *até* 'until', *Galiza* 'Galicia', etc. The pronoun *vosté* (StGal *vostede*, Pt *você* 'you [formal]') proposed by Reintegrationists is also used, as well as lexical items that diverge from standard Galician and coincide with Portuguese, such as *eleitoral* (StGal *electoral*), *aceitación* (StGal *aceptación* 'acceptance'), *gostar* (*gustar* 'like'), etc. Interestingly, in a discourse referring to language, more marked forms are encountered, such as the future subjunctive and inflected infinitive, which are regarded by some as indexes of a 'quality' language, despite the limited use of these tenses in Galician.

Notwithstanding the Portuguese influences in Lobeira's speech, the forms proceeding from Spanish are equally present: there are (i) lexical Castilianisms, such as such as *asignatura* 'subject' (StGal *materia*, Pt *matéria*) and *tasas* 'fees' (StGal and Pt *taxas*); (ii) syntactic constructions with reflexive pronouns, as in *quedámonos cortos* 'we have fallen short' (StGal *quedamos curtos*), and above all (iii) different phonological and phonetic features, that are very close to Spanish, and distant from Galician and Portuguese, such as the presence of a five stressed vowels system, as in Spanish (cf. Schulte in this volume for phonological influences of Spanish on Valencian Catalan).

With respect to Rebeca Bravo's language, generally speaking, Galician morphology is maintained, while some Portuguese elements are also added, especially verbal inflections, such as *conduz* 's/he drives' (StGal *conduce*) and *há* 'there is' (StGal *hai*). The most visible nominal morpheme is the suffix *-çom*, *-som*, where StGal presents *-ción* and Pt *-ção*. Similarly to Lobeira, the inflected infinitive is used, albeit at times in contexts where it is ungrammatical both in Portuguese and Galician. Again, lexical Lusisms abound and even hybrids are encountered. This contrasts with the phonetics used, which is much closer to that of Spanish than to standard Galician, and thus even further from Portuguese.

Using interactional sociolinguistics, Regueira demonstrates how the use of Portuguese features allows different types of identities to be constructed, such as political ideology (nationalism) as well as linguistic ideology (Reintegrationism, purism). He further proposes that the typical features of the "Spanish accent" act as indexing features of urban social origin: considering that Galician Spanish presents many of the Galician phonetic features and that especially the working class has greater contact with Galician, the phonetic characteristics exhibited by these speakers is indicative of their social background. Consequently, the use of phonetic features from Spanish acts as a social identity marker (not rurality nor lower class), while the use of Portuguese features contributes to the creation of an ideological identity and also to the strengthening of social, urban and class identity.

3 Convergence and divergence across Ibero-Romance varieties outside Europe

The second part of the volume looks into phenomena of convergent and divergent variation between standard and non-standard language varieties of Spanish and Portuguese outside of the Iberian Peninsula.

As has already been stated in the introduction, language contact may lead to various possible outcomes: for instance, it can produce processes of linguistic convergence through which a language shifts towards a target language and associated culture, but it can also lead to non-convergence (cf. Kaufman 2010), one possible outcome of which is contact-induced divergence, whereby a hybrid variety is created different from both input languages. The paper by **Wolf** defines the language used by Spanish speaking immigrant communities in the U.S., also called "Spanglish", as an example of the latter. The study argues that linguistic routines used by Spanglish speakers fulfil an emblematic function and should be analysed as an instrument for expressing their distinctive identity, both with regard to the U.S. culture and language, and the heritage ones.

The article starts with a critical assessment of two definitions of the term Spanglish. On the one hand, the notion has been dismissed by scholars such as Otheguy and Lipski, who see it as a superfluous expression for describing a wide set of Spanish varieties found in Spanish-English contact situations in the U.S. On the other hand, Spanglish has been proposed as a highly appropriate concept when referring to the hybrid identity situation (including the linguistic dimension) of Hispanic speakers in the U.S. Wolf argues that the most critical viewpoint does not take into account the fact that the specific language use referred to by Spanglish connects to the construction of a new divergent transcultural identity. The author hypothesizes that Spanglish equals an intentional discursive strategy, highlighting the biculturalism of its speakers. In such a view, the notion acquires a positive connotation.

The study basically relies on the idea that discourse should be conceived of as the union of language and practice; language and epistemic structures are inextricably interwoven, and together forge a collective identity. Concretely, Spanglish is argued to be a cultural practice which creates a discursive formation that conveys the shared knowledge of the speakers concerning their particular identity.

The empirical study that is undertaken to demonstrate the validity of this hypothesis uses a discourse analytical methodology. It examines to what extent linguistic patterns of code-switching are employed as discourse strategies to express the hybrid Hispanic identity. Four elements of identity formation, as defined by Gardt (2007) are analysed: (i) intertextual interconnectedness, (ii) language as interaction, (iii) discourse as expression of social thought patterns, and (iv) discourse as a stimulus for social change. The corpus contains over 150 posts proceeding from carefully selected bilingual blogs, written by members of the 2nd and 3rd generation of Hispanics in the U.S. The main part of the qualitative analysis is devoted to a discussion of the socio-pragmatic functions of patterns of language alternation. Five categories are distinguished: (i) clarification, emphasis and elaboration, (ii) linguistic routines, (iii) lexical needs, (iv) footing (by repeating a statement in another language), and (v) free switches. A general quantitative approach of the data show that bilingual bloggers switch languages mostly for the sake of lexical needs or clarification needs. These results pattern quite well with general tendencies of codeswitching observed in oral data.

The author concludes that language alternation patterns can be considered as cases of conscious processes of divergence, and that the initial hypothesis, according to which Spanglish is an instrument to express the distinctive identity of its users, can be confirmed. Switches may relate to the writers' need to punctually express a common transcultural identity, divergent from the dominant one.

The paper by **Mangialavori** focuses on a set of particular uses of the *estar hasta* construction in Spanish varieties, and compares instances found in Standard Spanish with those of Mexican Spanish. It contributes to a better understanding of the syntax and semantics of spatial prepositions in Spanish by exploring converging and diverging uses across national varieties. Moreover, comparisons between regional varieties are argued to provide a better comprehension of major empirical generalisations that are said to apply cross-linguistically. More specifically, the paper argues that the *estar hasta* constructions are instances of a productive pattern combining stative (locative) verbs and directional prepositions.

In Standard Spanish, the locative construction with *estar* combines with the non-directional boundary preposition *a* 'to', the non-bounded locative *en* 'in', and the non-bounded directional preposition *hacia* 'towards' or *adelante* 'in front of'. Similar uses are also found in Mexican Spanish. This study, however, focuses on structures in which the copular verb *estar* 'be' is combined with a Prepositional Phrase headed by the dynamic directional boundary preposition *hasta* 'until'. Given the inherent semantics of this preposition, it generally combines with dynamic verbs and not with stative ones, especially not copulas. In Standard Spanish, *estar hasta* is restricted to more abstract, non-locative, uses as in *estar hasta el borde de problemas* 'to be saturated with problems'. The construction is productively used to express saturation applied to any state or condition; the boundedness meaning of *hasta* coincides with a maximal point on an incremental scale, including a psychological scale. The Mexican Spanish cases, in which *estar hasta* conveys a spatial locative meaning, as in *la casa está hasta la punta del pueblo* 'the house is at the end of the village', are not observed in Standard Spanish. Instead of analysing these diverging uses as instances of coercion (meaning that a lexical item would be 'forced into' a construction it normally does not select), Mangialavori argues in favour of the existence of a different construction in Mexican Spanish. The selection of *hasta* is defined as a legitimate grammatical device, which alternates with other prepositions in a motivated way.

From these empirical observations two research questions arise: (1) is there a more general constraint on the combination of copulas and directional prepositions that motivates the particular alternation observed in Mexican Spanish?, and (2) is this particular use related to some innovative use of either the copula verb or the preposition? The answers to these questions are provided by an analysis formulated in terms of the Vector Space Semantics framework. As such, the author adheres to an aspectual definition of locative prepositions, which is based on vectors modelling spatial properties in terms of relative positions and paths between located objects and reference objects.

The key to the first question is provided by two cross-linguistic conditions constraining the combination of copula and directional prepositions, namely (i) the Measure Phrase Condition (according to which directional prepositions may be used with copula if accompanied by measure phrases), and (ii) the End Point Condition (meaning that directional prepositions may be used in specific cases where the location is understood as the endpoint of a *hypothetical journey*). Central to the argument put forward is the idea that the Prepositional Phrase introduced by *hasta* constitutes a path boundary, compatible with an endpoint interpretation. Applied to both the attributive (also observed in Standard Spanish) and locative (exclusively observed in Mexican Spanish) contexts, *hasta* introduces either a quantitative or spatial terminus of the path. These terminus readings are also observed in other languages, such as English (e.g., *The house is one mile from here*; *The Post Office is through the hill from here*).

With regard to the second research question, both the lexical properties of the verb and the preposition are said to be responsible for the particular use. What is crucial is that with *estar para*, the path is interpreted as a measure function with its point of saturation set at the point of the Prepositional Phrase. The difference between the locative boundary reading of *estar a* and the directional boundary of *estar hasta* relates to the possibility to syntactically realise either a simple boundary location (with *a*) or a complex one. The latter includes distance on a vector between the boundary expressed by the Prepositional Phrase expressed by *hasta* (as object location) and a second implicit boundary which coincides with a 'from here' reading (as reference location).

The paper by **Gras and Sansiñena** relates to the topic of divergence and convergence of discourse particles in varieties of Spanish. As a microstudy of dialect variation, it is one of the first contrastive analyses on peninsular and Latin American insubordination structures. Indeed, in the last decades, insubordination has increasingly become a topic of interest and has been addressed in different languages, but contrastive approaches remain rare. The main contribution of this article is that it provides a thorough account of insubordinate *que*-constructions in three varieties of Spanish, namely the ones of Madrid (Spain), Santiago de Chile (Chile) and Buenos Aires (Argentina). It classifies eight situated usages of discursive *que*-constructions, taking into account the discourse position they occupy and the pragmatic meanings they convey. The corpus-based analysis combines an interactional and constructional approach to grammar.

As a starting point for their study, Gras and Sansiñena argue that, in general, the regional variation, including contexts of convergence and divergence, of lexico-grammatical constructions expressing discourse-related functions remains understudied. This is also the case for the intralinguistic variation of discourse particles, including the *que*-construction. A contrastive variationist approach, showing shared and non-shared contexts among varieties, may provide additional evidence on how to model the polyfunctionality of the complex group of insubordination structures. In particular, diverging behaviour may point towards a different evolution of the same construction in several language varieties which are then becoming structurally more dissimilar.

The case study focuses on the initial complementiser *que* 'that' introducing non-embedded indicative *que*-clauses (IQCs). These are said to give rise to a limited list of interpretations depending on formal features (such as position and intonation) and on the discourse context in which they occur. The paper is methodologically informed by the analysis of the three subcorpora of the *Corpus Oral del Lenguaje Adolescente*, which contains spontaneous informal conversations between native Spanish speaking adolescents. Two kinds of formal parameters are taken into account: (i) turn position (initial or non-initial), and (ii) turn-type (initiation, preferred or dispreferred response, or response-initiation). The semantic-pragmatic analysis is based upon the meaning of the co-text and the participants' reactions.

A first set of interesting conclusions relates to the diverging regional distribution of discourse contexts. It is shown that, besides a high degree of functional convergence between the three varieties, some illocutionary types are characteristic of the peninsular variant and are not equally frequent in the Latin American varieties. The differences mostly relate to *que*-constructions occurring in initial position. These are very infrequent in Rioplatense Spanish and restricted to the function of emphatic contrast. Conversely, initial occurrences of *que*-constructions are widespread in Madrilenian Spanish, where they also adopt the widest range of communicative functions. Chilean Spanish is situated in between these extremes. It is further argued that the observed regional variation can be represented on a cline ranging from high to low discourse dependency. This cline is to be understood in terms of a divergence process by which the same construction gradually extends its scope towards new contexts (with lower degrees of discourse dependency) not (yet) available in other varieties.

A second objective of the analysis is to examine whether there is correspondence between the formal types of *que*-constructions previously identified in formalist literature (conjunctive, quotative and exclamative), and the situated meanings identified through the conversational analysis. The authors conclude that there is only partial correspondence as some illocutionary types coincide with different sets of formal features and/or are restricted to particular varieties.

That language contact may also be a trigger for divergence between varieties or for the formation of new varieties in post-colonial contexts is the main argument underlying **Afonso's** analysis of impersonal *se* constructions in the Portuguese of East Timor. The comparison of varieties of a language at different stages of their development, which might point towards contexts of convergence and divergence, are said to be important to understand particular behaviour of L2 varieties. Besides emphasizing the role of contact, the article presents empirical evidence that general processes of Second Language Acquisition (SLA) must also be taken into consideration when analysing the particular linguistic behaviour of a variety.

As a starting point, the author proposes to test two general theoretical hypotheses for Portuguese vernaculars. These include the already mentioned contact perspective, namely that vernaculars change due to contact with other languages, and the hypothesis of vernacular universals, based on evidence that vernaculars all over the world display many similarities. It is argued that, instead of looking for an exclusively language external or internal explanation, the interplay between contact and general tendencies of SLA must be investigated. The hypothesis is tested through an interesting case in point, namely the impersonal *se* construction, an overtly-coded construction whose main function is to demote the Actor participant from the event. The construction displays a wide range of morpho-syntactic variation in Portuguese vernaculars, which may be spoken both as a first language (L1) in Brazil and Portugal or as in a second language (L2). The observed patterns diverging from the construction's standard use are mainly of two kinds: impersonal constructions with deletion of the clitic *se*, and subject doubling constructions including for instance the indefinite overt subject *(a) gente*.

The analysis focuses on the Portuguese East Timorese variety. The particular historical background of East Timor has left important linguistic consequences and encourages the study of the development of Portuguese as L2 in that region. In concrete, in East Timor Portuguese is a non-dominant variety and presents a high degree of variation amongst its speakers. It has been strongly influenced by Tetun Deli, an Austronesian language, and has also been in a contact situation with Mambae. The data for the analysis come from a corpus of semi-guided conversations between speakers of East Timorese, recorded in Portugal in 2010–2011 and 2015. The corpus includes data from different generations representing diverse levels of proficiency in Portuguese (the older generations displaying a higher degree of proficiency than the younger ones).

The results show a complex situation underlying the emergence of divergent impersonal constructions in East Timorense. First, the degree of innovation clearly depends on the proficiency of Portuguese L2 speakers: the most innovative and divergent uses are found among less proficient speakers. Second, the omission of the clitic *se* is shared by other, more stable varieties of Portuguese, such as Brazilian, with a very different contact situation from the one observed in East Timor. Moreover, the subject doubling construction is (in a comparable version) also found in some L1 dialects of European Portuguese. These observations call into question the contact hypothesis. Third, it is shown that general tendencies of SLA, such as simplification of morphological patterns and the use of more transparent linguistic strategies, also play a role in the emergence of divergent innovative structures. While the deletion of the clitic is a simplification of the impersonal *se* construction, the subject doubling construction shows a complexification of the pattern which, however, leads to a higher degree of transparency of the construction.

4 References

Afonso, Susana, *Impersonal "se" constructions in the Portuguese of East Timor. Notes on the relation between language contact and second language acquisition*, in: Bouzouita, Miriam/Enghels, Renata/Vanderschueren, Clara (edd.), *Convergence and divergence in Ibero-Romance across contact situations and beyond*, Berlin/Boston, De Gruyter, in this volume, 281–305.

Álvarez-Pérez, Xosé A., *Language contact on the Spanish-Portuguese border. A contribution from the linguistic landscape perspective*, in: Bouzouita, Miriam/Enghels, Renata/Vanderschueren, Clara (edd.), *Convergence and divergence in Ibero-Romance across contact situations and beyond*, Berlin/Boston, De Gruyter, in this volume, 115–146.

Bouzouita, Miriam, *At the syntax-pragmatics interface. Clitics in the history of Spanish*, in: Cooper, Robin/Kempson, Ruth (edd.), *Language in flux. Dialogue coordination, language variation, change and evolution*, London, College Publications, 2008, 221–263.

Bouzouita, Miriam, *La posposición pronominal con futuros y condicionales en el códice escurialense I.i.6. Un examen de varias hipótesis morfosintácticas*, in: Kabatek, Johannes (ed.), *Lingüística de corpus y lingüística histórica iberorrománica*, Berlin/Boston, De Gruyter, 2016, 272–301.

Bouzouita, Miriam/Sentí, Andreu, *La gramaticalización del futuro y el condicional en el iberorromance del siglo XIV a partir de traducciones bíblicas paralelas. El caso del castellano y el catalán antiguos*, in: Enrique-Arias, Andrés (ed.), *Traducción bíblica e historia de las lenguas iberorrománicas*, Berlin/Boston, De Gruyter, in press.

Breitbarth, Anne/Bouzouita, Miriam/Danckaert, Lieven/Farasyn, Melissa (edd.), *The determinants of diachronic stability*, Amsterdam, John Benjamins, 2019.

Bucholtz, Mary/Hall, Kira, *Identity and interaction. A sociocultural linguistic approach*, Discourse Studies 7 (2005), 585–614.

Camus Bergareche, Bruno/Gómez Seibane, Sara, *Gender loss in accusative clitics in Basque Spanish. A contact-induced convergence phenomenon* in: Bouzouita, Miriam/Enghels,

Renata/Vanderschueren, Clara (edd.), *Convergence and divergence in Ibero-Romance across contact situations and beyond*, Berlin/Boston, De Gruyter, in this volume, 25–54.

Clyne, Michael, *Dynamics of language contact. English and immigrant languages*, Cambridge, Cambridge University Press, 2003.

Eckert, Penelope, *Three waves of variation study. The emergence of meaning in the study of sociolinguistic variation*, Annual Review of Anthropology 41 (2012), 87–100.

Enrique-Arias, Andrés, *El contacto de lenguas como inhibidor del cambio lingüístico. Castellano y catalán en Mallorca*, in: Montero Cartelle, Emilio (ed.), *Actas del VIII Congreso Internacional de Historia de la Lengua Española*, Santiago de Compostela, Meubooks, 2012, 2651–2662.

Fernández Ulloa, Teresa, *Análisis sociolingüístico del leísmo en el castellano del País Vasco (un corpus oral de Bermeo, Bizkaia)*, in: Echenique, María Teresa/Sánchez, Juan (edd.), *Actas del V Congreso Internacional de Historia de la Lengua Española*, Madrid, Gredos, 2002, 1687–1718.

Fernández-Ordóñez, Inés, *Isoglosas internas del castellano. El sistema referencial del pronombre átono de tercera persona*, Revista de Filología Española 74 (1994), 71–125.

Fernández-Ordóñez, Inés, *Leísmo, laísmo y loísmo*, in: Bosque, Ignacio/Demonte, Violeta (edd.), *Gramática descriptiva de la lengua española*, Madrid, Espasa Calpe, 1999, 1317–1397.

Fernández-Ordóñez, Inés (ed.), *Corpus oral y sonoro del español rural (COSER)*, Madrid, Universidad Autónoma de Madrid, 2005–present, www.corpusrural.es [last access: 16.07.2020].

Gardt, Andreas, *Diskursanalyse. Aktueller theoretischer Ort und methodische Möglichkeiten*, in: Warnke, Ingo (ed.). *Diskurslinguistik nach Foucault. Theorie und Gegenstände*, Berlin/New York, De Gruyter, 2007, 28–52.

Gómez Seibane, Sara, *Exploring historical linguistic convergence between Basque and Spanish*, in: Bouzouita, Miriam/Enghels, Renata/Vanderschueren, Clara (edd.), *Convergence and divergence in Ibero-Romance across contact situations and beyond*, Berlin/Boston, De Gruyter, in this volume, 55–85.

Gras, Pedro/Sansiñena, Sol, *Discourse structure, constructions and regional variation. Non-embedded indicative "que"-clauses in three regional varieties of Spanish*. in: Bouzouita, Miriam/Enghels, Renata/Vanderschueren, Clara (edd.), *Convergence and divergence in Ibero-Romance across contact situations and beyond*, Berlin/Boston, De Gruyter, in this volume, 245–280.

Harnisch, Rüdiger, *Divergence of linguistic varieties in a language space*, in: Auer, Peter/Schmidt, Jürgen Erich (edd.), *Language and space. An international handbook of linguistic variation*, vol. 1: Theories and methods, Berlin/New York, De Gruyter Mouton, 2010, 275–295.

Kaufmann, Göz, *Non-convergence despite language contact*, in: Auer, Peter/Schmidt, Jürgen Erich (edd.), *Language and space. An international handbook of linguistic variation*, vol. 1: Theories and methods, Berlin/New York, De Gruyter Mouton, 2010, 478–493.

Kühl, Kurt/Braunmüller. Karoline, *Stability and divergence in language contact. An extended perspective*, in: Braunmüller, Kurt/Hödder, Steffen/Kühl, Karoline (edd.), *Stability and divergence in language contact. Factors and mechanisms*, Amsterdam/Philadelphia, John Benjamins, 2014, 13–38.

Mangialavori, Eugenia, *Building locations from directional prepositions. Divergent uses of "estar hasta" in Spanish varieties*, in: Bouzouita, Miriam/Enghels, Renata/Vanderschueren, Clara (edd.), *Convergence and divergence in Ibero-Romance across contact situations and beyond*, Berlin/Boston, De Gruyter, in this volume, 209–244.

Matras, Yaron, *Language contact*, Cambridge, Cambridge University Press, 2009.

Matras, Yaron/Sakel, Jeanette, *Investigating the mechanism of pattern replication in language convergence*, Studies in Language 31:4 (2007), 829–965.

Palacios, Azucena, *Aspectos teóricos y metodológicos del contacto de lenguas. El sistema pronominal del español en áreas de contacto con lenguas amerindias*, in: Noll, Volker/Zimmermann, Klaus/Neumann-Holzschuh, Ingrid (edd.), *El español en América. Aspectos teóricos, particularidades, contactos*, Frankfurt/Madrid, Vervuert/Iberoamericana, 2005, 63–94.

Palacios, Azucena, *¿Son compatibles los cambios inducidos por contacto y las tendencias internas al sistema?*, in: Schrader-Kniffki, Martina/Morgenthaler García, Laura (edd.), *La Romania en interacción. Entre historia, contacto y política*, Madrid/Frankfurt, Iberoamericana/Vervuert, 2007, 259–279.

Palacios, Azucena, *Contact-induced change and internal evolution. Spanish in contact with Amerindian languages*, in: Chamoreau, Claudine/Léglise, Isabelle (edd.), *The interplay of variation and change in contact settings*, Amsterdam/Philadelphia, John Benjamins, 2013, 165–198.

Regueira, Xosé Luís, *Portuguese as a contact language in Galicia. Convergence, divergence, ideology and identity*, in: Bouzouita, Miriam/Enghels, Renata/Vanderschueren, Clara (edd.), *Convergence and divergence in Ibero-Romance across contact situations and beyond*, Berlin/Boston, de Gruyter, in this volume, 147–175.

Rodríguez Molina, Javier, *La gramaticalización de los tiempos compuestos en español antiguo. Cinco cambios diacrónicos*, PhD dissertation, Autonomous University of Madrid, 2010.

Schulte, Kim, *Structural convergence of two Ibero-Romance varieties. The case of colloquial Valencian as the outcome of contact between Catalan and Spanish*, in: Bouzouita, Miriam/Enghels, Renata/Vanderschueren, Clara (edd.), *Convergence and divergence in Ibero-Romance across contact situations and beyond*, Berlin/Boston, De Gruyter, in this volume, 87–113.

Silverstein, Michael, *Indexical order and the dialectics of sociolinguistic life*, Language & Communication 23 (2003), 193–229.

Silverstein, Michael, *The race from place. Dialect eradication vs. the linguistic "authenticity" of terroir*, in: Lacoste, Véronique/Leimgruber, Jakob/Breyer, Thiemo (edd.), *Indexing authenticity. Sociolinguistic perspectives*, Berlin/Boston, De Gruyter, 2014, 159–187.

Tuten, Donald N., *Koineization in medieval Spanish*, Berlin/New York, De Gruyter Mouton, 2003.

Winford, Donald, *Social factors in contact languages*, in: Bakker, Peter/Matras, Yaron (edd.), *Contact languages*, Berlin/Boston, De Gruyter, 2013, 363–416.

Wolf, Johanna *Linguistic perceptions on Spanglish discourse settings. Processes of divergence in constructing identity*, in: Bouzouita, Miriam/Enghels, Renata/Vanderschueren, Clara (edd.), *Convergence and divergence in Ibero-Romance across contact situations and beyond*, Berlin/Boston, De Gruyter, in this volume, 179–208.

Wright, Roger, *Convergence and divergence in world languages*, in: Hernández-Campoy, Juan Manuel/Conde-Silvestre, Juan Camilo (edd.), *The handbook of historical sociolinguistics*, Oxford, Blackwell, 2012, 552–567.

Part 1: Convergence and divergence in contact situations in the Iberian Peninsula

Bruno Camus Bergareche and Sara Gómez Seibane

Gender loss in accusative clitics in Basque Spanish

A contact-induced convergence phenomenon

Abstract: This paper describes the use of feminine *leísmo* for the variety of Spanish spoken in the Basque Country, i.e., the use of the unstressed dative pronoun *le* to refer to feminine direct objects. After reviewing its presence in historical texts, as well as its synchronic geographical and social distribution, we link *leísmo* in Basque Spanish with some grammatical characteristics of the other language spoken in this area, namely Basque. Taking this contact situation as our starting point, we put forward different arguments to corroborate our theory, including the existence of similar phenomena in other Spanish varieties in contact with languages whose pronominal systems are partly akin to those of the Basque language. Lastly, we will explain the phenomenon of feminine *leísmo* in Basque Spanish by assuming the models of contact-induced change and convergence developed by Palacios (2005) for cases in which gender has been eliminated in clitics in Latin American Spanish. In this way, we hope to contribute to a better understanding of little-known processes of grammatical convergence in Spanish in situations of contact with other languages.

Keywords: Basque Spanish, convergence, language contact, clitics, dative and accusative pronouns, gender loss

---

Note: This research is part of the project "COREC: Corpus Oral de Referencia del Español en Contacto. Fase I: Lenguas Minoritarias" headed by Azucena Palacios (Universidad Autónoma de Madrid) and Sara Gómez Seibane (Universidad de La Rioja), funded by the Spanish Ministry for Science and Innovation (Ref. PID2019-105865GB-I00). A previous version of this paper was presented at the *International Conference on Linguistics of Ibero-Romance Languages: Ibero-Romance in Contact and in Contrast*, Ghent University, December 14–16, 2015. We would like to thank those present for their comments and suggestions, which were helpful in improving this study. We also want to thank the two anonymous reviewers for their comments. Any errors are solely ours.

Bruno Camus Bergareche, Universidad de Castilla-La Mancha
Sara Gómez Seibane, Universidad de La Rioja

https://doi.org/10.1515/9783110736250-002

1 Introduction

The use of dative clitics *le* and *les* to refer the feminine direct object – as well as masculine ones, which constitutes the phenomenon known as *leísmo*, common throughout the whole of northern Spain – is widely documented in the Spanish variety spoken in the Autonomous Community of the Basque Country (onwards Basque Country) and in neighboring areas where we know that Basque was still spoken in the 18th century, such as the northern half of Navarre (Gómez Seibane 2012a; Camus/Gómez Seibane 2015b). This so-called feminine *leísmo* has been commonly accounted for as being one of the effects of contact between the two languages present in the region, Basque and Spanish (Fernández-Ordóñez 1999). In (1) we give an example of this phenomenon.[1]

(1) La chica$_i$ llegó a tal hora a su casa y el cura *le*$_i$ vio (COSER, Aulesti, Bizkaia). 'The girl arrived home at such a time and the priest saw her-DAT (DIRECT OBJECT) from his house'.

This paper is structured as follows: first we present the data and methodology that were used (section 2); Section 3 outlines the parameters on which the clitics in the Spanish spoken in northern Spain are based. Focusing on Spanish *leísmo* found in the Basque Country, section 4 describes its presence in historical texts and outlines its geographical, social, syntactic and semantic distribution. In section 5, we relate *leísmo* in Basque Spanish to the grammatical characteristics of Basque, the other language spoken in this area, taking into account its conditions of use and its syntactic distribution. We also offer examples of similar phenomena that occur relatively commonly in other Spanish contact varieties whose pronominal systems are partly akin to those of the Basque language. Using the previous, section 5 offers an explanation of feminine *leísmo* found in the Basque Country, based on the models of contact-induced change and convergence developed by Palacios (2005) for cases in which gender is lost in clitics in Latin American Spanish. More generally, we hope to contribute to a better awareness of grammatical convergence processes in contexts of language contact

---

[1] In the examples, clitics will be highlighted in bold, and referents will be underlined. When elements are co-referential, they will be co-indexed. *Leísmo* involves the use of dative *le/s* instead of the accusative *lo/s* or *la/s*. Therefore, the English glosses will mark *le/s* as DAT, and we will indicate the syntactic function in brackets (DIRECT OBJECT) when necessary. For a better understanding of the examples, we sometimes clarify the gender of the referent or the clitic in brackets (feminine as FEM, masculine as MASC, neuter as NEUT). PL is used for plural referents and SING for singular ones. Sources of used examples are mentioned, as well as their origin (town and province).

and, in particular, to draw attention to the interest of studies on lesser known Spanish varieties in contact with other languages.

2 Data and methodology

For a comprehensive description of *leísmo* found in the Basque Country, we used data gathered from various sources, as outlined below.
a. Linguistic corpora: oral data gathered from different corpora.
   - The open-access COSER corpus (*Corpus Oral y Sonoro del Español Rural*; 'Audible Corpus of Spoken Rural Spanish'), based on uneducated informants over the age of 60 from rural areas of Spain (Fernández-Ordóñez 2005–present). The interviews that have been included in this work were recorded in 2000 in Bizkaia, Gipuzkoa and Araba, the three provinces of the Basque Country.
   - An oral sample of ten bilingual speakers, with different degrees of proficiency in the Basque language, aged between 25 and 50, born and living in semi-urban areas of the Basque Country in x. This corpus contains semi-structured informal interviews conducted at informants' home. It has been also used for other contact studies (Gómez Seibane 2012b; 2012c). We will refer to this corpus as the Corpus of the Basque Country (CoBasCo).
b. Linguistic atlas: Oral data with *leísmo* found in rural areas adjacent to the Basque Country proceeding from the *Atlas Lingüístico y Etnográfico de Aragón, Navarra y La Rioja* (ALEANR; Alvar et al. 1979–1983).
c. A questionnaire on the acceptability of *leísmo*: it was conducted among twenty educated Basque Spanish-speaking adults from urban areas (Donostia-San Sebastián) and backed by a control survey with another twenty non-Basque adults from Castilla-La Mancha, Extremadura and Andalusia. They were asked to fill in the correct clitic in twenty sentences with different types of complements (direct and indirect objects) and referents (human/non-human, masculine/feminine, singular/plural). This survey will be referred to as the Direct and Indirect Objects Questionnaire (DIoQuest).
d. A comprehensive bibliographical analysis of empirical studies on *leísmo*.
   - Studies on historical documents relating to the Basque region (Gómez Seibane 2004; 2010; Camus 2015) and a corpus of letters written by three bilingual farm managers that worked for an aristocratic family in a rural area of Gipuzkoa (Gómez Seibane in this volume). Examples of this corpus will be quoted both as part of the corresponding published studies and as Historical Corpus of the Basque Country (HiCoBasCo).

- Corpus-based studies on Basque-Spanish contact, such as Urrutia (1988), Landa (1995), Echenique (1996), Fernández Ulloa (2002) and Paasch-Kaiser (2015).
- Studies of current oral corpora focusing on situations where Spanish is in contact with Amerindian languages like Quechua, Guaraní and Mayan languages (Lipski 1996; Palacios 1998; 2000; 2002; 2005; Fernández-Ordóñez 1999).

These sources provide empirical data for our presentation of the peculiarities of the phenomenon of *leísmo* found in the Basque region, seen from several different perspectives (geographic, social-historical, syntactic-semantic), while also facilitating a comparison of this type of *leísmo* with that of other areas in which Spanish is in contact with Amerindian languages that share to a certain extent typological features with Basque. The aims of this paper are as follows:

a. To document the presence of feminine *leísmo* from the first texts written in Castilian in the Basque Country territory.
b. To show the presence and acceptance of this phenomenon in different types of Basque Country speakers, such as monolinguals in Spanish, semi-speakers and bilinguals or (nearly) fully competent in both languages, following Campbell/Muntzel (1989). We do not aim to quantitative analyses, but rather want to describe qualitatively the general situation and main characteristics of the phenomenon under study.
c. To demonstrate the presence of this phenomenon in contiguous regions, such as the northern part of Navarre.
d. To connect and discuss similar results of feminine *leísmo* in other Spanish contact varieties in the Americas.

3 *Leísmo* in pronominal systems in Spanish

Leísmo involves the elimination of case and gender in unstressed third-person pronouns. Depending on the antecedent, a distinction can be made between the use of originally dative *le* for a masculine person (*A su hijo$_i$ le$_i$ castigaron en el colegio* 'His son (MASC), they punished him-DAT (DIRECT OBJECT) at school'), for a female one (*A la niña$_i$ le$_i$ llevaron al parque* 'The little girl (FEM), they took her-DAT (DIRECT OBJECT) to the park') and for an object, generally morphologically masculine in Spanish (*Ese libro$_i$ ya le$_i$ he leído* 'That book (MASC), I have already read it-DAT (DIRECT OBJECT)'). Although *leísmo* is a widespread phenomenon in Spanish, historically it has been more commonly used to refer to masculine antecedents than to feminine ones (Gómez Seibane 2013, 38–44). In the following section, an outline is given of the criteria that govern the selection parameters of a particular pronoun in Spanish (namely, case, animacy, (dis)continuity, gender and number). The differences in the organisation and importance of these parameters, among others, give rise to *leísmo*.

3.1 The etymological and *leísta* system

The etymological or case-distinguishing system, inherited from Latin, is widely known to base the use of third person clitics on three parameters: case, gender and number. Case is the most important parameter because, depending on whether the referent of the pronoun is an indirect or direct object, the dative *le/s* or the accusative *lo/s* and *la/s* will be selected, respectively. Following this initial rule, the antecedent's semantic features, more specifically its gender and number, play a decisive role, particularly in the selection of the appropriate accusative clitic (masculine *lo/s* and feminine *la/s*), since the dative clitic (*le/s*) does not exhibit any distinction for gender, just for number. The pronoun thus always reflects the syntactic function of the referent, together with the number of the antecedent (2a), whereas its grammatical gender is only visible in the case of the accusative pronoun (2b).

(2) a. A María$_i$ le$_i$ regalaron un pijama por su cumpleaños. A Pedro y a Juan$_i$ los$_i$ vieron por la calle.
'Maria, they gave her-DAT[2] some pyjamas for her birthday. Pedro and Juan, they saw them-ACC MASC PL in the street.'
b. La ropa$_i$ la$_i$ lava en casa. Los tomates$_i$ los$_i$ compra en la frutería.
'The clothes (FEM SING), she washes them-ACC FEM SING at home. The tomatoes (MASC PL), she buys them-ACC MASC PL at the greengrocer's.'

Within this system, we can find so-called *leísmo aparente* (apparent *leísmo*), i.e., the use of *le/s* with a series of verbs and constructions that permit this variation in the verb valency.[3] The uses described above are extended both geographically

---

2 See footnote 1.
3 The verbs that admit this accusative-dative variation include emotion verbs (such as *asombrar*, *encantar* or *halagar*), verbs whose direct object can be omitted (*atender*, *servir*, *pagar*), and verbs with alternating or preferential uses of the accusative and dative (*ayudar*, *obedecer*). As for constructions, mention should be made of infinitive clauses with verbs of influence (*ordenar* and *invitar a*), predicates with an unstressed pronoun and subject complement, the impersonal

and sociolinguistically. On the one hand, they are present in a large part of Spain, including the northern area in contact with the Basque Country (to the south and east), like La Rioja, the southern half of Navarre and Aragon (Gómez Seibane 2012a, 30). On the other hand, they are also characteristic of educated oral and written Spanish (Fernández-Ordóñez 1999, 1386–1390), since according to the Spanish Royal Academy (*Real Academia Española*; RAE), the use of *le* for a singular masculine person as a direct object is not considered wrong, given its widespread traditional use in educated language and by writers of recognised repute, although the use of *lo* is preferred (RAE/ASALE 2009, 1215). Given the above, this case-distinguishing system, which has come to be accepted as the standard one, exerts a certain influence on the local pronominal system used in the Basque Country.

3.2 The Cantabrian and the referential systems

In a large part of the north-west area of Spain which is in contact with the Spanish spoken in the Basque Country, the parameters that rule the use of pronouns follow a different system, leading to a usage different from that described in section 3.1. In comparison with the system outlined in the previous section, the pronominal paradigms described below reveal differences in the expression of case and gender, while they conserve the inflection for number. In these systems, *leísmo* is thus the result of the reorganisation of the pronominal paradigm according to different parameters.

In the two pronominal systems in contact along the western area of the Basque Country, case no longer plays a decisive role in the selection of the clitic. Instead, the determining factors are the antecedent's semantic features, and in particular the distinction between uncountable or countable nouns.[4] This distinction has

---

form *se* followed by a pronoun, and polite use of *leísmo* (Fernández-Ordóñez 1999, 1323–1339). Some authors consider the above contexts to be one of the possible factors that led the dative to replace the accusative (Lapesa 1968).

4 It is worth remembering that uncountable nouns refer to things that "can be endlessly divided while still conserving their intrinsic nature and name" (Bello cited by Bosque 1999, 8; translation is ours), like substances or materials (*water, air, sand*), qualities (*height, laziness, sobriety*), sensations or feelings (*love, enthusiasm*), states (*calm, fever*) and certain capacities (*memory, power*). However, no classification has been made of the semantic notions expressed by uncountable nouns, since many nouns behave grammatically like countable ones in some languages and uncountable ones in others. In contrast with uncountable nouns, countable ones "cannot be divided without losing their identity, as is the case of a *tree* or *table*" (Bello cited by Bosque 1999, 8; translation is ours).

important syntactic consequences in Spanish, associated with the possible combination (or not) of the noun with certain determiners and quantifiers (Bosque 1999, 10–13) and with pronominal usage in certain varieties of Spanish in northern Spain. Indeed, in a large part of northern Spain, neutral pronouns can express the uncountable nature of its referent, a phenomenon traditionally known as the mass neuter (Fernández-Ordóñez 2006; 2007). As illustrated in (3), when the nouns *caracoles* ('snails', masculine plural), *leña* ('firewood', feminine singular) and *remolachas* ('beetroot', feminine plural) are interpreted as uncountable, the neutral pronouns *lo* and *ello* can be used to refer to them due to *ad sensum* agreement, that is, agreement based on the word's semantic features as opposed to its lexical ones (masculine plural, feminine singular or feminine plural, respectively).

(3) a. ¿Había gente que se dedicaba a coger caracoles$_i$? – Habrán cogi[d]o muchos los chavales y se los$_i$ pagaban bien, pero ahora ya no vienen, venían muchos de Burgos y de Bilbao, venían a comprarlo$_i$ (Fernández-Ordóñez 2007, 426).
'Were there people dedicated to collecting snails (MASC UNCOUNT)? – The lads must have gathered a lot of them and they have paid them-ACC MASC PL well, but they don't come anymore. Many came from Burgos and Bilbao to buy it-ACC NEUT'.
b. [P]a[ra] este tiempo era mejor leña$_i$, metías un montón de *ello*$_i$ y no te calentabas casi (Fernández-Ordóñez 2006, 106).
'For this weather, firewood (FEM UNCOUNT) was better. You put on a pile of it-ACC NEUT but you barely warmed up'.
c. ¿Y cómo sacaban las remolachas$_i$ de la tierra? – Entonces con una horca se lo$_i$ solía sacar o con el ara[d]o. [...] Después había que sacudir*lo*, cortarles la hoja, limpiarlas para llevar*lo*$_i$ a la fábrica si *lo*$_i$ llevabas (Fernández-Ordóñez 2006, 107).
'And how did they get the beetroot (FEM UNCOUNT) out of the ground? – Back then, they used to get it-ACC NEUT out with a fork or plough. [...] After, you had to shake it-ACC NEUT, cut the leaves off, and clean them to take it-ACC NEUT to the factory if you took it-ACC NEUT'.

The prevalence of the antecedent's semantic features over its syntactic function takes place in a large part of Cantabria. As a result of this re-structuring, *le/s* is used for the masculine accusative and dative to refer to countable antecedents. Consequently, in this area, *leísmo* affects masculine countable words that are animate (4a) or inanimate (4b), while feminine countable words (4c) conserve their case and agreement with gender in the accusative.

(4) a. Unos *le*ᵢ llamaban pa[ra] sacar piedra pa una cabaña, otros *le*ᵢ llamaban pa[ra] hacer cosas [al marido] (Fernández-Ordóñez 1994, 105).
'Some called him-DAT (DIRECT OBJECT) to quarry stone for a hut, others called him-DAT (DIRECT OBJECT) to do things [her husband]'.
b. El carroᵢ *le*ᵢ tengo, ya no *le*ᵢ usan, porque resulta que se han hecho todos a un tractor (Fernández-Ordóñez 1994, 105).
'The cart (MASC), I have it-DAT (DIRECT OBJECT), they no longer use it-DAT (DIRECT OBJECT) because it turns out they've all got their hands on a tractor'.
c. Esa cerdaᵢ *la*ᵢ engordábamos pa matar*la*ᵢ. [...] Abrirle y ya sacar las morcillasᵢ, lavar*las*ᵢ. (Fernández-Ordoñéz 1994, 106).
'That sow (FEM) we fattened it-ACC FEM to kill it-ACC FEM. [...] Open it and take out the sausages (FEM), wash them-ACC FEM'.

According to Fernández-Ordóñez (2001, 422; 2012, 90–91), the origin of the Cantabrian pronominal paradigm seems to have been the result of dialect contact. Indeed, in this pronominal system *le* was adopted as an accusative pronoun, like in the Basque pronominal system (see 3.3), but it was adjusted according to the features that worked in the Cantabrian variety, gender and countability.

The second area where the noun's semantics prevail over case stretches from the north-western half of Castile to almost the middle of Spain. Here, uncountable and countable nouns can be formally distinguished and, in the latter case, attention is also paid to gender and number, but the non-distinction of case in the singular and plural is almost general. This readjustment of the pronominal system, known in this case as the referential system, has led the Spanish spoken in this area to be characterised not only by *leísmo* (5a), but by *laísmo*, i.e., the use of the accusative forms *la* and *las* instead of the datives *le* and *les* (5b), and also by *loísmo*, i.e., the use of the accusative forms *lo* and *los* instead of the dative *le* and *les* (5c).

(5) a. Al niñoᵢ *le*ᵢ llevaron al hospital. El tractorᵢ hace tiempo que *le*ᵢ vendimos (Fernández-Ordóñez 1999, 1361).
'The little boy, they took him-DAT (DIRECT OBJECT) to hospital. The tractor we sold it-DAT (DIRECT OBJECT) a long time ago'.
b. A la ovejaᵢ hay que esquilar*la*ᵢ teniendo cuidado de no dar*la*ᵢ cortes. A esa camisaᵢ *la*ᵢ quité el cuello para arreglar*la*ᵢ (Fernández-Ordóñez 1999, 1361).
'The sheep (FEM), we must shear it-ACC FEM, taking care not to cut it-ACC FEM. Lit. From that blouse, I took from it-ACC FEM (INDIRECT OBJECT) the collar off to repair it-ACC FEM'.

c. Según recogías la sangre_i del cerdo, *lo_i* revolvías, ibas dándo*lo_i* vueltas (Fernández-Ordóñez 1999, 1361).
'As you collected the blood (FEM UNCOUNT DIRECT OBJECT) from the pig, you stirred it-ACC NEUT (DIRECT OBJECT), stirring it-ACC NEUT (DIRECT OBJECT) round'.

Consequently, in western areas near the Basque Country, the paradigm is reorganised using the criterion of countability versus uncountability, which in turn influences the maintenance of case and gender (Table 1). The referential pronominal system used in most of Castile depends thus on both the categorisation of the antecedent into countable or uncountable and partially on its gender. With uncountable nouns, the agreement with gender and case disappears and *lo* is used. In the case of countable nouns, the morphological markers denoting feminine agreement are conserved but case disappears, so that *le* is used as a pronoun for masculine nouns and *la* for feminine ones. On the other hand, with the Cantabrian system, the clitics are distributed depending on whether a noun is countable or uncountable, partially on gender and case, although as not evenly as for the last parameter. *Le* is used for uncountable nouns if they are dative and *lo* if they are accusative, while the pronouns for countable nouns are still inflected for gender and case only in the feminine because *le* tends to be used if they are masculine.

Table 1: Pronominal uses in the referential and the Cantabrian systems.

System	Noun	Pronoun	Gender	Case
Referential	Uncountable	*Lo*	No	No
	Countable	*Le, les/La, las*	No (masc.)/Yes (fem.)	No
Cantabrian	Uncountable	*Le/Lo*	No	Yes
	Countable	*Le, les/La, las*	No (masc.)/Yes (fem.)	No/Yes

3.3 The Basque system

The peculiarities of the Basque pronominal system include the use of *leísmo* for animate masculine and feminine direct objects, including animals (6a) and humans (6b). The extension of the dative clitic *le/s* to the accusative with these types of antecedents means that animacy appears to be the main parameter on which the pronominal system depends: with animate entities, *le/s* is selected, with as a consequence that case and gender are eliminated.

(6) a. Se suelta el cerdo$_j$, el carnicero le$_i$ agarra de así. A mí me gustaban mucho las ovejas$_i$ [...] por eso les$_i$ tengo todavía (Fernández-Ordóñez 1999, 1350).
'The pig (MASC) is let loose, the butcher grabs it-DAT (DIRECT OBJECT) like this. I liked sheep (FEM) very much [...], that's why I still have them-DAT (DIRECT OBJECT)'.

b. Pues el domingo siguiente, primero les$_i$ llamó a las madres$_i$. Le$_i$ ponían de rodillas, medio agachada a la mujer$_i$ allí (COSER, Aulesti, Bizkaia).
'So the following Sunday, first he called them-DAT (DIRECT OBJECT) the mothers. They put her-DAT (DIRECT OBJECT) on her knees, crouching, the woman there'.

Le/s also tends to double the post-verbal lexical direct object as in (6b), although aspects relating to grammar or the sociolinguistic circumstances in which this phenomenon occurs are not adequately described yet (Fernández-Ordóñez 1994; 1999; Landa 1995). So far, the first results indicate that the differences in direct object doubling constructions in the Basque system are qualitative and quantitative, compared to data from central-peninsular Spanish (Gómez Seibane 2017; 2020a).[5]

Further, inanimate nouns maintain the case distinction since for the dative *le/les* is used whereas for the accusative *lo/s* or *la/s* can be used or the clitic can be omitted, as in (7).

(7) Los filetes rusos de mi madre$_i$ en casa Ø$_i$ solíamos hacer (Camus/Gómez Seibane 2015b, 227).
'My mother's breaded fillets, we used to make at home'.

The three phenomena that affect the Basque pronominal system (null object, clitic doubling and *leísmo*) have been considered as part of the object clitic agreement paradigm in which animacy hierarchies are crucial. As Landa (1995, 236–237) concluded "[the] null object construction stands for a [-animate] null pronominal in argument position agreeing with a phonologically covert clitic, whereas the object clitic doubled construction with [+animate] objects –

---

[5] Dialectal differences lie in cognitive and referential factors (Gómez Seibane 2017; 2020a). Cognitive factors, related to the accessibility of referents in the mind of speakers, indicate that the Basque corpus duplicates semi-active and inactive direct objects, while in the central variety corpus semi-active and active ones are preferred. As regards the referential factors, related to the type of co-referential accusative phrase, the Basque corpus duplicates nominal, human and animate, usually definite, but not always individuated, phrases. The central-peninsular variety selects nominal and pronominal referents, preferably inanimate, definite and individuated.

regardless of whether they are phonologically realised or not – represents verb object agreement instantiated by the object clitic *le*".

While further research on the characteristics of direct object doubling constructions in this Spanish variety remain pending, our proposal partially agrees with Landa (1995). As she pointed out already, animacy appears to be a determining parameter in the reorganisation of the Basque pronominal paradigm (Gómez Seibane 2020b). This entails the partial elimination of gender and case, above all for human antecedents. The preference for this parameter thus leads to a partial cancellation of both case – in keeping with the internal tendency in Spanish (section 3.1 and 3.2) – and gender, most likely because the latter is an inflectional category that does not exist in Basque (section 5). The models of contact-induced change and convergence outlined in section 5 offer insights into how this ordering came about.[6]

4 The distribution of *leísmo* in Basque Spanish

In this section, an outline is given of the extent to which *leísmo* has been (and still is) used in the Basque Country from the perspective of historical documentation, its current geographical and social distribution and the syntactic and semantic contexts in which the phenomenon occurs.

4.1 Historical presence

Historical studies of archival documents and private correspondence[7] in the Basque area[8] highlight the use of *leísmo* with masculine human antecedents as a more common phenomenon in the singular and as a growing one in the plural from the 16th century onward. In the case of feminine human antecedents, *le* was used for the accusative in the 16th and 17th centuries, as can be observed in the examples in (8a) and (8b), respectively. In the 17th century, the quantitative data available give a frequency of 7.2% (4/55) for this type of feminine *leísmo* in

---

[6] See also Gómez Seibane (in this volume).
[7] For some years, diachronic research has prioritised these sources since they are easier to tie in with a specific geographical region and to a specific moment in time and because there is no third-party interference when original documents are used.
[8] Prior to this date, in the Basque area there are relatively few documents written in Spanish.

singular (clitics referring to plural referents are very scarce), whereas the accusative clitic *la* is the preferred one (92.8%) (Gómez Seibane 2010).[9]

(8) a. Pareció Mancia de Ugarrio$_i$ [...] e dixo que le$_i$ recibiesen (Gómez Seibane 2010, 143).
'Mancia de Ugarrio appeared [...] and asked for them to receive her-DAT (DIRECT OBJECT)'.
b. Que a ella$_i$ le$_i$ había maltratado en algunas ocaciones (Gómez Seibane 2010, 143).
'That she, he had mistreated her-DAT (DIRECT OBJECT) on some occasions'.

During the 18th century, the use of *leísmo* increased with these two types of antecedents. In the case of feminine humans, using *le* instead of *la* in the singular, as in (9), rose to a frequency of 43% (9/21) in private letters from people who had migrated to the Americas, although these percentages should be taken with caution, given the limited number of occurrences.

(9) Dios le$_i$ tenga en su santa gloria. Y con esto no le$_i$ canzo más [mi mujer] (Gómez Seibane 2004, 44).
'May God keep her-DAT (DIRECT OBJECT) in his holy glory. And with this, I shall not tire her-DAT (DIRECT OBJECT) anymore [my wife]'.

In private 19th century correspondence, the use of *leísmo* with human masculine objects is widespread, amounting to 76.5% (62/81), while with feminine ones it seems to be a change in progress, accounting for a percentage of 24.1% (19/79) (Gómez Seibane in this volume). The importance of these data becomes clearer when compared with the frequencies obtained for a corpus of monolingual documents of the same type: for the masculine, the percentage of *leísmo* is 31.6% (31/98), while for the feminine it is 4.9% (2/41) and it is found in passages with formulaic forms.

The available data from 19th century allow us to characterize the feminine human *leísmo* in Gipuzkoa, at least, as a phenomenon present in both the middle socio-economic (10a) and high classes (10b). *Leísmo* appears in the letters of the three bilingual farm managers and in letters written by a member of the aristocratic family for whom they worked (for a detailed description of Zavala family, see Camus 2015).

---

[9] To provide a better understanding of the examples, the orthography and punctuation have been modernised up to a certain degree.

(10) a. Temprano a la Balbina_i ya estube a visitar*le_i* (Gómez Seibane in this volume).
'Early I went to visit her-DAT (DIRECT OBJECT), Balbina'.
b. Vi a aquel señor que *le_i* acompañó a la Dolores_i a Burdeos (Camus 2015, 1784).
'I saw that gentleman who accompanied her-DAT (DIRECT OBJECT), Dolores, to Bordeaux'.

4.2 Social and geographical distribution

Map 1 shows the area of Spain where the feminine *leísmo* has been detected. Both in northwest Navarre and the Basque Country, cases of this phenomenon have been found, as can be seen in the examples from COSER for inland Bizkaia (11a), Gipuzkoa (11b) and the northern edge of Araba (11c). It should be pointed out that this area coincides with points of intense contact between Spanish and Basque, particularly Gipuzkoa and inland Bizkaia.

Map 1: Area of feminine *leísmo* in the Basque Country and northern half of Navarre (based on Camus/Gómez Seibane 2015b and data from ALEANR).

(11) a. La chica_i llegó a tal hora a su casa y el cura *le_i* vio (COSER, Aulesti, Bizkaia).
'The girl arrived home at such a time and the priest saw her- DAT (DIRECT OBJECT)'.
b. Era costumbre de acompañar*le_i* a casa a la chica (COSER, Errezil, Gipuzkoa).
'It was customary to accompany her-DAT (DIRECT OBJECT) home, the girl'.
c. Resulta que la madre esperándo*le* [a la hija] (COSER, Luzuriaga, Araba).
'It turns out that the mother was waiting for her-DAT (DIRECT OBJECT) [her daughter]'.

As for its social distribution, the COSER corpus highlights that *le/s* is almost always used for feminine personal antecedents and that these uses are firmly established among older uneducated/lowly educated speakers living in Basque-speaking rural areas. Moreover, the frequency of use is lower in an oral corpus of bilingual speakers, aged between 25 and 50, who are highly educated and semi-urban (Gómez Seibane 2012c), since these speakers alternate *le/s* and *la/s* for feminine personal accusatives (12).

(12) Pues igual el primero que leí. [...]. De una niña$_i$ que era india, que con ocho años sus padres *la*$_i$ vendieron ya a un viejo verde y aquel pues ya con ocho años *la*$_i$ violaba y *le*$_i$ hizo de todo [...] Cuando creció mató al marido que *le*$_i$ violó (CoBasCo, Mendaro, Gipuzkoa).
'Well maybe the first I read. [...] About a girl who was Indian, whose parents sold her-ACC at the age of eight to a dirty old man, and he raped her-ACC at the age of eight and did all kinds of things to her-DAT (DIRECT OBJECT) [...] When she grew up, she killed the husband who had raped her-DAT (DIRECT OBJECT)'.

Indeed, studies based on urban and semi-urban localities agree that the feminine personal *leísmo* is not a systematic phenomenon, as speakers alternate dative and accusative clitics (Urrutia 1988; Fernández Ulloa 2002; Paasch-Kaiser 2015), probably due to pressure of the standard Spanish system (see 3.1). Nonetheless, the feminine personal *leísmo* is not used only by bilingual speakers. This phenomenon has also been found in the speech of three of twenty monolingual Spanish speakers analysed by Paasch-Kaiser (2015, 320–323). Moreover, a survey of the acceptability of this phenomenon among educated adult Basque Spanish-speakers born in Donostia-San Sebastián (DIoQuest) shows that such uses are regularly accepted. Many of these speakers even correct sentences where an accusative clitic *la/las* appears as Direct Object as in *Ana se encontró con sus hermanas y las acompañó a casa* 'Ana met her sisters and accompanied them-ACC FEM home', and insert *le/les* in its place. On the contrary, the answers of non-Basque speakers in DIoQuest are very different: they always reject sentences with feminine *leísmo*, but seem to have more doubts with masculine *leísmo*.

4.3 Syntactic-semantic contexts of occurrence

A description of the syntactic and semantic features of clauses with *leísmo* will now be given, paying special attention to the semantics of the antecedents, lexical aspect of the verbs involved, the degree to which the object is affected, and the type of syntactic construction in which the phenomenon occurs. The antecedents of pronominalised direct objects with *le/s* are characterised by the fact that they are human. This type of antecedent is the one commonly used and accepted by all speakers, whether they are bilingual or monolingual. *Leísmo* is also possible with non-human animate antecedents (13a), although not very common, and tends to be typical of rural speech. Cases with inanimate antecedents (13b), on the contrary, are also found in Basque-speaking rural settings, but Spanish speakers from urban areas seem not to accept them.[10]

(13) a. Atar*le*$_i$ a la yegua$_i$ allá pa[ra] que coma yerba (COSER, Luzuriaga, Araba).
'The mare (FEM), tie it-DAT (DIRECT OBJECT) there for it to eat the grass'.
b. – ¿Con la miel$_i$ qué hacían? – ¡Joé!, la miel$_i$ pues vender*le*$_i$. (Camus/Gómez Seibane 2015b, 291).
'– For what did they use honey (FEM)? – ¡Gosh! Honey? Well they sold it-DAT (DIRECT OBJECT)'.

As for the types of verbs, lexical aspect does not seem to play a decisive role in the presence of *leísmo*, since it is possible with states (14a), activities (11b), accomplishments (12) and achievements (14b). In contrast, the relationship between the direct object and the type of action expressed by the verb does seem relevant. Indeed, many cases of *leísmo* involve verbs of affectation and thus objects affected by the action of the verb (15) or verbs of cognitive activity that have experiencer subjects and affected direct objects as the theme, such as (14a) and (16).

(14) a. Aquí *le*$_i$ conocí a mi mujer$_i$ (Camus/Gómez Seibane 2015a, 219, note 4).
'Here I met her-DAT (DIRECT OBJECT), my wife'.
b. La Brígida no *le*$_i$ encontré en casa (Gómez Seibane in this volume).
'Brígida, I didn't find her-DAT (DIRECT OBJECT) at home'.

(15) a. No *les*$_i$ voy a dejar en la estacada a esta gente$_i$ (Gómez Seibane 2012b, 211).
'I am not going to leave them-DAT (DIRECT OBJECT) in the lurch, those people'.
b. [R]esulta que mi madre$_i$ *le*$_i$ llevaron el 3 de mayo a operar (COSER, Tolosa, Gipuzkoa).
'It turns out that, my mother, they took her-DAT (DIRECT OBJECT) for an operation on May 3rd'.

---

10 In this section, examples that have appeared before in the text are reproduced again to show different aspects of the phenomenon. Example (12) is partially reproduced in (14c) and (18b); examples (11b) and (14b) are the same; also (10b) and (17a); and (1), (11a) and (19a), as well.

(16) La Sor Juana nos dice que en la semana pasada le_i vio a Mercedes$_i$ (HiCoBasCo).
'Sister Juana tells us that last week she saw her-DAT (DIRECT OBJECT), Mercedes'.

As for the characteristics of syntactic constructions with *leísmo*, it should be noted that cases in which the pronoun doubles a direct object in the canonical position are very common (10b). There are also many examples of constructions where it doubles thematised objects or left-dislocated ones (17).

(17) Temprano a la Balbina$_i$ ya estube a visitarle_i (HiCoBasCo).
'Early I went to visit her-DAT (DIRECT OBJECT), Balbina'.

Leísmo also occurs in relative clauses with (18) co-referential and non co-referential relative pronouns (14c). Likewise, the direct object can occur in a previous clause (11a) or can even been found in another person's intervention (19).

(18) La otra$_i$ de diez y seis a diez y siete años [...] en la costura, mucho más adelantada, que le_i tuvimos en San Sebastián (HiCoBasCo).
'The other one of 16 or 17 [...] much more advanced in sewing, we had her-DAT (DIRECT OBJECT) in San Sebastian'.

(19) – Está Marile$_i$ arriba. – Ya le_i he visto (CoBasCo, Gernika, Bizkaia).
'– Marile is upstairs. – I have already seen her-DAT (DIRECT OBJECT)'.

5 Basque in contact with Spanish. Towards an account of feminine *leísmo*

The gender loss in accusative clitics has been associated with the influence of Basque on this variety of Spanish. As Echenique (1987) pointed out, *leísmo* is a simplifying and reorganizing phenomenon of the pronominal system. Along the same lines, Fernández Ulloa (2002) emphasised the importance of the lack of gender morphemes in the Basque language as a trigger for an opposition based on animacy in the pronominal system of this variety of Spanish. For Landa (1995, 154 footnote 7), however, the explanation of *leísmo* in terms of contact is not sufficient, as she considers that "this does not explain why Basque Spanish *leísmo* is limited to human referents".

Agreeing with the hypothesis of language contact as an external factor for the change, Fernández-Ordóñez (2012, 85–99) has considered that the origin of the use of dative morphology for accusative contexts could be explained in

Basque Spanish as an extension of Differential Object Marking (DOM) to the verb. In this variety, DOM is realised not only on the noun (by the preposition *a*), but also on the verb (morphologically marking with *le/s*). While considering the changes in the Spanish varieties in contact with non Indo-European languages, such as Quechua, Guaraní and Basque, with the same characteristics (i.e. lack of gender and object clitics, null agreement morphemes), Fernández-Ordóñez has posited that "there was a grammatical rearrangement or replacement of one category (gender) by another category (case)" (Fernández-Ordóñez 2012, 99).

As we will see, the information provided in the previous section clearly confirms the contact-based explanation for feminine *leísmo*. We will defend that intense contact between Spanish and other languages with no clitic pronouns or gender will eventually trigger a process of linguistic convergence. This process occurs in an area of Spanish where there exists already variation in the clitic pronouns system. This convergence affects the three relevant categories in terms of pronominal selection in Spanish: gender, number and case.

5.1 Gender in Basque

Firstly, Basque has grammatical features that tend to promote gender loss in Spanish pronouns used by Basque speakers. We must remember that in this language there is no category similar to the pronominal clitics in Spanish. Instead, the information that they provide is necessarily integrated in the verbal morphology. That is, in the case of accusative forms, the personal forms of the verb are necessarily inflected for number and person, and they agree with direct objects in the same sentence or the antecedents of which can be traced back to an earlier part of the discourse, or can understood contextually when implicit. The following examples illustrate this:

(20) a. Esta mañana he encontrado <u>esos libros</u>$_i$. *Los*$_i$ he comprado enseguida.
 'This morning I came across those books. I bought them-ACC at once'.
 b. Gaur goizean <u>liburu horiek</u>$_i$ aurkitu di*t*ut$_i$. Berehala erosi di*t*ut.
 'This morning I came across those books (DIRECT OBJECT). I bought them-ACC at once'.

Note how, in Spanish (20a), there is a first mention of the lexical direct object without clitic doubling and a second mention of the same direct object in the form of the clitic *los* in the following sentence, which is necessarily anaphorically interpreted. However, the Basque version of the same sequence (20b) incorporates an obligatory morphological third-person plural accusative marker -*it*- in the verbal form *ditut*, which, in the first sentence, agrees with the explicit lexical direct object and replicates it, whilst in the second the same marker -*it*- allows us to refer back to it without having to repeat it.

In addition to this striking structural difference between the Spanish pronominal system which includes anaphoric clitics and the Basque one with morphological agreement with the different verbal arguments, whether they are explicit or not, there is a fundamental difference in terms of how gender is marked. As we have just pointed out, Basque verbal morphemes indicate number and person but not gender. Indeed, pronouns in Basque, like other nominal categories or verbs, do not include formal markers that distinguish masculine from feminine antecedents or any other type of information reminiscent of Spanish grammatical gender.[11] Thus, as shown in sentences (21), a direct object referring to masculine entities, like *gizonak* 'men' (21a), and another one with a feminine referent, like *emakumeak* 'women', is expressed in exactly the same way in the auxiliary of the verbal form *aurkitu ditut* by using the third-person plural accusative marker -*it*-, as is also used in (20).

(21) a. Herriko gizonak aurkitu di*t*ut.
      'I came across the men of the town'.
   b. Herriko emakumeak aurkitu di*t*ut.
      'I came across the women of the town'.

In sum, Basque, the language in contact with Spanish in the Basque Country, not only necessarily identifies direct objects through the use of morphological markers, but it also lacks the nominal or verbal inflection for gender and does thus not mark the gender of nominal antecedents.

5.2 Contact between Basque and Spanish

Although the current contact situation between Spanish and Basque, detailed in section 5.1, provides a first explanation for the use of feminine *leísmo* in Basque Spanish, historical information on the links between Spanish and Basque as well as the geographical and sociolinguistic distribution of the phenomenon under study point unequivocally in the same direction (see sections 4.1 and 4.2).

---

[11] With the exception of the informal second-person singular pronoun, *hi*, which does incorporate a distinction between masculine and feminine in the verbal morphology, the other pronouns – including the more formal second person singular and more common *zu* – do not include this feature, which is also absent in the rest of the Basque grammar.

However, it must be kept in mind that the current scenario of strong contact between Basque and Spanish in areas where Basque is still L1 is, in fact, a pale reflection of what must have been the situation throughout the whole of the Modern Age, the period in which Basque started being displaced in most regions to the south of today's Basque speaking areas. The language's replacement and displacement intensified in the 19th century to the final decades of the 20th century and was aided by the spread of compulsory education and the region's industrialisation (Camus/Gómez Seibane 2010). Obviously, the process of language change included initially stages in which there was access to Spanish and bilingualism spread among the Basque speaking population, favouring the emergence of relatively stable language transfer phenomena. As already said, it is a situation that continues today, although education has ensured more organised access to knowledge of both languages and an increase in the number of balanced bilinguals, which limits the spread of transfers from one language to the other. Indeed, there are now hardly any monolingual Basque speakers and bilinguals with limited proficiency in Spanish are equally rare; and if found, they are invariably elderly people with rural backgrounds. Despite the evolving situation, it cannot be denied that, both historically and today, the Spanish variety spoken in large parts of the Basque Country is the product of a contact situation in which elements of Basque have been transferred, such as for instance feminine *leísmo*.

Indeed, as we have seen, gender loss in accusative clitics can be observed in Basque Spanish spoken in those areas of the Basque Country where Basque remained spoken until relatively recently. On the contrary, it is totally absent in areas where no historical evidence for Basque exists. This is the case of the most western areas of Bizkaia and Araba and southern areas of the banks of the Ebro in Araba and Navarre. As displayed in Map 1, in today's Spanish-speaking areas of Araba and Navarre, where Basque was spoken until at least the end of the 19th century, it is common to document the use of *le*, *les* for *la*, *las*. It is equally elucidating that the phenomenon is most common in the Basque-speaking areas of inner Bizkaia and northwest Navarre, together with Gipuzkoa (Camus/Gómez Seibane 2015a; 2015b) and is very significantly used in rural areas, where Basque is the first language for most of the population and Spanish is used less commonly (See the data cited above from COSER and from our corpus of oral interviews).

In this regard, we must again insist on the diastratic differences that can be inferred from the sources and interviews with urban speakers cited in section 3.2. Remember that it is among the monolingual Spanish-speaking urban population that the phenomenon is less common, although it might be accepted. Additionally, it increases in frequency as informants' knowledge of Basque increases, as is the case for the population for whom Spanish is an acquired language.

It can hence be concluded that there is a correlation between the feminine *leísmo* and knowledge of Basque (Camus/Gómez Seibane 2015a; 2015b).

5.3 Gender loss in Spanish in contact with Amerindian languages

Lastly, another argument corroborates the link between gender loss in the pronominal system and contact with Basque, to wit, the presence of the same trait in other Spanish varieties in contact with languages where, like Basque, gender is not marked. This link between the use of clitics in Basque Spanish and those in varieties of Latin American Spanish in strong contact with Amerindian languages has often been observed and has been described in detail in the last twenty years (Lipski 1996; Palacios 1998; 2005; Fernández-Ordóñez 1999, 1341; Gómez Seibane 2012a, 38–49). In what follows we will now provide clear illustrations of this. Concretely, we will exemplify this similarity with cases of Spanish varieties in contact with Quechua, Guaraní and Mayan languages.

5.3.1 Spanish in the Andes in contact with Quechua

In the highland or mountainous areas of Ecuador, Peru and Bolivia, Spanish has evolved in bilingual settings and is in heavy contact with Amerindian languages, particularly Quechua (in Ecuador known as Quichua) and, to a lesser extent, Aymara. These languages do not have an unstressed pronominal system (clitics) for the third person nor do they distinguish between masculine or feminine, unlike Spanish (Palacios 2005, 72). They further only incorporate an indication of the object in the verb if it has an animate referent. All these traits are evocative of the discussed characteristics of Basque. Moreover, as we will see now, they also appear in the Spanish spoken in this area of the Andes (Fernández-Ordóñez 1999; Palacios 2002; 2005; Gómez Seibane 2012a).

Firstly, in the Spanish variety spoken in the Ecuadorian mountains (which largely includes the variety spoken in the capital, Quito), the presence of a *leísmo*-type pronominal system, in which the originally dative form *le/les* is also widely used for both masculine and feminine accusatives, is well documented (Palacios 2005, 66–67; Gómez Seibane 2012a, 39–40), as can be seen in the following examples.

(22) a. *Les$_i$ van a matar [a ellos$_i$]* (Fernández-Ordóñez 1999, 1342).
 'They are going to kill them-DAT (DIRECT OBJECT) [them]'.

b. *Le*ᵢ vi <u>a la Rosa</u>ⱼ (Palacios 2005, example 2a)
   'I saw her-DAT (DIRECT OBJECT), Rosa'.

Although this widespread use of *le/s* seems to be frequent, particularly with animate antecedents, there are also examples with inanimate direct objects, like those in (23).

(23) a. *Les*ᵢ aplasté <u>a toditos</u>ⱼ para hacer un pastel [los plátanos] (Gómez Seibane 2012a, 40).
   'I squashed all of them-DAT (DIRECT OBJECT) to make a cake [the bananas (MASC)]'.
   b. *Les* cociné y *les*ᵢ metí al horno [<u>las papas</u>ᵢ] (Gómez Seibane 2012a, 40).
   'I cooked them-DAT (DIRECT OBJECT) and put-DAT (DIRECT OBJECT) in the oven [the potatoes (FEM)]'.

In this respect, it is important to note that Ecuadorian Highland Spanish also very frequently resorts to the omission of clitics, so-called null objects, if the direct object's antecedent is inanimate, as shown in (24), in a very similar way as in Basque Spanish (see section 3.3).

(24) <u>La leche</u>ᵢ Øᵢ vendían a 1,20 $ (Fernández-Ordóñez 1999, 1342).
   'They sold the milk at $1.20'.

A similar simplification can be found in the mountainous regions of Peru, Bolivia and northwest Argentina, areas with strong contact between Spanish and Quechua, or Spanish and Aymara. The loss or neutralisation of gender is here also observed in accusative clitics. In this case, however, the chosen form is not *le/s* but *lo*, both for the masculine and feminine – which is why they are referred to as *loísmo* varieties – and also for the singular and plural, as shown in (25).

(25) a. El hombre campesino por ejemplo <u>a la guitarra</u>ⱼ *lo*ᵢ tiene como ciencia (Palacios 2005, example 1a).
   'Peasants, for instance, the guitar (FEM SING) regard it-ACC MASC SING to be a science'.
   b. <u>A los de Huayranphue</u>ⱼ... yo he ido a vacunar*lo*ᵢ (Palacios 2005, example 1b).
   'Those from Huayranphue (MASC PL), I went to vaccinate them-ACC MASC SING'.

As a result, unlike in Ecuadorian Highland Spanish, these varieties neutralize gender and number, but continue to maintain the distinction between the dative (*le*) and the accusative (*lo*). It is important to highlight another common feature: like Basque and Ecuadorian Highland Spanish, in these varieties examples can also be found of the omission of accusative clitics, as illustrated in (26).

(26) a. A todas las mujeres$_i$ Ø$_i$ han llevado al mercado (Gómez Seibane 2012a, 41).
 'The women, they have taken to market'.
 b. Esos bultos$_i$ Ø$_i$ vas a llevar a la tienda (Gómez Seibane 2012a, 41).
 'These parcels, you are going to take to the shop'.

5.3.2 Spanish in contact with Guaraní

In Paraguay and also in the provinces of Misiones, Corrientes and the eastern side of Chaco and Formosa, in the northeast of Argentina near the border with Paraguay, there is also a strong language contact situation and, to a greater or lesser extent, bilingualism in Spanish and Guaraní. Like Quechua/Quichua and Aymara, Guaraní does not have pronominal clitics. Instead, it uses a pronominal construction with postpositions for the third person that does not distinguish between the accusative and the dative nor mark gender. These properties can also be seen in the Spanish of this whole area in different ways, as we will see now (Fernández-Ordóñez 1999; Palacios 2000; 2005; Gómez Seibane 2012a).

Firstly, gender loss is widespread throughout this whole area, normally with a preference for *leísmo*, like in Ecuador, as shown in (27).

(27) Le$_i$ vi ayer a María$_i$ (Gómez Seibane 2012a, 44).
 'I saw her-DAT (DIRECT OBJECT) yesterday, María'.

Cases with the pronoun lo are also documented in rural areas of Paraguay, Peru, Bolivia and northwest Argentina. As shown in the examples in (28), the form lo is used for feminine (28a) and masculine (28b) referents.

(28) a. El que puede se ha comprado una vaca$_i$ en su época y lo$_i$ va criando (Palacios 2000, 131).
 'He who could bought in his day a cow (FEM) and rears it-ACC MASC SING'.
 b. La familia a lo mejor prepara un serdito$_i$ (sic) o un serdo$_i$ (sic) para matar*lo*$_i$ en Navidad (Palacios 2000, 131).
 'Maybe the family will prepare a piglet (MASC) or a pig (MASC) to slaughter it-ACC MASC SING at Christmas'.

Distinctions in number are often eliminated too, particularly in Paraguay; as such, the form *le* ends up functioning in *leísmo* varieties as a single clitic for all kinds of objects.

(29) a. En Estados Unidos por ejemplo los norteamericanos *le*$_i$ tienen como animales [a los indios$_i$] (Gómez Seibane 2012a, 43)
'In the United States, for instance, North Americans regard them-DAT SING (DIRECT OBJECT) as animals [the Indians]'.
b. *Le*$_i$ saludo a la señora$_i$ (Fernández-Ordóñez 1999, 1348).
'I greet her-DAT (DIRECT OBJECT), the lady'.
c. Los peregrinantes$_i$ acuden de todos los puntos del país, sin importar*le*$_i$ los más duros sacrificios (Fernández-Ordóñez 1999, 1348).
'Pilgrims flock from all corners of the country, without that the harshest of sacrifices matters them-DAT SING'.

Once again, as in the Spanish contact varieties reviewed here, the omission of accusative clitics is also documented, albeit more often for objects referring to inanimate antecedents (30).

(30) El tronco$_i$ había que arrastrar Ø$_i$ hasta la picada (Gómez Seibane 2012a, 44).
'The trunk they had to drag to the forest trail'.

5.3.3 Spanish in contact with Mayan languages

Lastly, in areas of Guatemala where native Mayan languages are mainly spoken – for instance, in the Tzutujil area –, bilingual inhabitants speak a Spanish with simplified pronominal systems (Palacios 2005; Gómez Seibane 2012a). In this case, the pronoun that neutralizes gender for the accusative is *lo* and, as in Paraguay, it is also used indistinctly for the singular and plural. In (31), examples of these Guatemalan constructions with *lo* are given.

(31) Me fueron a dejar a la escuela, pero yo *lo*$_i$ quería soltar a mi mamá$_i$ (Gómez Seibane 2012a, 48).
'They went to leave me at school, but I wanted to let her-ACC MASC go, my mother (FEM)'.

Once again, these varieties usually exhibit null objects, particularly in the case of lesser educated speakers with lower proficiency in Spanish (32).

(32) [Y] el niño~i~ que tuvo no lo~i~ quería, prefirió ir a tirar Ø~i~ al río (Gómez Seibane 2012a, 48).
'[And] the little boy, she did not want him-ACC, she preferred to throw (him)in the river'.

A similar use of *lo* can be found in Mexico in the Mayan area (Yucatán), as well as among speakers of Nahuatl (Lipski 1996, 305–306; Gómez Seibane 2012a, 47–48), where *lo* can even be used for the dative (33).

(33) *Lo*~i~ van a dar de comer [a la gente~i~ en una fiesta] (Gómez Seibane 2012a, 48).
'They are going to give food to them-ACC MASC SING [to the people (FEM SING) at a party]'.

In sum, parallels in the clitics use in Basque Spanish and Latin American Spanish varieties in contact with Amerindian languages appear to support the existence of a shared explanation, following which a change has occurred due to long-lasting heavy contact. This is the hypothesis that we aim to explore in the following section.

6 Convergence between Basque and Spanish: The pronominal system in Basque Spanish

As Palacios has argued (2005, 71), it is reasonable to believe that contact contexts can give rise to general processes of change in which similar mechanisms can be found, with equally similar consequences and results. It is therefore legitimate to try to seek common explanations for phenomena found in such contact situations, like those in Latin American areas in contact with Amerindian languages. Palacios (2005) provides an explanatory model that, considering the parallels with Latin American situations, can be useful to explain what has occurred to the Basque Spanish.

6.1 A pronominal clitic convergence model

Palacios' analysis of the Latin American Spanish phenomena for which there is a reduction in the unstressed pronoun paradigm starts out from the observation that the social and linguistic conditions are very similar as there is heavy contact. The languages that coexist with Spanish all have pronominal systems with similar structural properties – no clitic pronouns nor gender – and it is in this grammatical aspect that Spanish displays a change. Due to convergence, similar structures from different coexisting languages – in this case the pronominal systems of Spanish and various Amerindian languages – exert a mutual influence on each other. Thus changes are set in motion that lead to the disappearance of previously existing differences, particularly in parts of the system where there was already a certain degree of variation and, hence, instability. The outcome is the contact-induced process of structural re-organisation or re-structuring, often resulting in the extension or simplification of a syntactic or morphological paradigm (Palacios 2005, 83–85). In the case of the unstressed pronoun or clitic paradigms of the aforementioned Spanish varieties in contact with Amerindian languages, this convergence has led to modifications that have a crucial impact on the three parameters that govern the pronoun selection, namely, gender, number and case. What then occurs is that at least one of them – and often two or even three – are eliminated or neutralised leading to the simplification of the original pronominal paradigm in Spanish.

As Palacios (2005) points out, the way in which the aforementioned morphological features are affected seems to respond to a set of general principles, and so the elimination of one or more of them does not seem to be random but based on a hierarchy, evidently associated with the characteristics of the languages in contact. According to this hierarchy, gender is the feature most likely to be neutralised, followed by number and case. Interestingly, this order seems to be corroborated by language acquisition data, namely the way in which children acquire these distinctions in the pronominal clitics in Spanish. As Palacios shows (2005, 75–76) from different studies with bilingual Spanish children under the age of three living in Los Angeles and Quechua speakers with Spanish as L2, the first distinction that they master is case (*le/lo*); this is generally followed by number, while the contrast between masculine and feminine comes last, which explains in turn why it is the first feature that is lost.

Considering all this, neither of the two ways of simplifying the pronominal paradigms documented in the Spanish in contact with Amerindian languages, is then surprising. On the one hand, we have the varieties with *loísmo* (Peru, Bolivia, northwest Argentina, Guatemala, and Mexico), where gender is lost for the accusative and sometimes number, but the resulting single form, *lo*, continues to be distinguished from the dative *le*. This choice of *lo* as a neutral pronoun with no reference to gender can be explained by its use in standard Spanish as an unmarked form, i.e. the form necessarily used in all cases with a joint masculine and feminine antecedent, and also in sentence and other types of anaphora. These circumstances no doubt facilitate its reading as a more comprehensive form.

On the other hand, there are the *leísmo* varieties of Spanish found in Ecuador or Paraguay, where gender loss (and number) favours the dative clitic *le*, which in turn implies the neutralisation of case. The reason for this more extreme option might be due to the fact that the forms of the dative do not incorporate gender in Spanish and can thus be used to refer to both masculine and feminine. This makes them the perfect candidate to function as pronouns with no gender marking. But, as Palacios also rightly notes (2005, 77), in the grammar of Spanish numerous changes affect the marking of datives and accusatives, often resulting in the extension of dative markers to the accusative. The phenomenon of *leísmo* found in the studied varieties of Spanish would merely be another example of this change brought about by an external agent, that is, contact with Amerindian languages.

In this respect, it is essential to bear in mind some external factors that are key when measuring the intensity of the contact: the level of the informants' education and, closely linked to this, their level of bilingualism or, rather, their proficiency in the various languages involved. In addition, the presence of a language with more marked or distinctive characteristics than that of the standard model is clearly conditioned by the community's level of proficiency in that language. It is possible to find striking variation in (a) incipient bilingual speakers with a low educational and low proficiency level in the language in question – for instance, in settings where Quechua or Guaraní is the first language –, (b) successive bilingual speakers with more proficiency in Spanish, and (c) balanced bilingual speakers. The resulting scenario, in areas of heavy contact, is the presence of an intricate continuum of linguistic varieties and, as a result, notable sociolinguistic variation. This is something that we have already proven in the case of Basque Spanish (Camus/Gómez Seibane 2015a), a variety to which we will now apply Palacios' explanatory model (2005).

6.2 The pronominal system in Basque Spanish

As discussed previously, Basque Spanish spoken is a variety of Spanish that has evolved in conditions of long-lasting heavy contact with Basque, a language which it has replaced in some areas and with which it continues to coexist in others. Not so long ago, this contact took place in conditions very similar to those that can still be found in the Latin American areas described above. As in these cases, Basque, the substrate language, has no morphological gender and treats direct objects with masculine and feminine antecedents in the same way. Moreover, Basque Spanish is characterised by an unstressed pronoun paradigm with a considerable degree of variation and instability, as shown in section

3, with different competing systems, some of which erase the differences between the accusative and the dative pronouns.

We believe that, given these contact conditions, the use of the unstressed pronouns in Basque Spanish can be regarded as the result of a convergence process, which partly coincides with the one described by Palacios (2005) for the uses in Latin American Spanish varieties in contact with Amerindian languages (Camus/Gómez Seibane 2015a, 214–216). The differences in between Basque and Spanish gradually faded for this particular grammatical aspect and modifications that can be interpreted as due to convergence between the two grammars showed up. On the one hand, as in Castilian Spanish, this new variety of Spanish partly tends to neutralize the case-related distinctions typical of the Castilian Spanish, generalizing it in the case of animate antecedents (*leísmo*). On the other hand, a new Basque-related innovation is also incorporated: the elimination of gender distinctions (the masculine and feminine *leísmo*), a phenomenon unknown in neighbouring Spanish dialects. Furthermore, as explained in section 3.3, the pronominal system of Basque Spanish is also characterised by two other innovations: the omission of accusative clitics when referring to inanimate antecedents and the pronominal doubling of direct object pronouns with human referents.

Our account of the contact-induced gender loss in Basque Spanish spoken is thus supported by the same arguments relating to Latin America Spanish contact varieties. As gender markers are at the bottom of the pronominal hierarchy scale, this makes them more prone to change, thus explaining their neutralisation in contact situations with a language that does not use them. Likewise, neutralisation through the form *le* can also be accounted for, namely by the fact that *le* is an ideal candidate for this function since in its traditional dative use, it refers indistinctly to feminine and masculine antecedents. We have also pointed out that the extension of this original form of the dative to the accusative (initially only in reference to masculine antecedents) is a sign of long-lasting evolutionary trends in Spanish: the extension of dative markers at the detriment of accusative ones. This is also the case for the preposition *a* to mark human (and, sometimes, animate) direct objects and, far more relevant to our case, the elimination of case-related distinctions in third person clitics that regularly occurs in Spain's mainland dialects with *leísmo*.

Lastly, processes induced by language contact must be taken into account. Also in the case of Basque, although the characteristics of the system of unstressed pronouns described in this paper – and, among them, feminine *leísmo* – are noticeably different from those of the standard variety of Spanish, the extent to which they are used by speakers will depend on the person's level of proficiency in Spanish. It is particularly noticeable in the case of incipient bilingual speakers (of which there are very few in the Basque case) or among successive bilingual speakers (who are far more numerous). On the other hand, even though large numbers of monolingual Spanish speakers may accept and occasionally use it, they tend to reintroduce the standard use of gender in the accusative and, as a consequence, they use the feminine *la* more regularly than the masculine *le*.

7 Concluding remarks

This paper examined the grammatical, historical, geographic, social and linguistic scope of feminine *leísmo* in Basque Spanish while taking into account the general context of the variations in the system of unstressed pronouns found in mainland European Spanish.

Its growing presence in written texts from the 16th century onward and its current use in Basque speaking areas and among older bilingual informants with a lower educational level who live in rural areas, have been detailed. In contrast, it occurs less among Spanish speakers living in urban areas or with a university education, although they do accept it as grammatical. We have further shown how it is particularly common when replacing human direct objects and in clitic doubling constructions.

Lastly, using Palacios' model (2005) developed for Spanish in contact with American languages, an explanation was proposed for this phenomenon in Basque Spanish, according to which convergence took place between the grammars Basque and Spanish with respect to the use of unstressed pronouns. This resulted in the (partial) loss of gender markers – that do not exist in Basque – and, following general evolutionary trends found in Spanish, dative forms extend overtaking accusative functions.

8 References

Alvar, Manuel/Llorente, Antonio/Buesa, Tomás, *Atlas lingüístico y etnográfico de Aragón, Navarra y Rioja*, Zaragoza/Madrid, Institución Fernando el Católico – La Muralla, 1979–1983 (= ALEANR).

Bosque, Ignacio, *El nombre común*, in: Bosque, Ignacio/Demonte, Violeta (edd.), *Gramática descriptiva de la lengua española*, Madrid, Espasa Calpe, 1999, 3–75.

Campbell, Lyle/Muntzel, Martha C., *The structural consequences of language death*, in: Dorian, Nancy (ed.), *Investigating obsolescence. Studies in language contraction and death*, Cambridge, Cambridge University Press, 1989, 191–196.

Camus, Bruno, *El castellano del País Vasco en el siglo XIX. Las cartas del Archivo Zavala*, in: García Martín, José María (ed.), *Actas del IX Congreso Internacional de Historia de la Lengua Española*, Madrid/Frankfurt, Iberoamericana/Vervuert, 2015, 1775–1789.

Camus, Bruno/Gómez Seibane, Sara, *Basque and Spanish in 19th century San Sebastian*, Ianua. Revista Philologica Romanica 10 (2010), 223–239.

Camus, Bruno/Gómez Seibane, Sara, *Nuevos datos sobre la omisión de objetos en el castellano del País Vasco*, Círculo de Lingüística Aplicada a la Comunicación 61 (2015), 211–236, doi.org/10.5209/rev_CLAC.2015.v61.48473 (= 2015a).

Camus, Bruno/Gómez Seibane, Sara, *La diversidad del español en Araba. Sistemas pronominales a partir de las encuestas de COSER*, Revista de Filología Española 95:2 (2015), 279–306 (= 2015b).

COSER = Fernández-Ordóñez, Inés (ed.), *Corpus oral y sonoro del español rural*, Universidad Autónoma de Madrid, 2005–present. www.corpusrural.es.

Echenique, Mª Teresa, *Historia lingüística vasco-románica*, Madrid, Paraninfo, 1987.

Echenique, Mª Teresa, *La lengua castellana hablada en el País Vasco. A propósito de los clíticos de tercera persona*, in: Briz, Antonio/Gómez, José Ramón/Martínez, Mª José (edd.), *Pragmática y gramática del español hablado. Actas del II Simposio sobre Análisis del Discurso Oral*, Valencia, Pórtico, 1996, 65–74.

Fernández-Ordóñez, Inés, *Isoglosas internas del castellano. El sistema referencial del pronombre átono de tercera persona*, Revista de Filología Española 74 (1994), 71–125.

Fernández-Ordóñez, Inés, *Leísmo, laísmo y loísmo*, in: Bosque, Ignacio/Demonte, Violeta (edd.), *Gramática descriptiva de la lengua española*, Madrid, Espasa Calpe, 1999, 1317–1397.

Fernández-Ordóñez, Inés, *Hacia una dialectología histórica. Reflexiones sobre la historia del leísmo, el laísmo y el loísmo*, Boletín de la Real Academia Española 81 (2001), 389–464.

Fernández-Ordóñez, Inés, *Del Cantábrico a Toledo. El "neutro de materia" hispánico en un contexto románico y tipológico (primera parte)*, Revista de Historia de la Lengua Española 1 (2006), 67–118.

Fernández-Ordóñez, Inés, *El "neutro de materia" en Asturias y Cantabria. Análisis gramatical y nuevos datos*, in: Delgados Cobos, Inmaculada/Puigvert Ocal, Alicia (edd.), *Ex admiratione et amicitia. Homenaje a Ramón Santiago*, Madrid, Ediciones del Orto, 2007, 395–434.

Fernández-Ordóñez, Inés, *Dialect areas and linguistic change. Pronominal paradigms in Ibero-Romance dialects from a cross-linguistic and social typology perspective*, in: de Vogelaer, Gunther/Seiler, Guido (edd.), *The dialect laboratory. Dialects as a testing ground for theories of language change*, Amsterdam/Philadelphia, John Benjamins, 2012, 73–106.

Fernández Ulloa, Teresa, *Análisis sociolingüístico del leísmo en el castellano del País Vasco (un corpus oral de Bermeo, Bizkaia)*, in: Echenique, Mª Teresa/Sánchez, Juan (edd.), *Actas del V Congreso Internacional de Historia de la Lengua Española*, Madrid, Gredos, 2002, 1687–1718.

Gómez Seibane, Sara, *Uso de los pronombres átonos de tercera persona en guipuzcoanos emigrados a Indias en el siglo XVIII*, Res Diachronicae Virtual 3: Estudios sobre el siglo XVIII (2004), 39–51.

Gómez Seibane, Sara, *Neutro de materia y otros fenómenos del sistema pronominal átono en Bilbao (siglos XV-XVII)*, in: Gómez Seibane, Sara/Ramírez Luengo, José Luis (edd.), *Maestra en mucho. Estudios filológicos en homenaje a la profesora Carmen Isasi Martínez*, Buenos Aires, Voces del Sur, 2010, 133–148.

Gómez Seibane, Sara, *Los pronombres átonos (le, la, lo) en el español*, Madrid, Arco/Libros, 2012 (= 2012a).

Gómez Seibane, Sara, *La omisión y duplicación de objetos en el castellano del País Vasco*, in: Camus Bergareche, Bruno/Gómez Seibane, Sara (edd.), *El castellano del País Vasco*, Bilbao, Universidad del País Vasco/Euskal Herriko Unibertsitatea, 2012, 193–214 (= 2012b).

Gómez Seibane, Sara, *Contacto de lenguas y orden de palabras. OV/VO en el español del País Vasco*, Lingüística Española Actual 34:1 (2012), 115–135 (= 2012c).

Gómez Seibane, Sara, *Los pronombres átonos (le, la, lo) en el español: aproximación histórica*, Madrid, Arco/Libros, 2013.

Gómez Seibane, Sara, *Español en contacto con la lengua vasca. Datos sobre la duplicación de objetos directos posverbales*, in: Palacios, Azucena (ed.), *Variación y cambio lingüístico en situaciones de contacto*, Madrid/Frankfurt, Iberoamericana/Vervuert, 2017, 143–159.

Gómez Seibane, Sara, *Leísmo y duplicación de objeto directo en tres variedades de español peninsular*, in: Blestel, Élodie/Palacios, Azucena (edd.), *Variedades del español en contacto con otras lenguas. Metodologías, protocolos y modelos de análisis*, Bern, Peter Lang, 2020, in press (= 2020a).

Gómez Seibane, Sara, *Animación y contacto lingüístico en la duplicación de objeto directo*, in: Palacios, Azucena/Sánchez Paraíso, María (edd.), *Dinámicas lingüísticas de las situaciones de contacto*, Berlin, De Gruyter, 2020, in press (= 2020b).

Gómez Seibane, Sara, *Exploring historical linguistic convergence between Basque and Spanish*, in: Bouzouita, Miriam/Enghels, Renata/Vanderschueren, Clara (edd.), *Convergence and divergence in Ibero-Romance across contact situations and beyond*, Berlin/Boston, De Gruyter, in this volume, 55–85.

Landa, Alazne, *Conditions on null objects in Basque Spanish and their relation to leísmo and clitic doubling*, PhD dissertation, Los Angeles, California, University of Southern California, 1995.

Lapesa, Rafael, *Sobre los orígenes y evolución del leísmo, laísmo y loísmo*, in: Baldinger, Kurt (ed.), *Festschrift Walther von Wartburg*, Tübingen, Max Niemeyer, 1968, 523–551.

Lipski, John, *El español en América*, Madrid, Cátedra, 1996.

Paasch-Kaiser, Christine, *El castellano de Getxo. Estudio empírico de aspectos morfológicos, sintácticos y semánticos de una variedad del castellano hablado en el País Vasco*, Berlin/Boston, De Gruyter, 2015.

Palacios, Azucena, *Variación sintáctica en el sistema pronominal del español paraguayo*, Anuario de Lingüística Hispánica 14 (1998), 451–474.

Palacios, Azucena, *El sistema pronominal del español paraguayo. Un caso de contacto de lenguas*, in: Calvo Pérez, Julio (ed.), *Teoría y práctica del contacto. El español de América en el candelero*, Frankfurt/Madrid, Vervuert/Iberoamericana, 2000, 122–143.

Palacios, Azucena, *Leísmo y loísmo en el español ecuatoriano. El sistema pronominal del español andino*, in: *Homenaje al Dr. Luis Jaime Cisneros*, Lima, Universidad Católica del Perú, 2002, 389–408.

Palacios, Azucena, *Aspectos teóricos y metodológicos del contacto de lenguas. El sistema pronominal del español en áreas de contacto con lenguas amerindias*, in: Noll, Volker/Zimmermann, Klaus/Neumann-Holzschuh, Ingrid (edd.), *El español en América. Aspectos teóricos, particularidades, contactos*, Frankfurt/Madrid, Vervuert/Iberoamericana, 2005, 53–94.

RAE/ASALE = Real Academia de la Lengua Española/Asociación de Academia de la Lengua Española, *Nueva gramática de la lengua española*, Madrid, Espasa Calpe, 2009.

Urrutia, Hernán, *El español en el País Vasco. Peculiaridades morfosintácticas*, Letras de Deusto 40 (1988), 33–43.

Sara Gómez Seibane
Exploring historical linguistic convergence between Basque and Spanish

Abstract: Null objects, female *leísmo*, i.e., the use of the dative *le/s* used as direct object pronouns for female referents, and the OV pattern with new information are frequent in spoken Basque Spanish. These (morpho)syntactic phenomena are absent (or extremely limited) in non-contact Spanish varieties and have their equivalent in Basque. Therefore, these structures are said to have been induced by the long-standing contact between Basque and Spanish.

I have explored these phenomena in a corpus of letters written by Basque-Spanish bilinguals during the 18th and 19th century, an important moment in the spread of Spanish to now bilingual areas due to literacy. These data have then been compared to those from personal letters written by Spanish monolinguals. I have performed descriptive and inferential statistical analyses, using IBM SPSS Statistics 22.0, and have also analysed the data qualitatively. Results show that variation is due to internal and external factors, caused by linguistic convergence mechanisms, similar to the processes of contact-induced grammatical replication.

Keywords: null objects, dative, *le/s*, female referents, OV, female *leísmo*, Spanish, Basque Spanish, convergence

1 Introduction

The use of null objects as in (1), dative *le/s* used as direct object pronouns for female referents (*leísmo*) (2), and a higher percentage of OV word pattern with new information (3) have been identified to be characteristic of the Spanish

---

Note: This research is part of the project "COREC: Corpus Oral de Referencia del Español en Contacto. Fase I: Lenguas Minoritarias" headed by Azucena Palacios (Universidad Autónoma de Madrid) and Sara Gómez Seibane (Universidad de La Rioja), funded by the Spanish Ministry for Science and Innovation (Ref. PID2019-105865GB-I00). I am very grateful to Lorena Saínz-Maza Lecanda for her helpful revision of the English translation. I gratefully acknowledge the constructive comments of the anonymous referees. A previous version of this work was presented at the *International Conference on Linguistics of Ibero-Romance Languages. Ibero-Romance in Contact and in Contrast*, Ghent University, on 14–16 Dec. 2015. All errors remain strictly my own.

Sara Gómez Seibane, Universidad de La Rioja

https://doi.org/10.1515/9783110736250-003

spoken in the Basque Country,[1] an autonomous community in northern Spain along the coast of the Bay of Biscay, where Basque and Spanish are in contact (Landa 1995; Gómez Seibane 2012a; 2012b; Camus Bergareche/Gómez Seibane in this volume).[2]

(1) *No encuentro mis llaves*
     not find.1SG my keys
     *Pensaba   que **Ø**   tenía   en el   bolsillo.*
     thought.1SG that NCL kept.1SG in the pocket
     'I can't find my keys. I thought I kept them in my pocket'.

(2) ***Le**ᵢ vi   a Maríaᵢ en la   escuela*
     CL   saw.3SG ACC Mary in the school
     'I saw Mary at school'.

(3) *Unos libros compró   ayer*
     some books bought.3SG yesterday
     'He bought some books yesterday'.

Different theoretical frameworks and methodologies have shown that language variation and change in language contact situations can be explained through both internal processes and external influence, although very often the precise role played by internal factors and contact is not clear (Aikhenvald 2007; Thomason 2010; Leglise/Chamoreau 2013). The processes and outcomes of contact settings depend on a number of sociohistorical and linguistic factors, including the duration and regularity of contact, the structure of the languages in contact, and the degree of speakers' bilingualism and awareness, among others.

---

[1] Nowadays, the Basque speaking territory is divided into seven provinces in Spain and France. Since the 1960s, the Basque language has undergone a standardisation process promoted by the Basque Language Academy. Since 1979, Basque has been one of the official languages in four Spanish provinces: Bizkaia, Gipuzkoa and Araba (all in the Autonomous Community of the Basque Country) and the north of Navarre. Especially in areas where Basque is co-official, the number of speakers of this minority language has increased in the last decades from below 600,000 to 775,000, according to data processed by Eustat, the Basque Statistics Office in 2006 (EUSTAT 2008).
[2] In the following examples, clitics and null objects (Ø), glossed as NCL, will be highlighted in bold, and referents will be underlined. When elements are co-referential, they will be co-indexed. Left-peripheral constituents at the beginning of the clause in preverbal position will also be underlined.

The contact between Basque, the only non-Indo-European language in Western Europe (Trask 1997, 358), and Romance has been taking place for about two millennia.[3] It is well known that Basque and Spanish are typologically different languages. Basque is a genetically isolated language with a subject-object-verb (SOV) configuration; it has a strongly agglutinating morphology and ergative alignment of case-marking (Trask 1997, 83). Spanish, on the contrary, is a Romance language with an SVO word order, a synthetic language (in particular, with relational synthesis), and displays an indirective alignment type (García-Miguel 2015). Notwithstanding this, typological differences do not exclude contact-induced changes. In fact, if two genetically unrelated languages are in contact and share a series of patterns or constructions, these have probably been transferred or borrowed from one to the other (Aikhenvald 2007, 2–4).

Basque and Spanish co-exist within their respective and complementary functional areas (Camus Bergareche/Gómez Seibane 2010, 227–231). From the end of the Middle Ages and during the Modern Period, for a large section of the middle and lower social classes, Basque was the native language that was used orally in everyday life, especially in rural areas. Spanish, on the contrary, was the written language for every document produced by any authority, be it the central or local government, and the church, as well as for trading relations. In fact, since the end of the 18th century, Spanish was the only language taught at schools and, therefore, people who reached a certain level of education were able to speak and write in Spanish. Consequently, a situation of diglossia persisted for centuries, and Basque-Spanish bilingualism was only present in the upper class.

---

3 The existence of Basque became known after the arrival of the Romans in Spain and Gaul in the 2nd and 1st centuries BC. However, it was not until the 10th century that documents with Basque proper names and place names were found in Araba and in some parts of the Castilian territory, where the presence of Basque might have been a consequence of medieval repopulation (Trask 1997, 35–42; Hualde 2003, 9). Although Basque was not an official language in historical times, in the French provinces of the Basque Country books were regularly published in Basque (songs, poems, prayers epitaphs and personal letters) in the 16th and 17th centuries. During these centuries, the northern boundary remained stable. Yet, in the four Spanish provinces, the language was constantly losing territory due to the pressure of Spanish, whose presence increased over the coming centuries when the Bourbon monarchy declared Spanish to be the national language and established it as the official language in schools (Camus Bergareche/Gómez Seibane 2010). Even though constant migrations of Spanish speakers to these four provinces at the beginning of the 20th century and Franco's dictatorship (1939–1975), during which the Spanish was declared Spain's only official language, accelerated the strong geographical recession of Basque, the new economic and cultural elite started several activities in favour of the Basque language and its traditions at the end of 19th century in order to protect and recover them (Trask 1997, 23–25; Hualde 2003, 10–11).

However, since the 19th century, native speakers of Basque who were in contact with Spanish in the cities (e.g. employees and servants of rich families) started to acquire some proficiency in Spanish. At the same time, during this century, more school attendance caused an increasing literacy rate in Spanish. The percentage of people who were able to read and write in Spanish in the Basque Country has thus been constantly growing, exceeding even the average for Spain (see Table 1).

Table 1: Literacy rate in the Basque Country and Spain (1860–1877) (Dávila Balsera/Eizagirre/Fernández 1995, 50).

	1860	1877
Gipuzkoa	19.6%	27.7%
Araba	41.5%	48.3%
Bizkaia	26.3%	35%
Spain	19.9%	24.5%

From this moment onwards, Basque-Spanish bilingualism experienced a progressive increase, not just in the Basque Country areas bordering the Spanish-speaking territories, such as the West of Bizkaia and the South of Araba, but increasingly throughout the entire Basque-speaking territories (Camus Bergareche/Gómez Seibane 2012, 4–8). This growth of the bilingual population also entailed the spread of the sub-standard variety of Spanish known as Basque Spanish. This variety has particular forms and patterns, many of which are the by-product of language contact. As a result, these linguistic features have turned into local features acquired by bilinguals and monolinguals in Spanish who have lived in the Basque Country for most of their lives.

In this paper, I focus on three contact-induced constructions resulting from linguistic convergence between Basque and Spanish. In brief, I will demonstrate that three Basque Spanish structures exhibiting internal variation have been activated and/or reanalysed due to exposure to the Basque language. This chapter is organised as follows: Section 2 provides a brief overview of the most important facts regarding contact-induced changes and linguistic convergence, while Section 3 presents the corpus and the methodology, which makes use of both quantitative and qualitative criteria. The empirical findings are then evaluated: null objects are discussed in Section 4, *le/s* for female referents as direct objects in Section 5, and the OV pattern in Section 6. Finally, Section 7 offers a few concluding remarks.

2 Theoretical framework: contact-induced changes and linguistic convergence

I assume the theoretical framework provided in Palacios (2007; 2013), which assumes two premises. First, linguistic changes in language contact scenarios are complex and are due to a combination of external and internal factors. Second, contact-induced changes arise from the communication needs of bilingual speakers, resulting thus from communication strategies in bilingual environments. I also adopt Matras' approach to language contact (2009) as a continuum of uses rather than as a system. In his view, the bilingual (or multilingual) speakers have a complex repertoire of forms and structures. This repertoire is not organised in different language systems but associated with social activities and regulated by the prescriptive attitudes of the speech community.

Based on these premises, Palacios (2007, 262) proposes a basic distinction between (i) *direct* contact-induced changes, which incorporate any lexical or structural features from one language to another and (ii) *indirect* ones, in which no linguistic material is incorporated directly from the other language. This paper focuses on the latter. In these indirect changes, linguistic *convergence* allows two languages, A and B, to become more alike with respect to certain features and structures, without necessarily sharing those forms (Aikhenvald 2007, 45; Palacios 2013, 194–195). Convergence will be perceptible in B due to (i) a change in the frequency of an existing phenomenon, (ii) the gaining of a new pragmatic meaning by a certain form, (iii) the expansion or simplification of a paradigm, and (iv) the increase or decrease of syntactic and semantic restrictions for a particular linguistic feature. Therefore, convergence is the result of bilingual speakers' syncretisation of processing operations present in the two languages, which allows them to apply similar mental organisation procedures to their communicative interaction in both languages (Matras/Sakel 2007, 835).

Concerning the permeability of linguistic systems, it seems that sufficient contact intensity and duration can trigger convergence in forms and structures at all levels of the grammar, including the morphological core. However, certain linguistic patterns, such as word order and pragmatic markers, are more likely to change in contact settings than other internal categories, like case markers and tenses, which appear to be more resistant (Aikhenvald 2007, 26–27). At the same time, specific areas of the grammar can be particularly weak because of internal variation (Palacios 2013), as we will see shortly.

As recently shown by Gómez Seibane (2014), some pragmatic and morphosyntactic features of oral Basque Spanish already appear in bilingual texts from the 19th century. This is the case for the use of (i) the *soler* + infinitive periphrasis with modal meaning, (ii) the *ya* adverb to emphasise a sentence affirmatively, (iii) the null objects, and (iv) the dative *le/s* for female direct objects. Furthermore, it is also demonstrated that in 19th century Basque Spanish there is a tendency to use a relatively freer constituent order due to the Basque OV pattern (Gómez Seibane 2015).

This paper pays attention to three (morpho)syntactic phenomena in Basque Spanish: null objects, *le/s* for female direct objects, and OV pattern. This study follows the methodology proposed by Poplack/Levey (2010, 398), whereby a contact-induced change "is present in the presumed variety and either 1) absent in the pre-contact or non-contact variety, or 2) if present [...] is not conditioned in the same way as in the source, and 3) can also be shown to parallel in some non-trivial way the behaviour of a counterpart feature in the source". The objectives of this paper are therefore (i) to empirically analyse the productivity of these phenomena in bilingual texts from the 18th and 19th centuries, and compare these findings with those from monolingual texts from the same period; (ii) to prove through empirical data that these structures are absent (or at times extremely limited) in non-contact Spanish varieties; (iii) to demonstrate that these phenomena belong to areas of the Spanish grammar that show internal variation and/or instability; and (iv) to show that these linguistic features have an equivalent in Basque. In view of all the above, it will be concluded that these phenomena are indirect contact-induced changes, which have arisen as a result of linguistic convergence.

3 Corpus, empirical data and methodology

3.1 Bilingual and monolingual corpus: private letters

The data collected come from private letters from a historical family archive, published partially by Zavala (2008). These originate from a rural area of Gipuzkoa, one of the southern Basque territories most resistant to shifting away from the minority language. The selected letters were written by three farm managers from one family: in 203 letters, dated between 1804 and 1882, these farmers inform their lords on aspects related to the organisation of the house, shopping, service to guests, and the news in the local town. Although the letters indicate a certain degree of familiarity towards the people they work for, the letter-writers also employ formal greetings, farewell and dating conventions and display good calligraphy, revealing a high literacy rate in Spanish. The language of the letters is the local variety, Basque Spanish, as described in Camus Bergareche/Gómez Seibane (2012), which includes the use of the adverb *ya* as an affirmative particle (4a), the indicative conditional (*estaría*) instead of subjunctive imperfect tense (*estaba/estuviera*) (4b), and code-switching (4c), among other features.[4] The writers appear to be stable Basque-Spanish bilinguals.[5]

(4) a. *Ha hecho   una huerta   muy hermosa*
       Have.3SG done.PART a vegetable-garden   very beautiful
       ***ya**   le   gustará   [a] usted.*
       already   CL   will-like.2SG   [to] you
       'He has grown a very beautiful vegetable garden. You will like it' (E 1825).
   b. *No me ocurrió   que **estaría***
       no CL thought.1SG that would-be.3SG
       en el   cesto.
       in   the   basket
       'I did not think that it would be in the basket' (E n.d.).
   c. *Para que proben   morcillas   de nuestro serdo*
       so   that taste.3PL   black pudding of our   pigs
       ederrac egon biar   dute
       superb   be   must   AUX.3PL
       'So that they taste black pudding of our pigs. It should be superb' (AM 1881).

Consequently, these texts written by non-professional writers present various oral features ("language of immediacy") and are an ideal source for observing the history of Spanish linguistic varieties (Elspass 2012, 160–161). To compare the data of this bilingual corpus, a control corpus with the same text typology was used: to wit, personal letters sent in the 18th and 19th centuries with a similar "register",[6]

---

4 The orthographic confusion of sibilant fricative sounds (*serdos* instead of *cerdos*) and the absence of diphthongisation (*proben* instead of *prueben*) in (4c) are also features of Basque Spanish.
5 In examples from the bilingual corpus, I will mark the authorship of the letter (Ana J. Echavarri = E, Manuel A. Machain = M, and Atanasio Mugica = AM), followed by its date. For the control corpus, I will add the bibliographical reference, followed by the number of the letter and its date. For ease of reading, the orthography and punctuation have been modernised to a certain degree.
6 Following Biber/Conrad (2001, 175), "we use the label register as a cover term for any variety associated with a particular configuration of situational characteristics and purposes. Thus, registers are defined in nonlinguistic terms."

but written by Spanish monolinguals.[7] Most of these letters were sent from Latin America to Spain, specifically, to the cities or towns where these migrant writers' native relatives lived, such as Cádiz, Málaga, Madrid, Salamanca, Burgos, Avilés or Santander (Pérez Murillo 1999; Martínez 2007). The remaining letters were sent to Latin America by relatives who lived in the Canary Islands (Arbelo García 2012) or in monolingual areas of the Iberian Peninsula (Martínez 2007).

3.2 Empirical data and methodology

As mentioned in the introduction, for the present study I empirically analyse the productivity and the linguistic characterisation of null objects, *leísmo* and the OV pattern, using qualitative and quantitative data from two corpora. For the first phenomenon, I will take into account the variation between null and pronominal objects referring to a definite direct object. Consider the examples below. In (5), the referent is introduced in the preceding clause, and in the next clause the pronoun can be omitted (Ø) (5a) or overtly realised (5b). It should also be noted that propositional antecedents as in (5a) will also be included in the analysis. Examples (6a) and (6b) are left-dislocated direct objects,[8] possible in main and subordinate clauses: the former expresses an overt pronoun, and the latter contains a null object.[9] On the contrary, mass nouns and

---

[7] Although letters from different monolingual dialectal areas were analysed, I grouped the results into a single set of data for each phenomenon, as no significant differences were found between the letters. For §4 and §5 I used letters 93–120 from Arbelo García (2012); and letters 99–101, 103–105, 108–109, 111–120, 131, 133–134, 137, 139, 140, 142–145, 153–154, 165, 172–175, 177, 179, 180–187, 189, 190, 192, 194–199, 203–204, 207, 226–227, 231–243, 252–253, 257, 258, 260–263, 273–276 from Martínez (2007). In addition to these letters, for §6, I also used letters 1–2, 5, 7, 9–41, 43–46, 48–54, 59, 64–68, 70–78, 80–92 from Pérez Murillo (1999); and from Zavala (2008), I selected letters between 1830 and 1855, sent by lawyers from non-contact areas (Madrid, Burgos and Valladolid) and by family members resident in Madrid. As concerns the authorship of these letters, whereas in asymmetrical written communication (e.g. formal letters) people tended to hire professional writers, since the 19th century an increasing number of (literate) people were able to write texts for personal needs in symmetrical and familiarity communicative settings (Elspass 2012).
[8] These are direct objects that appear at the beginning of the clause, in clause-internal position, and with a co-referential clitic.
[9] Although Bouzouita (2014) has observed that the syntactic properties of Left Dislocation constructions show a progressive grammaticalisation process from Old Spanish onwards, there is a lack of empirical data for the 18th and 19th centuries. Therefore, data from the control corpus will also allow us to elucidate the frequency of use of the co-referential direct object clitic with left-dislocated direct objects in monolingual varieties of Spanish.

bare noun referents (7) will be excluded as their pronominalisation is optional (see also §4).[10] Furthermore, semantic features of the referents, namely animacy, number and gender, have been taken into consideration.

(5) a. *Le dije que si traían alguna tramoya*
CL told.1SG that if brought.3PL some stage machinery
que me Ø dijeran pronto.
that CL NCL told.3PL soon
'I told him to tell me soon if they brought some stage machinery' (E 1838).
b. *Me han traído una niña para que **la** vea.*
CL have.3PL brought.PART a girl so that CL see1.PL
'They have brought me a girl so that I see her' (E 1838).

(6) a. *Porque los cuatro dientes de arriba₁ **los**₁ tiene rotos.*
Because the four teeth of top CL have.3PL broken.PART
'Because the four upper teeth are broken' (E 1831).
b. *La minuta₁ no me Ø₁ ha mandado*
the bill no CL NCL has.3SG sent.PART
hasta este mediodía.
until this noon
'The bill wasn't sent to me until noon' (AM 1880).

(7) *Me enviase vm. harina [...] aquí me (**la**)*
CL sent.3SG you flour here CL CL
traen muy negra.
bring.3PL very black
'To send me flour here. They bring it to me very black' (E 1832).

As for *leísmo*, the use of the dative *le/s* forms substituting the accusative *lo(s)/la(s)* when referring to direct objects, I extracted both masculine and feminine referents, human and (in)animate ones, with a direct object function. Syntactically, I considered the following contexts: (i) when the referent is mentioned in the previous discourse and needs to be pronominalised (8a), and (ii) cases in which the clitic is co-referential with either a noun or a prepositional phrase, both preverbally (8b) and postverbally (8c). In all these contexts, the distribution between accusative and dative pronouns is studied. Observe, nevertheless,

---

10 In (7a) the optionality of the pronoun is indicated using parentheses.

that the following cases will be excluded: (i) causative structures with *hacer* and *dejar*, influence (*enseñar*) or perception (*ver*, *oír*) verbs followed by an infinitive (9a), and (ii) when an adjective phrase refers to an object (9b), considering that both contexts show variation in the pronoun-case choice (Fernández-Ordóñez 1999, 1325–1328). Animacy, number, gender, and (in)formal address are the semantic features that have been incorporated into the present analysis. Further a variety of syntactic contexts (left-dislocated direct objects, dative clitics or infinitive constructions) has also been analysed.

(8) a. *La niña [...] está bien; siempre **la** tienen*
       the baby   is well   always CL hold.3PL
       en brazos.
       in arms
       'The baby is well. They are always holding her' (AM 1880).
    b. *A Federico$_i$ **le**$_i$ he entrado   en dos rifas.*
       ACC Federico CL have.1SG gotten.PART into two raffles
       'Federico, I have gotten him into two raffles' (E 1839).
    c. ***Le**$_i$ encontré a Echeverria$_i$.*
       CL met.1SG   ACC Echeverria
       'I met Echeverria' (AM 1878).

(9) a. *Al hortelano Prudencio$_j$, igualmente **le**$_j$ han*
       ACC gardener Prudencio also   CL have.3PL
       hecho   desocupar   su habitación.
       done.PART vacate-INF   his room.
       'Gardener Prudencio has been forced to leave his room' (M 1834).
    b. *En sus oraciones **la** tendrá   presente.*
       in his prayers   CL will-keep.3SG present
       'He will keep her present in his prayers' (E 1838).

As for the study of the variation in word order, verb-object (VO) and object-verb (OV), the following decisions were made: (i) declarative main sentences with lexical direct objects and subjects, and adverbs or adverbial phrases without finite verbs will be collected; (ii) as concerns the number of preverbal constituents, object clitic elements will not be counted as constituents as they are syntactically dependent on the verb (Sportiche 1998); and (iii) causative structures with a main verb of causation, influence or perception followed by an infinitive, as in (9a), will be excluded.

Finally, the quantitative data were subjected to the chi-square tests using a significance level of 0.05 (IBM SPSS Statistics 22.0). These tests measure how likely an observed distribution is due to chance. When appropriate, as for Table 10, I used Fisher's Exact Test.

4 Null objects or the omission of the accusative clitic

In Standard Spanish, the variation between the presence and absence of a pronoun referring to a direct object is explained in terms of the Animacy and Definiteness Hierarchies as illustrated in Table 2).

Table 2: Animacy and Definiteness Hierarchies (Aissen 2003, 437).

a. Animacy → Human > Animate > Inanimate
b. Definiteness → Tonic Pronoun > Proper Name > Definite Noun Phrase (NP) > Indefinite Specific NP > Indefinite Non-specific NP

If the referent is a tonic pronoun (10a), a proper name (10b) or a specific definite (10c) or indefinite NP (10d), the pronoun is obligatory. In contrast, with indefinite non-specific NPs, bare nouns (11a–b) and mass nouns (11d) included, two options emerge as the presence of the accusative clitic is optional (Leonetti 2011).

(10) a. *Solo **la**$_i$ quiero a ella$_i$.*
only CL love.1SG ACC her
'I only love her.'
b. *Vio a Juan en la calle pero no **lo** saludó.*
saw.3SG ACC John on the street but no CL greeted.3SG
'He saw John on the street but did not greet him.'
c. *El libro está en casa. Cóge**lo**.*
the book is.3SG at home take.2SG-CL
'The book is at home. Take it.'
d. *Compré un coche. Me gustaría que **lo** vieras.*
bought.1SG a car CL like.1SG that CL see.2SG
'I bought a car. I would like you to see it.'

(11) a. *¿Compró entradas para la próxima sesión?*
    bought.3SG tickets for the next session
    No (las) compró/(Las) compró.
    no CL bought.3SG/CL bought.3SG
    'Did he buy tickets for the next session? No, he did not/Yes, he did.'
  b. *¿Hay espectadores para la próxima sesión?*
    be.3SG spectators for the next session
    No (los) hay/(Los) hay.
    no CL be.3SG/CL be.3SG
    'Are there any spectators for the next session? No, there are not/Yes, there are.'
  c. *Él llevó dinero pero yo no (lo) llevé.*
    he brought.3SG money but I no CL brought.1SG
    'He brought money, but I did not.'

Interestingly, the omission of direct object pronouns beyond the contexts in (11) is not only a feature of Basque Spanish, but also of other language contact scenarios, such as Spanish in contact with the Amerindian languages (Palacios 2013). Indeed, in Basque Spanish bilingual and monolingual speakers may omit clitics referring to definite inanimate NPs,[11] particularly when occurring with left-dislocated constituents (12a), in sentences with dative clitics (12b), and in infinitive constructions (12c). Besides, null objects have been attested with human and animate referents (12d), mostly in events in which they do not actively participate, for example with infinitive constructions, imperfective tenses, and stative and perception verbs such as *have* (*tener*), *see* (*ver*) and *meet* (*conocer*) (Landa 1995).

(12) a. *La maratón de San Sebastián$_i$ Ø$_i$ hice en tres minutos.*
    the Marathon of San Sebastian NCL run.1SG in three minutes
    'The San Sebastian Marathon, I run in three minutes' (Camus Bergareche/Gómez Seibane 2015, 221).

---

11 However, differences in frequency of use have been perceived depending on the area of the Basque Country and the register used. The frequency of null objects increases considerably in areas where there is a higher degree of use and stability of the Basque language. Likewise, register crucially determines the frequency of clitic omission for non-human accusatives: the higher the degree of formality, the lower the clitic omission frequency. Therefore, this suggests a high degree of linguistic awareness of the phenomenon, which can probably be considered as a marker of cultural identity (Camus Bergareche/Gómez Seibane 2015).

b. *No sé   si me habéis visto   el gorro,*
no know.1SG if CL have.2PL seen.PART my cap
ya   me Ø habéis visto,   ¿no?
already CL NCL have.2PL seen.PART no
'I do not know if you have seen my cap. You have already seen it, haven't you?' (Camus Bergareche/Gómez Seibane 2015, 221).

c. *Bueno, vamos a retirarØ*
well go.1PL to remove-INF-NCL
[la comida].
[the food]
'Well, let's remove it' (Camus Bergareche/Gómez Seibane, 2015, 221).

d. *No le conozco   a la novia de Txetxu.*
no CL know.1SG ACC the girlfriend of Txetxu.
¿Tú Ø conoces?
you NCL know.2SG
'I do not know Txetxu's girlfriend. Do you know her?' (Landa 1995, 129).

It seems that the use of null objects depends on the semantic properties of the referents, and, to a lesser extent, on the syntactic constructions in which they appear. Some variationist research has revealed that animacy and number are the strongest constraints in the variation between null and overt pronouns: inanimate and plural referents increase the probability of use of null objects, while definiteness and specificity do not predict the presence or absence of the clitics, although they might interact with other linguistic constraints (Sainzmaza-Lecanda 2014a; 2014b). Syntactic factors that need to be considered in the use of null objects are left-dislocated direct objects and clauses in which dative clitics are present (Sainzmaza-Lecanda 2014b).

582 possible cases of null objects were analysed for the bilingual corpus, and 529 for the control corpus. Quantitatively, null objects represent 30% (175/582) of all contexts in the bilingual corpus, while for the control monolingual corpus null objects only constitute 1.5% (8/529) of all contexts. This difference is striking and, therefore, the comparison between these two corpora proves that null objects are much more frequent among bilingual speakers, as shown in Table 3.[12] Moreover, this difference in use between the bilingual and monolingual corpus is highly statistically significant.

---

[12] In oral data, null objects account for 60% in Basque Spanish and only 5.6% in Castilian Spanish (Sainzmaza-Lecanda 2014b).

Table 3: Frequencies of direct object pronouns and null objects.

Corpus	Direct object pronouns	Null objects
Bilingual	70% (407/582)	30% (175/582)
Control	98.5% (521/529)	1.5% (8/529)

$\chi^2 = 164.249; p < 0.001$

As can be seen in Table 4, the vast majority of all null objects in the bilingual corpus (93.7%, 164/175) are inanimate entities, while human referents (4.5%, 8/175) and animate antecedents (1.7%, 3/175) show similar low rates of use. The few cases of omission in the monolingual corpus are all related to inanimate referents. As can be seen from Table 4, the differences between the bilingual and monolingual corpus are apparent, despite the low number of cases for the latter. However, it should also be pointed out that neither gender nor number appear to be relevant categories in the omission of clitics (in both cases, the differences were not statistically significant).

Table 4: Frequency and semantic properties of null objects' referents.

Corpus	Human	Animate	Inanimate
Bilingual	4.5% (8/175)	1.7% (3/175)	93.7% (164/175)
Control	0% (0/8)	0% (0/8)	100% (8/8)

As concerns the syntactic properties of null objects, displayed in Table 5, in the bilingual corpus 50.3% (88/175) of the null objects occur with left-dislocated direct objects (13a). In 11.4% (20/175) of object clitic omissions, there is a dative clitic in the clause (13b), and in 8% (14/175) of the cases, null objects appear in infinitive constructions (13c).[13] Finally, null objects with the referent in the previous clause make up 30.3% (53/175) of the examples of the omission cases (13d). Turning now to the monolingual corpus, null objects occur exclusively within left-dislocated constructions (13e). The data clearly demonstrate that there is a significant difference between the bilingual and the monolingual corpus as regards the null objects and their syntactic contexts.

---

[13] When a null object appears in a sentence with a complex syntactic context, for example, with a left-dislocated construction and dative clitic, I count it as a single case and compute at the syntactic factor with fewer occurrences.

Table 5: Frequency and syntactic contexts of null objects.

Corpus	Left-dislocated direct object	Dative clitics	Infinitive constructions	Referent in previous clause
Bilingual	50.3% (88/175)	11.4% (20/175)	8% (14/175)	30.3% (53/175)
Control	100% (8/8)	0% (0/8)	0% (0/8)	0% (0/8)

(13) a. *Le dice   que el expediente de la casa de la calle de los*
  CL tells.SG that the file   of the house of the street of the
  Herreros$_i$ Ø$_i$ ha   entregado   a abogado.
  Herreros NCL has.3SG handed-in.PART to lawyer
  'He tells him that the file of the house on Herreros street, he has given it to a lawyer' (AM 1878).
  b. *[T]enía mal puesto el hueso y*
  had.3SG badly placed the bone and
  el sábado   le Ø   puso   Petriquillo.
  the Saturday CL NCL placed.3SG Petriquillo
  'He had his bone displaced and Petriquillo placed it back for him on Saturday' (E 1825).
  c. *[H]e   recibido   el adjunto real decreto y [...] por*
  have.1SG received.PART the attached Royal Decree and to
  enviar Ø cuanto antes,   lo envió por el correo.
  send-INF NCL more soon CL sent.3SG by the mail
  'I have received the attached Royal Decree, and in order to send it as soon as possible, he sent it by mail' (E 1839).
  d. *[R]ecibí la apreciable de usted y ayer domingo*
  received.1SG the significant of you and yesterday Sunday
  Ø   entregué   en propias manos a don Sarasola.
  NCL delivered.1SG in own hands to mister Sarasola
  'I received your significant letter and delivered it to mister Sarasola on Sunday' (M 1839).
  e. *[L]os cuatro restantes Ø   tengo*
  the four   remaining NCL have.1SG
  también percibidos.
  also received.PART
  'The remaining four, I have also received them' (Martínez 2007, 408, 1733).

Summarising, the data reveal higher frequency of null objects in the bilingual corpus, with syntactic and semantic properties quite similar to the contemporary Basque Spanish uses (Gómez Seibane 2012a). Null objects mostly refer to inanimate referents, occasionally to human and animate referents, as shown in Table 4, and often occur with left-dislocated direct objects, in clauses with dative clitics, and in infinitive constructions[14], among others, as seen in Table 5.

In view of these findings, it appears that null objects in Basque Spanish could have emerged as the result of internal factors related to Animacy and Definiteness constraints,[15] and external factors, such as language contact. Regarding the former, null objects appear to display interdialectal variation in Spanish. As seen at Table 2, the likelihood of accusative clitic omission in Basque Spanish follows the trajectory of the well-known Animacy Hierarchy, from inanimate to human referents in a process which is not yet completed (Gómez Seibane 2012a). Following this line of reasoning, it can be hypothesised that null objects in this contact scenario may follow the Definiteness Hierarchy from indefinite non-specific NPs (also possible in Standard Spanish) to definite NPs, an issue for further research.

In my view, an external factor triggers the semantic differences in the use of null objects: to wit, the intense contact with the Basque language. As already pointed out by Landa (1995, 188–219), the following characteristics of Basque may have triggered the disappearance of almost all restrictions for null objects. Firstly, Basque is an agglutinative language that lacks a pronominal system similar to Spanish, and in which the auxiliary verb agrees with ergative, absolutive (if any) and dative arguments (if any) (Trask 1997, 103–109). Consider example (14).

(14) Zuk   sagarra   erosi duzu
You.ERG apple.ABS buy   AUX.2SG
eta nik eskolara Ø   ekarri dut.
and I.ERG school it.ABS bring AUX.1SG
'You have bought an apple and I have brought it to school.'

---

14 Following Gómez Seibane (2012a, 205–206), in Basque Spanish oral speech, null objects (i) mainly refer to inanimate referents (96.2%, 104/108), (ii) appear in negative sentences (50.1%, 54/108), (iii) have the referent in a previous clause (29.6%, 32/108), (iv) appear in infinitive constructions (21.2%, 23/108), (v) co-occur with left-dislocated direct objects (12.9%, 14/108), and (vi) appear in clauses with dative clitics (7.4%, 8/108).
15 These factors are also decisive with regard to other phenomena such as differential object marking (Laca 2006) and clitic doubling (Gómez Seibane 2012a).

As can be seen, the finite auxiliaries (*duzu/dut*) provide information about the arguments subcategorised by these verbs, that is, ergative and absolutive (Trask 1997, 218–234). The morphemes *-zu* or *-t* specify the person and number of the subject, ergative 2nd person singular and ergative 1st person singular respectively; verbal morpheme *d-* encodes the absolutive (*sagarra*). Note that in the second clause the absolutive (*sagarra*) appears only in the form of verbal morpheme *d-*.

Considering this, I conclude that a process of linguistic convergence took place. As pointed out by Landa/Franco (1996), bilingual speakers draw parallels between the Basque construction, which encodes the direct object in the verb, and the Spanish possibility of omitting 3rd person direct object clitics which refer to indefinite non-specific NPs. This structural similarity appears to have facilitated the loss of semantic restrictions of null objects in Basque Spanish, resulting in the acceptance of null objects with definite referents and, in some contexts, human and animate NPs. In other words, a generalisation and broadening of contexts of use took place due to convergence, resulting in more internal variation. This most likely occurred before the 19th century.

5 *Le/s* for female referents in the accusative

The phenomenon known as *leísmo* entails the neutralisation of case and gender parameters in the unstressed 3rd person pronominal system.[16] Although it is a very common phenomenon in the history of the Spanish language, it tends to occur with masculine referents more often than with feminine ones (Gómez Seibane 2013a, 38–44). *Leísmo* is also one of the features of the so-called 'Basque pronominal system', observed among both bilingual and monolingual Spanish speakers in northern Basque Country and northern Navarre (Fernández-Ordóñez 1999). However, in contrast to other varieties of Spanish, *leísmo* in the 'Basque pronominal system' spreads to animate referents regardless of their gender, be they masculine or feminine.

It has been argued that both internal and external factors are responsible for the origin of *leísmo* (see a summary in Gómez Seibane 2013b). As for internal factors, the traditional hypothesis (Lapesa 1968) posited a distinction between animate (referred to by *le*) and inanimate ones (referred to by *lo/a*). This trend partially correlates with gender distinctions, as *le* is used for masculine, *la* for

---

16 For a synchronic study on *leísmo*, see Camus Bergareche/Gómez Seibane (in this volume).

feminine and *lo* for neuter forms, like in other paradigms, such as tonic pronouns (*él*, *ella*, *ello*) and demonstratives ones (*este*, *esta*, *esto*). Another semantic-pragmatic hypothesis (García 1975) views the variation between *le* and *lo* as the result of communication strategies that provide different degrees of participant activity in the event. According to this explanation, accusatives expressed by *le* are perceived as more active entities than others referred to via *lo/a*. Nevertheless, this hypothesis lacks explanatory power as the close relation between *le* and animate male referents, the lower diffusion of *le* for female entities and the usage of *le* targeting masculine inanimate entities remains unexplained.

Considering that *leísmo* is not an evolutionary trend in Romance languages, the third hypothesis proposes that language contact is the external trigger for this variation in the unstressed 3rd person pronominal system (Fernández-Ordóñez 2001, 428–430): it states that, in Basque and Spanish bilingual areas, *le/s*, prototypically animate as an indirect object and without gender marking, is the pronoun used to refer to animate entities, both male and female, due to the lack of gender markers in Basque. In this regard, the use of *le/s* for animate objects in this variety is a well-identified universal trend following which inflectional morphology is associated with prototypical arguments. This explanation would predict that, since dative clitics are usually linked to animate entities, they spread to all animate referents, including direct objects (Fernández-Ordóñez 2001).

From a historical perspective, the use of *le* instead of *lo/a* for masculine and feminine referents is well documented in Basque Spanish since the 16th century (Gómez Seibane 2013a): *le* could be selected in legal texts mainly for male referents, but also female ones. This tendency increased in the 17th century. In the following century, this situation expanded to other textual domains such as personal letters.[17] The use of *le* is also documented in the bilingual corpus of letters, as we will see shortly.

I found that bilingual and monolingual speakers selected accusative clitics for animate and non-human entities in the few attested cases (8/8); for inanimate referents, they were also preferred in almost all cases (bilinguals, 162/163 and monolinguals, 219/224). For human entities, I checked 81 clauses with male accusative referents expressed by a pronoun, and 79 with female accusative referents in the bilingual corpus. In the control corpus, there were 98 pronouns referring to male accusative entities, and 41 for female entities with the same function. The frequency of *leísmo* (i.e. the use of dative clitics) vs. the use of

---

17 In the 17th century *le* was used for female entities in the accusative with a frequency of 7.2% (4/55) (Gómez Seibane 2010). During the 18th century, the use of *le* instead of *la* in singular increased to 43% (9/21). However, caution is advised due to the limited number of occurrences (Gómez Seibane 2004).

accusative clitics referring to human entities with direct object function is shown in Table 6.

Table 6: Frequency of *le/s*, *la/s*, *lo/s* for human direct object NPs.

Corpus	Human referents	Dative clitics (*Le/s*)	Accusative clitics (*Lo/s – La/s*)
Bilingual	Male	76.5% (62/81)	23.5% (19/81)
	Female	24.1% (19/79)	75.9% (60/79)
Control	Male	31.6% (31/98)	68.4% (67/98)
	Female	4.9% (2/41)	95.1% (39/41)

Focusing now on direct object NPs with human referents, as Table 6 shows, bilinguals prefer dative clitics for male entities (76.5%, 62/81 *le/s* vs. 23.5%, 19/81 *lo/s*), but for female ones the accusative *la/s* is more common than the dative *le/s* (75.9%, 60/79 *la/s* vs. 24.1%, 19/79 *le/s*), although the dative pronoun still occurs in one in four cases, as is illustrated in (15). Among monolinguals, accusative clitics *lo/s* are selected for male entities in 68.4% (67/98) of all cases (vs. 31.6%, 31/98 with dative *le/s*), and for female referents in 95.1% (39/41) of all examples.[18] The data reveal that gender is statistically significant in the selection of the type of clitic, both for the bilingual corpus (χ^2 = 44.088; p = 0) and

---

18 In (i), there may be a structural priming effect (*le tenía*), while in (ii) *les* referred to the wife and sisters may be a formulaic expression or routinised sequence for farewell. It should be pointed out that in this letter the writer uses the familiar form of address (*tu esposo*).

(i) *[a tu hermana] el mucho amor que le tenía*
   [ACC your sister] the great love that CL had.1SG
   y le quería.
   and CL loved.1SG
   'The great love I had for her and I loved her' (Arbelo García 2012, 352, 1773).

(ii) *[esposa e hijas] De tu esposo que más*
    [wife and sisters] From your husband who more
    desea verles.
    desire.3SG see.INF-CL
    'From your husband who is looking forward to seeing you' (Arbelo García 2012, 382, 1812).

the control corpus (χ^2 = 11.429; p = 0.0007). The differences between the two corpora are also statistically significant for the male referents (χ^2 = 35.833; p < 0.001) as well as the female ones (χ^2 = 6.872; p = 0.009).

(15) a. **Le**$_i$ *he   tomado   a Josepa*$_j$.
CL have.1SG hired.PART ACC Josepa
'I have hired Josepa' (E 1838).
b. *La Brígida*$_j$ *no* **le**$_i$ *encontré en casa.*
the Brígida   no CL met.3SG in home
'Brígida, I did not meet her at home' (AM 1880).
c. *La otra [...]* **le** *tuvimos en San Sebastián.*
the other   CL had.1PL in San Sebastian
'The other [...] we had her in San Sebastian' (M 1827).

At the same time, *leísmo* may be influenced in both corpora by the polite forms of address (Fernández-Ordóñez 1999), as is exemplified in (16). The common procedure for expressing politeness and respect was to refer indirectly to the interlocutor. Therefore, *usted/es*, the grammaticalised form of *vuestra merced* (De Jonge/Nieuwenhuijsen 2012, 253) and other polite forms of address, such as *Señor* 'Sir' and *Señora* 'Madam' are used with 3rd person pronouns (*se*, *le/s*, *la/s*, *lo/s*, among others) and with an agreeing verb (Lapesa 2000, 340–341).

(16) a. *Me dijo que toda la defensa fue para usted, como*
CL told.3SG that all the defense was.3G for you because
todos   **le**$_i$ *atacaban a usted*$_i$.
everyone CL attacked.3PL ACC you
'He told me that you were strongly protected, because everyone attacked you.' (AM 1878)
b. *Muy señora mía   y   de mi mayor aprecio: tomo*
Very madam mine and of my greater appreciation take.1SG
*la libertad de molestar***le**   *de nuevo.*
the liberty of disturb.INF-CL of again
'Dearest madam: I take the liberty to disturb you again' (M 1829).

For the polite forms of address, *le* is the preferred choice, as opposed to accusative pronouns *lo* and *la*, to refer to *usted*, which has been interpreted as a way of emphasising that the reference of the 3rd person pronoun *le* must be sought in the communicative situation (Fernández-Ordóñez 1999, 1340). Although this tendency, known as *leísmo de cortesía* 'politeness *leísmo*', as in (17), has been explained as a procedure to disambiguate the formal 2nd person from the 3rd person, it has not yet been sufficiently investigated from a historical perspective.

(17) a. ¿**Le** llevo a casa?   [a usted/*a él]
      CL take.1SG to home [ACC you/*ACC him]
      'May I take you/*him home?'
    b. ¿**Lo** llevo a   casa? [a usted/a él]
      CL take.1SG to home [ACC you/ACC him]
      'May I take you/him home?'

In order to verify the possible influence of referents in the selection of clitic pronouns, I compared the frequency of accusative and dative pronouns referring to 3rd and formal 2nd person referents (*usted, señor, señora*), as seen in Table 7. The data show that the difference between the use of the dative or accusative pronouns and their referents is statistically significant for both corpora (bilingual corpus: χ^2 = 5.257; p = 0.022; and control one: χ^2 = 7.426; p = 0.006). The relative frequencies show that in the control corpus the dative clitic is more frequent for polite forms of address with 2nd person referents than in the bilingual one (60.6%, 20/33 vs. 27.2%, 22/81).

Table 7: Frequency of *le/s, la/s, lo/s* for human direct object NPs.

Corpus	Dative clitics		Accusative clitics	
	3rd person	2nd person (FA)	3rd person	2nd person (FA)
Biling.	72.8% (59/81)	27.2% (22/81)	87.3% (69/79)	12.7% (10/79)
Contr.	39.4% (13/33)	60.6% (20/33)	66% (70/106)	34% (36/106)

In sum, *leísmo* is much more frequent in the bilingual corpus than in the monolingual corpus, both for masculine and feminine human referents. In my view, the findings can be interpreted as an indirect contact-induced change in which both internal and external factors are crucial for its formation. When it comes to internal factors, it has been shown that the intrinsic evolutionary tendency of Spanish cancels the case parameter in the 3rd person pronominal system, which favours the dative case above the accusative, but only (or mainly) in the case of masculine referents. Gender agreement is better maintained in the feminine than in the masculine, akin to the evolutionary trends in Spanish (Fernández-Ordóñez

2001). It should be noted that gender and number are inherent qualities of nouns in Spanish and, consequently, these constitute internal and stable categories. Nevertheless, the masculine is less marked than the feminine at the morphological level (as in other Romance languages): for instance, masculine is the unmarked gender choice to refer jointly to masculine and feminine entities. Therefore, in Spanish, gender is a stable category, and feminine agreement must be particularly preserved, due to its morphologically marked status (Fernández-Ordóñez 2001, 436–442).

However, the Basque Spanish variety goes beyond these boundaries, since it extends the usage of *le/s* to both masculine and feminine human referents, because gender is not grammatically relevant in the Basque language. According to Trask (1997, 118, 255), Basque has no grammatical gender and, as a result, gender-marking of nouns is usually done lexically (*gizon* 'man' and *emakume* 'woman'), and very occasionally done by an adapted morpheme from Romance. Therefore, at least since the 19th century, it appears that bilingual speakers have partially restructured and simplified the Spanish unstressed 3rd person pronominal system through linguistic convergence. In the resulting system, animacy prevails over case (as in non-contact Spanish varieties), even for female referents, because gender is not relevant in the complex repertoire of forms and structures that bilingual speakers share in both languages (Matras 2009). In brief, we can conclude that the observed variation in this Spanish pronominal system has been reanalysed through exposure to Basque.

6 Word order: Spanish VO vs. Basque OV

Although word order in Spanish is relatively free, focus tends to appear after the verb (SVO) in declarative sentences within the matrix domain (18). Changes in word order are the result of information packaging and can occur at the left or right periphery of a clause. Left peripheral constituents may constitute cases of topicalisation or focalisation, containing topics and foci, usually associated in the literature with given and new information[19] respectively (Prince 1981; Zubizarreta 1999).

(18) Luis   vio   a su madre. (SVO)
      Luis see.3SG ACC his mother
      'Luis saw his mother.'

---

[19] The literature usually links topic with given information, for a critique of this, see Bouzouita (2015) who shows that new information is also possible.

(19) *Koldok   ama   ikusi zuen.* (SOV)
Koldo.ERG mother.ABS see AUX.3SG
'Koldo saw his mother.'

In contrast to Spanish, the unmarked word order configuration in Basque is SOV, as shown in (19), and focus is positioned immediately before the verb (Ortiz de Urbina 2003; Trask 1997, 109–110). Other structural patterns are also possible (SVO, OVS and OSV), but Erdocia/Laka/Rodríguez-Fornells (2012) demonstrated that SOV is the easiest to process, as the other patterns require more processing effort due to the extra syntactic operations involved.

Given the language contact scenario, one might hypothesise that Basque Spanish has increased the frequency of use of preverbal objects, and/or lost the discourse-pragmatic constraints of such objects. In fact, the order of clausal constituents and their pragmatic functions are highly diffusible cross-linguistically in contact scenarios (Aikhenvald 2007, 26–27). Nevertheless, Heine (2008) has demonstrated that contact does not always lead to a new word order in the influenced language: he suggests that "speakers recruit material available in R (the replica language) to create new structures on the model of M (the model language) and that, rather than being entirely new, the structures created in R are built on existing use patterns and constructions that are already available in R" (Heine 2008, 57). Thus, as Matras (2009, 4–5) points out, in language contact scenarios communication is the result of two primary pressures: loyalty to context-appropriate constructions and exploitation of the full expressive potential of linguistic structures.

As regards the interaction between information structure and word order among Basque-Spanish bilinguals, a previous study showed that bilinguals express new information in preverbal position more often than Spanish monolinguals, in addition to using fewer instances of discourse-continuous topics (Gómez Seibane 2012b). In this section, firstly, the frequency of OV and VO constructions in the bilingual and monolingual corpora will be determined and, secondly, OV constructions will be characterised from the discourse-pragmatic perspective. The word order patterns in 458 main clauses were examined for the bilingual corpus, and 183 clauses for the monolingual one, as shown in Table 8. The data show a higher frequency of preverbal direct objects in the bilingual corpus (18.8%, 86/458) than in the monolingual one (9.8%, 18/183). Besides, the bilingual corpus presents similar rates of preverbal direct objects in all three writers, which suggests this feature to be specific to this variety (Gómez Seibane 2015). Regarding the control corpus, results agree with historical data: from the 13th to the 16th century, preverbal direct objects occurred between 6.6% (92/1390) and 7.7% (79/1015) of the time and they would increase later on (Danford 2002 cited by Bouzouita 2014). In addition, there is a statistically significant difference between the corpora for the discussed word order patterns.

Table 8: Frequencies of preverbal and postverbal direct objects.

Corpus	OV	VO
Bilingual	18.8% (86/458)	81.2% (372/458)
Control	9.8% (18/183)	90.2% (165/183)

$\chi^2 = 7.691; p = 0.006$

Now that the frequencies of use of preverbal and postverbal objects have been explored, a fine-grained analysis aimed at checking whether preverbal objects maintain the same pragmatic functions and information-structural status in the two corpora will be undertaken. For this purpose, preverbal objects' behaviour will be analysed. Preverbal objects are usually described as given information and are commonly characterised as elements with discourse prominence (Prince 1981; Givón 1983);[20] for Spanish, following Silva-Corvalán (1984), we will use the term 'discourse link' (*enlace textual*).[21] In the bilingual corpus, preverbal objects appear to function primarily as discourse links (93%, 80/86), as exemplified in (20a).[22] The remaining preverbal objects (7%, 6/86) are mostly focalisations (20b), very often with (relatively) new information. In the monolingual corpus, preverbal objects are always discourse links (18/18).

(20) a. *La tienda$_i$ piensan ponerla$_i$* muy bien.
      the store plan.3PL put-INF-CL very well
      'They are planning to put the store really well' (E 1842).
   b. *Los anteojos me pidió*   Urrutia, el cura.
      the glasses CL asked.3SG Urrutia the priest
      'The priest Urrutia asked me for the glasses' (E n.d.).

---

20 I assume the given-new information taxonomy proposed by Prince (1981): (i) given information, known by the hearer or mentioned in the discourse (*evocated*); (ii) information that can be deducted, based on the speaker's beliefs (*inferable*); and (iii) *new entities*, that are first introduced in the discourse. New entities must sometimes be created by the hearer (*brand-new*), or are *unused*, but already known. For discourse prominence, I employ *referential persistence* that looks at how often a referent is mentioned in the subsequent discourse (Givón 1981).
21 For Silva-Corvalán (1984), discourse links are preverbal objects with [-new, -contrastive] information.
22 Some of these discourse links have null objects (see §4).

Nevertheless, discourse links in the bilingual corpus are more frequently new or relatively new entities (58.8%, 47/80), as shown in Table 9. In the control group, on the contrary, discourse links contain mainly evocated or inferred information (66.6%, 12/18). Discourse links in the bilingual corpus are thus quite different with respect to the information-structural status of the referent. However, the difference between both corpora is not statistically significant.

Table 9: Given-new information in discourse links.

Corpus	Information	
	Given (Evocated/Inferred)	New (New/Unused)
Bilingual	41.2% (33/80)	58.8% (47/80)
Control	66.6% (12/18)	44.4% (6/18)

$\chi^2 = 3.822; p = 0.051$

As shown in the examples below, first-time mentioned entities are quite common in preverbal position within the bilingual corpus. In contrast, these newly mentioned entities are already known by the hearer, as in (21). In this example, the writer tells the reader who she met in the festivities of a city. The people she mentions in her letter are well known to the writer and the addressee, but had not been previously introduced, or were not inferable from information given earlier in discourse. In the monolingual corpus, however, preverbal direct objects present mainly given information, usually mentioned in prior discourse, as in (22).

(21) <u>A la señorita$_i$</u> **la$_i$** vi   ayer,   pero de prisa [...] <u>Doña</u>
ACC the young lady CL saw.1SG yesterday but of hurry   madam
<u>Anita Colmenares y doña Joaquina$_j$</u> **las$_j$** vi también
Anita Colmenares and madam Joaquina CL saw.1SG also
y me preguntaron mucho de usted.
and CL asked.3PL more of you
'I saw the young lady yesterday, but in a hurry. I also saw madam Anita Colmenares and madam Joaquina and they asked about you.' (E 1853)

(22)　El legado de 1.500 reales [...] Los 1500 reales míos$_i$
　　　the legacy of 1.500 reals the 1.500 reals mine
　　　quisier a　　　　dejártelos$_i$,　　aunque tanto o más
　　　would-like.1SG leave.INF-CL-CL although much or more
　　　que tú **los** necesito.
　　　xthan you CL need.1SG
　　　'The legacy of 1,500 reals [...] I would like to leave you my legacy of 1,500 reals, although I need them as much or even more than you do' (Martínez 2007, 260, 1795).

In relation to discourse prominence, I analysed the persistence of discourse links with new or relatively new information. This kind of information shows no topic continuity in the previous discourse, but commonly exhibits referential persistence in the following discourse (Hidalgo Downing 2003, 290). This is indeed the case in the monolingual corpus (see Table 10): almost all (83.3%) discourse links conveying (relatively) new information continue in the following discourse. However, preverbal entities continue in the following discourse only half of the time in the bilingual letters (51%). There is not a statistically significant difference between both corpora with respect to the referential persistence in discourse links with (relatively) new information, according to the result of the Fisher Exact Test ($p = 0.204$).

Table 10: Referential persistence in discourse links with (relatively) new information.

Corpus	Referential persistence	Referential discontinuity
Bilingual	51.1% (24/47)	48.9% (23/47)
Control	83.3% (5/6)	16.7% (1/6)

Examples such as (23)–(24) illustrate this difference: in (23) the preverbal object introduces a new discourse topic (*su esposa*), which is resumed in the following clauses through 3rd person verb forms – in small caps –, while the preverbal object in (24) is not explicitly mentioned or addressed by any linguistic element in the subsequent discourse.

(23)　Su esposa$_i$ **la**$_i$ ha　　tenido　　bien achacosa y　ya
　　　his wife　CL has.3SG had.PART seriously ill　and already
　　　me dice　QUEDABA　tomando unos sudores por el mal
　　　CL tells.2PL stayed.3SG having.GER some baths for the sick

de la cabeza que *PADECE*.
of the head that suffers.3SG
'His wife has been seriously sick, and he indeed tells me that she used to take baths for her headache.' (Arbelo García 2012, 354, 1773)

(24) *La contribución$_i$ me Ø$_i$ han   bajado   a 200*
the contribution CL NCL have.3PL lowered.PART to 200
reales pero con este otro estamos como antes (E 1839)
reals but with this other are.1PL as before
'The contribution has been lowered to 200 reals, but with this one we remain the same' (E 1839).

In short, the Basque Spanish word order has developed from the Spanish internal tendency towards a relatively free constituent order. Although, as Heine states (2008, 57), it can be difficult to prove that contact is a decisive factor for a specific innovation, the findings presented here appear to demonstrate that the Basque language is a triggering factor for the OV pattern in Basque Country Spanish: the Basque word order (SOV) and the preverbal focus position have increased the frequency of use of preverbal objects with (relatively) new information and lower referential persistence in Basque Spanish, against the trend observed for non-contact varieties of Spanish.

7 Conclusion

In sum, it is clear that null objects, *le/s* for female direct objects, and OV pattern in Basque Spanish are indirect contact-induced changes resulting from linguistic convergence.
– The productivity of three features of Basque Spanish as the currently spoken have been documented in an 18th and 19th century corpus of letters written by bilinguals.
– Data have proved that these phenomena are absent (or extremely limited) in non-contact Spanish varieties: in comparison with the monolingual corpus, the results reveal higher frequency of null objects, *leísmo* for male and female accusatives, and preverbal objects with (relatively) new information and lower referential persistence in the bilingual group.
– Regarding Spanish grammar, it has been shown that internal variation in some domains of grammar has facilitated the loss of semantic restrictions of null objects, the partial restructuring and simplification of the unstressed 3rd person

pronominal system, and the surge of an alternative word order pattern, due to exposure to the Basque language. I refer particularly to the variation regarding the presence and absence of accusative pronouns referring to an indefinite non-specific NP, to the variation between *le/s* and *lo/s* for male direct objects, and to the internal tendency towards a relatively free constituent order. Bilingual speakers have taken advantage of the variation in these areas of Spanish grammar to apply their mental organisation procedures, complying with context-appropriate constructions and exploiting the full expressive potential of linguistic structures.
– As regards the Basque language, it has been shown that some linguistic features of this language could have triggered the emergence of these phenomena. In Basque, auxiliary verbs encode agreement with ergative, absolutive (if any) and dative arguments (if any), which may have led to the increased proportion of null objects. As a result of the lack of grammatical gender in Basque, gender appears not to be a relevant category for bilingual speakers, allowing them to link the dative clitics *le/les* with all animate referents in general, including accusative ones. Finally, Basque preverbal focus placement may have increased the frequency of OV pattern with (relatively) new information and lower referential persistence, contrary to the behaviour observed for non-contact varieties of Spanish.

8 References

8.1 Primary text sources

Arbelo García, Adolfo I., *Correspondencia canario-americana. Familia y redes sociales*, Santa Cruz de Tenerife, Idea, 2012.
Martínez, Mª del Carmen, *Desde la otra orilla. Cartas de Indias en el Archivo de la Real Chancillería de Valladolid (siglos XVI-XVIII)*, León, Universidad de León, 2007.
Pérez Murillo, Mª Dolores, *Cartas de emigrantes escritas desde Cuba*, Cádiz/Sevilla, Aconcagua Libros, 1999.
Zavala, Luis Mª (ed.), *Política y vida cotidiana*, Lasarte-Oria, Irargi, 3 DVD, 2008.8.2

8.2 Secondary literature

Aikhenvald, Alexandra Y., *Grammars in Contact. A Cross-linguistic Perspective*, in: Aikhenvald, Alexandra Y./Dixon, Robert M. W. (edd.), *Grammars in Contact. A Cross-linguistic Typology*, Oxford, Oxford University Press, 2007, 1–66.

Aissen, Judith, *Differential Object Marking. Iconicity vs. Economy*, Natural Language & Linguistic Theory 21 (2003), 435–483.
Biber, Douglas/Conrad, Susan, *Register variation. A corpus approach*, in: Schiffrin, Deborah/Tannen, Deborah/Hamilton, Heidi E. (edd.), *The handbook of Discourse Analysis*, Malden, Blackwell, 2001, 175–196.
Bouzouita, Miriam, *Left Dislocation Phenomena in Old Spanish. An Examination of their Structural Properties*, in: Dufter, Andreas/Octavio de Toledo, Álvaro S. (edd.), *Left Sentence Peripheries in Spanish. Diachronic, Variationist and Typological Perspectives*, Amsterdam/Philadelphia, John Benjamins, 2014, 23–52.
Bouzouita, Miriam, *Las dislocaciones a la izquierda en el español del siglo XIII. La accesibilidad referencial*, In: López Izquierdo, Marta/Castillo Lluch, Mónica (edd.), *El orden de palabras en la historia del español y otras lenguas iberorromances*, Madrid, Visor, 2015, 235–278.
Camus Bergareche, Bruno/Gómez Seibane, Sara, *Basque and Spanish in 19th century San Sebastián*, Ianua. Revista Philologica Romanica 10 (2010), 223–239.
Camus Bergareche, Bruno/Gómez Seibane, Sara, *Introducción. El castellano del País Vasco*, in: Camus, Bruno/Gómez Seibane, Sara (edd.), *El castellano del País Vasco*, Bilbao, Universidad del País Vasco, 2012, 1–17.
Camus Bergareche, Bruno/Gómez Seibane, Sara, *Nuevos datos acerca de la omisión de objetos en el castellano del País Vasco*, Círculo de Lingüística Aplicada a la Comunicación 61 (2015), 211–236.
Camus Bergareche, Bruno/Gómez Seibane, Sara, *A contact-induced phenomenon in Spanish. Gender loss in accusative accusative clitics in the Basque Country*, in: Bouzouita, Miriam/Enghels, Renata/Vanderschueren, Clara (edd.), *Convergence and divergence in Ibero-Romance across contact situations and beyond*, Berlin/Boston, De Gruyter, in this volume, 25–54.
Danford, Richard K., Preverbal accusatives, pronominal reduplication and information packaging. A diachronic analysis of Spanish, PhD dissertation, Ohio State University, 2002.
De Jonge, Bob/Nieuwenhuijsen, Dorien, *Form of address*, in: Hualde, José I./Olarrea, Antxon/ORourke, Erin (edd.), *The handbook of Hispanic linguistics*, London, Wiley-Blackwell, 2012, 247–262.
Dávila, Paulí/Eizagirre, Ana/Fernández, Idoia, *Leer y escribir en las escuelas de Euskal Herria*, In: Dávila, Paulí (ed.), *Lengua, escuela y cultura. El proceso de alfabetización de Euskal Herria siglo XIX y XX*, Bilbao, Universidad del País Vasco, 1995, 45–78.
Elspass, Stephan, *The use of private letters and diaries in sociolinguistic investigation*, in: Hernández-Campoy, Juan M./Conde-Silvestre, Juan C. (edd.), *The handbook of historical sociolinguistics*, Chicester, Wiley-Blackwell, 2012, 156–169.
Erdocia, Kepa/Laka, Itziar/Rodríguez-Fornells, Antoni, *Processing verb medial word orders in a verb final language*, in: Swart, Peter/Lamers, Monique (edd.), *Case, word order, and prominence. Interacting cues in language production and comprehension*, Dordrecht, Springer, 2012, 217–238.
EUSTAT = Euskal Estatistika Erakundea/Instituto Vasco de Estadística, *Estadística de población y viviendas 2006*, 2008, www.eustat.eus [last access: 22.08.2015].
Fernández-Ordóñez, Inés, *Leísmo, laísmo y loísmo*, in: Bosque, Ignacio/Demonte, Violeta (edd.), *Gramática descriptiva de la lengua española*, vol. 1, Madrid, Espasa-Calpe, 1999, 1317–1397.

Fernández-Ordóñez, Inés, *Hacia una dialectología histórica. Reflexiones sobre la historia del leísmo, el laísmo y el loísmo*, Boletín de la Real Academia Española 81 (2001), 389–464.

García, Erica, *The role of theory in linguistic analysis. The Spanish pronoun system*, Amsterdam, North Holland, 1975.

García-Miguel, José Mª, *Variable coding and object alignment in Spanish. A corpus-based approach*, Folia Linguistica 49:1 (2015), 205–246.

Givón, Talmy, *Topic continuity in discourse. An introduction*, in: Givón, Talmy (ed.), *Topic continuity in discourse. A quantitative cross-language study*, Amsterdam/Philadelphia, John Benjamins, 1983, 1–42.

Gómez Seibane, Sara, *Uso de los pronombres átonos de tercera persona en guipuzcoanos emigrados a Indias en el siglo XVIII*, Res Diachronicae Vitual 3: Estudios sobre el siglo XVIII (2004), 39–51.

Gómez Seibane, Sara, *Neutro de materia y otros fenómenos del sistema pronominal átono en Bilbao (siglos XV-XVII)*, in: Gómez Seibane, Sara/Ramírez Luengo, José L. (edd.), *Maestra en mucho. Estudios filológicos en homenaje a la profesora Carmen Isasi Martínez*, Buenos Aires, Voces del Sur, 2010, 133–148.

Gómez Seibane, Sara, *La omisión y duplicación de objetos en el castellano del País Vasco*, in: Camus, Bergareche, Bruno/Gómez Seibane, Sara (edd.), *El castellano del País Vasco*, Bilbao, Universidad del País Vasco, 2012, 193–214 (= 2012a).

Gómez Seibane, Sara, *Contacto de lenguas y orden de palabras. OV/VO en el español del País Vasco*, Lingüística Española Actual 34:1 (2012), 115–135 (= 2012b).

Gómez Seibane, Sara, *Pronombres átonos (le, la, lo) en español. Aproximación histórica*, Madrid, Arco Libros, 2013 (= 2013a).

Gómez Seibane, Sara, *El leísmo. Principales hipótesis sobre su origen*, Español Actual 100 (2013), 137–146 (= 2013b).

Gómez Seibane, Sara, *Cambios indirectos inducidos por contacto en el castellano del País Vasco del siglo XIX*, in: Ramírez Luengo, José L./Velásquez Upegui, Eva P. (edd.), *La historia del español hoy. Estudios y perspectivas*, Lugo, Axac, 2014, 97–111.

Gómez Seibane, Sara, *El español en contacto con la lengua vasca. Orden de palabras y estructura informativa en diacronía*, in: López Izquierdo, Marta/Castillo Lluch, Mónica (edd.), *El orden de palabras en la historia del español y otras lenguas iberorromances*, Madrid, Visor, 2015, 457–482.

Heine, Bernd, *Contact-induced word order change without word order change*, in: Siemund, Peter/Kintana, Noemí (edd.), *Language contact and contact languages*, Amsterdam/Philadelphia, John Benjamins, 2008, 33–60.

Hidalgo Downing, Raquel, *La tematización en el español hablado. Estudio discursivo sobre el español peninsular*, Madrid, Gredos, 2003.

Hualde, José I., *Introduction*, in: Hualde, José I./Ortiz de Urbina, Jon (edd.), A grammar of Basque, Berlin/New York, Mouton de Gruyter, 2003, 1–4.

Laca, Brenda, *El objeto directo. La marcación preposicional*, in: Company, Concepción (ed.), *Sintaxis histórica de la lengua española*, vol. 1, México, UNAM/Fondo de Cultura Económica, 2006, 423–478.

Landa, Alazne, *Conditions on null objects in Basque Spanish and their relation to leísmo and clitic doubling*, PhD dissertation, Los Angeles, University of Southern California, 1995.

Landa, Alazne/Franco, Jon, *Two issues in null objects in Basque Spanish. Morphological decoding and grammatical permeability*, in: Zagona, Karen (ed.), *Grammatical theory and Romance languages*, Amsterdam/Philadelphia, John Benjamins, 1996, 159–168.

Lapesa, Rafael, *Sobre los orígenes y evolución del leísmo, laísmo y loísmo*, in: Baldinger, Kurt (ed.), *Festschrift Walther von Wartburg*, Tübingen, Max Niemeyer, 1968, 523–551.
Lapesa, Rafael, *Personas gramaticales y tratamientos en español*, in: Cano, Rafael/Echenique, Mª Teresa (edd.), *Estudios de morfosintaxis histórica del español*, vol. 1, Madrid, Gredos, 2000, 311–345.
Léglise, Isabelle/Chamoreau, Claudine (edd.), *The interplay of variation and change in contact settings*, Amsterdam/Philadelphia, John Benjamins, 2013.
Leonetti, Manuel, *Indefinidos, nombres escuetos y clíticos en las dislocaciones en español*, Cuadernos de la ALFAL 3 (2011), 100–123.
Matras, Yaron, *Language Contact*, Cambridge, Cambridge University Press, 2009.
Matras, Yaron/Sakel, Jeanette, *Investigating the mechanism of pattern replication in language convergence*, Studies in Language 31:4 (2007), 829–965.
Ortiz de Urbina, Jon, *Word order*, in: Hualde, José I./Ortiz de Urbina, Jon (edd.), A grammar of Basque, Berlin/New York, Mouton de Gruyter, 2003, 448–459.
Palacios, Azucena, *¿Son compatibles los cambios inducidos por contacto y las tendencias internas al sistema?*, in: Schrader-Kniffki, Martina/Morgenthaler García, Laura (edd.), *La Romania en interacción. Entre historia, contacto y política*, Madrid/Frankfurt, Iberoamericana/Vervuert, 2007, 259–279.
Palacios, Azucena, *Contact-induced change and internal evolution. Spanish in contact with Amerindian languages*, in: Chamoreau, Claudine/Léglise, Isabelle (edd.), *The interplay of variation and change in contact settings*, Amsterdam/Philadelphia, John Benjamins, 2013, 165–198.
Poplack, Shana/Levey, Stephen, *Contact-induced grammatical change*, in: Auer, Peter/Jürgen E. Schmidt (edd.), *Language and space. An international handbook of linguistic variation*, Berlin, Mouton de Gruyter, 2010, 391–419.
Prince, Ellen, *Toward a taxonomy of given-new information*, in: Cole, Peter (ed.), *Radical pragmatics*, New York, Academic Press, 1981, 223–255.
Sainzmaza-Lecanda, Lorena, *Towards an understanding of null and overt object variation in Basque Spanish*, 43rd New Ways of Analyzing Variation (NWAV43) October 2014, Chicago (= 2014a).
Sainzmaza-Lecanda, Lorena, *A quantitative characterization of null objects in the contact variety of Basque Spanish*, Hispanic Linguistics Symposium (HLS) 2014, November 2014, West Lafayette, IN (= 2014b).
Silva-Corvalán, Carmen, *Topicalización y pragmática del español*, Revista Española de Lingüística 14:1 (1984), 1–19.
Sportiche, Dominique, *Subject clitics in French and Romance. Complex inversion and clitic doubling*, in: Sportiche, Dominique (ed.), *Partitions and atoms of clause structure. Subjects, agreement, case and clitics*, London, Routledge, 1998, 308–341.
Thomason, Sarah, *Contact explanations in linguistics*, in: Hickey, Raymond (ed.), *The handbook of language contact*, Malden/Oxford, Blackwell, 2010, 31–47.
Trask, Robert L., *The history of Basque*, London/New York, Routledge, 1997.
Zubizarreta, Mª Luisa, *Las funciones informativas. Tema y foco*, in: Bosque, Ignacio/Demonte, Violeta (edd.), *Gramática descriptiva de la lengua española*, vol. 3, Madrid, Espasa Calpe, 1999, 4215–4244.

Kim Schulte
Structural convergence of two Ibero-Romance varieties
The case of colloquial Valencian as the outcome of contact between Catalan and Spanish

Abstract: This paper is a case study aiming to exemplify how long-term diglossic contact between closely related languages can affect linguistic structure. After a brief socio-historical overview focusing on the shifting role and prestige of Valencian and Spanish over the centuries, a selection of phonological, lexical, phraseological, discourse pragmatic and morphosyntactic features are presented and analysed in order to determine whether structural convergence has taken place between these two Ibero-Romance varieties. Apart from the expected use of lexical loans and frequent instances of code switching between the two languages by bilingual speakers, it is shown that the influence of Spanish on colloquial spoken Valencian has affected its linguistic structure in a variety of ways. This includes contact-induced features taken from Spanish, but also contact-induced conservation of older features that have disappeared from other varieties of Catalan. Particular attention is paid to innovations in spoken Valencian that are based on a combination of Catalan and Spanish structural features, sometimes leading to a reduction of structural complexity or opacity.

Keywords: convergence, Catalan, Spanish, Valencian, colloquial, phonology, lexicon, phraseology, past tense, clitics

1 Introduction

The Romance languages are a classic example of diversification from a single parent language, but far less attention has traditionally been paid to the fact that numerous different contact scenarios between them have led, and are still leading, to a wide range of instances of linguistic convergence. That said, a considerable number of studies examining the outcome of specific Romance-Romance contact situations do exist; for the pair of languages examined in this article, Spanish and Valencian, a variety of aspects of language contact are analysed

Kim Schulte, Universitat Jaume I, Castellón

https://doi.org/10.1515/9783110736250-004

by scholars such as Montoya i Abad (1989), Blas Arroyo (1992; 1993), Gómez Molina (1998), Casanova (2001), Briz Gómez (2004) and Käuper/Guerreo Ramos (2008), to name just a few.

In this article, several contact-induced features commonly found in popular spoken Valencian will be presented and analysed.[1] While straightforward borrowing and transfer is the most common and obvious effect of language contact, the fact that the two languages involved in this case are structurally very similar and that many speakers are relatively balanced bilinguals also favours a different type of change, in which structures and paradigms are assimilated to one another in the two languages; this may result in an alignment of form-meaning mapping between the contact languages, a clear case of convergence[2] (cf. Matras 2011, 144), and also in the emergence of "pick-and-mix" paradigms, in which features from both languages are combined, generally leading to a reduction of structural complexity, via a process involving *levelling* and *simplification*, which is frequently associated with koineisation (Nida/Fehderau 1970; Siegel 1985, 363; Kerswill/Trudgill 2005, 197–198).

Prior to the presentation and analysis of the data, it is important to attempt to define the languages involved in the specific contact situation. Such definitions are always complex because every language consists of multiple regional and social varieties, which means that some kind of abstraction or idealisation is unavoidable. *Spanish* will, in this article, be used to refer to standard European Spanish as well as the regional variety of Spanish spoken in the contact area, which form part of a diastratic and diatopic linguistic continuum. *Valencian* is a cover term for a number of Catalan varieties spoken in the Valencian Community, i.e. along much of the south-eastern Spanish Mediterranean coast and in the mountainous hinterland. According to the traditional classification (Milá y Fontanals 1861, 462), Valencian belongs to the Western Catalan dialect group; it differs markedly, both in terms of phonology and morphosyntax, from Eastern Catalan as spoken in most of Catalonia.

It is important to distinguish standard Valencian from the vernacular varieties spoken in the Valencia region. As is the case with any standardised language, the number of functionally equivalent regional features accepted as part of the standard language must necessarily be limited for practical reasons. Furthermore, some Eastern Catalan features that are, in fact, atypical of vernacular Valencian have been incorporated into the standard variety due to a certain

---

[1] Some of the features analysed in this article are presented in Schulte (2018), a study aimed at comparing different contact scenarios.
[2] The term *convergence* refers to linguistic change in which prolonged contact between two or more languages leads to structural resemblance.

tradition, among Valencian philologists, to (over)emphasise the linguistic unity between Valencian and Catalan (Climent 2007, 50–59). At the same time, many widespread colloquial features of Valencian are considered non-standard and are thus stigmatised, often causing speakers to feel self-conscious about the use of their native language. Many of these non-standard, vernacular elements are features that have disappeared from other varieties of Catalan but are preserved in Valencian, while others are the result of more recent language-internal innovation. What will be examined here is the influence of the continuous close contact with Spanish, which has contributed both to innovation and to the preservation of older features.

Following a very brief outline of the historical and present-day sociolinguistic situation in the area where Valencian is spoken, in which particular attention is paid to the social status of the two contact languages, this article goes on to describe and analyse some phonological, lexical, phraseological, pragmatic and morphosyntactic features of the spoken vernacular that show signs of a certain degree of convergence with Spanish. Rather than simply listing lexical and structural loans (which would not be sufficient to support the claim that convergence is taking place), the aim is to provide examples of a more profound, structural combination and assimilation between the two languages.

As the languages involved in this contact situation are closely related and structurally very similar to begin with (at least from a cross-linguistic, typological perspective), care must be taken to distinguish contact-induced changes from parallel internal developments that just happen to coincide (cf. Poplack/Levey 2010), if indeed these two types can be clearly distinguished in contact situations characterised by a high degree of bilingualism. Furthermore, the data presented in this article confirms that contact can trigger internal change that goes beyond mere borrowing or calquing (cf. Palacios Alcaine 2007; 2013), making it difficult to draw a precise line between these two types of development. In general, the main criterion for considering a change to have been triggered by contact is the absence of the respective feature in closely related varieties or sister languages that have not been subject to the same degree of contact.

The linguistic data presented here stems from the observations of native Valencian speakers from Castellón, Valencia and the surrounding areas in everyday situations, between 2007 and 2016. To avoid the problems caused by the *observer's paradox* (Labov 1972, 209), speakers were not informed that their linguistic behaviour was being observed; had they been aware of the scrutiny of their linguistic performance, they would almost certainly have avoided colloquial or vernacular features in favour of the prescriptive standard, as awareness of the chasm between normative and colloquial usage is deeply engrained. To avoid ethical issues and for practical reasons, the data was not recorded and no information that could identify individuals appears in the examples provided in this article, as recommended by the Linguistic Society of America for data gathered via "anonymous observation of public behaviour, which often cannot involve consent" (LSA 2009, 1–2).

The present paper thus provides preliminary data for an in-depth corpus study in which the observed features can be confirmed, quantified and classified with respect to the groups of speakers whose speech they occur in, either regularly or occasionally. To accurately reflect actual language use, the corpus for such a study must consist entirely of natural speech, which rules out many established methods of linguistic data collection such as interviews and elicitation tasks. Dividing informants into different age groups might, furthermore, provide some evidence of recent and ongoing changes if certain features occur more frequently in the speech of the younger generations than in that of their parents and grandparents. Nevertheless, consideration should be given to the fact that language can and does change over a speaker's lifespan, which means that adult speech is not an exact reflection of the language acquired during childhood and adolescence (cf. e.g. Raumolin-Brunberg 2005; Kiesling 2011, 124; Hickey 2012). This factor can render the observation of language change in apparent time somewhat unreliable. In the case of Valencian, this is of particular relevance as recent social pressure to use the standard variety (cf. 2.3) is likely to have a similar effect on the linguistic behaviour of speakers in a wide range of age groups, leading to outcomes that do not fully correspond to those predicted by models of normal intergenerational change.

2 A very brief external history of the linguistic situation in the Valencia region

To understand the present-day sociolinguistic situation in the Valencian Community, it is important to take into account the simultaneous presence of both Spanish and Valencian over the past 800 years.

The history of Valencian can be said to begin with the conquest of the region from the Almohads by James I of Aragon between 1232 and 1245, which led to the subsequent repopulation of the area by a mix of settlers (cf. Guinot 2012) from Catalonia and Aragon, speakers of (Old) Catalan and (Old) Aragonese (an Ibero-Romance language in its own right), respectively. Old Valencian thus had input from two closely related Romance languages, making a koineisation scenario highly likely; in any case, features from both languages can be identified both historically (Martí Mestre 2012) and in the present-day language (Casanova 2011).

There is also a highly controversial theory regarding the contribution of Mozarabic, the Romance language spoken under Moorish rule until the 13th century, which in its extreme form claims that Valencian is not a dialect of Catalan, but a continuation of the local variety of Mozarabic (Peñarroja Torrejón 1990).

Contact between Valencian and Spanish is multidimensional, with different types of contact scenarios coexisting. Spanish is an adstrate as well as the prestige or H-language in a diglossic situation, and in recent years a reversal of attitudes in some sectors of society has also turned it into the less prestigious or L-language.

2.1 Spanish as an adstrate

The expulsion of the Arab-speaking Moriscos from the Kingdom of Valencia in 1609, who made up between a quarter and a third of the population, triggered large-scale immigration from almost all adjoining areas (Torres Morera 1966, 126–131). Though there is no consensus on the exact proportion of Spanish speakers among the new settlers, the partial population replacement that this involved is likely to have contributed to the shift towards Spanish in inland areas that were culturally and linguistically more similar to the adjacent Spanish- and Aragonese-speaking areas to begin with. In coastal areas, the varieties that were closer to Catalan were not under threat of language shift, but were most probably influenced by the influx of Spanish speakers, particularly since there was (and still is) a high degree of mutual comprehensibility between the two languages, which means that bilingual conversations, with each speaker communicating in their respective native language, are likely to have been the norm rather than the exception.

Another wave of immigration of Spanish speakers took place between 1960 and 1980 (Piqueras 2007, 176–177; Riera Ginestar 2009, 12) due to internal migration from economically disadvantaged rural areas of Spain, such as Andalusia, at a time when speaking Valencian was stigmatised and the majority of Valencian speakers were at least partially bilingual. In this sociolinguistic context, the influx of monolingual Spanish speakers almost certainly contributed to an increase in the use of Spanish in everyday situations outside the closest circle of family and friends. While the use of Valencian, or of Spanish with obvious Valencian features, was not socially accepted in formal settings and among speakers with a high degree of formal education (see 2.2), the frequent switch to Spanish in everyday conversations, paired with the fact that the mass media were only available in Spanish, led to a situation in which native Valencian speakers incorporated an increasing number of Spanish features into their language. In fact, it is remarkable that, at a time when Philologists were trying to establish the rules of "correct" Valencian, many actual native speakers were hardly aware of the distinction between the two languages, engaging in a complex combination of code mixing and code switching. Despite a certain degree of urban/rural divide, with the cities of Valencia and Alicante tending strongly towards the use of Spanish whereas Valencian is the first language in most rural areas, it is important to keep in mind that many speakers who grew up before Valencian acquired the status of a co-official language in the 1980s simply didn't draw a clear distinction between the two languages; their colloquial variety permitted mixing elements and structures from both.[3]

2.2 Spanish as a prestige/H-language

As early as the mid-15th century, the Valencian aristocracy adopted Castilian (cf. Duarte/Massip 1981, 86–87), turning it into the primary language of culture, both literature and music. After the dynastic union of the kingdoms of Castile and Aragon (the latter including Valencia) in 1479, a more general shift to Castilian by the upper social classes and the clergy took place during the 16th century, with sermons being delivered in Castilian (Palomero 2006), with the consequence that the general public had a greater degree of exposure to Spanish.

Following the War of the Spanish Succession at the beginning of the 18th century, the Kingdom of Aragon (covering the areas of Aragon, Catalonia and Valencia) was abolished as a political entity, and between 1714 and 1716 Castilian became the official language for all official and administrative purposes, leading to an increasing number of situations in which speakers were exposed to the Spanish language. Furthermore, the prohibition of the use of Catalan (including Valencian) in all schools by the Council of Castile in 1715[4] turned Castilian into the only language of education, thereby further entrenching its status as the prestige language. This was followed by more strictly enforced language policies in the second half of the 18th century, under Charles III, aimed at eradicating the regional languages in all official and educational settings.[5]

---

[3] One of the sources for this claim is personal communication with Amparo Tusón Valls, a linguist and philologist who grew up in exactly the linguistic situation described here; similar observations are made by numerous informants over the age of 50, especially those who grew up outside the larger cities.
[4] "[...] que en todas las escuelas de primeras letras, y de Gramática, no se permitan libros impresos en lengua catalana, escribir ni hablar en ella dentro de las Escuelas".
[5] "[...] para que en todo el Reyno se actúe y enseñe en lengua castellana. [...] y a este efecto derogo y anulo todas qualesquier resoluciones, o estilos, que haya en contrario, [...] Finalmente mando, que la enseñanza [...] se haga en lengua castellana generalmente, [...] cuidando de su cumplimiento las Audiencias y Justicias respectivas" (Royal Decree of 23 May 1768).

Until the 1980s, standard Spanish clearly remained the prestige language, used by the educated classes, in the education system and the media, in official settings, and more generally in the cities (Valencia, Alicante). Industrialisation, urbanisation and linguistic policies contributed to the dominance of Spanish during much of the 20th century (Blas Arroyo 2005, 409), leading to a situation in which most city dwellers were monolingual or dominant Spanish speakers, and the vernacular language was a varying mix of Spanish and Valencian, with the proportion of elements from the respective languages corresponding to a complex multidimensional continuum; Figure 1 is a strongly simplified illustration of some of the relevant factors.

Figure 1: Factors influencing the proportion of Spanish and Valencian features in everyday speech.

In many respects, the resulting linguistic situation is typical of diglossia (cf. Ferguson 1959), in that a single speech community uses two varieties for different social functions, typically a colloquial (L) and a formal (H) variety. Whilst the term is most commonly applied to situations in which two varieties of the same language are spoken, the arbitrariness of the distinction between varieties and languages must be kept in mind; standard (Swiss) German and the regional Swiss German varieties, for instance, are a classic example of diglossia, though the differences between them are, arguably, greater than those between Spanish and Catalan. Rather than the issue of whether we are dealing with varieties or languages, what is important in this context is that diglossia requires speakers to be aware of a degree of similarity between the H- and the L-variety (or language), which is certainly the case for Spanish/Valencian.

This long-standing and fairly stable diglossic situation, in which two closely related languages are spoken by a more or less bilingual population, provides ideal conditions for large-scale interference, transfer, and ultimately even for possible hybridisation (cf. Hulk/Müller 2000; Sanchez-Stockhammer 2011); until the late 20th century, most speakers perceived their (mixed) vernacular as little more than their local non-standard variety and the use of Spanish lexemes and morphosyntactic structures was not generally stigmatised within the community (cf. footnote 3).

2.3 Valencian/Catalan as the new prestige language

What makes the Valencian–Spanish contact situation particularly interesting, though by no means unique, is the recent status reversal of the two languages. Following legislation in 1979 and 1982, Valencian now has the status of co-official language and plays an important part in the education system, with an increasing number of schools using Valencian as their main vehicular language; the proportion of Valencians considering themselves literate in Valencian has increased from 7% in 1986 to 35% in 2015, and 51% of the population now feels confident speaking Valencian, according to a recent study by the regional government (Generalitat Valenciana 2015). The shift towards Valencian in educational and official settings has turned it into the new prestige language for certain sectors of society, particularly the established local middle classes, for whom the use of Valencian in official as well as private settings has, to some extent, become a way of setting themselves apart from other sectors of society, particularly those with a (domestic or international) migration background.[6]

Generally speaking, H-languages tend to be nobody's native variety in the region where they function as H-language. This is also the case of the present-day Valencian standard, which was established with strong influence from eastern Catalan[7] (i.e. the Catalan of Catalonia), as mentioned above in the introduction. The distance between the autochthonous varieties and standard Valencian is exacerbated by the fact that standard Catalan is accepted as an alternative in official settings and proficiency tests, whereas the majority of vernacular non-standard variants are considered incorrect. This has led to a stigmatisation of non-standard speakers for their use of so-called "barbarisms", reflected in the self-stigmatizing phrase *Jo parle molt malament* 'I speak very badly', frequently uttered by Valencian speakers whose native variety contains non-standard features.

The clear separation of Spanish and Valencian as two distinct languages with official standards has put pressure on both dialectal Valencian speakers and native Spanish speakers to learn standard Valencian. The effect of this

---

[6] No rigorous studies of this recent sociolinguistic phenomenon, a reversal of the H- and L-language status of the two languages for some speakers, have been published so far. However, observation of facts on the ground leave little doubt that this is the case. For instance, clearly Spanish-dominant teenage informants claim to speak Valencian as their first language, and parents of young children make a visible effort to speak Valencian in the presence of other adults they perceive as equivalent or superior in social standing, while their children answer in Spanish.

[7] The replacement of an existing Valencian standard by the "dialect of Barcelona" is decried by critics of the new Valencian standard, such as Puerto Ferre (2006).

increasing use of Valencian by native Spanish speakers is potentially quite complex. On the one hand, learners and L2-speakers of Valencian often make a conscious effort to avoid certain stigmatised non-standard features (especially Castilianisms), which are, in fact, stigmatised precisely because they are in widespread use among native Valencian speakers but considered incorrect according to the established standard. The increasing number of non-native Valencian speakers may thus effectively strengthen certain standard features across the speech community. On the other hand, L2 speakers are likely to increase the overall frequency of structures resembling those found in Spanish, which in turn may trigger their increased use by native Valencian speakers, thereby creating an additional pathway for further convergence.

3 Linguistic outcomes

The influence of contact on colloquial Valencian can be observed at all levels of linguistic description; it will be exemplified, in this section, for the areas of phonology, lexicon and phraseology, discourse-regulating elements, and morphosyntax. The resulting contact-induced features can be located along a continuum ranging from straight-forward borrowing to genuine hybrid structures.

3.1 Phonology

The influence of Spanish on the phonology of many varieties of Valencian is occasionally acknowledged in the literature (e.g. Segura Llopes 2003). Two areas that are particularly susceptible to simplification under the influence of Spanish are the vowel and sibilant systems.

Especially in the speech of younger speakers, the vowel system of spoken Valencian is increasingly assimilating to that of Spanish (cf. Beltrán-Calvo/Segura Llopes 2017, 141), which has five vowels (/i, e, a, o, u/), both in stressed and in unstressed position. In stressed position, the inherited seven-term vowel system of Catalan, including Valencian, distinguishes /i, e, ɛ, a, o, ɔ, u/, but a growing number of Valencian speakers no longer distinguish open /ɛ/ and /ɔ/ from closed /e/ and /o/.[8] On the other hand, the reduction from five unstressed vowels (/i, e, a,

---

8 Lleó/Cortés (2013, 116–117) provide evidence that the acquisition of this vowel distinction depends on the dominant language children are surrounded by (Spanish or Catalan) rather than on their parents' Catalan vowel system.

o, u/) to three (/i, ə, u/) that has taken place in standard Catalan is absent in most Valencian varieties; a factor favouring this resilience of the unstressed vowel system in Valencian is almost certainly the presence of the same set of unstressed vowels in Spanish.

In the sibilant system, a loss of voicing opposition is gradually spreading, with /z, ʒ, dʒ/ being devoiced and merging with /s, ʃ, tʃ/ (cf. Segura Llopes 2003, 8). This is a well-established phenomenon in some areas, notably in the "apitxat" variety spoken in and around the city of Valencia (Barnils 1914); it is generally accepted that the influence of Spanish, which has no voiced sibilants, is an important factor favouring this phoneme merger. Spanish is also the model for other wide-spread phoneme mergers such as that of the palatal lateral /ʎ/ with the palatal approximant /j/ (realised as /j/), and that of /b/ and /v/, both of which are the norm in standard Spanish, but not in most other Catalan varieties.

3.2 Lexicon and phraseology

Most lexical items are cognate in Spanish and all varieties of Catalan. Around 75–85% of basic vocabulary items share the same Latin root,[9] and the vast majority of loans from outside the Iberian Peninsula come from the same source languages (Arabic, learned Latin, French and, more recently, English). Adding to this shared lexical stock, borrowing from Spanish into colloquial Valencian is ongoing and frequent (Lacreu Cuesta 1995, 7). While older loanwords are often fully accepted and, given the general lexical overlap between the languages, not easily identifiable, more recent borrowings are, unsurprisingly, stigmatised by purists. On the other hand, there are lexical items that have been present in the language for centuries but are nevertheless stigmatised due to their similarity to Spanish, especially when a less Spanish-sounding synonym is available.

As can be expected in a long-term contact situation between sister languages, it is not always possible to distinguish clearly between borrowing and parallel developments in the two languages, especially in a context involving bilingual speakers. Table 1 shows some examples of lexical items that are considered incorrect by prescriptivists, but which nevertheless occur frequently in spoken Valencian; each item will be discussed individually below. The degree

---

[9] Different lists of basic lexical items provide varying cognacy percentages; according to one of the most recent ones, available at cobl.info, 78% of items in a basic 200-word-list are cognate, while Rea (1958, 147–149) finds 85% cognacy, using the Swadesh 100-word list.

and type of phonological and morphological adaptation to the recipient language is of particular interest, as a range of different patterns can be distinguished.

Table 1: Common borrowing patterns in colloquial Valencian.

	Spanish	Colloquial Valencian	Standard Catalan	English Translation
a)	tamaño	tamany	mida, grandària	'size'
b)	taladro	taladre	trepant	'drill'
c)	bandeja /-x-/	bandeja [-x-]	safata	'tray'
d)	albornoz /-θ/	albornós /-s/	barnús	'dressing gown'
e)	admi*tir*	admi*tir*	admetre	'to admit'
f)	*a*divinar	*a*divinar	*en*devinar	'to guess, divine'
g)	caradura lit. 'hard-face'	caradura lit. 'hard-face'	barra 'jaw/jawed'	'cheeky (person)'

It should be pointed out that the examples in Table 1 are commonly heard in the colloquial language, occurring in free variation with the standard Catalan terms, often even in a single speaker's idiolect.

a. Etymologically, *tamaño* and *tamany* come from Latin TAM MAGNUS; they are attested both in early Spanish and in early Valencian texts as adjectives meaning 'so big'.[10] With the exception of Alcover/Moll (1988), *tamany* 'size' does not generally appear in Catalan or Valencian dictionaries, despite its widespread usage. The shift in meaning and syntactic category from 'so big' (adj.) to 'size' (n.) may have taken place parallelly in both languages, or the Spanish noun may have been borrowed, with phonological adaptation based on regular correspondences between the two languages; the correspondence between Spanish words such as *año* /aɲo/ 'year', *baño* /baɲo/ 'bath' and *engaño* /eŋgaɲo/ 'deception' and the Valencian cognates *any* /aɲ/, *bany* /baɲ/ and *engany* /eŋgaɲ/ provides the model for analogical extension.

---

10 The Spanish 13th-century poet Berceo uses *tan manno* in *La vida de San Millán de Cogolla* (ca. 1230), and *tamanya* appears in the Valencian 15th-century novel *Tirant lo Blanch* (Martorell 1992), written in 1490.

b. Catalan *trepant* 'drill' is derived from the verb *trepar* 'to drill, to make holes', which is attested as early as the 14th century. Spanish *taladro*, on the other hand, is a continuation of Latin TARATRUM. This item appears not to have been preserved in Catalan, but it was later borrowed from Spanish (Alcover/Moll 1988), with a phonological adaptation of the final vowel based on the model of words like Spanish *cuadro* 'painting', *poliedro* 'polyhedron' and the respective Valencian *quadre, poliedre*.
c. *Bandeja* is a clear case of borrowing from Spanish; it is the default word for 'tray' in the entire Valencian region (Veny/Pons 2003, map 169), preserving the Spanish velar fricative /x/, a phoneme that is absent from the Valencian phonological system. Despite this lack of phonological adaptation, there is no indication that the non-native sound curbs its status as default word.
d. In this example, the Spanish and Catalan words stem from the same loan source, Arabic *burnūs*; the difference is that in Spanish the Arabic article *al-* was reanalysed as part of the noun itself. While a range of different forms of this word exist in Catalan/Valencian, both with and without *al-* such as *barnús, bernús, albernús, albornós* (Alcover/Moll 1988), the most common form in current colloquial Valencian is *albornós*. There is no way of knowing whether this form emerged independently in Valencian and gained popularity due to the resemblance to its Spanish counterpart, or whether Spanish *albornóz* was borrowed and adapted to the phonological system of Valencian by changing the final /-θ/ to /-s/, as /θ/ is not part of its phonological inventory.
e. This example shows how the influence of Spanish affects verbal morphology: whilst Catalan continues the Latin third conjugation in verbs like *admetre*, Spanish has incorporated the corresponding verbs into a simpler three-term conjugation system. By using the cognate Spanish verb *admitir* instead of *admetre*,[11] Valencian speakers effectively cause it to switch conjugations.
f. This verb has different prefixed prepositions in Spanish and standard Catalan. Both words ultimately go back to Latin DĪVĪNĀRE without a prefix, and it appears that the choice of prefixed preposition is an areal feature that makes no semantic difference: Spanish and Portuguese have *a-*, standard Catalan and Italian *en-/in-*, while French uses *deviner* without a prefix. A range of different forms can be found in different varieties of Catalan, including *adevinar, adivinar, endivinar, endevinar, divinar* and *devinar*, and it stands to reason that the choice of *a-* in colloquial Valencian is influenced by the cognitive presence of Spanish *adivinar*.

---

[11] According to Alcover/Moll (1988), this is a clear case of borrowing from Spanish.

g. This is an example of a lexical item that may either be a straight-forward loanword or a calque, as both elements of the compound (*cara* and *dura*) are the same in both languages; in fact, in a contact situation in which both borrowing and calquing are commonplace, no clear distinction can be drawn between these two processes. On the other hand, though not accepted as correct in Valencian by prescriptivists, this form-meaning combination may well have emerged simultaneously in both contact languages.

Numerous expressions and phraseological units are shared between the two languages; the examples in Table 2 below are all normatively accepted. Whether they are the result of calquing or of joint development as the result of ongoing close contact or convergence is difficult to determine;[12] in any case, their absence in some or all of the surrounding Romance sister languages[13] suggests that they are probably not inherited from Latin or common Western Romance, but rather joint innovations in Spanish and Catalan. In the final example, inheritance can be clearly ruled out as *propósito/propòsit* is a 14th-century learned loanword from Latin.

Table 2: Calqued or jointly developed expressions and phraseological units.

Spanish	Catalan	English Gloss and Translation
en lo que va de año	en el que va d'any	lit. 'in that which goes of year' 'so far this year'
al fin y al cabo	al cap i a la fi	lit. 'at the end and at the end' 'in the end, after all'
darse por vencido	donarse per vençut	lit. 'to give oneself for defeated' 'to admit defeat'
a propósito	a propòsit	lit. 'to intent' 'on purpose'

---

12 Calquing of phraseological units between the two languages is ongoing and extremely common, and it is important to point out that it goes in both directions. Prat Sabater (2016), for example, shows that non-standard calqued Catalan expressions are judged to be acceptable in colloquial Spanish by university students in Catalonia.

13 The expression *en lo que va de año* has spread to Galician and is gradually also entering Portuguese, where *no que vai de ano* is currently still very rare. Portuguese *ao fim e ao cabo* is calqued on the Spanish expression (Botelho de Amaral 1938), while French expressions such as *à la fin et au bout* may also be calqued and are, in any case, very infrequent. *Dar-se por vencido* does exist in Portuguese, but there is no comparable expression in French.

3.3 "Discourse-regulating" elements

As observed by Matras (1998, 326) "'Discourse-regulating grammatical elements' are usually borrowed from the dominant language in a contact situation, i.e. the language used for communication with those outside a linguistic minority group." This is certainly true for Valencian. As exemplified in Table 3, discourse markers (DM) are generally borrowed from Spanish (cf. Vila i Moreno 1996, 201), whilst the Catalan cognates are often used as the corresponding "content words" (CW).

Table 3: Discourse markers borrowed from Spanish.

Spanish DM & CW	Colloquial Valencian DM	Valencian CW	Normative Valencian DM	Notes
bueno lit. 'good' 'well, ...'	bueno 'well, ...'	bo(n) 'good'	bé 'well'	Diphthong /we/ clearly marks loan.
pues/pos lit. 'because' 'well, then ...'	pues/pos 'well, then ...'	doncs 'so'	doncs 'so'	
vale lit. 'it is worth' 'ok'	vale 'ok'	val 'it is worth'	entesos lit. 'understood. PL'	Final /-e/ in 3rd sg. clearly marks loan.

Example (1) illustrates the natural use of borrowed discourse markers, even in the context of a discussion of "good Catalan usage"; while speakers are advised against the use of *d'acord*, probably because of its similarity to Spanish *de acuerdo*, the even more obviously borrowed discourse markers *pues* and *vale*, the latter a synonym for *entesos*, are used to comment this prescriptive rule.

(1)   Es recomana dir "entesos", enlloc de "d'acord". Pues, vale.[14]
      'It is recommended to say *entesos* instead of *d'acord*. Well, ok then.'

---

[14] From *Parleu bé en català, entesos?*, http://www.rac1.cat/elmon/blog/parleu-be-en-catala-entesos.html [last access: 21.7.2017].

Discourse-structuring elements in colloquial Catalan and Valencian are also frequently influenced by the Spanish model, as shown in Table 4. They can either be straight-forward loans, as in the case of *desde luego*, or incomplete calques with non-native morphosyntax, as in the other two examples.

Table 4: Discourse-structuring elements influenced by Spanish.

Spanish	Colloquial Valencian	Normative Valencian	English gloss/ translation	Notes
desde luego	*desde luego*	*per descomptat*	lit. 'since afterwards' 'of course'	Diphthong /we/ clearly marks loan.
por lo tanto	*per lo tant*	*per tant*	lit. 'for it so much/for so much' 'so therefore'	In standard Valencian, *per lo* would be contracted to *pel*.
a lo mejor	*a lo millor*	*potser, a la millor*	lit. 'at the best/ can-be' 'perhaps'	In standard Valencian, *lo millor* would be *el millor*, contracted to *al millor*.

Certain interjections are also adopted from Spanish without phonological adaptation. For instance, *jo!* [xo] ('crikey!', 'blimey!') retains the Spanish velar fricative [x] despite the fact that it is not part of the Catalan/Valencian phonemic inventory.

3.4 The past tenses: convergence in Spanish and Valencian

3.4.1 Agreement in the perfect tense

The *have*-perfect is an example of structural convergence between Spanish and Valencian. On the one hand, Spanish, Portuguese and all varieties of modern Catalan (including Valencian) have lost the *have/be*-dichotomy that existed in the medieval languages[15] and has survived in many other Romance languages, which may be due to areal convergence (cf. Drinka 2017), though it is also a cross-linguistically common development in the grammaticalisation process

---

[15] Detailed accounts of this process in Spanish can be found in Rodríguez Molina (2010) and Rosemeyer (2014).

leading to the emergence of present perfect tenses, e.g. in English and, to some extent, in Romanian.

Valencian, however, has gone one step further in converging with Spanish than most other varieties of Catalan, which generally have gender and number agreement between direct object and past participle in sentences such as (2); such agreement was obligatory in the Ibero-Romance languages in medieval times but has since disappeared from colloquial Valencian, as it has from Spanish and Portuguese.

(2) L'   Ana, l'   he   vist   / ?*vist-a   avui
    DEF.ART Ana OBJ have.1SG   see.PTCP / ?*see.PTCP-F   today
    'Anna, I've seen her today.'

Like the *have/be*-dichotomy, this loss of agreement, which appears to have originated in Navarre and then spread from there (Rodríguez Molina, 2010), is also cross-linguistically common and could easily have arisen language-internally. However, the fact that Valencian shares this feature with Spanish, which it has been in closer contact with than other varieties of Catalan have, combined with the gradual diatopic expansion of the feature (Rodríguez Molina 2010, 1782–1783), does suggest that contact has played its part in this development.

It should be noted that the less complex structure has ousted the more complex one in this particular convergence scenario; it is well known that structural simplification is a common outcome of contact-induced morphosyntactic change, though the opposite effect can also occasionally be observed under specific circumstances, such as early bilingualism (Trudgill 2011, 15–61).

3.4.2 The functional range of the different past tenses

The aspectual contexts triggering the use of the *have*-perfect are virtually identical in Spanish and Catalan (including Valencian),[16] setting them apart from surrounding Romance languages such as French on the one hand, and Portuguese, Galician, and Asturian on the other. While French follows the central European areal pattern of generalising the use of the *have*-perfect in the spoken language and relegating the other past tenses to formal registers and the written language,

---

16 In Spanish and Catalan, the functional range of this tense is similar to that of the English present perfect: it is used for events and actions that have taken place in the same time unit as the utterance (today, this week, this year, etc.) and those that have an ongoing effect at the time of the utterance ('I have read/eaten it').

the western Ibero-Romance languages have either not developed this periphrastic tense at all, or they use it in very specific semantic contexts only (Schmitt 2009, 404). In Portuguese, for example, the functional range of the [*ter* + past participle] construction is far more restricted; it is used only for events that have begun in the past but are still ongoing.

The functional range of the non-perfective past tenses is also identical in both languages. While the synthetic preterite has been replaced by the analytic *anar* + infinitive ('go + INF') construction in all but the most conservative varieties of Catalan, the three-way functional contrast between the preterite, the imperfect and the *have*-perfect is exactly the same as in Spanish, showing that the two languages have developed a parallel distribution of the past tenses, based on precisely the same aspectual distinctions. Taking into account that the past tenses have evolved very differently in other Romance languages, it is more than likely that contact and bilingualism played an important part in this joint development.

3.4.3 The pronominal system: convergence and divergence

3.4.3.1 Syntax: clitic pronoun position

The position of clitic pronouns, i.e. whether they appear in pre- or post-verbal position, has evolved in exactly the same way in Spanish and Catalan (including Valencian) since the Middle Ages, in contrast to the neighbouring Romance languages French and Portuguese. It is determined exclusively by whether the verb form is finite or not; thus, all non-finite verb forms (infinitive, imperative and gerund) require unstressed pronouns to be enclitic, whilst finite verb forms have proclitic personal pronouns. Historically, this system emerged in Catalan and then spread to Castilian (Fernández-Ordóñez 2011), which goes to show that the process of convergence is by no means unidirectional.[17]

3.4.3.2 Clitic pronoun allomorphy

Spoken Valencian does not adopt the standard Catalan allomorphy within the clitic pronoun system (1SG, 2SG, 3SG/PL REFL, 1PL), resisting pressure from the "metropolitan standard", instead preserving the pattern shared with Spanish, as shown in Table 5.

---

17 Similarly, Bouzouita (2016, 294–295) suggests that the increasing grammaticalisation of the Spanish future and conditional tense forms may have been triggered or supported by earlier such developments in neighbouring varieties such as Occitan, Catalan and Aragonese.

Table 5: Lack of pronominal allomorphy in Valencian.

	Standard Catalan		Colloquial Valencian		Standard Spanish	
	proclitic	enclitic	proclitic	enclitic	proclitic	enclitic
1SG	em	-me	me	-me	me	-me
2SG	et	-te	te	-te	te	-te
3SG/PL REFL	es/se/s'	-se	se	-se	se	-se
1 PL	ens	-nos/'ns	mos	-mos	nos	-nos

Whilst it is, of course, perfectly possible for a variety such as Valencian not to have participated in this innovation without any outside influence, there is documentary evidence that the morphological differentiation between pro- and enclitic pronouns of standard Catalan was also emerging in medieval Valencian; for instance, in *Tirant lo Blanc* (Martorell 1992), a famous chivalric romance written in Valencian in the second half of the 15th century, both variants can be found in preverbal position, in apparent free variation, as shown in examples (3)–(6).

(3) La sperança [...] que tinch [...] **me** dóna ànimo
 the hope that have.1SG OBJ.1SG gives courage
 de pregar-te...
 of ask.INF-OBJ.1SG
 'My hope encourages me to ask you...'

(4) ¿Què **em** fa a mi?
 what OBJ.1SG does to 1SG
 'What do I care?'

(5) no **se** pot sperar longua vida posseir
 NEG REFL.3SG can.3SG expect.INF long life have.INF
 'You can't expect to have a long life.'

(6) no **es** pot cremar
 NEG REFL.3SG can.3SG burn.INF
 'It can't be burnt.'

So why, then, did this change not become generalised in the same way that it did in standard Catalan? It stands to reason that the availability of the Spanish model in a largely bilingual environment was a factor, particularly because the standard Catalan pattern is somewhat complex: the choice between the allomorphs is determined (a) by the position in relation to the verb, and (b) by the initial phoneme of the verb, as shown in the following examples:

(7) *sense repetir-se* without repeat-3SG.REFL 'without repeating himself'

(8) *no es pot* not 3SG.REFL can.3SG 'you can't/it's forbidden'

(9) *no se sap* not 3SG.REFL know.3SG 'it is not known'

(10) *no s'espera* /sə/ not 3SG.REFL expect.3SG 'it is not expected'

(11) *sense enrecordar-me* without remember-1SG.REFL 'without (me) remembering'

(12) *no em coneix* not OBJ.1SG know.3SG 'he doesn't know me'

(13) *no m'espera* /mə/ not OBJ.1SG expect.3SG 'he doesn't expect me'

Whilst an increase in complexity is, in itself, certainly no barrier for structural change, the continuing presence of a less complex alternative pattern (that of Spanish, in this case) may have tipped the balance in favour of the latter.

3.4.3.3 Reorganisation of the pronominal system (plural indirect objects)

Most Spanish and Catalan varieties distinguish direct and indirect object pronouns. However, while in standard Spanish, accusative *lo, la* (M/F SG), *los, las* (M/F PL) contrast clearly with dative *le* (M+F SG), *les* (M+F PL), the system is less transparent in standard Catalan, as the masculine and feminine plural forms of the indirect object pronoun coincide with the masculine plural form of the direct object pronoun, shown in bold type in Table 6.

While there is a clear form–function correspondence in Spanish, the standard Catalan system is somewhat opaque. On the one hand, the relationship between the singular and plural indirect object pronouns (*li–els*) is not transparent, as they have less in common than the singular direct object pronoun with the plural indirect object pronouns (*el–els*). Furthermore, the fact that the feminine plural indirect object form (*els*) coincides with the masculine plural direct object pronoun (*els*), but not with the feminine plural direct object pronoun *les*, highlights the opacity in the standard Catalan system. Colloquial Valencian remedies

Table 6: Direct and indirect object pronouns in Catalan, Spanish and colloquial Valencian.

Function + number	Standard Catalan		Spanish		Colloquial Valencian	
	Masculine	Feminine	Masculine	Feminine	Masculine	Feminine
Direct obj. sg.	el (-lo)	la (-la)	lo	la	el/lo (-lo)	la (-la)
Direct obj. pl.	els (-los)	les (-les)	los	las	els/los (-los)	les (-les)
Indirect obj. sg.	li	li	le	le	li	li
Indirect obj. pl.	els (-los)	els (-los)	les	les	lis	lis

this lack of transparency by following the model of the more transparent Spanish system, replacing the plural indirect object pronouns with *lis* by adding the plural marker /-s/ to the singular forms. It should be noted that this is not an instance of straight-forward borrowing, as the morphological material is Catalan/Valencian; what has been imported from Spanish is the greater degree of system-internal clarity, in which functional relatedness is reflected by formal similarity.

3.4.3.4 Introducing the [+/- human] parameter

In the Spanish pronominal system, the case distinction between dative and accusative (indirect vs. direct object) is gradually being replaced by a human/non-human distinction. Due to the fact that indirect objects (beneficiaries) are almost always human, the Spanish indirect object pronouns are in the process of being reanalysed as [+human] object pronouns, leading to an extension of their use to (masculine) human direct objects, the so-called *leísmo* phenomenon.[18]

Whilst standard Catalan resists this redistribution of pronouns, in colloquial Valencian the extension of *li* from indirect object to human direct object is not uncommon, as seen in (14).

(14) L'   ha   visitat el   metge
     3SG.ACC.OBJ.M has visited the doctor
     ↓
     Li   ha   visitat el   metge
     3SG.HUM.OBJ.M has visited the doctor
     'The doctor has visited him.'

---

[18] See Gómez Seibane as well as Camus Bergareche/Gómez Seibane in this volume for an account of *leísmo* as a convergence phenomenon due to contact between Basque and Spanish.

This is closely related to the functional expansion of the preposition *a*, modelled on Spanish Differential Object Marking (DOM). In addition to its function as indirect object marker, *a* is also commonly used to mark human direct objects, which confirms that for human referents, the distinction between direct and indirect objects is somewhat blurred in modern colloquial Valencian.

(15) **A.l**   seu pare, li   ha visitat el metge
      DOM.DEF.SG his father 3SG.HUM.OBJ.M has visited the doctor
      'His dad, the doctor has visited him.'

3.4.3.5 Adverbial pronouns: divergence

Considering the instances of structural convergence, described so far, which often lead to a reduction in complexity, this tendency might be expected to apply across the board. However, the clitic adverbial pronouns *hi* and *en*, which are absent from modern Spanish whilst constituting a morphosyntactic area of some complexity in Catalan, show no signs of falling victim to convergence-driven simplification.

Broadly speaking, *en* (< Lat. ĪNDE) is used to substitute adverbial PPs headed by the preposition *de*, whilst *hi* (< Lat. HĪC + ĪBĪ) substitutes most other adverbial PPs, particularly locative and allative ones. While such "adverbial" pronouns are not uncommon in the Romance languages, they add both morphological and syntactic complexity to the Catalan pronominal system: they participate in a variety of contraction processes (e.g. *et hi* 'you there' is contracted to *t'hi*, *et en* 'you from there' to *te'n*), certain clitic pronoun combinations are not permissible and trigger substitution by a different pronoun (e.g. *ho en* 'it from' is substituted by *l'hi* or *l'en*), and the rules governing the order and contraction of sequences of three clitic pronouns are also a matter of some complexity.

The corresponding adverbial pronouns also existed in Old Spanish (*ende*, *y*), but in contrast to Catalan (including Valencian) they disappeared by the late 15th century (Meilán Garcia 1994; Matute 2016). Meyer-Lübke (1925) cites them as an example to show that many of the syntactic differences between Spanish and Catalan have emerged in relatively recent times; it might, indeed, be claimed that these pronouns are part of an ongoing process of divergence, as their use has, furthermore, been expanded for the purpose of semantic distinction. Thus, the Valencian verb *vore* 'to see' is semantically distinct from *vore-hi* [see + ADV.PRON] 'to be able to see (i.e. not to be blind)', and *anar* 'to go' is distinct from *anar-se'n* [go + REFL + ADV.PRON] 'to go away, to get going'; a reduced and contracted fossilised 1PL form of *anem-nos-en* [go.1PL + 1PL.REFL + ADV.PRON], *mone* 'let's go', is in fact considered an emblematic features of the speech of Castellón, used in both

Spanish and Valencian. However, bilingual speakers hardly ever use *en* and *hi* in Spanish, limiting their use of these pronouns to discourse in Valencian. It can thus be observed that, despite long-lasting close contact and bilingualism in this area, there are certain morphosyntactic features that clearly resist the general trend of convergence, perhaps as a visible and symbolic marker of linguistic distinctness and identity.

4 Conclusions

The data presented in this paper is the result of linguistic observation, and the presence of the features described is furthermore confirmed (and often criticised) by members of the local population who aim to speak or teach standard Valencian. While this data can and should serve as a basis for an in-depth sociolinguistic corpus study, which would most likely provide valuable insights regarding the frequency with which different groups of speakers employ these non-standard features, the primary aim of the present study has been to identify and analyse the ways in which long-term diglossic contact between closely related languages affects linguistic structure.

Perhaps unsurprisingly, lexical loans and calques between the two languages are pervasive; as observed by Sankoff (2001, 642), mixing lexical items from both contact languages is commonplace among fellow bilinguals, which is the case for almost all Valencian speakers. Wholesale borrowing of morphosyntactic structures, on the other hand, is not common; instead, a certain degree of hybridisation, in which features from both languages are combined, takes place in specific areas; a good example of this is the reorganisation of the personal pronoun paradigm (3.4.3.3).

Furthermore, a semantic alignment of structures with originally partly overlapping functional ranges in the two languages can be observed; the alignment of the functional ranges of the three past tenses (3.4.2) and the extension of the functions of the indirect object pronoun to human direct objects (3.4.3.4) both fall into this category. To some extent, the outcome of this alignment process resembles that of syntactic or structural calquing (cf. Molnár 1985, 54–57), but the fact that the corresponding structures are present in both languages to begin with means that this is a distinct phenomenon. In fact, it is sometimes difficult to identify in which of the two languages the respective pattern originated, as its propagation is often virtually simultaneous in both languages. It is, furthermore, noteworthy that there is no need for a pair of semantically/functionally aligned structure to be cognate (or even similar) in terms of their internal morphosyntax, as seen in the case of the preterite tenses, which have exactly the same functional range in both languages, although the Spanish form is a continuation of the Latin perfect tense, whilst contemporary Catalan (including Valencian) uses an idiosyncratic periphrastic construction.

A further insight that can be drawn from the data presented here is the fact that contact between closely related and mutually intelligible languages appears to favour the reduction of opacity within paradigms, at least if a more transparent or less complex model is available in the H-language. Examples of this are the resistance to the complex allomorphy in the object pronoun paradigm that has developed in standard Catalan, in favour of retaining the simpler system shared with Spanish (2.4.3.2), as well a move towards a more transparent pronominal paradigm (3.4.3.3), in which syncretism is reduced by copying a structural feature from Spanish, without borrowing the actual morphological material.

The question whether language contact leads to simpler or more complex grammatical structure has been extensively discussed in the literature (e.g. Trudgill 2001; 2011; 2012). It is often observed that contact situations in which one of the languages is acquired as a second language by a large number of adult speakers tend to lead to simplification, due to the perpetuation of features arising from imperfect language learning (e.g. Trudgill 2004, 306; McWhorter 2005, 265), though these studies focus primarily on the genesis of creole languages, a rather special case of contact-induced change. On the other hand, there is also evidence that "contact among languages fosters complexity" (Nichols 1992, 193; Maitz/Németh 2014). In any case, the linguistic outcome of a particular contact situation depends heavily on the prevalent sociolinguistic conditions as well as the similarity or relatedness between the languages involved.

The contact situation examined here has some of the hallmarks typically associated with the emergence of koiné varieties, notably contact over several generations and mutual intelligibility between the languages involved (Siegel 1985, 376), which often lead to the emergence of a variety in which a general tendency towards evening out the differences in favour of the simpler variant is complemented by the maintenance of certain iconic features of one of the contributing varieties or languages (Tuten 2003). The fact that koineisation can progress at different speeds for different speakers, e.g. in urban versus rural areas (Siegel 1985, 375), also coincides with the situation in parts of the Valencian-speaking region, where the more rural communities have been resisting contact-induced changes to a greater extent than urban areas such as Castellón de la Plana.[19]

---

[19] The larger cities, particularly Alicante, have undergone language shift from Valencian to Spanish to a greater degree over the past centuries, which means that the majority of their inhabitants are now non-native L2-speakers of standardised Valencian.

It should be pointed out that L-language structures with no counterpart in the H-language (e.g. the adverbial pronoun system, cf. 3.4.3.5) are not necessarily under threat; the data presented here suggests that convergence between related languages primarily affects existing similar structures, aligning them semantically or adjusting them morpho-syntactically. Finally, it remains to be seen what the effects of the recent (partial) inversion of the H/L-language relationship between Spanish and Valencian will be.

5 References

Alcover, Antoni Maria/Moll, Francesc de Borja, *Diccionari Català-Valencià-Balear. Inventari lexicogràfic i etimològic de la llengua catalana en totes les seves formes literàries i dialectals*, 10 vol., Palma de Mallorca, Moll, 1988.
Barnils, Pere, *El parlar "apitxat"*, Butlletí de dialectologia catalana 1 (1914), 18–25.
Beltrán-Calvo, Vicent/Segura Llopes, Carles, *Els parlars valencians*, Valencia, Publicacions de la Universitat de València, 2017.
Berceo, Gonzalo de, *La vida de San Millán de Cogolla*, ed. Dutton, Brian, London, Tamesis, 1984.
Botelho de Amaral, Vasco, *Dicionário de dificuldades da língua portuguesa*, Oporto, Educação Nacional, 1938.
Bouzouita, Miriam, *La posposición pronominal con futuros y condicionales en el códice escurialense I.i.6. Un examen de varias hipótesis morfosintácticas*, in: Kabatek, Johannes (ed.), *Lingüística de corpus y lingüística histórica iberorrománica*, Berlin/Boston, De Gruyter, 2016, 272–301.
Blas Arroyo, José Luis, *Consecuencias del contacto de lenguas en el español de Valencia*, Español Actual 57 (1992), 81–100.
Blas Arroyo, José Luis, *La interferencia lingüística en Valencia (dirección: catalán– castellano). Estudio sociolingüístico*, Castellón de la Plana, Universitat Jaume I, 1993.
Blas Arroyo, José Luis, *Sociolingüística del español. Desarrollo y perspectivas en el estudio de la lengua española en contexto social*, Madrid, Cátedra, 2005.
Briz Gómez, Antonio, *El castellano en la Comunidad Valenciana*, Revista Internacional de Lingüística Iberoamericana 4 (2004), 119–129.
Camus Bergareche, Bruno/Gómez Seibane, Sara, *Gender loss in accusative cliticis in Basque Spanish. A contact-induced convergence phenomenon* in: Bouzouita, Miriam/Enghels, Renata/Vanderschueren, Clara (edd.), *Convergence and divergence in Ibero-Romance across contact situations and beyond*, Berlin/Boston, De Gruyter, in this volume, 25–54.
Casanova, Emili. *La frontera lingüística castellano-catalana en el País Valenciano*, Revista de Filología Románica 18 (2001), 213–260.
Casanova, Emili, *Influencia histórica del aragonés sobre el valenciano*, Archivo de Filología Aragonesa 67 (2011), 201–235.
Climent, Josep Daniel, *Les normes de castelló. L'interés per la llengua dels valencians al segle XX*, Valencia, Acadèmia Valenciana de la Llengua, 2007.
Drinka, Bridget, *Language contact in Europe. The periphrastic perfect through history*, Cambridge, Cambridge University Press, 2017.

Duarte, Carles/Massip, Àngels, *Síntesi d'història de la llengua catalana*, Barcelona, Magrana, 1981.
Ferguson, Charles A., *Diglossia*, Word 15 (1959), 325–340.
Fernández-Ordóñez, Inés, *La lengua de Castilla y la formación del español*, Madrid, Real Academia Española, 2011.
Generalitat Valenciana, Conselleria d' Educació, Investigació, Cultura i Esport, Subdirecció General de Política Lingüística, *Coneixement i ús social del valencià 2015*, Valencia, Generalitat Valenciana, 2015.
Gómez Molina, José Ramón, *Actitudes lingüísticas en una comunidad bilingüe y multilectal. Área metropolitana de Valencia*, Valencia, Publicacions de la Universitat de València, 1998.
Gómez Seibane, Sara, *Exploring historical linguistic convergence between Basque and Spanish*, in: Bouzouita, Miriam/Enghels, Renata/Vanderschueren, Clara (edd.), *Convergence and divergence in Ibero-Romance across contact situations and beyond*, Berlin/Boston, de Gruyter, in this volume, 55–85.
Guinot, Enric, *El repoblament aragonés. Colonització i llengües (segles XII i XIII)*, Caplletra. Revista Internacional de Filologia 32 (2012), 85–94.
Hickey, Raymond, *Internally and externally motivated language change*, in: Hernández Campoy, Juan Manuel/Conde-Silvestre, Juan Camilo (edd.), *The handbook of historical sociolinguistics*, Malden, Wiley-Blackwell, 2012, 401–421.
Hulk, Aafke/Müller, Natascha, *Bilingual first language acquisition at the interface between syntax and pragmatics*, Bilingualism. Language and Cognition 3 (2000), 227–244.
Käuper, Anna Anja/Guerreo Ramos, Carlos J., *El habla de los grauveros. Peculiaridades del castellano de los jóvenes del distrito portuario de Castellón*, in: Sinner, Carsten/Wesch, Andreas (edd.), *El castellano en las tierras de habla catalana*, Madrid/Frankfurt, Iberoamericana/Vervuert, 2008, 133–154.
Kerswill, Paul/Trudgill, Peter, *The birth of new dialects*, in: *Dialect change. Convergence and divergence in European languages*, Cambridge, Cambridge University Press, 2005, 196–220.
Kiesling, Scott F., *Linguistic variation and change*, Edinburgh, Edinburgh University Press, 2011.
Labov, William, *Sociolinguistic Patterns*, Philadelphia, University of Pennsylvania, 1972.
Lacreu Cuesta, Josep, *Vocabulari de barbarismes*, Valencia/Oliva, Generalitat Valenciana/Colomar, 1995.
Lleó, Conxita/Cortés, Susana, *Modelling the outcome of language contact in the speech of German-Spanish and Catalan-Spanish bilingual children*, International Journal of the Sociology of Language 221 (2013), 101–125.
LSA (Linguistic Society of America), *Ethics statement*, 2009, https://tinyurl.com/y8wp5r7o [last access: 29.06.2020].
Maitz, Péter/Németh, Attila, *Language contact and morphosyntactic complexity. Evidence from German*, Journal of Germanic Linguistics 26 (2014), 1–29.
Martí Mestre, Joaquim, *Afinidades léxicas aragonesas en el valenciano del siglo XIX*, Archivo de Filología Aragonesa 68 (2012), 143–176.
Martorell, Joanot, *Tirant lo Blanch*, edd. Hauf, Albert Guillem/Escartí, Vicent Josep, 2 vol., Valencia, Generalitat Valenciana, 1992.
Matras, Yaron, *Utterance modifiers and universals of grammatical borrowing*, Linguistics 36 (1998), 281–331.
Matras, Yaron, *Explaining convergence and the formation of linguistic areas*, in: Hieda, Osamu/König, Christa/Nakahawa, Hirosi (edd.), *Geographical typology and linguistic areas. With special reference to Africa*, Amsterdam, John Benjamins, 2011, 143–160.

Matute, Cristina, *Entre pronombres y adverbios: mecanismos de cambio en la historia dialectal peninsular de hi/ý < ibi*, Boletín de la Real Academia Española 96 (2016), 201–237.

McWhorter, John H., *Defining creole*, Oxford, Oxford University Press, 2005.

Meilán García, Antonio J., *Funcionamiento y valores del pronombre ende en el castellano antiguo*, Revista de Filología de la Universidad de La Laguna 13 (1994), 245–262.

Meyer-Lübke, Wilhelm, *Das Katalanische. Seine Stellung zum Spanischen und Provenzalischen sprachwissenschaftlich und historisch dargestellt*, Heidelberg, Winter, 1925.

Milá y Fontanals, Manuel, *De los trovadores en España*, Barcelona, Joaquín Verdaguer, 1861.

Molnár, Nándor, *The calques of Greek origin in the most ancient Old Slavic gospel texts. A theoretical examination of calque phenomena in the texts of the archaic Old Slavic gospel codices*, Weimar, Böhlau, 1985.

Montoya i Abad, Brauli, *La interferència lingüística al sud valencià*, Valencia, Generalitat Valenciana, 1989.

Morera, Juan R., *Repoblación del Reino de Valencia después de la expulsión de los moriscos*, Saitabi 16 (1966), 121–148.

Nichols, Johanna, *Liunguistic diversity in space and time*, Chicago, University of Chicago Press, 1992.

Nida, Eugene A./Fehderau, Harold W., *Indigenous pidgins and koines*, International Journal of American Linguistics 32 (1970), 146–155.

Palacios Alcaine, Azucena, *¿Son compatibles los cambios inducidos por contacto y las tendencias internas al sistema?*, in: Schrader-Kniffki, Martina/Morgenthaler García, Laura (edd.), *La Romania en interacción. Entre historia, contacto y política*, Madrid/Frankfurt, Iberoamericana/Vervuert, 2007, 259–279.

Palacios Alcaine, Azucena, *Contact-induced change and internal evolution. Spanish in contact with Amerindian languages*, in: Chamoreau, Claudine/Léglise, Isabelle (edd.), *The interplay of variation and change in contact settings*, Amsterdam/Philadelphia, John Benjamins, 2013, 165–198.

Palomero, Josep, *Valenciano y castellano en la Comunidad Valenciana*, in: Barcia, Pedro Luis (ed.), *III Congreso Internacional de la Lengua Española. Identidad lingüística y globalización*, Buenos Aires, Academia Argentina de Letras, 2006, http://tinyurl.com/nyc5upq (Centro Virtual Cervantes) [last access: 29.06.2020].

Peñarroja Torrejón, Leopoldo, *El mozárabe de Valencia. Nuevas cuestiones de fonología mozárabe*, Madrid, Gredos, 1990.

Piqueras, Andrés, *Capital, migraciones e identidades Inmigración y sociedad en el País Valenciano. El caso de Castellón*, Castellón de la Plana, Universitat Jaume I, 2007.

Prat Sabater, Marta. 2016. *Las unidades fraseológicas temporales utilizadas en el contexto bilingüe español/catalán*, in: Polch Olivé, Dolors (ed.), *El español en contacto con las otras lenguas peninsulares*, Madrid/Frankfurt, Iberoamericana/Vervuert, 2016, 265–295.

Poplack, Shana/Levey, Stephen, *Contact-induced grammatical change. A cautionary tale*, in: Auer, Peter/Schmidt, Jürgen Erich (edd.), *Language and space. An international handbook of linguistic variation*, vol. 1: *Theories and methods*, Berlin/New York, Mouton de Gruyter, 2010, 391–419.

Puerto Ferre, Teresa, *Lengua valenciana: una lengua suplantada*, Valencia, Diputación de Valencia, 2006.

Raumolin-Brunberg, Helena, *Language change in adulthood. Historical letters as evidence*, European Journal of English Studies 9:1 (2005), 37–51.

Rea, John A., *Concerning the validity of lexicostatistics*, International Journal of American Linguistics 24:2 (1958), 145–150.

Riera Ginestar, Joaquín, *Apuntes sobre la inmigración en la Comunidad Autónoma Valenciana*, Espacio, Tiempo y Forma. Serie VI: Geografía 2 (2009), 11–20.

Rodríguez Molina, Javier, *La gramaticalización de los tiempos compuestos en español antiguo: cinco cambios diacrónicos*, PhD dissertation, Universidad Autónoma de Madrid, 2010, https://tinyurl.com/y8z9eg9m [last access: 29.06.2020].

Rosemeyer, Malte, *Auxiliary selection in Spanish. Gradience, gradualness, and conservation*, Amsterdam, John Benjamins, 2014.

Sanchez-Stockhammer, Christina, *Hybridization in language*, in: Stockhammer, Philipp Wolfgang (ed.), *Conceptualizing cultural hybridization. A transdisciplinary approach*, Berlin/Heidelberg, Springer, 2011, 133–157.

Sankoff, Gillian, *Linguistic outcomes of language contact*, in: Trudgill, Peter/Chambers, Jack K./Schilling-Estes, Natalie (edd.), *Handbook of sociolinguistics*, Oxford, Blackwell, 2001, 638–668.

Schmitt, Christina, *Cross-linguistic variation and the present perfect. The case of Portuguese*, Natural Language & Linguistic Theory 19 (2009), 403–453.

Schulte, Kim, *Romance in contact with Romance*, in: Ayres-Bennett, Wendy/Carruthers, Janice (edd.), *Manual of Romance sociolinguistics*, Berlin/Boston, De Gruyter, 2018, 587–618.

Siegel, Jeff, *Koines and koineization*, Language in Society 14:3 (1985), 357–378.

Segura Llopes, Carles, *Variació fonètica i estandardització al País Valencià*, Noves SL. Revista de Sociolingüística 4:3 (2003), https://tinyurl.com/y7ouqsxd [last access: 29.06.2020].

Trudgill, Peter, *Contact and simplification. Historical baggage and directionality in linguistic change*, Linguistic Typology 5 (2001), 371–374.

Trudgill, Peter, *Linguistic and social typology. The Austronesian migrations and phoneme inventories*, Linguistic Typology 8 (2004), 305–320.

Trudgill, Peter, *Sociolinguistic typology. Social determinants of linguistic complexity*, Oxford, Oxford University Press, 2011.

Trudgill, Peter, *On the sociolinguistic typology of linguistic complexity loss*, in: Seifart, Frank/Haig, Geoffrey/Himmelmann, Nikolaus P./Jung, Dagmar/Margetts, Anna/Trilsbeek, Paul Anna (edd.), *Potentials of language documentation. Methods, analyses, and utilization*, Honolulu, University of Hawai'i Press, 2012, 90–95.

Tuten, Donald N., *Koineization in medieval Spanish*, Berlin, De Gruyter Mouton, 2003.

Veny, Joan/Pons i Griera, Lídia, *Atles lingüístic del domini català*, vol. II: *2. El vestit; 3. Les ocupacions domèstiques*, Barcelona, Institut d'Estudis Catalans, 2003.

Vila i Moreno, Francesc Xavier, *Transcodic markers and functional distribution in Catalan*, in: Pujol Berché, Mercè/Sierra Martínez, Fermín (edd.), *Las lenguas en la Europa Comunitaria*, vol. 2: *Las lenguas de minorías*, Amsterdam/Atlanta, Rodopi, 1996, 195–212.

Xosé A. Álvarez-Pérez
Language contact on the Spanish-Portuguese border
A contribution from the linguistic landscape perspective

Abstract: This paper studies the linguistic landscape of two distant border-crossing areas, located in the municipalities of Verín (Spain)-Chaves (Portugal) and Vilar Formoso (Portugal)-Fuentes de Oñoro (Spain). The research is based on a corpus of 306 texts promoted by public bodies and private entities or individuals. It examines the presence and weight of the languages in which they are written, as well as the linguistic accuracy of the collected texts, interference phenomena and mixed statements that combine both languages. The results obtained demonstrate the complexity of the linguistic landscape on the borderland, a place with intense interpersonal contact and, at the same time, an area where national identity is often vindicated. In this sense, convergence whereby linguistic systems of neighbouring languages become similar due to the borrowing of material from the neighbour's language or, on the contrary, non-convergence, i.e. the lack of such converging and thus the tendency to not use the neighbour's language in the texts placed into the public space, can serve as an indicator of language loyalty and, as such, of the strength of the national identity.

Keywords: Linguistic landscape, (non-)convergence, language contact, language policy, identity, Spanish-Portuguese border, Spanish, Portuguese

1 Introduction

The linguistic landscape of a given territory can be defined as the set of written testimonies visible in the public space. It is not confined to those texts located in

---

Note: This contribution was funded by a *Ramón y Cajal* Fellowship granted by the Ministry of Economy and Competitiveness (reference RYC-2013-12761). It was also developed in the framework of the research projects *Frontera hispano-portuguesa: documentación lingüística y bibliográfica* (FFI2014-52156-R, Ministry of Economy and Competitiveness of the Spanish Government, 2015–2017), for which I am responsible. I would like to thank the reviewers of this text for their interesting feedback.

Xosé A. Álvarez-Pérez, University of Alcalá, UAH

the streets, but also includes linguistic statements placed in the showcases window displays of commercial establishments, such as menus in a restaurant, and even in private homes (property rental adverts, protest banners displayed in a window, and the like), provided that such messages can be seen from a public space.

The choice of the linguistic code for a sign identifies explicit and implicit language policies, both at the private and the public level. Therefore, the theoretical framework provided by the research on the linguistic landscape, combining linguistic data and demographic, economic, political and social information, can provide an innovative methodology in contact analysis that links linguistic and cultural relationships. The analysis of the linguistic quality of the texts collected during the study is also important, since they may reveal cases of linguistic interference, as well as processes of convergence/divergence between varieties that are in close contact. Observation of the linguistic landscape is a relatively new perspective within linguistics. Among the pioneers are Rodrigue Landry and Richard Y. Bourhis who, in a work published in 1997, called attention to the dual role of written texts on public roads, namely an informative function that delineates the territory in which a certain language is used, and a symbolic function that reveals the status of a linguistic variety in a given community. That is, the analysis of the distribution of texts can address many sociolinguistic issues that also have implications from the viewpoint of Sociology or Human Geography, such as the quantitative weight of each variety in a bilingual territory, the existence of spheres of use restricted to a particular language, the hierarchy of languages in multilingual texts (as determined by font size or position of the text), the balance of languages in official texts, the visibility of migrant communities' languages, the role of English as a *lingua franca* and its association with the commercial and tourist worlds, and so forth.

For more than a decade, several studies about the Spanish linguistic landscape from the perspective proposed by Landry/Bourhis (1997) have been produced.[1] Among them, some useful contributions can be mentioned, such as Castillo Lluch/Sáez Rivera (2011) on Madrid, Pons Rodríguez (2012) on Seville, and, finally, a monographic issue with contributions on various cities: Almería, Barcelona, Basque Country, Galicia and Madrid (with a focus on Arabic) (Castillo Lluch/Sáez Rivera 2013). Studies on the linguistic landscapes in Portugal are far fewer. I will mention three contributions from different perspectives. There is a work by Clemente et al. (2013) that examines a neighbourhood in the

---

[1] As various editorial events have delayed the publication of this work, it should be noted that, in order to assess the validity of the presented results, the fieldwork was carried out in the summer of 2015 and that the data analysis and bibliographic work was concluded in early 2017.

city of Aveiro and touches on many theoretical and programmatic issues. Torkington (2016) examines the British lifestyle of migrants in the Algarve and, linked to this line of research, some works on the linguistic landscape of tourist areas in this region have appeared. Finally, Solonova et al. (2016) studied graffiti on the walls of Coimbra using an approach that combines semiology, sociology and more specific issues pertaining to linguistic landscape.

After having carried out this research, I became aware of the publication of the work *El paisaje lingüístico de la frontera luso española. Multilingüismo e identidad* (Pons Rodríguez 2014). However, it must be noted that, despite the title of the work, it only examined the Portuguese side of the border; moreover, the studied area in each locality is quite limited in relation to their overall surface area.

This paper adopts a transnational perspective. It examines the contact of Spanish and Portuguese in the linguistic landscape of two border regions. More specifically, it analyses the degree of presence and spheres of use of Portuguese in written records visible from the public space in the Spanish borderland and the use of Spanish in public signs placed in Portugal. This specific geographical area was chosen for two reasons: the intense contact between the Spanish and Portuguese people and the identity issues that are intrinsically linked to border areas, as will be explained in the following lines.

Along the borderland, the dialogue between border identity and state identity has always been difficult and tense (Godinho 2009a). The state boundary has clear symbolic and identity values attached to it but, at the same time, there is a strong feeling of belonging to a supranational community because of the intense cross-border relationship. The Spanish-Portuguese border has been a meeting point of languages, occurring via the extensive population movements between the countries, both temporal and permanent, such as sales, smuggling, pilgrimages, tourism, intermarriage, work migration, etc. Throughout the centuries, strong solidarity between the two sides of the border has developed. In fact, border villages are often *mirror-localities*, a binomial distribution placed symmetrically on the borderline, the members of which have traditionally maintained a closer relationship with each other than with other villages and cities in the same country. Furthermore, the entry into force of the Schengen Agreement (1995) has led to the disappearance of border controls, a fact that has increased daily commerce and tourism between the two countries significantly.

Considering that situation, this paper aims to analyse the following questions:
– Is the intense cross-border mobility between Spain and Portugal reflected in the linguistic landscape of the borderlands?
– Which foreign language is predominant in the borderlands: Spanish/Portuguese, the languages of the neighbouring countries, or English, a language clearly identified with the tourist sector?

– Do Portuguese and Spanish have a similar presence in official and private texts? What is the attitude of public bodies regarding these languages?
– Are there differences in language choice depending on the geographic typology of the border? In particular, I will seek differences between cross-border conurbations and *Eurocities*, which are medium-sized populations that have signed a cross-border agreement to share infrastructures and activities.
– What is the degree of linguistic correctness of statements written in the border area? Are there linguistic interferences? If so, are they more likely to occur in certain text types?

2 Methodology and data

Most linguistic landscape studies include an extensive introduction to the emergence of this line of research, the establishment and consolidation of the theoretical frameworks and the diversification of methodological approaches. In fact, the reader may sometimes have the impression of reading the usual litany of citations and references, considering that "On the whole the main discourses on LL methodology are in agreement and many researchers point out the same problems even if some discourses vary" (Clemente et al. 2013, 117). Because of space limitations, this section must be concise; therefore, I will focus on the discussion of my methodological choices in the delimitation and classification of the corpus, while I will refer to the studies mentioned above in 1 to provide more information about the development of the linguistic landscape and a thorough review of the existing literature. In this regard, special attention is paid to Gorter (2013), which combines the analysis of pioneering research and the examination of recent studies that opened the field to new perspectives and applications.

2.1 Corpus delimitation

Regarding the physical support on which the text is displayed, this research considers any type of static text visible from public areas. In other words, the corpus consists of both stable texts, written messages on rigid media that are intended to be permanent (such as a plaque that describes a monument), and ephemeral texts on walls, such as advertising posters that may be rapidly covered by others. Digital screen panels have been also included (see 3.1.3.1). Mobile texts (such as those found in newspapers, buses, private vehicles, etc.) have been excluded because of the technical complications linked to the study thereof.

The delimitation of the *unit of analysis* is a key issue in research on the linguistic landscape but, as there is no consensus among scholars, several studies differ in the definition of this unit. I will explain in 2.1.1 below that my choice is justified because of the special nature of this research, which is not a description of a multilingual territory, but is an examination of Portuguese and Spanish in contact. This specific purpose also justifies the exclusion of some typologies of sign, such as so-called *shared texts* (see 2.1.2).

The corpus includes all texts written entirely or partly in a language other than the official language(s) of the country concerned. In other words, in a Portuguese village, all statements written in English, French, Spanish, German and so on will be collected. Even though this paper focuses on Portuguese and Spanish, an inventory of all signs composed in foreign languages is essential to shed light on the linguistic hierarchy in the territory and to determine whether the language of the neighbouring country enjoys the same vitality and belongs to the same spheres of use as do other varieties. In 2.1.3, I will discuss some issues concerning language identification.

2.1.1 Delimitation of textual units

There is no agreement regarding the delimitation of textual units of analysis inside commercial or official establishments. Several studies – including the aforementioned research on the Portuguese border carried on by Pons Rodríguez (2014), who followed the proposal by Cenoz/Gorter (2006) – have grouped all texts from the same establishment into a single object of study. However, in this research, I have chosen to analyse each sign individually. In my view, the overall vision is useful for general studies of multilingual societies, where the priority is the identification of foreign languages. However, this particular research, focused on Spanish and Portuguese in contact, must examine the degree of presence, position within the sociolinguistic hierarchy and the spheres of use of each foreign language; thus, an individual examination of each text is essential for this purpose.

Image 1[2] is enlightening in this respect. A restaurant in Vilar Formoso displays a menu (that is, a relatively stable list of dishes) in its shopfront, with versions in four languages (French, English, Portuguese and Spanish). However, the dishes of the day are written only in Portuguese, but are preceded by a

---

[2] For editorial reasons, the images referred to in this paper have been placed in a gallery available at http://arcanaverba.org/artigos/IberoCon/images_landscape.html, where they may be downloaded and viewed at full size. They are offered under a Creative Commons Attribution-ShareAlike 4.0 International (CC BY-SA 4.0) license.

trilingual header, from which Spanish has been excluded (it appears in Portuguese, French and English). Considering the showcase of the restaurant overall, one could say that it is a multilingual sign: English, French, Portuguese and Spanish. However, the individual examination of texts shows a tri-level hierarchy: first, Portuguese; second, English and French; and third, Spanish, despite being the language of the adjacent country.

2.1.2 Exclusion of shared texts

Franco-Rodríguez (2009) provided an interesting revision of the concept of the linguistic landscape's unit of analysis. A key aspect of his proposal is the concept of the *actor*, "the entity (business, institution, or individual) or joined entities that compose a text" (Franco-Rodríguez 2009, 2–4). He identified three types of texts that are composed by external actors, and not by the primary actor (the responsible for the place where the text appears):

- *Guest texts*: The statement has been produced by a third party and has no relationship with the commercial or service activities of the establishment in which it is placed. A few examples of this typology are event announcements, edicts, jobs or property rental adverts affixed to the showcase of a shop.
- *Borrowed texts*: The content is directly related to the services, items, or activities advertised by the primary actor. The primary author could have produced the texts, but he chose to borrow them from a third party, because of commercial reasons or purely for convenience. One example is the "open/close" sign displayed on a soft drink company's logo at a restaurant's main entrance
- *Shared texts*: The external actor usually has a commercial relationship with the primary actor or performs a supervisory activity. Some examples are stickers placed by security companies, ratings of hotels given by a tourist board or travel guide, smoking warnings issued by health authorities, etc.

Shared texts are foreign to the local linguistic communities, which have no opportunity to choose which languages would be used in the sign, the order thereof, specific formats associated with each idiom and the like. These issues are determined by private enterprises (*Le Routard, TripAdvisor, MasterCard*, amongst others) or by public legislation, common for the entire country. Image 2 is an excellent example. The picture shows a sign prohibiting smoking and a sign that announces the existence of a smoking area. The format of these Portuguese signs is dictated by Law 37/2007, which determines trilingual presentation (in Portuguese, English and French), regardless of whether such signs are placed at the door of a bar that is located 200 metres away from the Spanish border or in a

Lisbon restaurant. Besides, shared texts are overrepresented, especially mandatory signs, such as the aforementioned non-smoking sticker, which must be affixed to the door of any bar, restaurant or public service.

Even if their small size and reiteration make them much less noticeable than other elements in the configuration of the linguistic landscape, each instance should be counted as an independent sign; thereof, their inclusion in the corpus may alter the overall results of the language distribution and the hierarchy to a significant degree. For all these reasons, they have been excluded from the corpus.

2.1.3 Linguistic adscription

The linguistic classification of signs has not been without problems. There have been two major issues.

First, Portuguese (and Spanish, to a much lesser extent) is very likely to incorporate foreign words without adaptation. That is, words that retain the spelling of the original language but which, because of their frequency of use, can also be considered as lexical elements in the target language. Thus, recurring appearances in the corpus, such as *outlet*, *design* or *stand* (on signs located in Portugal), are difficult to interpret with regard to their linguistic description. The applied criterion was the inclusion of the dubious elements in two reference dictionaries – *Diccionario de la Lengua Española* (DRAE) and *Dicionário da Língua Portuguesa* –, regardless of whether they appear indicated as anglicisms, because I am interested in their vitality, and not in the academic discussion on their relationship with the standard language. Accordingly, the aforementioned words were classified as Portuguese because they appeared in the second dictionary and were thus excluded from the corpus.

Second, as Portuguese and Spanish are extremely close linguistic varieties, it is often the case that a specific word is identical in both languages. When this occurred, the text was assigned to the official language of the country in which it was located, based on the assumption that, if the composer/promoter of the sign had wished to write a statement in a foreign language, he/she would have opted for a clearly foreign form, or, more likely, by adding the local designation, as documented in (1). This criterion led to the classification of (2) as a bilingual Spanish-Portuguese sign, since the text was collected in Portugal, and *bazar* can be used in both languages; however, *España* is clearly written in Spanish, since the grapheme <ñ> does not exist in Portuguese. The case in (2b) seems to confirm this decision, since it is clear that the Portuguese form was used as generic designation of the establishment, whereas the name of the store and a commercial slogan were presented in Spanish.

(1) *Ourivesaria – Joyería* 'jewellery' (Vilar Formoso), Image 3.

(2a) *Bazar España* 'Bazaar Spain' (Vilar Formoso).

(2b) *Comércio El Navarro* || *Todo para el hogar* 'El Navarro's retail || Homeware' (Vilar Formoso), Image 4.

Two additional cases, which were excluded from the corpus, must be discussed. The sign for a candy store had a Brazilian flag and a puzzling statement that imitated Portuguese (2c) but was linguistically incorrect (it should read *doce baía*). In (2d), Portuguese is present in the proper name of this bakery, but only because it is the owner's surname.

(2c) *Dolce Bahía* (Image 67).

(2d) *Pan Da Cunha* (Image 68).

2.2 Corpus classification

After conclusion of the fieldwork, each unit of analysis was classified using a *Filemaker* database with the following structure:
1. Nature of the text (*top-down/bottom-up*).
2. Multilingual (Y/N).
3. Languages.
4. Including linguistic errors. (Y/N).
5. Country.
6. Locality.
7. Support (fixed, semi-stable, graffiti).
8. Typology (road sign, tourist information, commercial advertisement, name of an establishment and so on).

The distinction between texts issued by an official body (*top-down*) and those produced by individuals or private entities (*bottom-up*) is particularly relevant for the purpose of determining the degree of the presence of Spanish and Portuguese and the factors involved in their contact.

The first category includes signs at official buildings, road signage, information campaigns, tourist information promoted by public entities, and prohibitions issued by any authority. The latter category includes the names of shops, publicity, posters announcing festivals or celebrations, graffiti on walls, etc. It is evident that top-down texts can be largely influenced by the official language policy since the legal framework may determine whether a certain linguistic variety may appear in official texts and under what conditions: as the only language, subordinate to the main language in position and size, or under identical conditions. On the other hand, code choice is usually freer in bottom-up texts, because there are not usually external restrictions on the motivations of the actor choosing the language and the content of a certain message. However, it should be noted that bottom-up texts are not exempt from legal interference either.

A clear example is a peninsular territory frequently studied within the linguistic landscape approach, to wit the Raval neighbourhood (Barcelona). This is a multi-ethnic area with a strong presence of Pakistani, Filipino and Moroccan immigrants who are highly active in commercial life. The linguistic analysis of the labels placed in their establishments reveals that Catalan has a strong weight, as opposed to its more reduced oral use in this trade context. This apparent contradiction is explained because of regional government (*Generalitat de Catalunya*) legislation, which obliges local businesses to write all their public information (such as opening hours and descriptions of products) in at least the Catalan language.

This is not an exceptional regulation. In fact, regarding this study, there is at least one similar restrictive rule, but it has never been strictly enforced. More specifically, Article 7 of the Portuguese *Código da Publicidade* 'Publicity Code' stipulates that:

> 3 – the use of languages from other countries in the advertisement is only permitted, even in conjunction with the Portuguese language, when it has foreigners as the exclusive or main recipients, without prejudice to the following paragraph. || 4 – the exceptional use of words or expressions in languages of other countries is permitted when necessary to obtain the intended effect of the message design (https://dre.pt/web/guest/legislacao-consolidada/-/lc/74450489/201901161046/diploma?rp=indice&did=34537375; last access: 10.06.2021. Author's translation).

2.3 Timeframe of the fieldwork. Synchrony and diachrony in the linguistic landscape

The fieldwork was conducted on different days in July 2015. All the signs were photographed in situ using a digital camera (Canon EOS 700), although it was sometimes necessary to use a camera integrated into a mobile phone.

Research into the linguistic landscape is intrinsically synchronic. The corpus used in this study corresponds to a particular historical moment and would have been different had it been compiled a year earlier or a year later. The geographical reality mutates, and the process of change is more dramatic along the Spanish-

Portuguese borderland because it has been subject to on-going alterations in recent years, such as the opening of high-capacity cross-border roads. These divert traffic away from towns and villages, with the resulting decline in economic activity and closure of commercial establishments with their concomitant signs and texts.

A distinction should be made between the synchrony of the corpus and the chronology of the collected elements. The corpus captures the linguistic landscape at a certain moment. However, each individual element has its own chronology. There may be texts that were created on the same day of the corpus collection (for example, a menu written in chalk at the front door of a restaurant) and other elements with varying degrees of age, such as a poster for a concert given in the previous summer, a plaque that commemorates the inauguration of a monument, or even a sticker of an airline that closed twenty years ago, as occurred in the corpus collected for this research – see (14).

However, future research into the linguistic landscape may take other time frames into account. Just as digital photography and audio recordings were a breakthrough for fieldwork linguists, more recent technological innovations may lead to significant changes in the procedure of data collection. This is clarified by providing an example. Image 5 is a screenshot taken from *Google Street View*, dated 2009, located in the Galician town of Feces de Abaixo. It shows the bar *Portugalicia*, which no longer exists. This establishment had an iconic name – it is no surprise that it was mentioned in anthropological works, such as Godinho (2009b; 2013) – but it is also very interesting because there are many Portuguese elements on the main awning, such as *sandes, bifanas, tostas mistas* and *presuntos* ('sandwiches, fillets, toasted cheese and ham sandwich, ham').

2.4 Geographical area

This paper examines two different sections of the Spanish-Portuguese border, approximately 150 km away from each other in a straight line. Therefore, three different typologies of border will be analysed:
a. Chaves and Verín, two cities with over 10,000 inhabitants that are the economic centres of their area of influence. They are about 22 km apart;
b. A 2,500-metre-long section of the cross-border road that connects the rural villages of Feces de Abaixo and Vila Verde da Raia;
c. The cross-border conurbation of Fuentes de Oñoro and Vilar Formoso, which is the focus of much of the road and rail traffic between Spain and Portugal. Images 6 to 8 show the areas studied in each of these zones.

Chaves (Portugal) is the capital of a large municipality with 18,500 inhabitants in its urban area (2011 data). On the Spanish side, Verín has 10,600 inhabitants in the town centre (2014). These localities were chosen because of the existence of the *Eurocity Chaves-Verín* (http://www.eurocidadechavesverin.eu), a pioneering initiative that started in 2007 (Trillo/Lois/Paül 2015). It is an agreement between historically related cities but belonging to different EU states in order to share resources and to establish joint policies in economic and sociocultural fields. Therefore, the question arises what the linguistic reflection of this experience of cross-border cooperation, which has received several European awards for joint development strategies, would be. In both cities, the main arteries of the city centres have been examined.

Feces de Abaixo has 420 inhabitants (2011). It belongs to the municipality of Verín and it is crossed by the national road N-525. Its Portuguese counterpart, Vila Verde da Raia (municipality of Chaves), has 993 inhabitants and is also situated on the same road axis, which is called the N-103 in Portugal. This crossing point traditionally had intense interstate circulation (7,524 per day in 2008), however, the opening of highways A-24 (Portugal) and A-75 (Spain) has greatly altered the dynamics of the area, limiting national roads to local traffic. The studied area was the stretch of road along which major commercial establishments in the area are located. The route starts at Feces de Abaixo, continues past the old Spanish customs building – which has been restored and serves as the headquarters of the Eurocity – goes through the abandoned Portuguese customs area, and crosses the shopping area of Vila Verde da Raia until it reaches the junction of the new highway.

Area c) is composed of two neighbourhoods of the municipality of Fuentes de Oñoro (Salamanca, Spain) – *Colonia de la Estación* and *Pueblo Nuevo*, built around railway and customs facilities – and the shopping and service area of Vilar Formoso (municipality of Almeida, district of Guarda, Portugal), which is located between the railway and the national road N-332. These municipalities have a combined population of 3,500 inhabitants. It should be noted that Fuentes de Oñoro is the smaller of the two (1,070 inhabitants), and that more than a third of its census has Portuguese nationality, mainly consisting of people who have emigrated for economic, social or labour reasons. This conurbation is one of the more important border passes, with daily traffic of 10,615 vehicles (of which one-third is trucks). The border is still crossed by the national road, but it is planned that highways A-25 and A-62 will be connected in 2020, which will transform the reality of this nucleus radically. Finally, it is also one of the three operational railway links between Spain and Portugal.

3 Discussion of materials

After having analysed the materials collected during the fieldwork and having expunged the texts that did not conform to the criteria explained in 2.2, the corpus consisted of 306 elements, which were texts written entirely or partly in one or more languages other than the official language of the country in which the sign was located.

The corpus is quite balanced between the countries, with 143 entries from Spain and 163 from Portugal. It is also well proportioned with regard to the actors' natures, namely public bodies (top-down signs) and private individuals or entities (bottom-up signs), as shown in Table 1.

Table 1: Typology of texts by country and nature of the issuer.

	Portugal	Spain
Top-down (public)	22 texts (13.5%)	18 texts (12.5%)
Bottom-up (private)	141 texts (86.5%)	125 texts (87.5%)

However, the national sub-corpora showed discrepancies in the number of languages involved in the creation of a sign (Table 2). In Spain, monolingual and multilingual texts were virtually matched, whereas Portugal preferred multilingual statements.

Table 2: Distribution of texts according to the number of languages.

	Portugal	Spain
Monolingual	60 texts (36.8%)	71 texts (49.6%)
Multilingual	103 texts (63.2%)	72 texts (50.4%)

3.1 The linguistic landscape in the Portuguese border area

3.1.1 Idiomatic distribution

The 163 texts collected in Portugal were distributed across 47 different language combinations; the more dominant choices are shown in Table 3.[3]

Table 3: Dominant linguistic choices used in the signs collected in Portugal.

Portuguese – English	50 texts (30.5%)
English	30 texts (18.5%)
Spanish	19 texts (11.5%)
Portuguese – Spanish	13 texts (8%)
Portuguese – French – English	10 texts (6%)
Other combinations	41 texts (25%)

Half of the results reveal Portuguese-English bilingual texts (30.5% of the corpus) and monolingual English signs (18.5%). However, there are other combinations in which English is also present. In all, 108 of the collected signs (66.26%) contained English forms, either entirely or in part. With regard to the nature of promoters, 93 of these texts with English elements came from the private sector (bottom-up) and 15 from public bodies (top-down).

Spanish is the second language used in the corpus, but at a great distance from English, since it only appears in 44 of the collected statements (27%); it is very close to French (19%). Regarding the promoters of the texts, the proportion is quite similar to the one described in the previous paragraph, with 35 private statements (79.5%) and nine public signs (20.5%). However, as will be explained in 3.1.3., these figures must be considered with caution.

What is most striking is the reversal of the ratio between monolingual and bilingual texts. In the case of texts written in Spanish, these are mostly monolingual signs (19 items), whereas there were only 13 Spanish-Portuguese bilingual

---

[3] To facilitate comprehension and clarity, the classification considers only the languages that were used in the production of the signs; it does not take into account the order of appearance of languages in the text, the extension occupied by each linguistic code, typographic hierarchy, or the like. Thus, for the purposes of this paper, a Spanish-Portuguese sign is merely a text in which both Spanish and Portuguese (and they alone) have been used, regardless of which language came first.

statements. Some important notes about these texts will be provided in the next section.

3.1.2 Monolingual statements in Spanish

A typological analysis explains the striking vitality of the monolingual texts. More than half of these signs were graffiti or paintings on walls. They are particularly common in the underground passage connecting the two neighbourhoods of Vilar Formoso separated by the railway line. Texts (3), (6) and (7) below were sourced here.

Because of their semantic content, lexical selection and use of colloquialisms, it follows that the authors of (3), (4) and (5) are Spaniards. However, the signature of text (6) is crucial for identifying the provenance of the author: the proper name is Portuguese, as is the header of the signature, *Ass.* (*assinado* 'signed').

(3) *Viva españa | lo mejor de la | tierra* 'hurrah for Spain | the best in the world'.

(4) *Ricotetos*[4] *de Verin | guapos* 'Flics from Verín | cute' (Vila Verde da Raia, older customs buildings) (Image 9).

(5) *De puta madre* 'fucking great' (Chaves).

(6) *Te Quiero* || *Ass. Filipa P.* 'I love you | sign[ed] Filipa P' (Image 10).

There is discursive unity, judging by the handwriting and spelling, in the three examples of graffiti found in the abovementioned underground passage. These inscriptions were written in Spanish by a feminine collective, as deduced from the pronoun *nosotras* in (7a). They contained accusations targeted at another group, possibly Portuguese, because of the conscious insertion of the Portuguese term *cuecas* ('panties, underpants') in (7c).

---

4 *Picoletos* was originally a colloquial term for the civil guard. The painting has since been overwritten. The resulting word, *ricotetos*, is unknown to the author.

(7a) *Solo teneis envidia de nosotras* 'you just have envy of us'.

(7b) *No habeis venido* || *25-5-07* 'you have not come || 25-5-07'.

(7c) *Teneis kaka en las | cuecas* 'you have poop in your underpants' (Image 11).

Excluding the graffiti, the corpus contained only seven monolingual Spanish statements. They were produced by private actors (bottom-up) and were advertising and publicity texts clearly aimed at Spanish people. It must be taken into account that coffee, furniture and household textiles are typical products imported from Portugal. Text (8) was a billboard in Vila Verde da Raia, with a Spanish contact phone number, and (9) was a sign in front of a shop in the same village. Examples (10) to (12) were placed in commercial establishments in Vilar Formoso. Finally, (13) was a billboard placed at a road junction in Vilar Formoso used by many Spaniards to enter Portuguese highways.

(8) *Espacio disponible* 'space available'.

(9) *Muebles | Armarios | Cocinas | Aquí* 'furniture | wardrobes | kitchens | here'.

(10) *Café-Monte|negro | a | precio | "especial"* || *El auténtico* 'coffee Monte|negro | "special" prize | the authentic one' (Image 12).

(11) *6 toallas | 19.50 €* '6 towels | 19.50 €'.

(12) *El Navarro.*[5]

(13) *2º encuentro ibérico de rehalas* || *Prueba de trabajo de perros conejeros* || *Carrera de galgos* || *Prueba de San Huberto* || *Exposición de rehalas de caza mayor* || *Demonstración de cetrería.* 'Second Iberian meeting of packs of hounds || test of dogs bred to hunt rabbits || greyhound race | competition of San Huberto | exhibition of packs of hounds for big game hunting | falconry spectacle' (Image 13).

---

5 This is the name of a business establishment. The current owner explained that *El Navarro* ('The Navarre') was the nickname of her father, the establishment's founder, because they had lived in Tafalla (Navarre, Spain) for a long time; when the family returned to Portugal, their car still had Spanish number plates with the provincial sign (NA).

(14) *Viasa. La línea aérea de Venezuela* 'Viasa. The airline of Venezuela' (Image 71).[6]

3.1.3 Signs in which Spanish was present

3.1.3.1 Top-down texts

In 3.1.1, it was noted that nine bilingual texts from the corpus collected in Portugal were top-down texts. However, this affirmation must be qualified. I have counted two signs with a minimal presence of Spanish as bilingual, namely a plaque located at the main entrance of the *Centro de Documentação da Rede Ibérica de Entidades Transfronteiriças* (Image 14) and an announcement of works in Vilar Formoso (Image 15). In these cases, the corporate logo of the cross-border cooperation programme is bilingual, but the variable text, the information provided by the plaque, is only available in Portuguese. Similarly, the map *Uma fronteira que nos une* ('a boundary that binds us together') has also been categorised as being bilingual. In fact, this map of the municipality of Almeida is written in Portuguese, but the legend headers are bilingual (Spanish appears in Italics, with a smaller font type) – see Images 16 and 16b.

Finally, another element could be better defined as "potentially multilingual" because it is a touch screen panel with information about Chaves that can be accessed in several languages (English, Spanish, Portuguese and French), although it is shown initially in Portuguese by default.

Therefore, there were only five texts promoted by public actors in which Spanish maintained a certain balance with Portuguese. Even so, the presence of Spanish is not always remarkable, as in (15), where the sequence is fixed, with some repetitions, to the door of the tourist office in Vilar Formoso.

(15) *agro-raia · agro-raya* 'agro-[border]line'.

Two of the bilingual signs were maps. The map reproduced in Image 17a occupied the other side of the panel on which the map in Image 16 was fixed. However, linguistic distribution and weight of each language are different. The map is divided into eight columns with the same structure: a title (only in Portuguese), a bilingual description of the main territories (Spanish appears in italics and has a smaller font and is in a clearer colour) and a list of places of interest

---

[6] Sticker in the shopfront of a travel agency in Chaves. This sign proved to be an excellent example of anachronisms in linguistic landscape research, since this airline disappeared in 1997.

(in Portuguese, with a bilingual header). Image 17b shows an enlarged cross-section in order to reveal the aforementioned distribution. The Spanish translation sometimes differs from the original Portuguese text, and it is linguistically poor, as will be shown in 3.1.4. The other map is located in Chaves; in the urban centre, there are bilingual tourist maps in Portuguese-Spanish (Image 18a) and in French-English (Image 18b).

Of particular interest in terms of linguistic hierarchy are two signs placed very close to each other, almost on the borderline. Image 19 shows a notice board that provides information regarding where foreign vehicles can pay the electronic tolls on Portuguese highways. The official sign is trilingual: Spanish-French-English (16). However, an anonymous hand, perhaps offended by the absence of the national language on a board created by a public entity, added a Portuguese word (*portagens*), expanded the abbreviation *km* and pinpointed the exact location of the toll station (*Alto de Leomil*).

(16) *Telepeaje* | *Télépéage* | *Electronic Toll* | 11 *km.*

Image 20a depicts a bilingual plaque (17) fixed to the building that housed the former joint Spanish-Portuguese police station. Symmetrically, a few metres away, on the Spanish side of the border, there is another plaque (Image 20b), with an inversion of the languages (18) and the same spelling error (missing accent) in *comisaría*.

(17) *Posto misto de fronteira luso-espanhol* | *Vilar Formoso / Fuentes de Oñoro* ||
      Comisaria común de frontera luso-española | *Vilar Formoso / Fuentes de Oñoro* (Image 20a).

(18) *Comisaria común de frontera luso-española* | *Vilar Formoso / Fuentes de Oñoro* || *Posto misto de fronteira luso-espanhol* | *Vilar Formoso / Fuentes de Oñoro*
      'joint Spanish-Portuguese border police station Vilar Formoso / Fuentes de Oñoro' (Image 20b).

3.1.3.2 Bottom-up texts

As regards private texts, the largest sphere of use of Spanish is in the hospitality and catering sectors. There are bilingual or multilingual texts on two restaurant menus (Chaves and Vilar Formoso) and on five signs placed at hotels and guesthouses (Vilar Formoso). Image 21 shows a Portuguese-Spanish-English-French warning about the payment of tolls that is fixed to the door of a restaurant and souvenir shop in Vilar Formoso. Curiously, this private notice had a Portuguese version, whereas the official sign issued by a public entity (16) lacked one.

The other five texts containing Spanish were from the commercial sector. There were two signs at a custom agent's office in Vilar Formoso, two labels in establishments in the same locality and a notice asking customers to ring a bell to enter a shop in Vila Verde da Raia.

Text (19) is particularly interesting. The intended use of a bilingual label clearly solves a communication problem. Although Portuguese and Spanish are closely related Romance languages, some terms are completely different; thus, a foreigner without linguistic skills may not be able to understand their meaning. Obviously, this has unfortunate consequences when the opaque word designates the type of a certain establishment. Therefore, there is need for clarification, and bilingual signs are a good tool to ensure that Spanish visitors will understand that an *ourivesaria* is the same as a *joyería* ('jewellery shop'). On the Spanish side of the border, this phenomenon can be repeatedly observed at butchers' shops, since the Spanish and Portuguese designations – *carnicería* and *talho*, respectively – are very different (see 3.2.3).

(19)　*Ourivesaria – Joyería* (Vilar Formoso) 'jewellery shop' (Image 22).

3.1.4 Linguistic errors

Overall, the Spanish texts in the corpus that were collected in Portugal are quite correct, except for the aforementioned tourist map of the municipality of Almeida (Image 16), which provides many of the examples below: (25) to (29) and (31) to (33).

First, I will present the orthographic errors. Examples (20) to (24) are completely void of accents. This does not seem to be a product of interference, since the content of (21) has direct correspondence with the Portuguese *autêntico*, with an accent mark, and texts (21) to (24) are apparently graffiti produced in Vilar Formoso by Spaniards. The following two examples show the incorrect use of accent marks. Text 25 confuses the relative pronoun *cual* with the interrogative one *cuál*, which should have an accent; the Portuguese correspondent is *qual* for both forms, always without a mark. Image (26) is clearly a transposition of Portuguese rules of accentuation. Phrases (27) to (29) have incorrect capital letters in the Spanish version of the text. Finally, (30) shows interferences in the writing of consonant groups (see the Portuguese *demonstração*).

(20) El aut_entico 'the authentic one'.

(21) Solo ten_eis envidia 'you just feel envy'.

(22) No hab_eis venido 'you have not come'.

(23) _Alvaro y Jeni... 'Alvaro and Jeni'.

(24) Ten_eis kaka en las cuecas 'you have poop in your underpants'.

(25) de la cu_ál se extrae 'from which is extracted'.

(26) eje vi_ário internacional 'international road axis'.

(27) los _Monolitos 'monoliths'.

(28) La _Arquitectura es típica de los... 'the architecture is typical of...'

(29) Desde la _Boda de D. Dinis 'since D. Dinis' wedding'.

(30) Demon_stración de cetrería 'spectacle of falconry'.

There are other types of interferences. In (31), the Spanish noun *paisaje* is feminine because of the influence of the Portuguese *paisagem*. In (32), the composers borrow the Portuguese *florir* instead of using the correct Spanish verb, *florecer*, while (33) presents an interesting case of semantic interference. The Portuguese term *freguesia* designates an administrative entity into which municipalities are divided. However, there is no equivalent in the Spanish organisation of territories; the Spanish cognate would be *feligresía* ('members of a parish', without the administrative sense), and not the inexistent *fregesía* (perhaps a typo of *freguesía*?). Finally, the sign reproduced in Image 23 uses the form *hostal* as a synonym for 'rooms'. A literal translation, coherent with the versions in other languages, should be *habitaciones*.

(31) L_as maravillos_as paisajes 'the wonderful landscapes'.

(32) _florir los almendros 'the almond trees blossom'.

(33) Freg_esías 'parishes'.

3.2 The linguistic landscape in the Spanish border area

3.2.1 Idiomatic distribution

The 143 texts included in the corpus collected in Spain present 28 different language combinations; the main combinations are represented in Table 4. It should be noted that there is less internal diversity than there is in the corpus collected in Portugal, which contained up to 47 language combinations.

Table 4: Main linguistic choices used in the signs collected in Spain.

Portuguese	30 texts (21%)
Spanish – English	27 texts (19%)
English	25 texts (17.5%)
Spanish – Portuguese	19 texts (13%)
Mixed Spanish – Portuguese	5 texts (3.5%)
Other combinations	37 texts (26%)

The linguistic hierarchy is also quite different, since English and Portuguese are relatively balanced in this corpus, while the statements collected in Portugal showed a predominance of English, present in more than 66% of texts, while Spanish barely attained 27%.

Specifically, 61 of the 143 records (42.66% of the corpus) contained some English forms. These were divided between 25 monolingual statements, 27 bilingual Spanish-English texts, and 9 multilingual texts. Regarding the producer, only seven texts were promoted by an official body. Portuguese was present in 55 of the records that constituted the corpus (38.46%). Thirty are monolingual statements and nineteen are bilingual Spanish-Portuguese signs. As regards the promoter, 47 were private and eight public. The third language in the collection is French, which had a much lower incidence, with just 11 texts (18.03% of the corpus).

It was necessary to introduce an additional linguistic classification, namely mixed Spanish-Portuguese signs. Bilingual texts show either a functional distribution of languages – in (2a) and (2b), the category of the establishment is coded in one language, while the proper name uses another linguistic variety – or a complete or partial repetition of information, as in (16). However, mixed statements such as (34) and (35) combine Spanish and Portuguese without an apparent criterion on a list of products that are available in these shops in Feces de Abaixo and Fuentes de Oñoro, respectively.

(34) *Calzados | Perfumeria | Limpieza* [...] | *Ferragens* | *Bolachas* | *Caramelos* [...]
'shoes | perfumery | cleaning [...] | hardware | biscuits | candies' (Image 24).

(35) *2º andar | Perfumaria | Presentes | Brinquedos | Lingerie | W.C. | 3º andar | Decoracion*[7] *| Lar Textil P. Electrodomestico* '2nd floor | perfumery | presents | toys | lingerie | W.C. | 3rd floor | decorations | home textile small electrical appliances (Image 25).

3.2.2 Monolingual statements in Portuguese

The corpus includes 30 monolingual statements in Portuguese, a significant number that is even higher than the amount of monolingual English texts collected in this territory.

The biggest novelty is one top-down Portuguese monolingual text. There was no equivalent in the linguistic landscape examined in Portugal. This sign is an advertising poster for a thermal tourism programme (*termalismo saudável* 'healthy hydrotherapy') funded by a provincial public body, the Deputación de Ourense. It was fixed to the door of the premises of the *Eurocity Chaves-Verín*, based in the old Spanish customs building in Feces de Abaixo (Image 26).

Another striking difference from the corpus collected in Portugal was the large quantity of guest texts placed in shop windows and on the doors of establishments to announce various activities such as religious festivals, bullfights, rallies and concerts. These events were going to be held in different Portuguese towns and villages, and they were announced in Spain via a monolingual Portuguese poster (presumably, the same one that was used in Portugal). There are nine cases in the corpus; Images 27 and 28 represent two examples from Fuentes de Oñoro.

In addition to the aforementioned guest texts, another phenomenon was commonly observed in the frontier culture, which could be termed *rendered objects*. The material support on which the signs appeared was bought in Portugal but was used in Spain. Therefore, in a street in Fuentes de Oñoro, I observed a mailbox engraved in Portuguese (36), and in the road that traverses Feces de Abaixo, there is a rental advert with a Spanish phone number, but with the predefined text in Portuguese (37).

---

[7] The possibility of a mistake cannot be excluded, since the rest of the statement was written in Portuguese, with the exception of this single word, which may be a form that was left untranslated.

(36) *Correio* 'post' (Image 29).

(37) *Aluga-se* 'for rental' (Image 30).

As mentioned in 3.1.2, a significant number of signs were placed at commercial establishments to advertise certain products. Nine cases were found during the fieldwork, none of them in the *Eurocity Chaves-Verín*. Examples (38) and (39) were located in Feces de Abaixo, in a general store that sold food and hunting items. In Fuentes de Oñoro, there were signs such as (40) at a roadside restaurant that advertised the sale of roasted chickens. Most of these texts contained linguistic errors, usually spelling mistakes – see also 3.2.4, and texts (55), (59) and (64).

(38) *Polvo | Vitela || Bacalhau | Noruega* 'octopus | veal | cod | Norway' (Image 31).

(39) *Mais de 30 modelos | de carabinas (chumbos) | calibres 4.5 5.5 y 6.35* 'more than 30 models of carbines (bullets) | calibre 4.5 5.5. and 6.35' (Image 32).

(40) *Frangos asados* 'roast chicken'.

(41) *Mercearia | congelados* 'grocer's shop | frozen food store' (Image 35).

(42) *Cabeleireiro de homens | peluquero de hombres* 'gentlemen's hairdresser' (Image 36).

There were also two external texts that advertised deep-frozen cod (Image 33) and advertised the services of a generator rental company (Image 34). These adverts were also written in Portuguese, but they originated in Portugal, unlike the signs described above.

It is no surprise that, in border villages, the neighbours' language may be used in the names of establishments, both for the generic designations and for proper names. Example (41) is placed at the awning of an establishment in Feces de Abaixo; while the second word has the same form in Spanish and Portuguese, the first is unmistakably Portuguese: *Mercearia congelados* (Image 35). Example (42) is particularly interesting. It is a sticker that publicises a hairdresser in Vilar Formoso. The entire text is written in Portuguese. As the designation *cabeleireiro de homens* 'men hairdresser' was opaque, somebody (the advertisers themselves?) wrote the Spanish translation *peluquero de hombres* by hand, in order to cancel out the linguistic distance (Image 36).

In the same way that there is a top-down statement related to the tourist sector, there was also a bottom-up sign, which was a notice board for the bus company Anpian (Ourense), placed at the bus station in Verín and which provides information about international connections. Nonetheless, above the printed Portuguese poster, there is a handwritten text in Spanish: *Confianza, Seguridad y Confort* ('trust, security and comfort') (Image 37).

Finally, with respect to graffiti, while there were many examples in Portugal, only one was found in Spain, in Fuentes de Oñoro, which was a declaration of love written on a lamppost (43).

(43) *Amo-te, Joel* 'I love you, Joel' (Image 38).

3.2.3 Signs with the presence of Portuguese

3.2.3.1 Top-down texts

Only seven records have public promoters. In fact, it should be noted that presence of Portuguese in some of these texts is minimal; thus, the real weight of Portuguese in this sphere of use is even lower.

Image 39 is a parallel case to that of Image 15 – (see 3.1.3.1). It is an informative panel about construction works, which is written entirely in Spanish, except for the bilingual logo of the cross-border cooperation programme. However, it seems that there was no coherent information policy, because some metres away there was another informative panel about the same project (Image 40); in this case, the headers and predefined sections were in Portuguese, whereas the description of the works was written in Spanish. Verín, the municipal capital, has an informative panel about the Chaves-Verín stretch of the Way of St. James (Image 41a). It was classified as bilingual because there was a Portuguese logo in a corner of the poster (44), but the poster itself was in monolingual Spanish, despite its geographical scope and the large number of Portuguese pilgrims who walk that route. See http://www.cpisantiago.pt; last access: 10.06.2021).

(44) *Caminho | Português | Interior de | Santiago* 'Interior Portuguese Road of St. James' (Image 41b).

Therefore, only five official texts showed a clear presence of Portuguese, and two of them have already been commented upon: the plaque at the former joint police station (3.1.3.1) and the information panel mentioned in the previous paragraph (Image 40).

In Feces de Abaixo, next to the old Spanish customs building, there was a hapax, that is the only text in this corpus that combined Portuguese and

Galician[8]. The sign was a poster advertising a "eurocitizen identity card" allowing access to certain infrastructures and services (45). The alternation of languages was chromatically indicated in red and blue: on the left side, Portuguese was in red and Galician in blue; on the right side, the opposite was the case. The poster contained the logo of the Eurocity using the form *eurocidade*, which is common to Galician and Portuguese; the same logo is also attached to the former customs building, now the administrative premises of the Eurocity.

(45) *Compartimos servizos | Compartilhamos serviços || Descubra todas as vantagens | do novo cartão do eurocidadão | Descobre todas as vantaxes | da nova tarxeta do eurocidadán* 'we share services | discover all the advantages of the new euro citizen card' (Image 42).

Another interesting text can be defined as being top-down, since it is fixed to the door of the Spanish police station in Fuentes de Oñoro. However, it has no official status (no signature, no seal and no letterhead). Thus, it seems more like an informal brief written by somebody to escape from recurrent questions.

(46) *No tenemos | ningún tipo de | información | sobre los peajes | de la A-25 || Nao dispomos de | qualquer tipo de | informaçao | sobre portagens | da A-25* 'We have not any of information about the tolls of A-25' (Image 43).

3.2.3.2 Bottom-up texts

The cases included in the corpus of bottom-up texts were all sourced in the municipality of Fuentes de Oñoro; Verín shunned any presence of Portuguese, as explained in further detail in the conclusion, and Feces de Abaixo opted for monolingual Portuguese statements.

I have identified three typologies of bilingual or multilingual statements. The first, the clarification of opaque designations, was already commented upon when analysing the corpus collected in Portugal. When linguistic distance obscures the identification of a certain establishment, bilingual labels are created (47). On occasion, there is no direct correspondence, as in (48). The Spanish term is a generic designation ('supermarket'), whereas the Portuguese word ('butcher') provides information about the availability of certain products that are in high demand by Portuguese shoppers. Example (49) is a curious case of bilingualism.

---

[8] There were, however, other examples some years ago. For example, Lois (2013, 318) reproduced a Galician-Portuguese poster that publicised a food collection campaign carried out around Christmas 2010.

The generic designation of the establishment is given only in Portuguese (*rebuçados* 'candies'), even though the store is located in Spain and the Spanish form is quite different (*caramelo*); the proper name *La Cabra* ('the goat') refers to a prestigious brand of candies from Logroño.

(47) *Carnicería – Talho* 'butchery' (Images 44 and 45).

(48) *Supermercado – Talho* 'supermarket – butchery' (Images 46 and 47).

(49) *Rebuçados La Cabra* 'candies La Cabra' (Image 48).

On other occasions, Portuguese is used to advertise a certain product or service. The door of the pharmacy in Fuentes de Oñoro (Image 49) is remarkable for its internationality. It has a welcome sign written in eight languages (in addition to Spanish and Portuguese, the languages are English, Arabic, French, German, Russian and Chinese). However, for the purpose of research into the linguistic landscape, its shopfront (Image 50) is far more interesting. The main services provided by the pharmacy are described on bilingual lists that clearly indicate hierarchies: Spanish has a bigger font size, while the Portuguese version is a poor translation and sometimes lacks information included in the Spanish version.

By contrast, the advertisements for the booking offices of the bus company *Eurolines* (Image 51) demonstrate full equivalence between Portuguese and Spanish, both in the position and size of the forms and in terms of content, with the exception of a small mistake in the second line of the Portuguese text (cf. section 3.2.4, example 58).

The last type refers to information about opening hours and access to commercial establishments. Spanish and Portuguese follow different procedures to create the names of the days. The former adopts pagan references, such as *martes* 'day of Mars', for Tuesday, whereas the other uses the Christian calendar – Tuesday is *Terça-feira*, the 'third fair', because the count begins on Sunday, the holy day. As a result, the designations for weekdays (but not for Saturday and Sunday) are completely different. Furthermore, Spain and Portugal are located in different time zones and have a one-hour difference. Because of this, it is common for establishments with a high flow of cross-border clients to display two different notices about service hours in order to minimise the risk of confusion (50). Similarly, linguistic distance may complicate even simple acts such as entering a shop, since the action of pulling a door is *puxar* in Portuguese and *tirar* in Spanish. This explains bilingual statements such as (51). Linguistic errors, underlined, will be discussed in 3.2.4.

(50) *(Hora española) | De lunes a sábado | Mañanas: 9:00 horas – 14:00 h | Tardes 15:30 horas – 20 h* || *(Hora portuguesa) | De Segunda a <u>Sabado</u> | <u>Manha</u> 8.00 horas – 13 H | Tardes 14.30 Horas – 19.00 H* '(Spanish time) | (Spanish hour) | From Monday to Saturday | Mornings: 9 – 14 | Afternoons: 15.30 – 20 || (Portuguese hour)) | From Monday to Saturday | Mornings: 8 – 13 | Afternoons: 14.30 – 19' (Image 52).

(51) *Por favor | llame al | timbre* || *Toque | a | campainha* || *Tirar | Puxe* 'please, ring the bell || pull' (Image 53).

Finally, I would like to draw attention to a circumstance that is highly interesting from the perspective of the linguistic landscape. On the 21st of May 2015, the group Gildo – founded by Hermenegildo Bravo, who was born in Fuentes de Oñoro – inaugurated the refurbishment of its supermarket placed in this locality, 650 meters from the borderline. This establishment, now associated with the brand Carrefour, is essentially bilingual in all external labelling (Images 54 and 55) and in most of the internal signage – see Images 56 and 57.[9] Moreover, the catalogue of products is published in both languages. Therefore, this marketplace is a true point of contact between two communities, beyond the political frontier and on an equal footing from a linguistic point of view.

3.2.4 Linguistic errors

The linguistic errors in the Portuguese texts produced in Spain are far more frequent on the orthographic level.

The first group – (52) to (56) – is characterised by the absence of accent marks and tildes. The causes are diverse. The lack of tildes (~) may be a consequence of technical problems in most cases, since they are absent from Spanish keyboards. In addition, (56) could be explained as an interference from the Spanish accentuation system, but it could also be a simple mistake or misprint. Finally, other mistakes are hard to explain, since the Spanish cognate of the word would also require an accent, as in *sábado* (53).

Another group of texts revealed insufficient knowledge of Portuguese orthography. It is possible to distinguish between three different types.

---

[9] Clearly, these indoor texts and other similar cases have not been taken into consideration in the quantitative study, since they are not visible from the public space.

Firstly, there are clear interferences from the Spanish graphic system; (57) and (58) present a very common interference between Spanish and Portuguese orthographic systems, as the Portuguese conjunction *e* (pronounced [i]) is transcribed as *y*, the Spanish one, which sounds the same. Example (62) can be also explained by processes of interference, since regional Spanish has only one unvoiced alveolar fricative [s], written <s>, whereas Portuguese makes a distinction between voiced and unvoiced fricatives: <s> ([z]) and <ss> [s], as in *assados*. Finally, the second part of (64) can be also explained by interference from the Spanish system, since the author has used the digraph <ll> instead of <lh>.

A second group consists of texts overtly influenced by pronunciation; the correct written forms in (59) to (61) would be *binóculos, cassetes, infravermelho* and *análises*.

Finally, a third section groups other spelling errors that arose because the composers were unaware of certain peculiarities of Portuguese orthography; the correct forms would be (63) *presunto*, (64) *melancias* and (65) *pequeno-almoço*.

(52) *Nao* [...] *informaçao* [...] 'no [...] information' (Image 43).

(53) [...] *Sabado | Manha* [...] 'Saturday | Morning' (Image 52).

(54) *melao; almondegas; leitao* 'melon; meatballs; roast suckling pig' (Image 58).

(55) *armazem; meloes* 'warehouse; melons'(Image 59).

(56) *relogios* 'watches' (Image 61).

(57) *calibres 4.5 5.5 y 6.35* 'calibres 4.5 5.5 and 6.35', (Image 32).

(58) *reserva y venda* 'reservation and sale' (Image 51).

(59) *binoclos; R. cassets* 'binoculars radio-cassette'

(60) *infrabermelho* 'infrared' (Image 61).

(61) *análeses* 'analyses' (Image 50).

(62) *asados* 'roasts'.

(63) *presumto* 'ham' (Image 58).

(64) *melançias*; *maravil<u>l</u>a* 'watermelon; wonderful' (Image 59).

(65) *pequeno<u> </u>almoço* 'breakfast' (Image 60).

Text (66) is very curious: maybe it is a morphological interference (use of Spanish article *el*, instead of *o*) or, more likely, an oversight when writing the translation over the original text. Text (67) contains incorrect translations: it retains the Spanish word *embutidos*, instead of *enchidos*, and ignores the existence of the Portuguese form *esparguete*. Finally, (68) is an incomplete translation, since the original Spanish text, shown in another part of the showcase, is *Dermofarmacia Infantil* 'children's dermopharmacy'.

(66) *prato del dia* (Image 60).

(67) *embutidos variados*; *spaguetti* 'mixed cold meat' (Image 58).

(68) *crianças* 'children' (Image 50).

4 Conclusions

The quantitative and qualitative analysis of a large corpus of material collected during the fieldwork allowed me to reach conclusions about the cross-border vitality of Portuguese and Spanish, their spheres of use, their linguistic accuracy and phenomena of interference.

One of the initial hypotheses I intend to verify is whether the existence of the *Eurocity Chaves-Verín* – a cross-border entity established to strengthen economic, social and territorial cohesion via joint initiatives and the joint use of infrastructure and services – leads to a better appreciation of the neighbour's language, more vitality and, obviously, a greater presence in the public landscape. The answer is strongly negative. Moreover, it would be more realistic to affirm that what exists is a complete ignorance of the neighbour's language; in fact, some cases even suggest the existence of a "making invisible" strategy. Images (62a) and (62b) show information plaques placed at tourist sites. The format and layout are similar on both sides of the border, but the languages are different. Signs located in Chaves are written in Portuguese and English; in Verín, they are written in Spanish and English. Therefore, Spanish is absent from Chaves and Portuguese is absent from Verín. Meanwhile, Galician was absent from both towns, although a logo showed that the Galician regional government sponsored this publicity campaign. The common language of the *Eurocity* seems to be English.

No top-down text that used Portuguese was found in Verín, with the exception of the inclusion of a tiny logo, as discussed above in (44). However, English in present in several tourist texts (Images 63,[10] 64 and 65).

Regarding bottom-up texts, the situation is even worse, at least from a quantitative perspective. The corpus is composed of 55 signs written in languages other than Galician and Spanish, mainly in English, but there are also French, German, Romanian and Chinese texts, among others. However, only three examples that contained Portuguese were collected: two guest texts – the advertisement for a party in Chaves (Image 66) and the extremely degraded billboard for a bullfight celebrated in Portugal some months previously – and the aforementioned notice board at the bus station (Image 37).

Its counterpart, Chaves, has a similar linguistic landscape, if not worse, particularly in the private sector. Apart from the small bilingual logo of the cross-border cooperation programme, Spanish was only present in two of the nine top-down texts containing foreign languages. With regard to bottom-up signs reflecting the presence of Spanish, Chaves was a linguistic wasteland. Of the 79 signs with foreign forms collected in our corpus, only three contained Spanish forms: the graffiti (69), presumably produced by Spaniards, a restaurant menu (also available in English and French – see Image 70) and the sticker for a Venezuelan airline that disappeared 19 years ago (Image 71).

(69) *De puta madre* 'fucking great' (Image 69).

This clearly demonstrates that, despite the language contact setting, no convergence between Spanish and Portuguese appears to be taking place in the linguistic landscapes of Chaves and Verín. On the contrary, one could state that we are dealing with a non-convergence case (cf. Kaufmann 2010) as the presence of the neighbour's language is quite limited. In fact, the border between these places may be characterised as "distant", a boundary that points out the differences and settles national identities by rendering the neighbour invisible by concealing his or her language, among other procedures. This situation becomes even more paradoxical given the existence of a *Eurocity*. It is possible to adopt, in this sense, the conclusions of Pons Rodríguez (2014, 88–89, my translation):

---

[10] Note that, even though the thermal path is designated by its Portuguese name, *Rota termal e da água*, this language is entirely neglected in the tourist information.

> The differences between the two localities we have studied are relevant [...] but it is even more striking a coincidence: marginalisation of Spanish [...]. It seems that there is an ongoing self-definition of being Portuguese from the linguistic landscape which, far from be driven by the values granted to borders by new policies, consolidates the idea of separation and difference. While the boundary is something political, it is social when an opaque or porous value is assigned. With respect to linguistic landscape, this border scenario is a non-hybridisation place. Physical and linguistic proximities are broken in the linguistic landscape, where there is a limitation of the other.

Nevertheless, it would be wrong to extend this limiting vision to the entire Spanish-Portuguese border. Pons Rodríguez explored a geographical framework in which there was no close relationship on either side of the border. While the cities of Chaves and Verín are located 22 km from each other, Castro Marim and Vila Real de Santo António, studied by Pons Rodríguez, are closer to their Spanish counterparts in a straight line but, as the borderline follows the course of the river Guadiana, cross-border mobility requires using the ferry or taking a detour on the highway that was inaugurated in 1991.

However, there is a closer, more intimate border there where daily contact has existed for decades, instance when crossing the border only entails a short walk to the grocery store. For this part of the research, two different zones were studied, Feces de Abaixo/Vila Verde da Raia and Vilar Formoso/Fuentes de Oñoro. On the Spanish side of this "close border", nine top-down texts were collected, and Portuguese was present in seven of these statements. It is missing only in two signs in Fuentes de Oñoro, namely the instructions for a phone booth (Image 72) and a plaque commemorating the inauguration of the new customs facilities (Image 73); interestingly, as this plaque was placed on the borderline, Latin was chosen as a neutral language because it is valid for both states. On the Portuguese side, Spanish has a lower presence, although it is more visible than in Chaves. I would like to point out, as a curiosity, that Portuguese cabin booths also neglect the language of the neighbouring country (Image 74). It is also significant that the information available at the railway station about connections to Spain (and France) was written only in Portuguese and English (Image 75).

As regards bottom-up texts, 70 statements were collected on the Spanish side, and Portuguese was present in 53 of them. In Portugal, our corpus collected 62 signs, and roughly half (32) included Spanish forms. The latter is not a particularly high percentage, but it must be said that Spanish was the main foreign language in the area, since English appeared in 30 statements and French in only 14; in any event, this linguistic landscape clearly differs from the reality encountered in Chaves.

Therefore, it can be stated that close cross-border contact is a direct reflection of the linguistic landscape in the border area, particularly with regard to bottom-up texts. There is a greater presence of Portuguese in Spain than there is of Spanish in Portugal, possibly because the Spanish side of the border concentrates on commercial activities. As one moves further away from this "close border" into municipal capitals or major towns, this situation fades, and the languages of the neighbouring country vanish, replaced by tourism's major languages (English and French), as well as via a process of the affirmation of national identity.

5 References

Castillo Lluch, Mónica/Sáez Rivera, Daniel Moisés, *Introducción al paisaje lingüístico de Madrid*, Lengua y migración 3:1 (2011), 73–88.

Castillo Lluch, Mónica/Sáez Rivera, Daniel Moisés (edd.), *Paisajes lingüísticos en el mundo hispánico*, Madrid/Frankfurt, Iberoamericana, 2013 [= Revista internacional de Lingüística Iberoamericana 21].

Cenoz, Jasone/Gorter, Durk, *Linguistic landscape and minority languages*, International Journal of Multilingualism 3:1 (2006), 67–80.

Clemente, Mariana Ribeiro/Vieira, Rui/Martins, Filomena/Andrade, Ana Isabel, *Linguistic diversity in Aveiro, Portugal. Exploring linguistic landscape methodologies in the "Beira Mar" neighborhood*, Internet Latent Corpus Journal 3:1 (2013), 116–133.

Dicionário da Língua Portuguesa, Porto, Porto Editora, 2003–2019, https://www.infopedia.pt [last access: 03.07.2020].

DRAE = Real Academia Española, *Diccionario de la lengua española*, [23]2014, http://www.rae.es [last access: 03.07.2020].

Franco-Rodríguez, José Manuel, *Interpreting the linguistic traits of linguistic landscape as ethnolinguistic vitality. Methodological approach*, Revista Electrónica de Lingüística Aplicada 8 (2009), 1–15.

Godinho, Paula, *Discursos palacianos*, in: Cairo Carou, Heriberto/Godinho, Paula/Pereiro, Xerardo (edd.), *Portugal e Espanha. Entre discursos de centro e práticas de fronteira*, Lisboa, Colibri, 2009, 73–91 (= 2009a).

Godinho, Paula, *Entre Chaves e Verín. Mediadores, fronteira útil e fronteira fútil*, in: Medina, Eusebio (edd.), *Fronteras, patrimonio y etnicidad en Iberoamérica*, Málaga, Signatura, 2009, 137–152 (= 2009b).

Godinho, Paula, *Re-signification of the past in the northern Portugal/Galicia border. Amenity, heritage and emblem*, in: K. Stokłosa, Katarzyna/Besier, Gerhard (edd.), *European border regions in comparison*, New York/ London, Routledge, 2013, 149–168.

Gorter, Durk, *Introduction. The study of the linguistic landscape as a new approach to multilingualism*, in: D. Gorter, Durk (ed.), *Linguistic landscape. New approach to multilingualism*, Clevedon, Multilingual Matters, 2006, 1–6.

Gorter, Durk, *Linguistic landscapes in a multilingual world*, Annual Review of Applied Linguistics 33 (2013), 190–212.

Kaufmann, Göz, *Non-convergence despite language contact*, in: Auer, Peter/Schmidt, Jürgen Erich, *Language and space. Theories and methods*, Berlin/New York, De Gruyter Mouton, 2010, 478–493.

Landry, Rodrigue/Bourhis, Richard Y., *Linguistic landscape and ethnolinguistic vitality. An empirical study*, Journal of Language and Social Psychology 16:1 (1997), 23–49.

Lois, María, *Re-significando la frontera. El caso de la eurociudad Chaves-Verín*, Boletín de la Asociación de Geógrafos Españoles 61 (2013), 309–327.

Pons Rodríguez, Lola, *El paisaje lingüístico de Sevilla. Lenguas y variedades en el escenario urbano hispalense*, Sevilla, Diputación Provincial de Sevilla, 2012.

Pons Rodríguez, Lola, *El paisaje lingüístico de la frontera luso española. Multilingüismo e identidad*, in: Bravo-García, Eva/Gallardo Saborido, Emilio/Santos de la Rosa, Inmaculada/Gutiérrez, Antonio (edd.), *Investigaciones sobre la enseñanza del español y su cultura en contextos de inmigración*, Sevilla/Helsinki, Universidad de Helsinki/Grupo de Investigación Estudios lingüístico-culturales y Enseñanza del Español como Lengua Extranjera (HUM 927) de la Universidad de Sevilla, 2014, 69–89 (CD-ROM).

Solovova, Olga/Matos, Ana Raquel/Nolasco, Carlos, *E se as paredes falassem? Análise discursiva de inscrições no espaço público urbano de Coimbra*, in: Nolasco, Carlos/Matos, Ana Raquel/Solovova, Olga (edd.), *Ways of seeing, ways of making seen. Visual representations in urban landscapes*, Coimbra, Centro de Estudos Sociais, 2016, 43–61, http://hdl.handle.net/10316/81065 [last access: 03.07.2020].

Torkington, Kate, *Os impactos das mobilidades turísticas e migratórias na paisagem semiótica do Algarve*, in: Nolasco, Carlos/Matos, Ana Raquel/Solovova, Olga (edd.), *Ways of seeing, ways of making seen. Visual representations in urban landscapes*, Coimbra, Centro de Estudos Sociais, 2016, 26–42, http://hdl.handle.net/10316/81065 [last access: 03.07.2020].

Trillo Santamaría, Juan Manuel/Lois González, Rubén Camilo/Paül Carril, Valerià, *Ciudades que cruzan la frontera*, Cuadernos Geográficos 54:1 (2015), 160–185.

Xosé Luís Regueira
Portuguese as a contact language in Galicia
Convergence, divergence, ideology and identity

Abstract: Portuguese is not generally regarded as a contact language with Galician. Both languages shared a common written form in the Middle Ages, but at the end of that period they became differentiated. Today, standard Galician encourages some convergence in aspects of vocabulary and grammar, and some minority groups take (mainly written) Portuguese as the main reference for standard Galician. This paper addresses some public discourses which show numerous grammatical and lexical forms appropriated from written Portuguese but in which, in an apparently paradoxical manner, many (mainly phonetic) features of Spanish as a contact language also appear. In the wake of studies on identity construction in linguistic interaction, and by using the concept of indexicality, this study demonstrates that the contact forms taken from Portuguese and from Spanish contribute to the construction of social, political and ideological identities in a way that, far from being contradictory, reinforce each other in some respects (urban, non-lower class, educated). In more general terms, this article shows that the understanding of language contact can benefit greatly from the sociolinguistic work based on the agency of speakers and from the studies of identity construction in interaction.

Keywords: Galician, Portuguese, language contact, divergence, convergence, identity, ideology, parliamentary and political discourse, indexing features

---

Note: This paper was written within the context of the "Contacto, cambio lingüístico e ideoloxía en contextos de minorización lingüística" project, funded by the Ministry of Education, Innovation and Universities of the Spanish Government (PID2019-110352GB-I00) and the European Regional Development Fund (multiannual financial framework 2014 2020), and within the "Tecnoloxías e Análise dos Datos Lingüísticos" network, funded by the Xunta de Galicia (ED431D 2016/011). I would like to thank Jose Manuel Dopazo for his help with the transcription of the recordings, and two anonymous reviewers for their suggestions and comments, which helped to improve the manuscript.

Xosé Luís Regueira, Instituto da Lingua Galega – Universidade de Santiago de Compostela

https://doi.org/10.1515/9783110736250-006

1 Introduction

Studies on language contact tend to focus on linguistic codes, regarded as entities that are external to the people who speak them and which can be analysed as if they were natural objects (hence the frequent metaphors taken from biology or other areas: languages are born, die, decay or are purified, hybridise, etc.). This perspective dominated linguistics during the 20th century, as encapsulated in the idea expressed explicitly by Saussure (1995, 31): "La langue, distincte de la parole, est un objet qu'on peut étudier séparément". This perspective, which regards language as a natural object, also dominated studies of linguistic change: "'language changes' – it is not (necessarily) speakers that change it" (Lass 1980, 120). Contact studies have followed a similar path since their very foundation (Weinreich 1953), although in recent decades other, more comprehensive perspectives have made inroads, from works such as that of Le Page/Tabouret-Keller (1985), or more recently, the most valuable and complex visions of linguistic contact developed by Blommaert (2010). However, these studies are still limited regarding contact between the Iberian languages, and Romance languages in general.

Galician, the Ibero-Romance language spoken in north-western Spain, is closely related in genetic terms to Portuguese. The common written and literary language in the Middle Ages, known as Galician-Portuguese, led to both languages emerging at the end of the Middle Ages, as Portuguese developed a standard language based on Lisbon dialects and departed from the northern varieties, while Galicia remained under the rule of the Kingdom of Castile and Galician vanished as a written language. From that point on, Galician has been in contact with Spanish and separated from Portuguese by a political border. In this situation, Portuguese is not usually regarded as a contact language for Galician.

From the literary Renaissance in the 19th century and the recovery of Galician as a written language, kinship and shared history with Portuguese has been invoked as a feature of prestige and Portuguese has an important role as a language of reference, whether as a preferred language for the adoption of loans, through proposals for greater alignment between the two languages, or unification of the written standard. This has led to different grammatical and lexical features, taken from the Portuguese, currently being found in standard and literary Galician. Moreover, some minority groups (known as "Reintegrationist") advocate further alignment with Portuguese spelling and grammar or simply the adoption of the Portuguese standard for written Galician. At the same time, the continuity of phonetic, grammatical and lexical features between linguistic varieties of Galicia and northern Portugal, which were historically maintained across the political border (Cintra 1971), are disappearing due to the diffusion of standard Portuguese on the south side of the political border (Regueira/Ginzo 2019), and of standard Galician, and also contact with Spanish on the north side (González et al. 2002).

In this context, the apparent paradox of numerous features being taken from written Portuguese (mainly lexical and grammatical), while at the same time forms of contact with Spanish appearing (especially phonetic and grammatical, but also lexical and other kinds), can be encountered in some public discourses. On the basis of sociolinguistics focused on the agency of speakers (Eckert 2012; 2018) and the theory of indexical orders (Silverstein 2003), this article intends to demonstrate that these are resources used by speakers to build and strengthen identities at different levels (social, ideological and political, amongst others). At another level, it can be argued that some of these Reintegrationist groups constitute an alternative public sphere (Habermas 1962), or more precisely what Fraser (1990) refers to as *subaltern counterpublics*.

Regarding the organisation of this article, it will begin with an introduction to the relationship between Galician and Portuguese, focusing on linguistic continuities detected across the political border and the divergence between the standards of both linguistic communities, as well as the importance of Portuguese in the standardisation of Galician. Subsequently, the method employed is described, and the corpus considered for this study analysed, before the results are discussed in the conclusion.

2 Galician and Portuguese: continuity and divergence

The Galician and Portuguese languages have their origin in Ibero-Romance linguistic varieties spoken in the ancient Kingdom of Galicia. This kingdom extended southward with the *Reconquista* (the conquest and recovery of lands held by the Arabs), and by the end of the 11th century the southern part of the Miño river became the County of Portugal, which became an independent kingdom in the first third of the 12th century. Although Galicia and Portugal were already different kingdoms when this area stopped using Latin and began to use Romance in documents, translations, chronicles and, later, as a literary language, on both sides of the border a fundamentally similar language was written, which is known as Galician-Portuguese.

This unity was ruptured when, at the end of the Middle Ages, Portuguese started the standardisation of the language based on the variety spoken in the power centres of Lisbon and Coimbra, located in the southern centre of the country, far from Galicia and the County of Portugal (Neto 1979, 381–390; Teyssier 1982, 35; Vázquez 1998; Venâncio 2019). As Teyssier affirms (1982, 40): "E assim é que o galego, que nas origens da língua tanto contribuiu para definir a língua literária, veio a encontrar-se no pólo oposto desta mesma norma" ('And that is how Galician, which when the language was originating contributed so much to defining its literary language, came to be at the opposite pole of this same norm'). In standardisation processes undertaken during the following centuries, the trends towards unification continued to act "no sentido desgaleguizador e latinizante" ('in the distancing from Galician and Latinising sense') (Vázquez 1998, 59), increasingly separating standard Portuguese from the language spoken in the north of the country (and from Galician) (see Venâncio 2019, 105–150). Galicia, meanwhile, was subjected to the crown of Castile and eventually annexed by the kingdom of Spain. The Galician language ceased to be written in the early 16th century, until it was recovered in the 19th century as a literary and written language and initiated an independent standardisation process. Currently, Galician is the official language of Galicia, along with Spanish.[1]

In the 20th century, social changes, the urbanisation of society, education and the media have caused standard languages to extend to all corners of both Portugal and Galicia, where Spanish spread as the language of the Spanish state, and in recent decades standard Galician also. One of the effects of this has been that the longstanding linguistic continuity between Galician territory and northern Portugal, which persisted through the centuries in traditional rural society on both sides of the political border, has started to fade away quite quickly. This process seems to be more advanced in Portugal (Regueira/Ginzo 2019). For example, the Linguistic Atlas of the Iberian Peninsula (ALPI, data collected in 1953–1956, presented partially in Cintra 1971) detects the preservation of a system of six fricative sibilants, as well as another system of four sibilants, two apico-alveolars and two postalveolars, with voice opposition in each pair (which contrasts with the standard system, with two lamino-dentals and two postalveolars, cf. Mateus/D'Andrade 2000, 13–14), while Martins/Saramago (1993) show that in the Atlas Linguarum Europae (ALE, data obtained in 1975) the presence of these systems is already greatly reduced. Note that these atlases list the most conservative forms of rural speech patterns, with NORM speakers (non-mobile, old, rural, males). Furthermore, Cintra (1983 [1958], 27) states:

---

[1] For a linguistic comparison of current Galician and Portuguese, see Dubert/Galves (2016).

"No Norte e no Centro de Portugal [...] o facto de grande parte das diferenças existentes em relação à linguagem normal ser sentida muito vivamente como rusticismo e evitada na medida do possível, desde que haja algum conhecimento da linguagem-padrão, obrigou-nos a escolher quase sempre aldeias isoladas, fora das principais vias de comunicação"

('In Northern and Central Portugal [...], the fact that most of the differences related to the normal language are perceived very strongly as backward, and have been avoided as much as possible ever since there was some knowledge of the standard language, has forced us to almost always choose isolated villages, away from the main thoroughfares').

These features that are "perceived as backward" largely coincide with Galician. It would seem, therefore, that the continuities presented in ALPI are not representative of the general state of the language up to the 1950s, and that the loss of the native varieties was already far advanced. In Regueira/Ginzo (2019), with data of university students from central and northern Portugal, these systems that diverge from the standard language are no longer registered. Moreover, in the Galician part, the divergent standard systems that displayed continuity in the north of Portugal are disappearing (González et al. 2002), even though in general greater dialectal diversity is retained.

In spite of this, the Galician phonetics of "traditional" speakers (i.e., who speak Galician as L1 and live in Galician-speaking environments) differs in many aspects from Spanish and is even closer to Portuguese phonetics with regard to nasalisation (Carvalho 1988; Regueira 2010), or the word-final unstressed vowels (Regueira 2007). The pronunciation of stressed vowels is also very similar to that of Portuguese, with a system of seven vowels with contrastive differentiation between mid-high and mid-low vowels: /e/ *bebe* 'drink' (imperative) ['beβɪ] vs. /ɛ/ *(el/ela) bebe* ['bɛβɪ] '(s/he) drinks'; /ɔ/ *bóla* ['bɔlɐ] 'ball' vs. /o/ *bola* ['bolɐ] 'bun' (see Regueira/Fernández Rei in press). Some recent developmental processes also seem to approximate Galician to Portuguese phonetics, such as the development of [ʃ] at the end of words in certain rural dialects (*meses* ['meṣɪʃ] 'months', Pt ['mezɨʃ], cf. Regueira/Ginzo 2019), or the lowering of the mid vowels in pretonic position, mainly in learned words such as *electricidade* [ɛlɛktriθi'ðaðɪ] 'electricity' or *obsesión* [ɔbsɛ'sjoŋ] 'obsession' (cf. Regueira 2008, 276–280; Martínez-Gil 2019), coinciding with a similar process in Portugal (Mascarenhas 1996; Barbosa 1988).

In Galicia, there was a process of rapid urbanisation, accompanied by increasing language substitution. According to data from the *Mapa Sociolingüístico de Galicia (Sociolinguistic Map of Galicia)* (RAG 1994), speakers with L1 Spanish went from 11.3% in the oldest generations to 45.9% in the youngest; in the MSG 2004 (RAG 2007), 37.2% of speakers between 16 and 25 claim to have L1 Spanish and 32.5% more Spanish than Galician. Although some of these young people use Galician, to a greater or lesser extent, it is obvious that contact with Spanish is very high in the majority of the population, especially in urban environments. Furthermore, most of the media is received in Spanish (television, radio, the Spanish press, and also most of the Galician media), which continues to be the language of the state.

Galician is the majority language used in the regional and local administration. A radio station and two television channels that are local in scope broadcast in Galician, as is the case for different programmes on Spanish networks broadcast in Galicia. It is also present in education at all levels, and cultural and political life takes place mostly in Galician. Galician employed in public life therefore displays the effects of contact with Spanish, especially in phonic aspects, and therefore a greater separation between public Galician and the media, and the Galician of "traditional" speakers, is taking place (Regueira 1994; Kabatek 1996).

3 The standardisation of Galician and its convergence with Portuguese: the debate on linguistic norms

From the start of the recovery of Galician as a written language, Portugal and the Portuguese language played a prominent role in Galician culture. The frequent references to the Portuguese language, as the "legitimate daughter of Galician" (Hermida 1996), stem, as stated González Seoane (1996, 123), from "un desexo de subliña-la importancia do galego como berce dunha moderna lingua de cultura" ('a desire to emphasize the importance of Galician as the cradle of a modern cultural language'). To highlight the similarities and the close historical relationship with the language of a colonial empire and an important literature is a method for the legitimisation of Galician, Galician identity and cultural sovereignty (Torres 1999, 273).

Despite these statements, Portuguese played a marginal role in the standardisation of Galician until the 1970s. In the final years of the dictatorship of General Franco (1939–1975), Galician recovered social spaces while at the same time the political recognition of Galicia as a nation or a "historic nationality" within the Spanish state was requested. At the end of that decade, Galician began to be used in compulsory education, administration, political and cultural acts, and thus began a process of "linguistic normalization" (Regueira 2006).

Part of that process was the "corpus planning" or standardisation (see Fernández Salgado/Monteagudo 1995; Alonso 2006; Ramallo/Rey-Doval 2015). The *Real Academia Galega* (RAG) (Royal Galician Academy) and the *Instituto da Lingua Galega* (ILG) (Institut of Galician Language) were the main actors in this process, and despite some disagreements both institutions promoted a language form based upon the literary tradition since the *Rexurdimento* ('Resurgence') in the 1860s and upon the spoken language. That was when a debate on the form of standard Galician took place.

This debate had its starting point in an article by Rodrigues Lapa (1973), in which he disqualified attempts to recover Galician for learned communication from the spoken language as "ineffective" and "ridiculous" and formulated the proposal to adopt Portuguese: "Nada mais resta senão admitir, que sendo o português literário actual a forma que teria o galego se o não tivessem desviado do caminho próprio, este aceite uma língua que lhe é brindada em salva de prata" ('There is nothing left to do but admit that with literary Portuguese being the current form that Galician would have had if it had not been deviated from its own path, the latter should accept a language which is offered to it on a silver platter') (Lapa 1973, 286). Lapa's argument, in addition to being an exercise in counterfactual history, consciously ignores the fact that the Portuguese standard was built on the southern models, at a remove from the Portuguese of the north and from Galician (see above 2). Lapa (1973, 283) comments, among other, on a Galician expression found in a poetry translation, arguing that "quadrará ao labrego que se deixa cair para baixo do ervedeiro, com a barriga ao leu e a camisa encharcada em suor" ('it would suit the farm worker who lays down beneath the arbutus, with his belly bare and his shirt soaked with sweat'), but that it is not consistent with "modos decentes e a compostura do caçador de ocios" ('decent manners and the composure of the leisure seeker'). The contrast made by Lapa is revealing of his social and cultural prejudices towards Galician and linguistic diversity in general.

Lapa´s proposal was rejected by the leading figures of the Galicianist movement, such as Ramón Piñeiro (1973) and Álvaro Cunqueiro (1973). The answer of the latter, who was a writer and journalist, in the journal *El Faro de Vigo* was clear and direct: "bríndasenos unha lingua que non é a nosa" ('we are being offered a language that is not ours'). He accuses Lapa of being a "colonialist" and reminds him that a language into which Shakespeare, Rilke, Yeats, or Elliot were translated, is capable of expressing Heidegger's thought (*Vom Wesen der Wahrheit* was translated into Galician before Spanish) has proven that it is suitable for learned communication. This proposal did not, therefore, have major repercussions at the time, but would be resumed some years later (see below).

In 1982, the Galician government established the *Normas ortográficas e morfolóxicas do idioma galego* ('Orthographic and Morphological Norms of the Galician Language'), as developed by the *Real Academia Galega* and the *Instituto of Lingua Galega* in 1982 (RAG/ILG 1982). At that time, Galician was already an official language, together with Spanish, and the "language of Galicia", as established by the Statute of Galician Autonomy, passed in 1981.

In the official standard, a certain convergence with Portuguese is promoted. In the official normative it is expressly stated that:

> "As escollas normativas deben ser harmónicas coas das outras linguas, especialmente coas romances en xeral e coa portuguesa en particular [...]. Para o arrequecemento do léxico culto, nomeadamente no referido aos ámbitos científico e técnico, o portugués será considerado recurso fundamental, sempre que esta adopción non for contraria ás características estruturais do galego" (RAG/ILG 2012, 10).

> ('Normative selections must be in keeping with those of other languages, especially with the Romance languages in general and in particular with Portuguese [...]. For the enrichment of learned lexicon, particularly in regard to scientific and technical fields, Portuguese will be considered a primary resource, provided that this adoption is not contrary to the structural features of Galician').

Since the 1970s, the Galician linguistic standard has experienced a gradual drift towards Portuguese (Regueira 2003). This approach may be seen in morphological aspects, such as the selection of certain forms of co-occurrence with Portuguese (such as the plural form of the oxytonic nouns and adjectives ending in *-l*, such as *animais* 'animals', or verbal forms such as *sexa* (3rd p. present subjunctive of *ser* 'to be', instead of other variants such as *seña* or *sea*), *ía* (3rd p. imperfect of *ir* 'to go', instead of the most frequent *iba*), in the selection of lexical variants (*igrexa* 'church', *parafuso* 'screw', etc., instead of *eirexa ~ iglesia ~ ilesia*, and *tornillo*, see Regueira 2003), as well as in the adoption of learned terminology and lexicon: *orzamento* 'budget', *adestrar* 'to train', *vestiario* 'wardrobe', amongst others. There are also variants that are not present in the vernacular language, but which coincide with Portuguese, such as the suffix *-bel*, together with *-ble* (*amábel ~ amable* 'kind'), the suffix *-aría*, together with *-ería* (*zapataría ~ zapatería* 'shoe shop'), or forms such as *até ~ ata* 'until', *se callar* 'maybe' etc.

However, around the time when Galician became an official language, alternative proposals appeared which, based on Lapa's idea that Galician had been deviated from its natural path by Spanish colonisation, accused the official standard of being a castilianised form of Galician, proclaiming the need to "reintegrar o noso idioma no seu espazo natural, o galego-portugués" ('reinstate our language in its natural environment, Galician-Portuguese') (Rodríguez 2008), hence the name of this movement: *Reintegracionismo*.

Proponents of these proposals were divided into two main groups: on the one hand, the "minimum Reintegrationism" position, which maintained a "Reintegrationist" discourse that postulated Portuguese as the main guideline for standard Galician, but in practice only diverges from the official normative in minor aspects; and on the other hand, "maximum Reintegrationism", which adopted numerous written, grammatical and lexical features from standard Portuguese, but not the phonetic features (for example, the written representations -s-/-ss- and -j-, -g-/-x- were introduced, but not the distinction between voiced and unvoiced fricatives, the -z- and -ç- spellings are read as [θ], a fricative inexistent in Portuguese, etc.). Numerous differential features are maintained with Portuguese (nasal vowels are not represented, the morphology is basically that of Galician, the lexicon contains many more Lusisms but retains features which differentiate it from Portuguese). This was the position of the *Associaçom Galega da Língua* (AGAL, see AGAL 1983; 1985).

During the 1980s and 1990s, "minimum Reintegrationism" enjoyed a social presence of some significance because it was adopted officially by the main nationalist party, the BNG (Galician Nationalist Bloc), and the most important trade union in Galicia, the CIG (Galician Inter-Union Confederation), linked to the BNG. Standard Galician therefore became a political battleground, in which an important part of Galician nationalism fought the official normative as a way of symbolizing opposition to the current law (Galicia as an "autonomous community" within the Kingdom of Spain) that was felt to be insufficient. In 2003, an agreement was reached between representatives of this tendency with the RAG and ILG, which led to certain modifications in the selection of variants of this norm being made (the greater relevance of some variants that match Portuguese, like -*bel*, -*aría*, *ao*, *até*, *Galiza*, amongst others, with respect to the more usual variants -*ble*, -*ería*, *ó*, *ata*, *Galicia*). From 2003, therefore, the BNG, CIG and associations within the nationalist spectrum use the official standard, but "maximum Reintegrationism" continued to be used by some cultural (*Asociaçom Galega da Língua, Academia Galega da Língua Portuguesa*) and separatist groups (most importantly, *Nós-Unidade Popular*, formally dissolved in June 2015).

The products that emerge from the linguistic practices of maximum Reintegrationism are not, therefore, texts in Portuguese, since they maintain a form of differentiated Galician (in the spelling, phonetics, grammar, and partly in the lexicon). On the other hand, the texts are conditioned by the low level of knowledge of Portuguese in Galicia, despite the similarities and linguistic proximity. There are certainly intellectual minorities who have a good knowledge of the literary language and erudite knowledge of aspects of Portuguese history and culture, but the language and culture of Portuguese ordinary life is scarcely known. As stated by the Portuguese anthropologist Antonio Medeiros (2003, 335–336): "As referências ao país vizinho feitas no discurso galeguista podem ser caracterizadas como apropriação de aspectos muito selectivos da cultura portuguesa. Surgem-nos como percepções estereotipadas, invariavelmente positivas, mas por regra muito desfasadas do que é familiar e julgado relevante no quotidiano dos nativos do país vizinho" ("References to the neighbouring country made in Galicianist discourse can be characterised as the appropriation of highly selective aspects of Portuguese culture. They appear to be stereotyped perceptions, invariably positive but usually very removed from what is familiar and judged relevant in the daily life of the natives of the neighbouring country"). Thus, the texts produced by these groups very often fail to meet their objective of approximating Galician to Portuguese. In that sense, Medeiros (2003, 330) comments on the "maximum Reintegrationist" texts: "Foi em textos que observavam esta regra – sobretudo aqueles que a aplicavam de forma mais imaginosa, mimando tanto quanto possível a ortografia portuguesa – que encontrei algumas das dificuldades mais intrincadas de compreensão do galego" ("It was in texts that observed this rule – especially those who applied it more imaginatively, mimicking Portuguese orthography as much as possible – that I found some of the most intricate difficulties of understanding Galician"). Even in texts supposedly written in Portuguese, this type of problem often appears, as indicated by Tiago Vidal, a teacher of Portuguese, concerning an article published in the journal *A Trabe de Ouro*, which "pasaría, para a redacción da revista e para moitos lectores, como escrito en portugués. Pero non é certo. [...] O texto [...] está composto cunha extravagante mestura de ingredientes da lingua galega, española e portuguesa" ("it would, for the writing of the journal and for many readers, pass for Portuguese. But it is not true. [...] The text [...] is made up of an extravagant blend of ingredients ranging from Galician and Spanish to Portuguese") (Vidal 1994, 142; see also Venâncio 2019, 193–194, 227–230, 233–235).

In spite of the discourses of approximation to Portugal, there is still little cultural exchange and virtually no social communication with Portugal. Each country´s media shape disconnected communicative spaces, and all Spanish electronic media and press are received in Galicia, in contrast to those from Portugal. Even those that can be received (like radio in the southern part of Galicia) are not followed by the Galician public. The Galician and Portuguese public and political spheres remain, as such, disconnected (Regueira 2016). After more than two decades after the disappearance of the border, following the Schengen Agreement of 1992, the border is still there: "La desaparición completa de los controles fronterizos y de cualquier marca visible de división no ha supuesto la desaparición de la 'frontera mental'" ("The complete disappearance of border controls and any visible mark of division has not meant the disappearance of the 'mental border'") (Kavanagh 2011, 45).

4 Method

The corpus on which this work is based is formed by three recordings that are part of the *Corpus Oral Informatizado da Lingua Galega* (Computerised Oral Corpus of Galician) (CORILGA) (García-Mateo et al. 2014; Seara et al. 2016). They consist of two statements made by Bieito Lobeira, a BNG deputy, in the Galician Parliament in 2010 and 2012, and a speech read at the closing ceremony of the VII Nós-Unidade Popular National Assembly by spokesperson Rebeca Bravo in 2013.

These discourses have been selected because they are some prime examples of the public use of Reintegrationist Galician, which usually only appears in peripheral areas (Herrero 2011, 75). These can be cultural events in certain groups or associations, which tend to not go beyond the scope of the group itself, or certain acts of political protest, precisely where the "non-standard" linguistic form conveys some ideological contents of Lusophile or countercultural nationalism (Herrero 2011, 73–79), and as such is very visible in graffiti (Rodríguez/Ramallo 2015). I try not to use written texts as they do not have a phonetic form and are affected by a corrective factor (the author's own or that of other people). However, Rebeca Bravo's speech consists of the reading of a written text, and this factor must be considered when assessing deviations that may arise. In examples in this text, I have followed the spelling used by the *Associaçom Galega da Língua* (AGAL 1985) and the manual by Maurício Castro (1998), a former leader of Nós-UP.

The deputy Bieito Lobeira is one of those political figures who have declared themselves to be Reintegrationist and who occupy a space of political relevance, although within a party that since 2003 has abandoned Reintegrationist discourse. Therefore, although a Reintegrationism supporter, he finds himself in a situation (delivering a formal speech in Parliament) in which standard Galician is the usual variety, and as a representative of a party that is not officially Reintegrationist. On the other hand, Nós-UP was the most important party that defined itself as a defender or the "maximum" Reintegrationist position until its dissolution in 2015, but was nevertheless marginal in the Galician political scene (at the 2005 Galician elections it won its best election result, a total of 1749 votes, or 0.12%).[2]

The first statement by Lobeira is a response during a debate concerning a popular legislative initiative in defence of the Galician language in the plenary session held on 14.12.2010, with a duration of 6 minutes, and the second is the defence of a non-legislative proposal on Marine SAR (*Servizo Aéreo de Rescate*

---

[2] See article "Nós-Unidade Popular" in Galician Wikipedia: https://gl.wikipedia.org/wiki/N%C3%B3s-Unidade_Popular [last access: 12.07.2020].

'Air Rescue Service'), in the plenary session which took place on 27.06.2012, with a duration of 10 minutes 32 seconds. These are two oral speeches that are available on the Galician Parliament website and also on YouTube.[3] These parliamentary sessions were attended by representatives of public organisations that defend Galician and representatives of seafarers, respectively.

Rebecca Bravo read a speech, lasting 16 minutes and 40 seconds, which contains the main conclusions of the conference as well as the presentation of the political lines to be followed by the formation.[4] The event took place in a hotel in the municipality of Teo, near Santiago de Compostela on 30.11.2013, and members of the group and guests from other parties and organisations are present.

The interventions were transcribed using the ELAN program (Brugman 2004), which allows transcripts to be aligned with the sound file. From there, a description was given of the most significant aspects, taking standard Galician into account, features of Portuguese which are introduced and do not form part of standard Galician, as well as the forms introduced from Spanish as a contact language. It should be noted that the presence of Spanish in Galicia spans for several centuries (Mariño 2000) and many forms (mostly loanwords, but also some grammatical features) historically taken from Spanish are part of vernacular Galician, although they are not admitted in the standard language.

The analysis and interpretation of these oral texts will be undertaken on the basis that the speakers are not monolithic entities who employ linguistic codes that are susceptible to being analysed as objective entities external to themselves (see 1), but who engage in linguistic practises "in which speakers place themselves in the social landscape through stylistic practice" (Eckert 2012, 93–94), therefore focus will be placed, following Blommaert/Rampton (2011, 5), on "the ways in which people take on different linguistic forms as they align and disaffiliate with different groups at different moments and stages".

This approach is consistent with a constructionist view of identity, which understands identity as "the product rather than the source of linguistic and

---

[3] The statements can be found on the Galician Parliament´s website: http://mediateca.parlamentodegalicia.gal/library/items/actos-institucionales-8-lexislatura-pleno-2010-12-14, and http://mediateca.parlamentodegalicia.gal/library/items/pleno-ordinario-2012-06-27 [last access: 12.07.2020]. On YouTube: https://www.youtube.com/watch?v=XgHvulg_fJ0&ab_channel=BloqueNacionalistaGalego(BNG), and https://www.youtube.com/watch?v=APSVFlOO1f4&ab_channel=galicia24horas [last access: 12.07.2020].

[4] The recording of the event can be accessed at https://www.youtube.com/watch?v=xMW24iHOch4&ab_channel=IrmandadeTV and also at http://gzvideos.info/?p=8956&lang=pt [last access: 12.07.2020].

other semiotic practices and therefore is a social and cultural rather than primarily internal psychological phenomenon" (Bucholtz/Hall 2005, 585; see also Joseph 2004; 2010; Benwell/Stokoe 2006; Bucholtz/Hall 2010; Bamberg et al. 2011). The mechanism through which identities are produced is indexicality (Silverstein 2003; Johnstone 2010; Blommaert 2010). Indexicality acts at different levels or orders (Silverstein 2003), therefore a form which can signal geographical or social origin in a primary way, can index ideological values or those of another kind, such as loyalty to a social group, a social or linguistic ideology, etc. in another order (Silverstein 2014, 183). Indexicality acts at different levels simultaneously to produce identity, and this process occurs through linguistic interaction. In the words of Bucholtz/Hall (2005, 607–608):

> "The linguistic resources that indexically produce identity at all these levels are therefore necessarily broad and flexible, including labels, implicatures, stances, styles, and entire languages and varieties. Because these tools are put to use in interaction, the process of identity construction does not reside within the individual but in intersubjective relations of sameness and difference, realness and fakeness, power and disempowerment".

Therefore, in the analysis presented here, the focus falls on features from different levels, such as the pronunciation of some phonetic segments, the employment of grammatical forms, syntactic structures, lexicon, set expressions and other discursive elements, in order to show identity creation practices that emerge in each case. From there, the function that linguistic elements of Portuguese perform will be discussed in relation to the identitarian practices displayed.

5 Linguistic description

5.1 Parliamentary statements by Bieito Lobeira

The current standard of Galician allows a reduced number of morphological variations that are revealing of the users' linguistic ideologies, as were the subject of lengthy discussions and debates before the 2003 orthographical agreement, including the preposition *ata/até* 'until' or the suffix *-ble/-bel* (*amable/amábel* 'kind'). The first forms were proposed in the official normative, and those that were defended by Reintegrationist groups are in second place (cf. Pt *até*, *-vel*).[5] Similarly, the name of the country has been the subject of debate and

---

5 Abbreviations used: fem. = feminine; masc. = masculine; pl. = plural; Pt = Portuguese; Sp = Spanish; StGal = Standard Galician.

continues to have a dual use: *Galicia* (the official name)/*Galiza* (the medieval form recovered in the 20th century in written uses and used mostly by nationalist groups, cf. Pt *Galiza*). The deputy Lobeira always use the forms closest to Portuguese: *até* 'until', *Galiza*, *favorábel* 'favourable', *posíbel* 'possible', *estabelecer* (< *estábel*) 'establish', etc.

On the other hand, he also uses the pronoun *vosté* (StGal *vostede*, Pt *você* 'you [formal]'), which was a form proposed by the "minimum Reintegrationist" normative sponsored by the BNG before 2003. It uses lexical forms that diverge from standard Galician and coincide with Portuguese: *eleitoral* (StGal *electoral*), *aceitación* (StGal *aceptación* 'acceptance'), *gostar* (*gustar* 'like'), *parlamentar* (*parlamentario* 'paliamentary'), *sofrer* (*sufrir* 'suffer'), *inteiras* (*enteiras* 'whole'), *nen... nen...* (*nin... nin...* 'neither... nor'), *cúmplice* (*cómplice*), etc.

In the statement referring to the language (Stat-1), with the presence of a public from cultural associations and teachers, the use of a greater amount of marked forms is registered, especially in grammatical forms such as the future subjunctive (*cando dos debates de lingua se tratar*) and inflected infinitives: *falaren*, *aproveitárense*, etc. Note that these forms are amongst those that some Galician linguists regard as indexes of a "quality" language: "A calidade do galego recoñécese en trazos concretos: o uso do futuro de subxuntivo, do infinitivo flexionado, das interpolacións pronominais entre outros aspectos que non detallarei agora" ("The quality of Galician is recognised in specific traits: the use of the future subjunctive, inflected infinitive, pronominal interpolations amongst other aspects which I will not detail at this point") (Moure 2011, 108; see also Freixeiro 2009). The future subjunctive is not used in vernacular Galician and has a very limited use in the written language; the inflected infinitive is losing ground in spoken Galician, although it is employed in the contexts of formal speeches and written language. Conversely, both tenses are frequently used in Portuguese.

Lexical Lusisms also appear in this statement, such as *suceso* (StGal *éxito*), significantly in a self-correction: "é a proba empírica do éxito... do suceso, da política lingüística do Partido Popular" ("This is the empirical proof of the success (StGal)... success (Pt) of the language policy of the Partido Popular"). Another lexical Lusism is *crianzas* 'children', alongside the corresponding Galician term: "prohiben que até crianzas, nenos e nenas de tres anos, poidan aprender a ler e escribir no idioma propio deste país" ("they prohibit even children (Pt), three-year old children (StGal), from learning to read and write in the language of this country"). Furthermore, at this point he ends the speech with an *Obrigado*, an expression of gratitude taken from Portuguese, although both at the beginning and the end he uses the standard Galician form, *grazas*: *grazas, señora presidenta*; *Obrigado. Moitas grazas* ('Thank you (StGal), Madame President';

'Thank you (Pt). Thank you (StGal) very much.'). These traits are not found in statements concerning Marine SAR (Stat–2).

However, the use of forms taken from Spanish, as a contact language in Galicia, is also significant: there are lexical forms, syntactic structures, and above all different features of the phonological and phonetic system, which I shall discuss below.

Some lexical Castilianisms appear, such as *asignatura* 'subject' (StGal *materia*, Pt *matéria*) (Stat 1), *tasas* 'fees' (StGal and Pt *taxas*) (Stat–2), *cortos* 'short' (StGal and Pt *curtos*) (Stat–2), *acomplexados* 'complexed', pronounced with [ʃ] (StGal and Pt [ks]) (Stat–1). There are also some morphological Castilianisms, such as *moito desorde* 'a lot of disorder' (masc.; StGal *moita desorde*, Pt *muita desordem*, fem.) (Stat–2), and expressions such as *con arreglo a* 'in accordance with' (StGal *consonte, de conformidade con*; Pt *consoante, de conformidade com*) (Stat–2). In Stat–2, syntactic structures with reflexives that are typical of Spanish also appear: *quedámonos cortos* 'we have fallen short' (StGal *quedamos curtos*) or *pensarse: vai haber moita xente no mar [...] que se vai pensar dúas veces a posibilidade de chamar ou non ao servizo de salvamento* ('there are going to be a lot of people who work at sea [...] who are going to think twice about calling the rescue services or not') (StGal *que vai pensar*) (Stat–2). Most of these lexical and grammatical Castilianisms are common in spoken vernacular Galician, but are not part of the standard language (cf. Schulte in this volume for a similar observation in vernacular Valencian Catalan).

The most striking aspect of these speeches is the use of a phonological system that is very close to the Spanish one, and distant from Galician and Portuguese. Particularly notable is the presence of a system of five stressed vowels, coinciding with Spanish, given that there is no distinction between mid-low and mid-high vowels: *prop[o]n a instauraci[o]n* (StGal [ɔ]/[o]) 'proposes the installing', *t[e]n que l[e]r* ([ɛ]/[e]) 's/he has to read', and the same happens in the words in which a mid-low vowel is expected but which are pronounced with a mid-high vowel: *fix̱era* 'had made', *mesmo* 'same', *cóbrase* (6 times) 'is charged', *Bloque* (Bloc, the name of his party), *logo* 'then', *trintesete* 'thirty-seven', *leva* 'carries', *noso* 'our', *cento* 'hundred', *a pé* 'on foot', etc. In fact, an acoustic analysis[6] of all the stressed vowels of these statements reveals a triangle of 5 vowels, with slight differentiation between the back mid-vowels, as shown in Figure 1 (cf. for a similar convergence pattern in phonetics of Colloquial Valencia due to contact with Spanish, see Schulte in this volume):

---

[6] The acoustic analyses were carried out with Praat (Boersma/Weenink 2016).

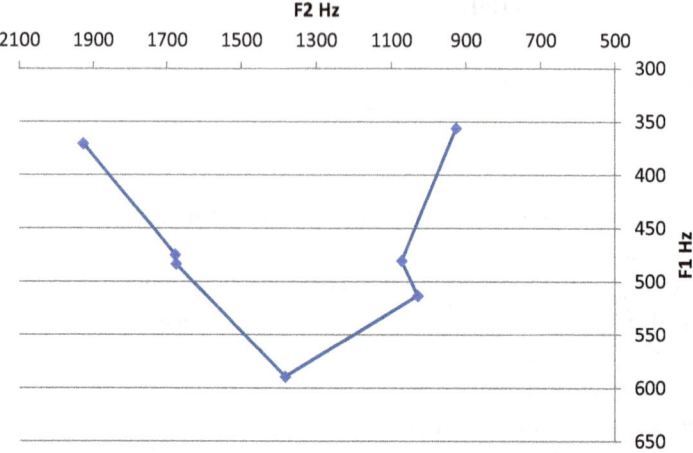

Figure 1: Triangle of Lobeira's stressed vowels in the two parliamentary statements (the vowels from left to right, following the line [i, e, ɛ, a, ɔ, o, u]).

Moreover, the word-final unstressed vowels are closest auditorily to their counterparts in Spanish and not Galician, although vernacular Galician and spoken Portuguese present striking similarities in this respect, as demonstrated by Regueira (2007), who presents and compares acoustic results for stressed and unstressed word-final vowels of recordings of two sets of speakers of vernacular Galician and Northern Portuguese (Braga).

Furthermore, as concerns the consonant system, sufficient differentiation between the apical [s̺] and postalveolar [ʃ] sibilants does not manifest itself, although these sibilants are quite differentiated in Galician, except in certain marginal dialects and the speech of some speakers whose first language is Spanish (Regueira/Ginzo 2019). Lobeira, instead, presents numerous cases in which a sibilant that is very close to the apico-alveolar is detected where one would expect a lamino-postalveolar: *xa* 'already', *inxenuos* 'ingenuous', *lexislatura* 'legislature', *xestionouse* 'was organised', *fixera* 'had done', *Xunta* (the Galician government), *demagoxia* 'demagogy', *axuda* 'help', *sexa* 'may be', *xeral* 'general', *baixo* 'beneath', *axilidade* 'agility', etc.

5.2 Speech read by Rebeca Bravo at the Nós-UP VII National Assembly

In the variety used by advocates of maximum Reintegrationist, an orthographic, morphologic, syntactic and lexical approximation to Portuguese is sought, since they argue that Galician and Portuguese are the same language: Galician-Portuguese. However, a full identification is not sought, but the existence of many differential traces, at all levels, as can be seen, for example, in *Manual de iniciaçom à língua galega* ('Beginner's Manual for Galician'), by Mauricio Castro Lopez (1998), who at the time was a member of Nós-UP and also the *Fundaçom Artabria*, as was Rebeca Bravo. In this manual, "Galician" is used to refer to the variety of Galician-Portuguese spoken in Galicia. As usual in this type of manual, the focus falls on the written language, and it is not a matter of the phonetics or phonology of the language, although from the few references made to pronunciation (when discussing orthographical representations, for example), it is deduced that it would be the phonetics and phonology of standard Galician.

Given that the present description is of an oral text, and there thus no written representation is, I employ the AGAL system of spelling to transcribe the speech (as stated earlier in 3), although spelling will not be the focus of this analysis. Therefore, the presence of features taken from Portuguese is limited to grammatical and lexical items. In this language model, the morphology generally maintains the characteristics of Galician while introducing some elements taken from Portuguese, especially in the verbal inflections, where forms such as *conduz* 's/he drives' (StGal *conduce*) and *há* 'there is' (StGal *hai*) can be found. However, it generally maintains Galician conjugation: *fago* 'I do' (Pt *faço*), *atoparedes* 'you (pl.) will found' (Pt *atopareis*), etc.

In the nominal morphology, the most visible element is that of the endings *-çom, -som* (according to the written representation proposed by AGAL 1983 or Castro 1998), where StGal presents *-ción* and Pt *-ção*. Despite this partial assimilation to the Portuguese spelling, it is not accompanied by the pronunciation, as the Galician phonological system is maintained: ['θoŋ], cf. StGal ['θjoŋ], Pt ['sẽw̃]. And this is the pronunciation found in Bravo's speech: *configuraçom* 'configuration', *consolidaçom* 'consolidation', *refundaçom* 'refoundation', *naçom* 'nation', amongst others. In the same way, *fusom* 'fusion', *cohesom* 'cohesion' [-'şoŋ], cf. StGal [-'şjoŋ], Pt [-'zẽw̃]. However, there are also cases of *-ción, -sión*: *satisfacción* 'satisfaction', *expulsión* 'expulsion'.

In the same way as Lobeira, whose discourse was analysed previously (see 4.1), the current speaker also uses the inflected infinitive: *crescermos* 'to grow (we)', *sermos* 'to be (we)'; however, it also appears in contexts where it is considered ungrammatical both in Galician and Portuguese: *por iso queremos abrirmos de par en par as portas da unidade popular* ('this is why we wish to open ajar the doors of popular unity').

Variants such as *depois* 'after' (StGal *despois*), *naquele* 'in that' (StGal *naquel*), *sim* 'yes' (StGal *si*), *quase* 'almost' (StGal *case*) are taken from standard

Portuguese, and so are the non-contracted sequence of preposition *com* + article (in contrast with the contracted form in Galician, *co/coa*): *com a* [koŋ a] *patria* 'with the country', *com a súa práctica* 'with his/her practical'.

Lexical loans are common: *pena* 'pen' (StGal *pluma*), *efeitos* 'effets' (StGal *efectos*), *eleitoral* 'electoral' (StGal *electoral*), *carregados* 'loaded' (StGal *cargados*), *parlamentar* 'parliamentary' (StGal *parlamentaria*), *autóctone* 'autochthonous' (StGal *autóctono*), *rumo* 'course' (StGal *rumbo*), *greves* 'strikes' (StGal *folgas*), *protestos* 'protests' (StGal *protestas*), *maciça* 'massive' (StGal *masiva*), *factos* 'facts' (StGal *feitos*), *polícia* 'police' (StGal *policía*), *democracía* 'democracy' (StGal *democracia*), *pessoal* 'personal' (StGal *persoal*), *embora* 'however' (StGal *aínda que*). However, in some cases hybrid forms appear: *leiçom* 'lesson' (StGal *lección*, Pt *lição*), *respeituoso* 'respectful' (StGal *respectuoso*, Pt *respeitoso*), *útis* 'useful (pl.)' (StGal *útiles*, Pt *úteis*).

Despite being read from a written text, occasional recourse to the standard forms is observed, such as when the speaker says: *satisfacción per | pessoal* 'personal satisfaction', in which the standard from *satisfacción* is read and corrects itself as *persoal*. Also, the phrase *face a* is used in the sense of the Galician *cara a* 'towards': *avançando face ao precipício a que nos conduz o capitalismo espanhol* ('Approaching the precipice to which the Spanish capitalism is driving us'). Some words are pronounced following Spanish and not standard Galician or Portuguese: *complexos* 'complexes', *complexa* 'complex', are pronounced with [ʃ] and [s̩] respectively (adapting the Spanish words *complejos*, *compleja*, pronounced with [x], after other equivalences between Sp [x] = Gal [ʃ], such as Sp *jamón* = Gal *xamón* 'ham'), as opposed to the StGal and Pt [ks]); *seductora* (pronounced as [θt]) 'seductive' (StGal and Pt *sedutora*), *estructurais* [kt] 'structural' (StGal and Pt *estruturais*), *paradigma* [xm] 'paradigm' (StGal and Pt [gm]), or *reforzarla* 'reinforce it' (StGal *refozala*, Pt *reforça-la*).

In addition to Lusisms, there is a remarkable emergence of a number of lexical Castilianisms, such as *pertrechos* 'gear', *oleage* 'swell', *dietas* 'allowances', *plasmar* 'to project', *enemigo* 'enemy', *corsé* 'corset' (*abandonar o corsé español* 'abandon the Spanish corset'), *timoratismos* 'spineless acts', *diferencia* 'difference' (together with *diferença*). Some other words that are shared by Spanish and Portuguese are used in the figurative senses pertaining to Spanish public discourse. In some cases, hybrid forms based on Spanish appear: *cansanço* 'fatigue' (Sp *cansancio*, StGal *cansazo*, Pt *cansaço*), or *curtoplacismos electorais* 'electoral short-termism', on the basis of the Sp *cortoplacismo* (note also *electorais*, as compared with *eleitoral* in other places). It also employs the periphrasis *vamos a rematar* 'we are going to finish', regarded as a Castilianism in vernacular Galician (StGal *imos rematar*, Pt *vamos rematar*).

This abundance of above all lexical elements taken from Portuguese in the written text contrasts sharply with the phonology employed and the phonetics with which the speech is pronounced: indeed, the phonetics of the Nós-UP spokesperson is much closer to that of Spanish than to standard Galician, and therefore even further from the Portuguese system. As with Bieito Lobeira, the vowel system comprises five phonemes, as shown in Figure 2, which represents the vowel triangle resulting from the acoustic analysis of stressed vowels of this read text:

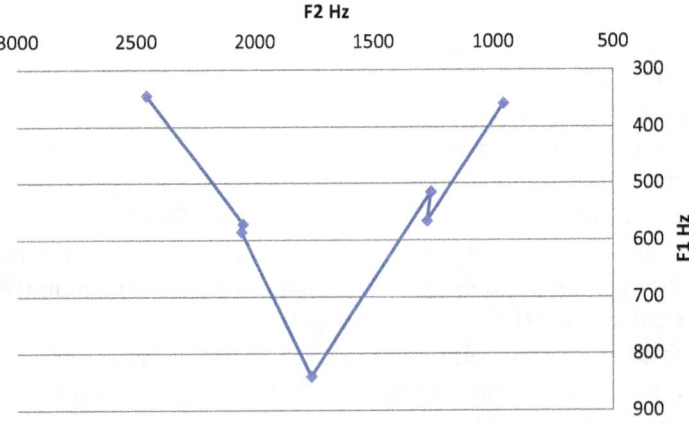

Figure 2: Triangle of Bravo's stressed vowels in the reading of his speech (the vowels from left to right, following the line [i, e, ɛ, a, ɔ, o, u]).

There is no opposition or appreciable difference, therefore, between the realisation of the mid-low and mid-high vowels: *tamén sempre tivemos e temos* [ẹ ẹ ẹ ẹ] (cf. StGal [ɛ ɛ ɛ e]) ('also we always had and have had'), and throughout the speech. The contractions necessary for understanding the text are not formed either: *forza expulsión* [ɐ] is heard, regarding *forza a expulsión* [aː] ('it forces the expulsion'). Word-final vowels occasionally present pronunciations that are more similar to Spanish than Galician: *máis fortes* [e] (for [ɪ]) 'stronger'. Occasionally the diphthong [ow] appears reduced to [o], as in Spanish or certain varieties of Portuguese: *entregó* (for *entregou*) 's/he submitted', *Pachi Vázquez o Besteiro* (for *ou* 'or').

With respect to the consonant system, Bravoalso deviates from Galician at the more difficult points for speakers who come from the phonological system of Spanish: the opposition between the sibilants [s̺] and [ʃ] and the pronunciation of the velar nasal [ŋ]. In sibilants, cases in which a fricative apico-alveolar [s̺] is found, sometimes more backed (apico-postalveolar [s̺]), instead of the lamino-postalveolar [ʃ], are frequent: *tra[ʂ]ecto* 'journey', *[ʂ]enuinamente* 'genuinely', *[ʂ] uventude* 'youth' etc. There is no contrast in fricatives in words like *se̠ja* [ʂ s̠] (StGal [s̠ ʃ]) 'to be (subj.)', or *men̠sage* [ʂ s̠] (StGal [s̠ ʃ]) 'message'.

Regarding the velar nasal [ŋ], it is replaced by an alveolar nasal [n] in most cases where it appears systematically in Galician. Such is the case with the indefinite article: *u[n]a casualidade* 'a coincidence', *u[n]a alternativa* 'an alternative', *u[n]a vida de suor* 'a life of toil', *nu[n]a organizaçom* 'in an organisation', etc. (StGal [ŋ] in all cases). On some occasions, she places a velar at the end of a word before a vowel (*u[ŋ] apelo* 'an appeal', for example), but mostly she pronounces an alveolar: *Unio[n] Europeia* (2 cases) 'European Union', *se[n] enganos* 'without deceit', *e[n] España* 'in Spain', *so[n] organizaçons* 'they are organisations', etc. (StGal [ŋ] in all cases). This includes at the end of words before a pause: *nova tripulaço[n]* (StGal [ŋ]).

Finally, there are also other cases of consonants from Spanish and not Galician, such as *apo[ɟ]o* 'support', *ma[j]oria* 'majority' (StGal and Pt [j]), or as a result of the delateralisation of [ʎ], one of the points where Galician separates from Portuguese and coincides with Spanish, or which in Galician can present different phonetic variants (Regueira 2008), but not as open as we find in this speaker: *ve[j]as* (StGal [ɟ] or [ʎ], Pt [ʎ]) 'old (fem. pl.)'.

All these features, together with other issues of prosody, mean that this speech causes a very similar aural impression to that of Spanish and quite distant from Galician phonetics, and even more so from Portuguese phonetics in any of its varieties.

6 Discussion

In the current sociolinguistic situation in Galicia, Spanish is the language associated with cities, prestigious professions and social success, as shown in studies on linguistic attitudes and perceptions:

> "Os que se expresan nas variedades con acento galego percíbense como un grupo social pouco dotado para o éxito social, mentres que os que o fan en lingua galega cunha fonética similar á do castelán son caracterizados como un grupo innovador e socialmente competente, se ben espertan escasos sentimentos de empatía social na mocidade" (González 2003, 185).

> ('Those that speak in varieties with a Galician accent are perceived as a social group poorly equipped for social success, while those who do so in Galician with phonetics similar to Spanish are characterised as an innovative and socially competent group, although they would have awoken scarce feelings of social empathy among young people').

Therefore, the characteristic features of the "Spanish accent" act as indexical features (first-order indexicality, in the sense of Silverstein 2003) of urban social origin. If we take into account that the Spanish of Galicia presents many of the features of Galician phonetics (such as the velar nasal, mid-open and -closed vowels), especially in classes that have greater contact with Galician (the working class, cf. Faginas 1998), the phonetic characteristics presented by these speakers would indicate their origin from non-lower classes. This is most notable in the case of Bravo, with characteristics that reveal little contact with Galician-speaking social groups (at least with L1 Galician).

Furthermore, the level of the language used, in keeping with parliamentary and political discourse, abundant in learned words and foreign loans (what Agha 2003 and Silverstein 2003 call *enregisterment*), indexes professional competence, while users are aware of the linguistic and discursive practices of this register. These speakers place themselves, therefore, in a certain *order of discourse*, in the terms of Foucault (1996 [1971]) (see also Blommaert 2005; 2010). This fact is especially notable in the statements by Lobeira, who employs the resources of parliamentary discourse (Galician and Spanish). However, Galician political discourse is inscribed within the scope of political Spanish discourse (Regueira 2016), and often shows a great dependence upon it, whilst being generally disconnected from political discourse in Portuguese.

Furthermore, the inclusion of unusual items in Galician political discourse (mainly loans from Portuguese), as well as marked forms (inflected infinitives, the future subjunctive, amongst others), expresses a concern about the linguistic shape of their speeches. In the case of Lobeira, he approaches what Freixeiro (2009) calls a *língua de calidade* ('quality language'), a linguistic ideology which advocates a "learned" Galician that is "liberado de interferencias espurias" ('freed from spurious interferences') and "máis auténtico" ('more authentic') (Freixeiro 2009, 7), which in certain respects approaches Portuguese ("cada vez máis galego-portugués e menos galego-castelán" ("increasingly more Galician-Portuguese and less Galician-Spanish") (Freixeiro 2009, 7), on the basis of the rejection of popular language, "distorted" by contact with Spanish. Lobeira clearly expresses that very linguistic ideology (a kind of "ideology of the standard", Milroy/Milroy 1993) in his speech on the initiative concerning Galician (Stat-1), in which many more marked items, more Lusisms and less Castilianisms appear, whereas in his speech on Marine SAR, on the contrary, forms of contact with the Spanish are much more frequent.

Regarding the use of features taken from the Portuguese, we have a sample of what Medeiros (2003, 335) denominates the "apropriação de aspectos muito selectivos da cultura portuguesa" ("appropriation of highly-selective aspects of Portuguese culture"). In Bravo's speech, they are much more abundant and used more systematically. This said, we must not forget that she reads out a speech written in the "maximum Reintegrationist" standard. From the point of view taken in this paper, I argue that the use of Portuguese plays a role in the construction of social and ideological identities: on the one hand, of linguistic ideologies (Reintegrationist, approaching Portuguese), on the other, of ideological identities that are linked to nationalism. Although, as Herrero states (2011, 77), "seria um erro fazer uma inferência rígida que identifique o indepententismo com o reintegracionismo político" ("it would be a mistake to make a rigid inference that identifies the pro-Galician independence movement with the political Reintegrationist position"), the use of a linguistic form that symbolically (in written and lexical aspects, especially) is much closer to Portuguese symbolises a rejection not only of (i) Spanish (the language and the political structure of the Spanish state), but also of (ii) "official Galician" of the Galician autonomous institutions, and especially the Galicianists and nationalist groups who accept, to a greater or lesser extent, the game of political institutions. That way, "a maior parte dos usos do galego lusista apresentam uma ideologização evidente de orientação linguística e cultural, inserida no nacionalismo galego lusófilo" ("the majority of uses of Lusist Galician present an evident ideologisation that is linguistic and cultural in nature, inserted into Lusophile Galician nationalism") (Herrero 2011, 75), in such a way that it represents in itself a political and linguistic ideology (Cordal 2009).

In this sense, Nós-UP lies symbolically within a different political sphere than that occupied by the BNG, which defended "minimal Reintegrationism" and eventually accepted the official normative. In addition, the BNG is a party present in the institutions: it formed part of the Galician government during 2005–2009 and runs various city councils. The linguistic and ideological uses made by Reintegrationists firmly cohere with what Bucholtz/Hall (2007, 383–385), using Bourdieu's (1979) term, call tactics of *distinction*, "the mechanism whereby a salient difference is produced". Through this tactic, they emphasise the difference between their openly separatist position and less radical nationalist groups like the BNG itself, and also with respect to other non-nationalist groups.

Galician occupies a series of public spheres (in political and cultural activity, etc., see Regueira 2016), for which Reintegrationism is seen as occupying marginal positions (Herrero 2011). In her criticism of the theory of the public sphere of Habermas (1962), Nancy Fraser (1990, 67) argues that "they are parallel discursive arenas where members of subordinated social groups invent and circulate counter discourses, which in turn permit them to formulate oppositional interpretations of their identities, interests, and needs", and denominates these alternative spheres as "subaltern counter publics". Given that cultural groups and Reintegrationist politicians define themselves as an alternative to language ideologies and policies dominant in society overall, and to those that are dominant in the ideological nationalist field, it can be argued that a counter political and public sphere is being constructed that very clearly demarcates borders with dominant ideologies through visible linguistic labels (and hence all the issues related to writing stand out above all others) (cf. Venâncio 2019, 221). Alternative orthography functions as a symbol that demarcates this public counter sphere.

In this sense, the use of features from a linguistic repertoire that builds an ideological, pro-independence, radical, advanced and modern identity, becomes compatible with the use of markers of urban, modern and non-lower class in social origin. Given that this kind of language ideologies has its best expression in university and cultural fields (Herrero 2011), the use of a Reintegrationist standard and the use of a phonetic form that largely corresponds to Spanish are not incompatible, but they are reinforced as they are sharply distinct from the speech of the lower and rural classes, which use a Galician variant that is closer to Portuguese phonetically, but which lexically displays many Spanish features.

The linguistic behaviour and the identity moves of the two speakers analysed here are not per se emblematic of all reintegrationists nor do we conclude that they are representative of their ideological or linguistic groups, although similar situations are quite frequent in the public space. Since identity is understood here as a product of linguistic interaction, it is contextually mediated, and significant differences have been found not only between both speakers, but even between the two speeches of Lobeira (see 4.1). The main objective of this paper is thus to show how these speakers use some Portuguese linguistic features, along with others of Spanish origin, to create identity in different and complex ways.

7 Conclusion

Portuguese occupies an important place in the recovery process of Galician as a written language and as a language of culture, and also in recent decades in the process of standardisation of the language. If, during the 19th century and most of the 20th century, it was primarily a resource employed to confer prestige upon Galicia, in the last 40 years the impact has been much greater, both from the linguistic and sociolinguistic point of view. "Reintegrationist" proposals seeking to "reinstate" Galician in its "natural" place (that is, like another variety of Portuguese) have led to a certain confluence or convergence with Portuguese occurring in the standard language, through the selection of variants from Portuguese shared by Galician and also of features taken from standard European Portuguese, albeit in a minority and marginal manner.

However, the approach to Portuguese by these groups is relatively shallow and is generally limited to a few written morphological and lexical features. Hence, it is a language variety used in the internal communication of different minority groups in the political and cultural sphere, with little impact on most of society, although with a certain social and public visibility in the areas in which these groups operate, particularly in literary culture and in political nationalism.

This paper has analysed three speeches by two Galician nationalist politicians whose ideology is "Reintegrationist". The first two were given by the deputy of the Galician Parliament, Bieito Lobeira, a leading member of the BNG (a group that does not currently defend Reintegrationism) and the third by Rebecca Bravo, spokesperson for the pro-independence party, Nós-UP (a party that defends "maximum" Reintegrationism) at the closing of the assembly where she was elected to her position. In her speech, there are elements from both Portuguese and Spanish. However, it should not be forgotten she was reading a written version of her discourse, while the statements by Bieito Lobeira were oral. They also take place in two very different contexts: in the Galician Parliament, before members of the plenary and with an audience in attendance that is related to initiatives that the Nationalist deputy is defending (one regarding Galician and another Marine SAR), whilst Bravo speaks for an audience made up by fellow party colleagues and by guests from affiliate organisations.

Using interactional sociolinguistics, and more specifically the theory of identity construction in linguistic interaction, with the concept of indexicality, I have shown how the use of features from Portuguese allows identities to be constructed, both as regards political ideology (nationalism) as well as linguistic ideology (Reintegrationism, purism). These indexical features are, moreover, compatible with characteristics from standard Galician and even with material taken from Spanish, in the lexicon and especially in the phonology and phonetic systems. Given that Spanish and Galician with Spanish phonetics have greater prestige in society (González 2003), in terms of indexes from an urban middle-class background, I argue that the use of phonetic elements that clearly coincide with Spanish acts as a social identity feature (not rurality nor lower class), while the use of features from Portuguese contributes to the creation of an ideological identity and also to the strengthening of social, urban and class identity, concretely in being fundamentally an urban ideology present mostly in university environments.

It therefore becomes clear that study of language contact should appropriately address the agency of speakers, their performance in specific speech acts in a specific context and with specific interlocutors. From the point of view that languages are not something external to the speakers and that speakers build their identities through linguistic and semiotic acts, the analysis of speakers' performance can serve to elucidate the role that different linguistic elements play in a particular discourse, in a specific speech act. In order to realise these objectives, speakers avail of different linguistic repertoires to which they have access (Blommaert 2010). The presence of Portuguese in certain Galician social and political circles has increased the wealth of these repertoires in such a way that they are available for the symbolisation of political and ideological differences, for the construction of new identities and the creation of *subaltern counter publics*.

8 References

AGAL 1983 = Associaçom Galega da Língua, *Estudo crítico das normas ortográficas e morfolóxicas do idioma galego (ILG-RAG 1982)*, s.l., AGAL, 1983.
AGAL 1985 = Associaçom Galega da Língua, *Prontuário ortográfico galego*, s.l., AGAL, 1985.
Agha, Asif, *The social life of cultural value*, Language & Communication 23 (2003), 271–273.
Alonso Pintos, Serafín, *O proceso de codificación do galego moderno (1950–1980)*, A Coruña, Fundación Pedro Barrié de la Maza, 2006.
Bamberg, Michael/De Fina, Anna/Schiffrin, Deborah, *Discourse and identity construction*, in: Schwartz, Seth J./Luyckx, Koen/Vignoles, Vivian L. (edd.), *Handbook of identity theory and research*, Berlin/New York, Springer, 2011, 177–199.
Barbosa, J. Morais, *Notas sobre a pronúncia portuguesa nos últimos cem anos*, Biblos 64 (1988), 329–382.
Benwell, Bethan/Stokoe, Elizabeth, *Discourse and identity*, Edinburgh, Edinburgh University Press, 2006.
Blommaert, Jan, *Discourse. A critical introduction*, Cambridge, Cambridge University Press, 2005.
Blommaert, Jan, *The sociolinguistics of globalization*, Cambridge, Cambridge University Press, 2010.
Blommaert, Jan/Rampton, Ben, *Language and superdiversity*, Diversities 13:2 (2011), 1–20.
Boersma, Paul/Weenink, David , *Praat. Doing phonetics by computer*, 2016, http://www.fon.hum.uva.nl/praat/ [last access: 15.07.2017].
Bourdieu, Pierre, *La distinction. Critique du jugement social*, Paris, Minuit, 1979.
Brugman, Hennie/Russel, Albert, *Annotating multimedia/multi-modal resources with ELAN*, in: Lino, Maria Teresa/Xavier, Maria Francisca/Ferreira, Fátima/Costa, Rute/Silva, Raquel (edd.), *Proceedings of LREC 2004, Fourth International Conference on Language Resources and Evaluation*, Lisbon, LREC, 2004, 2065–2068. Computer program downloadable at the site of Max Planck Institute for Psycholinguistics, The Language Archive, Nijmegen, The Netherlands http://tla.mpi.nl/tools/tla-tools/elan/ [last access: 02.12.2016].

Bucholtz, Mary/Hall, Kira, *Identity and interaction. A sociocultural linguistic approach*, Discourse Studies 7 (2005), 585–614.

Bucholtz, Mary/Hall, Kira, *Language and identity*, in: Duranti, Alessandro (ed.), *A companion to linguistic anthropology*, Oxford, Blackwell, 2007, 369–394.

Bucholtz, Mary/Hall, Kira, *Locating identity in language*, in: Llamas, Carmen/Watt, Dominic (edd.), *Languages and identities*, Edinburgh, Edinburgh University Press, 2010, 18–28.

Carvalho, Joaquim Brandão de, *Nasalité et structure syllabique en Portugais et en Galicien, approche non linéaire et panchronique d'un problème phonologique*, Verba 15 (1988), 237–263.

Castro Lôpez, Maurício, *Manual de iniciaçom à língua galega. Sociolingüística, morfosintaxe, ortografia e léxico*, Ferrol, Fundaçom Artábria, 1998.

Cintra, Luís F. Lindley, *Nova proposta de classificação dos dialectos galego-portugueses*, Boletim de Filologia 22 (1964–1971), 81–116.

Cintra, Luís F. Lindley, *Os inquérigos realizados em Portugal para o "Atlas Linguístico da Península Ibérica" e o seu interesse para a dialectologia brasileira*, in: *Estudos de dialectologia portuguesa*, Lisboa, Sá da Costa, 1983, 21–54 [Prev. publ. in *Anais do Primeiro Congresso Brasileiro de Língua Falada no Teatro (1956)*, Rio de Janeiro, 1958].

Cordal Fustes, Xabier, *A ideoloxía reintegracionista*, A Trabe de Ouro 79 (2009), 27–47.

Cunqueiro, Álvaro, *A recuperación literaria do galego*, El Faro de Vigo, 9.09.1973.

Dubert García, Francisco/Galves, Charlotte, *Galician and Portuguese*, in: Ledgeway, Adam/Maiden, Martin (edd.), *The Oxford guide to the Romance languages*, Oxford, Oxford University Press, 2016, 411–446.

Eckert, Penelope, *Three waves of variation study. The emergence of meaning in the study of sociolinguistic variation*, Annual Review of Anthropology 41 (2012), 87–100.

Eckert, Penelope, *Meaning and linguistic variation. The third wave in sociolinguistics*, Cambridge, Cambrige University Press, 2018.

Faginas Souto, Sandra, *As realizacións do /e/ no castelán da Coruña*, Cadernos de Lingua 17 (1998), 83–103.

Fernández Salgado, Benigno/Monteagudo Romero, Henrique, *Do galego literario ó galego común. O proceso de estandarización na época contemporánea*, in: Monteagudo, Henrique (ed.), *Estudios de sociolingüística galega. Sobre a norma do galego culto*, Vigo, Galaxia, 1995, 99–176.

Foucault, Michel, *A ordem do discurso*, transl. Fraga de Almeida Sampaio, Laura, São Paulo, Loyola, 1996 [*L'ordre du discours*, Paris, Gallimard, 1971].

Fraser, Nancy, *Rethinking the public sphere. A contribution to the critique of actually existing democracy*, Social Text 25–26 (1990), 56–80.

Freixeiro Mato, Xosé Ramón, *Lingua de calidade*, Vigo, Xerais, 2009.

García-Mateo, Carmen/Cardenal, Antonio/Xosé, Luis/Luís Regueria, Xosé/Fernández Rei, Elisa/Martínez Maqueira, Marta/Seara, Roberto/Varela Fernández, Rocío/Basanta, Noemí, *CORILGA. A Galician multilevel annotated speech corpus for linguistic analysis*, in: *Proceedings of LREC 2014, 9th Language Resources and Evaluation Conference (Reykjavik, 26–31 mayo 2014)*, http://www.lrec-conf.org/proceedings/lrec2014/pdf/739_Paper.pdf [last access: 12.07.2020].

González, Manuel (ed.), *O galego segundo a mocidade*, A Coruña, RAG, 2003.

González González, Manuel/Juncal, Luis Antonio/Folgar, Esteban, *El subsistema "arcaico" de las fricativas dentoalveolares del gallego. Una reliquia en vías de extinción*, in: Díaz

García, Jesús (ed.), *Actas del II Congreso de Fonética Experimental (Sevilla, 2001)*, Sevilla, Universidad de Sevilla, 2002, 215–219.

González Seoane, Ernesto X., *O debate sobre a independencia do galego na última década do século XIX*, in: Lorenzo, Ramón/ Álvarez Blanco, Rosario (edd.), *Homenaxe á profesora Pilar Vázquez Cuesta*, Santiago de Compostela, Universidade de Santiago de Compostela, 1996, 121–131.

Habermas, Jürgen, *Strukturwandel der Öffentlichkeit. Untersuchungen zu einer Kategorie der bürgerlichen Gesellschaft*, Darmstadt/Neuwied, Luchterhand, [14]1983, [1]1962.

Hermida, Carme, *Galego e português durante o século XIX (1840–1891)*, in: Lorenzo, Ramón/ Álvarez, Rosario (edd.), *Homenaxe á profesora Pilar Vázquez Cuesta*, Santiago de Compostela, Universidade de Santiago de Compostela, 1996, 107–119.

Herrero Valeiro, Mário J., *Guerra de grafias e conflito de elites na Galiza contemporânea*, s. l., Através, 2011.

Johnstone, Barbara, *Locating language in identity*, in: Llamas, Carmen/Watt, Dominic (edd.), *Languages and identities*, Edinburgh, Edinburgh University Press, 2010, 29–36.

Joseph, John E., *Language and identity, national, ethnic, religious*, Houndmills/New York, Palgrave Macmillan, 2004.

Joseph, John E., *Identity*, in: Llamas, Carmen/Watt, Dominic (edd.), *Languages and identities*, Edinburgh, Edinburgh University Press, 2010, 9–17.

Kabatek, Johannes, *Die Sprecher als Linguisten. Interferenz- und Sprachwandelphänomene dargestellt am Galicischen der Gegenwart*, Tübingen, Niemeyer, 1996.

Kavanagh, William, *Identidades en la frontera luso-española. Permanencias y transformaciones después de Schengen*, Geopolítica(s) 2:1 (2011), 23–50.

Lapa, Manuel Rodrigues, *A recuperação literária do galego*, Grial 41 (1973), 278–287.

Lass, Roger, *On explaining language change*, Cambridge, Cambridge University Press, 1980.

Le Page, Robert B./Tabouret-Keller, Andrée, *Acts of identity. Creole-based approaches to language and ethnicity*, Cambridge, Cambridge University Press, 1985.

Mariño Paz, Ramón, *Historia de la lengua gallega*, München, Lincom, 2000.

Martínez-Gil, Fernando, *Galician mid-vowel reduction. A stratal optimality theory account*, in: Gibson, Mark/Gil, Juana (edd.), *Romance phonetics and phonology*, Oxford, Oxford University Press, 2019, 299–350.

Martins, Ana Maria/Saramago, João, *As sibilantes em português. Um estudo de geografia linguística e de fonética experimental*, in: Lorenzo, Ramón (ed.), *Actas do XIX Congreso Internacional de Lingüística e Filoloxía Románicas (Santiago de Compostela, 1989)*, vol. 4, A Coruña, Fundación Pedro Barrié de la Maza, 1993, 121–142.

Mascarenhas, Maria Isabel de Vilhena, *Estudo da variação dialectal entre Lisboa e Porto das vogais átonas [-rec] e [+arred] em contexto inicial*, MA Diss., Lisboa, Universidade de Lisboa, 1996.

Mateus, Maria Helena/d'Andrade, Ernesto, *The phonology of Portuguese*, Oxford, Oxford University Press, 2000.

Medeiros, António, *Discurso nacionalista e imagens de Portugal na Galiza*, Etnográfica 7:2 (2003), 321–349.

Milroy, James/Milroy Lesley, *Authority in language. Investigating Standard English*, London/ New York, Routledge, [3]1993.

Moure, Teresa, *Ecolingüística, entre a ciencia e a ética*, A Coruña, Universidade da Coruña, 2011.

Neto, Serafim da Silva, *História da língua portuguesa*, Rio de Janeiro, Presença, [3]1979.

Piñeiro, Ramón, *Carta a Don Manuel Rodrigues Lapa*, Grial 42 (1973), 389–402.
RAG 1994 = Real Academia Galega, *Lingua inicial e competencia lingüística en Galicia*, A Coruña, RAG, 1994.
RAG 2007 = Real Academia Galega, *Mapa sociolingüístico de Galicia 2004*, vol. 1: *Lingua inicial e competencia lingüística en Galicia*, A Coruña, RAG, 2007.
RAG/ILG 1982, 2012 = Real Academia Galega/Instituto de Lingua Galega, *Normas ortográficas e morfolóxicas do idioma galego*, A Coruña, RAG/ILG, ^{23}2012, ^{1}1982.
Ramallo, Fernando/Rei-Doval, Gabriel, *The standardization of Galician*, Sociolinguistica 29:1 (2016), 61–82.
Regueira, Xosé Luís, *Modelos fonéticos e autenticidade lingüística*, Cadernos de Lingua 10 (1994), 37–60.
Regueira, Xosé Luís, *Lingua falada e estándar escrito, o galego desde o Rexurdimento á modificacion ortografica do 2003*, in: Vázquez Fachini, Ana María (ed.), *Galicia desde Salamanca 4*, Salamanca, Universidad de Salamanca, 2003, 185–220.
Regueira, Xosé Luís, *Política y lengua en Galicia. La "normalización" de la lengua gallega*, in: Castillo-Lluch, Mónica/Kabatek, Johannes (edd.), *Las lenguas de España. Política lingüística, sociología del lenguaje e ideología desde la Transición hasta la actualidad*, Madrid/Frankfurt am Main, Iberoamericana/Vervuert, 2006, 61–93.
Regueira, Xosé Luís, *Vocais finais en galego e en portugués. Un estudio acústico*, in: González, Helena/Lama, María Xesús (edd.), *Actas do VII CIEG*, Sada, O Castro, 2007, 859–875.
Regueira, Xosé Luís, *Cambios fonolóxicos no galego actual*, in: Brea, Mercedes/Fernández Rei, Francisco/Regueira, Xosé Luís (edd.), *Cada palabra pesaba, cada palabra medía. Homenaxe a Antón Santamarina*, Santiago de Compostela, Universidade de Santiago de Compostela, 2008, 275–286.
Regueira, Xosé Luís, *Nasalización en gallego y en portugués*, Estudios de Fonética Experimental 19 (2010), 71–110.
Regueira, Xosé Luís, *La lengua de la esfera pública en situación de minorización, español y portugués como lenguas de contacto en el lenguaje político gallego*, in: Poch Olivé, Dolors (ed.), *El español en contacto con las otras lenguas peninsulares*, Madrid/Frankfurt am Main, Iberoamericana/Vervuert, 2016, 39–59.
Regueira, Xosé Luís/Ginzo, María José (2019), *A cross-linguistic study of voiceless fricative sibilants in Galician and European Portuguese*, in: Gibson, Mark/Gil, Juana (edd.), *Romance phonetics and phonology*, Oxford, Oxford University Press, 62–76.
Regueira, Xosé Luís/Fernández Rei, Elisa (in press), *Phonetics and phonology*, in: González Seoane, Erenesto/Sousa, Xulio (edd.), *Manual of Galician linguistics*, Berlin/New York, De Gruyter.
Rodríguez, Francisco, *Galego-portugués*, [2008] http://arquivo.bng-galiza.org/opencms/opencms/BNG/global/contidos/columnistas/frodriguez/artigos/artigo_0014.html [last access: 12.07.2020].
Rodríguez Barcia, Susana/Ramallo, Fernando, *Graffiti y conflicto lingüístico. El paisaje urbano como espacio ideológico*, Revista Internacional de Lingüística Iberoamericana 25 (2015), 131–153.
Saussure, Ferdinand de, *Cours de linguistique générale*, ed. di Mauro, Tullio, Paris, Payot, 1995.

Schulte, Kim, *Structural convergence of two Ibero-Romance varieties. The case of colloquial Valencian as the outcome of contact between Catalan and Spanish*, in: Bouzouita, Miriam/Enghels, Renata/Vanderschueren, Clara (edd.), *Convergence and divergence in Ibero-Romance across contact situations and beyond*, Berlin/Boston, De Gruyter, in this volume, 87–113.

Seara, Roberto/Martínez Maquieira, Marta/Varela Fernández, Rocío/García-Mateo, Carmen/Fernández Rei, Elisa/Luís Reguieira, Xosé, *Enhanced CORILGA. Introducing the automatic phonetic alignment tool for continuous speech*, in: *Proceedings of LREC 2016, 10th Language Resources and Evaluation Conference (Portorož, Eslovenia, 23–28 mayo 2016)*, http://www.lrec-conf.org/proceedings/lrec2016/pdf/1074_Paper.pdf [last access: 12.07.2020].

Silverstein, Michael, *Indexical order and the dialectics of sociolinguistic life*, Language & Communication 23 (2003), 193–229.

Silverstein, Michael, *The race from place, dialect erradication vs. the linguistic "authenticity" of "terroir"*, in: Lacoste, Véronique/Leimgruber, Jakob/Breyer, Thiemo (edd.), *Indexing authenticity. Sociolinguistic perspectives*, Berlin/Boston, De Gruyter, 2014, 159–187.

Teyssier, Paul, *História da língua portuguesa*, Lisboa, Sá da Costa, 1982.

Torres Feijoo, Elias, *Cultura portuguesa e legitimação do sistema galeguista. Historiadores e filólogos (1880–1891)*, Ler História 36 (1999), 273–318.

Vázquez Corredoira, Fernando, *A construção da língua portuguesa frente ao castelhano. O galego como exemplo "a contrário"*, Santiago de Compostela, Laiovento, 1998.

Venâncio, Fernando, *Assim nasceu uma língua. Sobre as origens do português*, Lisboa, Guerra & Paz, 2019.

Vidal Figueiroa, Tiago, *Carta*, A Trabe de Ouro 20 (1994), 141–143.

Weinreich, Uriel, *Languages in contact. Findings and problems*, The Hague, Mouton, 1968 [originally publ. in New York, Linguistic Circle of New York, 1953].

Part 2: **Convergence and divergence across Ibero-Romance varieties outside Europe**

Johanna Wolf
Linguistic perceptions on Spanglish discourse settings
Processes of divergence in constructing identity

Abstract: By analysing four English-Spanish bilingual blogs, the present paper demonstrates that discursive practices like code-switching play a crucial role in constructing a divergent Spanglish identity in specific discourse settings and that this may have effects on the epistemic structures of the Hispanic society in its entirety. Immigrant communities need to negotiate which processes of convergence or divergence would be accepted by their speakers in order to construct a kind of hybrid identity that offers an appropriate frame of reference to its members. Although the second generation of Hispanics in the United States, and even more the third generation, will have converged to the target culture in many perspectives (e.g. organisation of daily-life-routines), members of this group still want to accentuate their own identity. Thus, they try to diverge in other perspectives in order to keep a link to their origins. Above all, concerning the Hispanic community, an idiosyncratic use of the heritage language helps to guarantee distinctiveness by using processes of divergence in their linguistic behaviour. In accordance with the hypothesis that language use strongly relates to the expression of identity, this paper focuses on these processes and suggests a more targeted use of the term Spanglish taking into account that Spanglish fulfils a mere emblematic function and serves as a label for the complex and multifaceted identity of second and third generation Hispanics in the United States. This includes the dimension of language and its specific use: linguistic routines used by Spanglish speakers are seen as a means for expressing their distinctive identity, that is, divergence concerning linguistic behaviour in a double sense. On the one hand divergence is created with regard to a U.S. specific culture, on the other hand in reference to the original one. Specifically, the use of code-switching is defined as a discursive practice which precipitates changes in sociocultural episteme, knowledge and understanding and is able to transport shared epistemic knowledge, by creating linguistic divergence.

Keywords: Spanglish, Hispanic community, language contact, divergence, code-switching, discursive practice, construction of transcultural identity

Johanna Wolf, Universität Salzburg

https://doi.org/10.1515/9783110736250-007

1 Introduction: Hispanic population and language behaviour

Already in 1987, Appel and Muysken pointed out that language and language behaviour are always closely connected to the collective identities peoples are constructing in the course of lifetime, because "the history of languages is tied up with and is a reflection of the history of people [...]" (Appel/Muysken 1987, 1). For monolingual societies this crucial function of language (as a means to express identity) is relatively clear. The interweaving of specific linguistic features and epistemic structures in the forging of a collective identity that includes discursive practices, conceptual knowledge, semantic frames etc., which in turn create a consensual understanding of shared values and the roots of the community, can be analysed as a process of convergence in the identity construction. For multilingual communities this is not valid to the same degree – even more so if it comes to immigrant communities who normally need to adapt to the majority language if their members strive for social advancement. In communities, where linguistic behaviour is affected by language contact, one can observe phenomena like language loss or language maintenance – both depending on multiple factors like prestige, status or speakers' proficiency (cf. Apple/Muysken 1987, 11–21; Negrón 2018, 121–122). Particularly the second and the third generation of immigrants often have to deal with the problem that neither the target language nor their heritage language can fulfil the function of a key element in their construction of identity. So, they are need to find specific ways to express the hybridity of their bicultural imprint. An example of how this requirement can be linguistically implemented is provided by the Hispanic population[1] in the U.S. Hispanic speakers in the U.S. use linguistic practices, e.g. code-switching, borrowings, lexical and syntactic calques, in order to create an emblematic variety (cf. Zentella 1997; Betti 2008; 2015; 2017a; 2017b) – a language use for which the term "Spanglish" is reserved here in a restrictive way.

In the following, we will analyse this specific linguistic behaviour and language choice as a means to create divergence with regard to the U.S. specific culture and with reference to their heritage culture with the objective of creating a discursive practice that is able to express their inner conflict and their desire to construct an identity proper. Referring to Gardt, below, a discursive practice is defined as a special use of language for the expression of social think patterns

---

[1] *Hispanic* refers to any person coming from a country where Spanish is spoken whereas the term *Spanish* refers to "Spaniards and people of Spanish ancestry" (Field 2011, 14; for a definition of the term *Hispanic* see also Garrido 2008, 18).

and as a means to express the perception of identity of a group whose members do not only feel interconnected by sharing the same heritage language and culture, but also, as a consequence of having the same cultural heritage, by sharing, a similar way of thinking and feeling (cf. Gardt 2007).

According to the 2010 Census, the Hispanic population constitutes 16.3% of the total population of the United States and, as shown by the latest *ACS 5-Year Population Estimate* (ACS 2010–2014), this population is still growing. Consequently, there has also been an increase of the use of Spanish – a fact that is clearly demonstrated by the statistics of the U.S. Census Bureau. The *ACS 5-Year Estimates* report places the percentage of the Spanish-speaking population at 13% (ACS),[2] which means that approximately 38 million people over the age of 5 are using Spanish in daily communication. The majority of this 13% report speaking English "very well" (57.1%), but 42.9% admit to having a lower proficiency[3] in English than in Spanish. A closer look at the age breakdown of respondents who stated speaking English "not very well" offers additional information. Only 21.4% of the youngest generation report speaking English "not very well", while 63% of the eldest generation (65 years and older) report the same. These numbers highlight a generational shift within the Spanish-speaking population of the United States and show that the typical bilingual behaviour of individuals belonging to this population differs by age. It also appears that what may be driving higher proficiency in English is the loss or reduced use of Spanish by second-generation Hispanics in the U.S. Scholars have widely noted (Hurtado/Vega 2004; Lipski 2008; among others) that Spanish normally lasts only one generation after immigration to the United States and a loss of Spanish competence is almost always observed in the second generation. Despite this pattern of reduced use of Spanish by younger generations, overall, the statistics reveal a clear presence of Spanish as an unofficial second language in the United States (cf. Montes-Alcalá 2009, 97), and in doing so they highlight the significance of bilingualism within the Spanish-speaking population. Unlike other language contact situations, where bilingual behaviour is considered a common and normal scenario (bilingualism is, in fact, the *norm* in these situations (Gafaranga 2007), the Spanish-English contact situation in the U.S. has been and remains in the headlines. The seemingly never-

---

2 Unfortunately, the Census does not distinguish between the different Spanish varieties. Only the report of *Detailed Languages Spoken at Home and Ability to Speak English for the Population 5 Years and Over for United States: 2009–2013* separates Spanish from Ladino and Pachuco (Release October 2015).
3 Regrettably the report does not explain what is understood by "very well" or "not very well". The statements about language proficiency depend on the self-evaluation of the interviewees and do not, therefore, reflect a veridical view of the real proficiency level.

ending debate about the status of the varieties resulting from this Spanish-English contact is still controversial. As Montes-Alcalá points out, the lingering controversy often leads to a nearly "traditional stigma that Hispanics' way of speaking" is a "bastardised" language (Montes-Alcalá 2009, 97) and not an expression of an autonomous transcultural identity. To describe the continuum of linguistic behaviour resulting from the Spanish-English contact situation in the United States, people often use the term "Spanglish" as an umbrella term to delineate any and all varieties of mixed English-Spanish language used in casual oral communication as well as in written contexts (cf. Otheguy/Stern 2010, 86). In the following sections, we will propose a targeted use of the term "Spanglish" and will reserve it to the emblematic function Spanglish fulfils. Based on the hypothesis that linguistic patterns like code-switching are used in an autonomous and conscious way by bilinguals and this linguistic behaviour being part of the creation of a discursive formation, four blogs of writers that use Spanglish will be analysed in order to examine whether code-switching can be used as a symbol of an identity sustaining language in written contexts of that kind of internet communication.

2 Approaching a definition of Spanglish

Among linguists there is still confusion concerning the term "Spanglish" and whether it is really necessary or useful for describing the complex linguistic situation resulting from language contact. This uncertainty surely results from the polysemous nature of the term: *Spanglish* can refer to the language (linguistic system level) used by speakers in Spanish-English contact situations as well as to the linguistic situation itself (pragmatic and contextual level/discursive and epistemic level). It is not always differentiated whether it applies to transfer phenomena due to unconscious acquisition processes in bilingual speakers (i.e. transfer phenomena that may occur at different stages of interlanguage) or conscious processes dealing with the construction of a transcultural identity. However, *prima facie*, there seems to be a consensus among non-linguists – as well as among some linguists – about labelling any Spanish-English alternation that contains the linguistic device of code-switching utterances as Spanglish (Rothman/Rell 2005, 516). On closer inspection, scholars differ in their perspectives on the Spanglish phenomenon. While Otheguy (Otheguy 2009; Otheguy/Stern 2010) declares that the term "Spanglish" is completely superfluous and even harmful, because it might transmit a damaging view of the Spanish-speaking community in the United States, there are many researchers pleading for the necessity of the term as an adequate description of a new form of communication within a new socio-cultural group (Fresneda 1998; León Jiménez 2003; Betti 2008; 2009; 2015; 2016a; 2016b; 2017a; 2017b). They are convinced that the term is needed to legitimise an identity proper for this group – especially concerning second and third-generation Hispanics in the United States (Rothman/Rell 2005; Ducar 2009): "To the extent that opinion is implicit in the analysis of Spanglish, there is no clear much less totally unbiased answer to the question on the status of its legitimacy as a language proper" (Rothman/Rell 2005, 533).

Otheguy argues that the use of a special term (one that is explicitly reserved for the Spanish-English contact situation within the United States) creates an environment of exclusion and disparagement. This is exacerbated by the fact that the term can be described morphologically as a blending derived from the lexical morphemes "Spanish" and "English", which inevitably connects the concept to the idea of a hybrid variety and therefore, as Otheguy says, has a negative connotation as being considered less prestigious as is, for example, the term "Spanish of the United States" or, even simpler, just Spanish (Otheguy/Stern 2010, 97–98).[4] Otheguy and Sterns' argument is based on a strict structural perspective on language, which focuses on acquisition and low proficiency problems. According to these authors, contact-induced changes only result in a variety of Spanish whose speakers – the bilingual speakers of Spanish and English – are at different levels of acquisition, but these changes do not lead to an entirely "new language" (Otheguy/Stern 2010, 96).[5] This claim is supported by empirical data showing clearly that the impact of English on the syntactic and morphological level in Spanish is quite limited and accounts only for a small proportion of structural convergence (Otheguy/Stern 2010; Erker/Otheguy 2016). Corresponding to their findings, a speaker's variety is mainly shaped by two forces: dialect levelling and linguistic convergence (Erker/Otheguy 2016, 132). According to this perspective, socio-cultural factors are only secondary and language use resulting from a contact situation just reflects a rather natural process of language contact (cf. Salaberry 2002; Fairclough 2003). Hence, the contact-induced changes to English (as the target language) or to Spanish (as the heritage language) cannot be considered a deterioration of the English or Spanish language, nor do they constitute the construction of a new communication system. Rather, these changes represent one particular form of variation, not unlike other forms of variation to which all varieties of English or Spanish are subject. They just reflect normal phenomena of language acquisition processes.

---

4 In 2009 Otheguy proposed to replace Spanglish with "español popular de los Estados Unidos".
5 These varieties can potentially be equated with so-called learner varieties (different stages of interlanguage) which illustrates the proximity of Otheguy's perspective to the domain of SLA research (Ellis 2015).

As a result, there is no need to label this particular process of language change with a specific term (cf. Salaberry 2002).

A similar criticism of the term "Spanglish" as a label for Spanish varieties used in the United States is expressed by Lipski, who also sees the exclusionary dimension of the concept and its harmful and derogatory connotations (cf. Lipski 2008, 39). As Lipski points out, the use of the term "Spanglish" involves the risk of damaging the self-confidence of any Spanish speaker living in the United States and of creating a climate of intolerance and disparagement towards them (Lipski 2008; see also Otheguy/Stern 2010). Following Otheguy's and Lipski's arguments, the Spanish spoken by the Hispanic population in the United States is a local form of Spanish.

So far, we mainly discussed a mere systemic perspective towards the term "Spanglish" as a label for the linguistic behaviour of the Spanish speaking community in the U.S. and evaluated language choice in the light of linguistic correctness and deficient language competence that evokes negative connotations which in turn may provoke negative forecasts regarding the economic and social career of Hispanic speakers. This may mislead to believe that language choice is a decision that predominately depends on social factors concerning social rise, recognition and progress[6], all of them producing processes of linguistic convergence to the target language and a tendency to shift completely to the target language as well as to the target culture.

However, as bilingual communities are in need of negotiating how to construct their transcultural identity, language shift also has to be discussed under the aspect of identity construction. Starting from the idea that language choice does not only depend on functional differentiation – as is the case in situations of diglossia (Fishman 1980, 8) – but also on the community's decision on how much identical potential is attributed to the maintenance of its heritage language, the creation of a hybrid variety is considered a process of creating divergence by a specific linguistic behaviour. From this perspective, Spanglish has to fulfil an emblematic function: it has to ensure the transfer and sharing of common cultural values and roots of the community and as such is a key element indicating identity and membership (Appel/Muysken 1987, 130). If the community decides to maintain the heritage language as a cultural symbol of its identity with the goal to express its individual identity, it has to make sure that every communicative situation can be handled with this language. This

---

[6] Surely, it would be necessary to discuss the different forms of interlanguages that exist among Spanish speakers in the U.S. But as we will focus on the emblematic and social function of Spanglish, we will hardly touch upon these aspects of language acquisition. For more details about educational aspects see Villa (2010) and Dumitrescu (2013).

implies that the linguistic system is adapted to every possible communicative need – exactly as English and Spanish are as majority languages. As a consequence of such a decision, the main goal of Hispanics should be to attain a proficiency in both languages (target and heritage language), which allows them to express themselves in any given written or oral context, regardless of whether they encounter a context requiring the language of proximity or one requiring a language of distance.[7] This implies a definition of bilingualism as a perfect mastering of both languages.

Note that this view of bilingualism often is connected to questions of language acquisition. The focus is on the different proficiency levels and the accuracy of language use that a language learner attains, and it seems that Otheguy and Lipski are concentrating on this dimension when approaching the "Spanglish-debate". This view reduces the complexity inherent in the term "Spanglish" and also neglects the fact that this term is used to refer to the split Hispanic-U.S.-American identity of Spanglish speakers. This split identity, typical of second and third generation immigrants, is the result of people being raised with dual identities that reflect both their Hispanic heritage and the U.S. culture.[8] The use of Spanglish as a means to express this identity has to be considered as a process of creating divergence with a twofold significance: on the one hand, divergence is created towards the heritage culture, on the other hand also towards a U.S. specific one.

In contrast to this structural view of the Spanish-English contact situation in the United States and the use of Spanglish, which focuses on the acquisition aspects of each language and the influences the language contact has on the respective linguistic systems, other researchers have focused on the cultural and ethnic dimensions connected to the term "Spanglish".[9] Here we find mainly perspectives dealing with transcultural constructions of identity. This approach has become famous primarily through the works of Ilan Stavans. In his often polemic contributions to the literature, he regards the use of Spanglish as a way for speakers to construct an autonomous transcultural identity by way of using a proper linguistic device reflecting this autonomy (Stavans 2003). A similar way of thinking about Spanglish as a term describing the multifaceted identity

---

[7] See Koch/Oesterreicher (2007) for more details with regard to the concept of language of proximity and language of distance.
[8] This critique on one-dimensional perspectives to Spanglish has already been formulated by Rodríguez-González/Parafita-Couto (2012) who are explicitly calling for an interdisciplinary approach to Spanglish.
[9] See the works of Betti or Potowski for detailed argumentations in support of this view, e.g. Betti (2008; 2009; 2015; 2016a; 2016b; 2017a; 2017b); Potowksi (2012; 2013; 2016).

situation, especially that of second and third generation Hispanics, is proposed by several researchers (Morales 2002; Zentella 2002; 2007; López García-Molins 2015; Betti 2016b; 2017a; 2017b). In this perspective, Spanglish no longer refers merely to a linguistic dimension, but rather to an identity situation which includes the linguistic dimension (in general, reduced to code-switching phenomena) and is intimately connected to it. This perspective leads to the consideration of whether the term Spanglish is an acceptable way to make a clear distinction between these two dimensions: one interested in questions of language change or language acquisition concerning language as a system and one interested in the connection between identity and language use. In the current study, the description of any linguistic system resulting from approaches interested in questions stemming from the research domain of language acquisition will be treated as learner varieties or varieties of Spanglish-English contact.

In contrast, descriptions dealing with issues that connect a specific language use to the construction of a new transcultural identity will be designated with the term Spanglish, which, of course, includes the linguistic phenomena of code-switching. Thus, the term Spanglish would be available to any interdisciplinary perspective which goes beyond a purely linguistic approach. As a consequence, we suggest making the following distinction when talking about code-switching as a linguistic phenomenon appearing in language-contact situations: a) the use of code-switching as a way of communication due to lack of proficiency in one or more languages versus b) using code-switching to create a transcultural discursive identity (which is related to the first distinction).

This suggestion is strengthened by a statement made by one of the evaluated bloggers with regard to frequently used typical Spanglish utterances (like for example *llamar (para) atrás, el rufero* etc.), phenomena which often serve to illustrate what Spanglish is (cf. Ardila 2005). In this case, Spanglish seems to be reduced to these stereotypical prefabs and is therefore seen by many as being a language consisting solely of phrases like these, which is an inadequate understanding of the communication possibilities that Spanglish offers its speakers. The blogger points out that the correct use of both languages is important: Standardised English is necessary for being treated as equal to native English-speaking white Americans and standardised Spanish is necessary for being considered as belonging to the heritage community. In her opinion, as a blogger and not as a linguist, statements like the following, collected by the blogger for her blog entry and corrected by herself, have nothing to do with Spanglish – which seems to negate Otheguy's and Lipski's understanding of the term:

> "The kind of conversation that annoys me to no end:
> Pues rellene un aplicacion para que puedo pagar el bil del dish, estoy esperando que me llamen para atrás.

Mi esposo parquea en el parqueo cuando trabaja de rufero.
Lleve mis ninos al parqueo y a la libreria.
En lugar de...
Pues hice un solicitud para poder pagar la factura del antena parabólica. Estoy esperando que me regresan la llamada. ['So I made a request to pay the satellite dish bill. I hope they will call me back'].
Mi esposo se estaciona en el estacionamiento, cuando trabaja de techador. ['My husband parks in the parking lot, when he works as a roofer'].
Lleve mis niños al parque y a la biblioteca. ['I take my children to the park and to the library']" (elenamary 2008).[10]

Roberto González Echevarría echoes the distinction discussed above regarding the possible reasons for code-switching, by stating that there is an essential difference between language mixing because one is not able to communicate otherwise (acquisitional dimension referring to proficiency and the mastery of the linguistic system), and language mixing, i.e., code-switching in the current study, as a legitimate strategy of constructing a proper identity which allows for expressing the historical and socio-cultural background of its members (González Echevarría 2008, 116). Finding new and distinct ways to label the different processes and aims of communication is the first step towards accommodating these different perspectives on language use, specifically the use of code-switching, in the Spanish-English contact situation.

Interestingly, several recent studies have pointed out that the educational discourse[11] concerning the term Spanglish seems to have shifted from having a negative connotation to having a more positive one (Villa 2010; Dumitrescu 2013; Sánchez-Muñoz 2013).[12] Faced with the fact that most heritage learners do

---

10 Quotations from the analysed blogs are cited in the following manner: Name of the blog, year of the entry.
11 This term refers to the discussions about teaching and learning Spanish in classroom settings and to questions of whether it makes sense to broach the issue of Spanglish there in order to help bilingual Hispanics to become more self-confident, so that they will no longer consider their use of Spanish as a diminished variety, but rather as an expression of their specific identity. In this way, 'educational discourses' are dealing with questions of language acquisition as well as with questions of self-perception of the scholars. The main goal is to reach a valorisation of the vernacular and its use as a pedagogical resource. For describing the development of the linguistic repertoire of bilinguals and their linguistic behaviour in classroom settings that should not be equated to code-switching, Otheguy/García/Reid (2015) use the term 'translanguaging' (cf. Otheguy/García/Reid 2015; for a detailed analysis of the situation bilinguals are exposed to in the educational context see García 2009. For descriptions of the special case of Hispanics in the U.S. see Postma 2013; Sayer 2008).
12 This trend may also be linked to the merits of research in the field of multilingualism and the sociocultural approaches to SLA.

not master the so-called literate or sophisticated register of Spanish required in written (academic) contexts and that their vernacular differs from a register required in language-of-distance-settings (especially academic settings, cf. Sánchez-Muñoz 2013, 440), researchers in the educational field tend to define "Spanglish", according to Stavans' proposals, as a way of constituting identity – an identity which is able to cope with the complex and hybrid background of second or third generation Hispanics in the United States:[13]

> "[...] Spanglish is a way for the students to deal with complex linguistic and ethnic identity issues in a creative manner. In a way, the use of Spanglish creates another level of meaning where the hybridity of the Chicana/o experiences are negotiated. In this sense, Spanglish is a way to construct and reconstruct a third space of Chicana/o identity, a linguistic *nepantla*" (Sánchez-Muñoz 2013, 44).

According to this perspective, the use of Spanglish is a specific and intentional discursive strategy that aims to highlight the biculturalism of its speakers and by doing so, Spanglish is developing a more positive connotation.

Given these different positions on the term "Spanglish" – a) *Spanglish* as a superfluous term for describing the varieties of Spanish found in the Spanish-English contact situation in the United States and b) *Spanglish* as a helpful term for describing the links between identity-construction and language use –, it is necessary to make a clear distinction between the different contexts in which a type of Spanish is identified as Spanglish, what the term "Spanglish" refers to, and which ideology might be involved in determining whether to use the term Spanglish. In an attempt to answer the call for interdisciplinary approaches to address the complex issue of Spanglish and its different meanings (Rodríguez González/Parafita-Couto 2012), the present contribution determines the role that the linguistic device of code-switching utterances plays in constructing a discursive formation. By using code-switching as an intentional discursive practice that can transmit a virtual concept of transcultural identity and one that helps to legitimise the autonomy of this concept, the use of Spanglish can be defined as a conscious reflex of identity construction – in a nutshell, the use of Spanglish as a discursive practice implies a process of linguistic convergence that allows to symbolise cultural diversity.

---

[13] The study of Sánchez-Muñoz focuses on Latinos, who describe themselves as *Chicano/Chicanas* (Sánchez-Muñoz 2013).

3 Discursive strategies: constructing episteme by language use

As it has theoretically been stated, language can be used as a means to create and define identity, especially in the case of minority groups or people that have to deal with the situation of language contact and who use specific linguistic behaviours as discourse of legitimation. Following this thought, in the sections to come we will assume that Spanglish can be used as an instrument of legitimation – a hypothesis that will be tested by analysing the blogs of Spanglish writers. The language behaviour and linguistic speech patterns associated with Spanglish, like code-switching, are typical phenomena resulting from the Spanish-English contact situation in the U.S. and perceived as a symbol of the speaker's own cultural heritage and transcultural identity. The use of Spanglish on the one hand creates an inner sense of belonging to the group of Hispanics raised with dual identities, and on the other hand contributes to the distance between the speaker and others who do not belong to this group. According to this perspective, Spanglish in the current study is conceived as a cultural practice used by Hispanics in the United States to create a discursive formation to convey the shared conceptual knowledge of their transcultural identity.

Following the hypothesis that language is inextricably related to identity and based on the postulation that Spanglish functions as a linguistic identity constructor, where the construction of the cited mixed-race culture is reflected by discursive language patterns, discourse in the current study is defined in the sense of Michel Foucault (cf. Foucault 1960; 1969). In Foucault's conceptualisation, the term "discourse" is not just a linguistic concept, but it brings together *language* and *practice* (Hall 1992, 44). As Stuart Hall explains:

> "A discourse is a group of statements which provides a language for talking about – i.e., a way of representing – a particular kind of knowledge about a topic. When statements about a topic are made within a particular discourse, the discourse makes it possible to construct the topic in a certain way. It also limits the other ways in which the topic can be constructed.
>
> A discourse does not consist of one statement, but of several statements working together [...]" (Hall 1992, 201).

Following this definition of discourse, one has to analyse how linguistic patterns – in the present contribution only iterative structures of code-switching will be considered – interact in order to create or to construct a potent discourse that will be able to respond to the desideratum of a *proper transcultural identity* of the majority of Hispanics in the U.S.

If code-switching is used as a discursive strategy to construct an influential line of discourse capable of creating identity in the epistemic structures of knowledge, these patterns form part of this identity and also define it. In this way the discursive practice as well as the specific discursive formation can be detected by members who share this epistemic knowledge. The creation of a discursive formation by using specific discursive practices, for example code-switching, is only possible if, at least, the following four elements are given: a) intertextual interconnectedness which is here interpreted as a connectedness concerning the writing and discourse style of the analysed blogs, b) language as interaction, which is used as a means to create a specific form of c) discourse that could serve as expression of social thought patterns and d) discourse as a stimulus for social change (Gardt 2007). After having given a brief overview of the different linguistic aspects of code-switching utterances, the use of this linguistic device of bilingual bloggers will now be analysed against the background of these four elements.

4 A short overview of the main linguistic characteristics of Spanglish and their discursive functions

Describing the main characteristics of Spanglish, Ardila distinguishes between superficial phenomena like borrowing (e.g. the use of very frequent lexemes like *casa* or *lunch*[14] in an English or Spanish discourse respectively), code-switching (e.g. *¿Piensas que mañana we could go to the beach after returning from la casa de mi abuelita?* – these are also called shallow phenomena) and deep phenomena like lexical-semantic (e.g. spangl. *escortar* or *sala de emergencies*)[15] and grammatical features (e.g. spangl. *esperar por mi esposa*), for example subject pronoun use (e.g. Spangl. *Yo he estado pensado* vs. Span. *He estado pensado*), word order flexibility or verbal morphology (cf. Ardila 2005, 68–77). Most studies working with Spanglish corpora have focused on shallow phenomena like borrowing, code-mixing and code-switching as socio-pragmatic functions of language choice (Poplack 1981; Zentella 1997). Research focusing on aspects of deep phenomena is rarer and deals mainly with questions of language acquisition and proficiency in bilingual speakers (e.g. syntactic convergence, phonological and grammatical

---

14 All examples were taken from Ardila (2005).
15 In this case of a literal translation from engl. *emergency room* to span. *sala de urgencias* also lexical borrowing can be discussed.

adaption, cf. MacSwan 2005; Otheguy/Zentella 2007). The present contribution, however, is limited to the scope on shallow phenomena as these seem to be more important for the construction of a discourse formation that legitimates the creation of a transcultural identity. This hypothesis is guided by the reflection that shallow phenomena are easy to detect by the reader, even if he or she is not bilingual. Therefore, their symbolic character is accessible and at the same time, their use as a discursive pattern remains transparent. So, bilinguals can use shallow phenomena in written contexts in a conscious and intentional way in order to create a discursive formation.

Some researchers differentiate between code-switching as inter-sentential switches and code-mixing as intra-sentential switches (Zentella 1997). The present paper follows the definition Myers-Scotton gives with regard to the insertion of elements belonging to another language into the grammatical frame of the dominant language (Myers-Scotton 1997). As a consequence, every insertion is subsumed under the category of code-switching phenomena. In addition to this and according to Poplack's proposal that code-switching functions as an ethnic discourse marker (Poplack 1980; 1981), the speech contained in the presented data will be defined broadly as code-switching (inter-sentential and intra-sentential as the two main strategies). Thus, code-switching phenomena occurring in the presented data range from single lexical items to complex constructions and are defined as language alternation patterns used as communicative strategies.[16]

Poplack adds a third strategy with respect to switching behaviours that belongs to the shallow phenomena: tag-switching. Tag-switching is intended to mark a monolingual utterance as belonging to a bilingual context and means "the insertion of a tag in one language into an utterance which is entirely in the other language" (Poplack 1980, 589; Romaine 1989, 122). Hence, it has a more symbolic character aimed at emphasizing the bilingual background of the speaker (Appel/Muysken 1987). Frequent examples of tag-switching are discourse markers like *well, so* or *anyway*,[17] but, as the present contribution suggests, examples of tag-switching can also be prefabricated constructions[18] or idiomatic expressions due to their possible emblematic character (e.g. *a la verga, vale, basta*, etc.).

---

16 Therefore, *borrowing* is reserved for labelling switches of lexical items in the speech of speakers of low proficiency or monolinguals where they were caused by a lack of vocabulary.
17 Examples were taken from the collected data of the current study.
18 Prefabricated constructions or prefabs are defined here as conventionalised multi-string words (cf. Bybee/Torres Cacoullos 2009, 188).

5 Creating a Spanglish identity: language use as discursive practice in blogs

The data collected for this contribution are textual data and they are explored inductively using typical philological methods, such as content analysis to generate categories and explanations.[19] For example, all bloggers exhibited different behaviours with regard to conceptualizing their hybrid identity, which made it impossible to subsume them under one label or to pretend that a "typical" bilingual behaviour or identity concerning the self-perception of Hispanics (immigrants or belonging to the borderlands) exists. Consequently, conclusions must be considered as tendencies that have been found in the linguistic behaviour of selected individuals and need to be strengthened in future research by extended data collection and evaluation.

In the scope of the present contribution, linguistic behaviour, which reveal specific discursive practices and are used to construct a discursive formation can be compared to the linguistic behaviour found in the works of bilingual writers in order to demonstrate similar strategies to create a discursive formation (cf. Aparicio 1993; Sebba/Mahootian/Jonsson 2012). The discursive construction of these concepts is described by Anzaldúa in a quite radical way:

> "*Deslenguadas. Somos los del español deficiente.* We are your linguistic nightmare, your linguistic aberration, your linguistic *mestizaje*, the subject of your *burla*. Because we speak with tongues of fire we are culturally crucified. Racially, culturally and linguistically *somos huérfanos* – we speak an orphan tongue" (Anzaldúa 1987, 80; italics as in the original).[20]

The following analysis attempts to examine whether code-switching is employed, as Anzaldúa claims, to shift from an "orphan tongue" to a symbol of an autonomous, identitary language use.

---

[19] This method is also used by Ziem/Wengeler (2014) to explain how discourse formations concerning the term 'crisis' are formed and perceived by communities.
[20] Interestingly, one of the bloggers, Elena Mary, expresses very similar feelings in a quite identical way: "My Spanish comes from colonialism. My Spanish is seen as inferior and discouraged in public spaces. My English is viewed as inferior because of the influence of my Spanish. My Spanish made me a 'high risk' student. My Spanish is now mocked as inferior to the variety spoken in Spain. My Spanish is resilience, and despite being discouraged from using it in this country, the fact I have maintained any of it should be applauded for my resistance [...]" (elenamary 2017).

5.1 Blog analysis: description of data and method

In the current study, four bilingual blogs, created in the period from 2007 to 2016 were analysed. It is not easy to find blogs that really use Spanglish and treat issues of creating a transcultural identity at the same time – mostly bloggers decide to write either in English or in Spanish. In order to find the selected blogs, it proved/turned out to be useful to rely on the different "blogtitlan" provided by the blogs' authors. By analysing the interconnectedness of the authors, it was possible to detect a kind of blogosphere containing blogs that use Spanglish in its emblematic function and that evaluate issues dealing with the construction of a hybrid identity. These were key elements that decided whether a blog was selected or not as was the language choice. Only blogs with phenomena classifiable as Spanglish language use were considered. Blogs containing separate English and Spanish versions of the posts or translated pages were excluded.[21] Individual style obviously plays an important role in language choice. For levelling this effect and for the sake of comparability and in order to obtain a reliable result, the number of analysed posts was adjusted down to the number of posts produced by the least productive blog, so that 38 posts per blog, selected at random, were analysed. The data analysed therefore includes 152 posts in total. The selected posts differ in length and range, depending on the individual writing style and the interconnectedness of the author – for example, the author of *yonderliesit* often writes in verse form whereas the author of *elenamary* prefers a very academic style when she illustrates the problems of Spanglish and its specific function.[22]

All evaluated blogs are so-called "free-style-blogs", meaning that the posts are not filtered and may be classified as a kind of online-diary where one can find a wide range of very different topics treated, composed using very individual writing styles (Montes-Alcalá 2007, 162). These are the four bilingual blogs analysed in the present contribution:

a. http://elenamary.com/ (female, Ph.D. student, Ohio, U.S., born in the U.S., dominant English language use). Average of words per post: #505.6 words, frequency of posting on average #1.4 per month.

---

[21] One of the blogs under investigation unfortunately went inactive during the analysis and stopped in 2013 (*aislinn the albino bean*), one of them only started in 2009 (*lifeinspanglish*).
[22] Regrettably, none of the blogs contains a statistics about its readership or the visitor numbers – what is available is the average of comments per post. But these seem to be a very unreliable criteria to measure the range of a blog so it is neglected here.

b. http://www.yonderliesit.org/aztlan/ (male, Spanish teacher, Sweden/Mexico/ California, not born in the U.S., dominant Spanish language use). Average of words per post: #352.7 words, frequency of posting on average #1.3 per month.
c. http://thealbinobean.blogspot.de/ (inactive since august 26, 2013) (female, unemployed, Cabo, Mexico, dominant Spanish language use). Average of words per post: #375.5 words, frequency of posting on average 0.7 per month.
d. https://lifeinspanglish.com/ (female, student, Los Angeles, U.S., born in the U.S., dominant English language use). Average of words per post: #473.4 words, frequency of posting on average #0.9 per month.

5.2 Results

All bloggers are of Mexican origin, and all address in their posts, more or less, the topic of being transcultural, though to a varying extent. But the difficulty of how a proper transcultural identity can be constructed is a common topic among all bloggers. *Elenamary* and *yonderliesit*, in particular, dedicate a considerable number of posts to this topic. As Montes-Alcalá (2009, 165) has already pointed out, nearly all of the bilingual bloggers tend to write in English and switch to Spanish, except Aislinn, who is living in Cabo, Mexico, and who is mainly writing in Spanish with switches to English. The author of *yonderliesit* writes approximately half of his posts in English and half in Spanish and only switches in posts written predominantly in English. Elena Mary tends to avoid the mix of the two languages and only uses switches in posts explicitly dedicated to topics of Spanglish culture, Hispanic heritage, or the like. Christina from *lifeinspanglish* declares explicitly that she uses both languages to express her specific identity and does so by using a very individual kind of switching which underlines the function of code-switching both as emblem and as a means to create divergence:[23]

> "So this is my attempt at getting current with the Spanglish lifestyle in LA... and by that I mean the capacity to understand and live both worlds, cultures, ideas, etc. in English and Spanish simultaneously. You know how it goes. In my case, I usually think 'in English' and then Spanish suddenly creeps in. I'm not just referring to being bilingual or that other word they like to call us... pochos comes to mind! ('They' being the language purists.) Even though I try to stick to one language and use proper grammar, if I know you speak Spanish, are of Hispanic descent or are even curious about the Latino culture, then both languages will collide! No puedo evitarlo. So I hope if this blog gains any traction and gets any hits you'll bear with me and understand my lingo" (lifeinspanglish 2009).

---

[23] In fact, Christina uses mostly free switches without an obvious socio-pragmatic function. It seems almost as if she simply wanted to inject a certain symbolic significance into her writings.

The dominant language of her blog remains English. This tendency of second and third generation bilingual speakers to use English predominantly has been supported recently by a study released by the *Pew Research Center* (PRC) indicating that 71% of Hispanics do not think that it is necessary to speak Spanish to be considered Latino (Lopez 2016). Note, that even in 2012 a similar trend of reporting English as the dominant language was found by the PRC, but 95% of the Hispanics interrogated thought it important for future generations to be still able to speak Spanish (Taylor et al. 2012). It becomes evident that the bloggers use linguistic behaviour here to create a discourse/discursive formation as a means to express the social thought patterns they are – or perhaps they feel – confronted with. Language in this sense becomes a tool to interact between the self-perception as members of a minority group and the society they are living in. This claim can be strengthened by the following metalinguistic comments that the bloggers made concerning their linguistic behaviour in order to explain the reasons for their switching.

An important topic of bilingual bloggers is the gap between their English and Spanish proficiency, which they take notice of evaluating their own linguistic behaviour. One of the evaluated bloggers, Christina from *lifeinspanglish*, explicitly describes her blog as an attempt to address her bilingualism: "Life in Spanglish is just a little experiment to see if I can get away with publishing the weird word combos that pop up in my mind, en inglés y en español y todo mixed together… Is there anything more frustrating than not having the correct translation of a thought or word and needing it immediately?" (lifeinspanglish 2009).

While Christina is dealing with the problem that she isn't always immediately able to access the lexical item required in the language she is currently speaking and seems to perceive her bilingualism as a proficiency problem that she solves mostly by using switches (perhaps even borrowings in this case), Elena Mary from *elenamary* goes one step further by explaining her motivation for using code-switching: "I try to tell people interested in interpreting, that knowing a language isn't achieved by knowing a vocabulary. Knowing a language is cultural, it is becoming the language, being part of the ethos, it is a change in personality and perspective" (elenamary 2011).

The above observations reveal the main strategy adopted by all bloggers when they are using linguistic patterns typical for language contact: code-switching as a social and communicative strategy and therefore as a discursive practice. Hence, discourse becomes a useful strategy to express social thought patterns and may perhaps – in a further step – turn into a way to influence these patterns in the sense of changing the social perception of Spanglish as an inferior variety to a perception of Spanglish as an emblematic variety created and used to express a special identity.

Both quotations show that there can be different reasons for switching. On the one hand, switching can stem from a lack of semantic knowledge concerning concepts and frames that are matched to the particular item and evoked by its use.[24] On the other hand, switching of lexical items may often be employed as an intentional discursive practice of distinction – e.g. the use of Spanish items like *tapa, borracho, gente*[25] should evoke a typical Spanish atmosphere and can probably be seen as a game with cultural stereotypes.

But these are only two of the possible socio-pragmatic functions that have been suggested by several studies investigating spoken and written code-switching (cf. Zentella 1997; Montes-Alcalá 2007; 2013). According to the traditional classification with regard to the socio-pragmatic functions of code-switching, findings are generally classified under the following categories: quotations, emphasis, clarification or elaboration, lexical need, linguistic routines or formulaic speech (including idiomatic expressions), contextual switches and stylistic switches (Montes-Alcalá 2013, 218). Based on the analysis pattern in Montes-Alcalá (2013), the present contribution suggests five categories of analysis: a) Clarification and elaboration (incl. parenthetical comments), b) Linguistic routines (incl. tags, formulaic language and idiomatic expressions,) c) Lexical needs (incl. product-names, contextual switches and stylistic switches), d) Emphasis and topic shift, and e) Free switches (i.e. switches without apparent specific function).

The term crutch-like mixes is avoided because there was no evidence that a switch was caused by a momentary loss of words, or because the writer lacked the word in the other language due to a problem of language mastery. This is surely due to the fact that posts are planned and not spontaneous texts, even if they pretend to preserve a kind of orality as proof of authenticity. It is also important to note that not every switch is related to a specific function, as Zentella (1997, 99) makes clear: "[...] pinpointing the purpose of each code switch is a task as fraught with difficulty as imputing the reasons for a monolingual's choice of one synonym over another, and no complete accounting may ever be possible".

In total, 623 switches were found, and Table 1 summarises the number of switches per category:

---

[24] Even when reaching a high proficiency, it can still be a problem for bilingual speakers to match the complete semantic information to lexical items, so that switches of single lexical items may reflect an uncertainty concerning conceptual knowledge (cf. Jiang 2000).
[25] Examples of the collected data.

Table 1: Number of switches per category.

	Total number of switches	Lexical items	Clarification	Free switches	Linguistic routines	Emphasis and topic shift
Number	623	197	134	119	94	79
Percent	100	31.62	21.51	12.68	15.09	19.10

The results of the study support the findings of Montes-Alcalá (2007; 2013). She already illustrates that the categories Lexical need and Clarification are the most frequently used socio-pragmatic functions. In the examined data, the most frequent type of switch is Lexical need (31.62%), followed by Clarification and elaboration (21.51%). In the following, examples for every category are given to illustrate the effects of code-switching as a strategy to establish a specific linguistic behaviour that could be read as a symbol of a discursive formation:

A) Lexical need:
   (1) En mi cabecita pienso que canto muy bien, me *rockstareo* (aislinnthealbinobean 2009).
   (2) Según yo me veía muy cool con una camisetilla con lentejuelas que compre. Me sentía muy *Glam Rock*. Edith me dijo que parecía *Figure Skater*. [...] También vino efra y su nueva *roomie* gringa Kate? A la hora del postre, y de allí nos fuimos a mi casita a ver una *movie* y comer *mixed nuts*. ['I felt very cool with my sequined shirt that I bought. I felt very Glam Rock. Edith said that I resembled the Figure Skater. Efra and his new white roomie Kate came too? When it was time to have dessert, we went to my house and watched a movie and ate mixed nuts'][26] (aislinnthealbinobean 2008).
   (3) I would stop at a bakery on my way to class and buy a sweet roll, my favorite were the *borrachos* ['fried pastries'] coated in sugar and strips of pink dye through the inner doughy layers. I would eat while either drinking a steaming cup of *cafe con leche* ['coffee with milk'] or *atole* ['drink containing corn'] (elenamary 2007).
   (4) *El Indio* TEZZY never forgets his GENTE ['folk'] no matter where they may be at! (yonderliesit 2007; capital letters as in the original).
   (5) Like a *taco* ['toasted shell'] stand, a green leaf came to my eyesight, between your mouth opening wide and your arm folding to take the *taco* to your beautiful lips I couldn't make out if it was a radish leaf or a cilantro one [...] (yonderliesit 2016).

---

[26] All translations are made by the author.

Examples A (2), A (3) and A (4) show clearly that the socio-pragmatic functions of lexical need, context-induced and stylistic switches are engaging and that they fulfil the writer's need to construct a discursive formation that can convey the sensation of transcultural identity, despite writing mainly in one specific language. Shared cultural knowledge is evoked by the semantic concepts and frames related to the lexical items.

The second most frequently used category by the blog-authors was Clarification and Elaboration:

B) Clarification and elaboration:
   (1) Facebook is an outlet for my brain farts, but very superficial, I prefer to complain on my blog. *El face es pa chistes y memes* ['Facebook is for jokes and memes'] (aislinnthealbinobean 2013).
   (2) Most women don't know that *las enfermedades del corazón* ['illness of the heart'] are the #1 killer of women in the US, more than any form of cancer or other diseases (lifeinspanglish 2015).
   (3) Last weekend AGI won the Director's Guild of America award and he was especially sentimental during his speech. *Se le salieron las lagrimas* ['He was crying'] (lifeinspanglish 2016).

Each of the examples fulfils the same function: the previous statement is clarified once more. In B (1), it seems to be easier for the reader to guess what is meant by the part written in Spanish. In B (2) and B (3), the contexts only give some hints for the correct interpretation. This kind of switching may be interpreted as a means to establish a sort of exclusive discourse because for a monolingual speaker it is difficult to understand. Possibly there is a tendency to use code-switching not only as a means of integration, but also as a means of exclusion. Thus, the aim of switching as a discursive practice fulfils two conditions of group formation: the integration of the group's members that are able to use the same code and the exclusion of everyone else.

Free switches form the third most-prolific category used by the blog authors. This category groups all switches that do not seem to have a special function except to demonstrate the blogger's proficiency in both languages and to create an individual style that is intended to prove the existence of an autonomous Spanglish identity, i.e. they function as discursive practice.[27]

---

[27] Surely the ranking is highly influenced by the small number of blogs evaluated. For example, one defining characteristic of Christina's writing (*lifeinspanglish*) is her extensive use of free switches, which may be responsible for the high number of free switches in the overall data.

C) Free switches examples:
   (1) *Aqui estaré* ['Here I am'] blogging in Spanglish (lifeinspanglish 2009).
   (2) *Durante pleno Spring Cleaning se me ocurrió que estos libros* ['During the whole Spring Cleaning it strikes me that all the books...'] either I'm done with them or I'm not going to finish reading them (Abu Ghraib *es muy deprimente* ['it's so sad']) *o de plano no me surten efecto* ['or, speaking freely, it has no effect on me'] (lifeinspanglish 2009, fat letters as in the original).
   (3) A veces pienso cuan fácil sería mi vida si en realidad fuera lesbiana ['Sometimes I think that my life would be easier if I was a lesbian']... but I really can't deal with the whole unshaven leg/armpit feminist thing (aislinnthealbinobean 2008).

Linguistic routines are also used frequently with the aim of creating the already mentioned discursive formation:

D) Linguistic routines examples:
   (1) All monolinguals will defend *a capa y espada* ['defend by all means'] their language but they can't understand that bilinguals hence have two identities to deal with (yonderliesit 2008).
   (2) I'm just bored... and I keep wondering what would happen if I just said A LA VERGA CON TODO? ['Go fuck yourself'] (aislinnthealbinobean 2008; capital letters as in the original).
   (3) *Anyway*, pensé en hacer Linchburg Lemonade, pero al final me decidí por una Sangría Blanca... que como se hace? (aislinnthealbinobean 2007).
   (4) *Well* no mucho lo mio la verdad, pero si me gusta (aislinnthealbinobean 2009).
   (5) *Pues sí* ['Well'], maybe you've noticed que I've been absent for a while, as I try to regroup and focus on new items for the blog (lifeinspanglish 2012).
   (6) *El otro día* ['the other day'] as I was walking down the halls of South Coast Plaza [...] (lifeinspanglish 2013).

Examples of this category are twofold: examples D (3), D (4) and D (5) include discourse markers that are utilised to produce a coherent and well-structured discourse where information is easily available for the listener/reader (cf. Schiffrin 2001). In the examples D (3), D (4) and D (5), discourse markers are employed to introduce a topic shift. This use of discourse markers occurs very often, the switching seems to be applied to call the reader's attention: introducing the new topic by using discourse markers in English or in Spanish and proceeding in the other language provokes that the listener's/reader's attention is attracted to the new topic (Schiffrin 2001). This kind of interactive discourse structuring often underlies the use of linguistic (here: pragmatic) routines that every speaker has stored in the mental lexicon. This also applies to example D (6). Examples D (1) and D (2) are different: here, linguistic routines refer to prefabricated chunks, in this case idiomatic expressions. Both are used to evoke an emotional reading. In D (1), the blogger probably seems to use the idiomatic expression *a capa y espada* to highlight the importance of heritage languages for the construction of identity. But, as he belongs to the group of bilingual speakers, the use of both languages on the one hand underlines the problem of constructing a hybrid identity and illustrates the inner conflict of the speaker; on the other hand, it makes his discourse more expressive. Example D (2) stages the effect of switching in a similar way: the author writes in English, but switches to Spanish (*A LA VERGA CON TODO?*) to make her discourse more expressive. At the same time, she is provoking a comical effect: switching to the other language when using strong language or swear words is a frequent phenomenon. Montes-Alcalá (2007, 168) explains that this behaviour is probably due to the lack of a similar expression in the other language. But this explanation seems to be not quite appropriate in the concrete case because all authors master both languages with native-like proficiency. So, a pragmatic interpretation of this phenomenon (provoking a comical effect, rising expressivity) appears to be more adequate.

Switches belonging to the category Footing were used less frequently than all other types of switches in the four blogs:

E) Emphasis and topic shift examples:
   (1) We were trouble-making friends, frequently tinkering on the line of suspension from school, often being called out for our shenanigans and being told *que nos llevábamos demasiado pesado* ['that we were annoying']. (elenamary 2016)
   (2) El recuento de los daños, o más dramático... *where did I go wrong*. (aislinnthealbinobean 2013)
   (3) But enough already. *Ya basta*. ['That's enough!'] It's a Friday, it's summer and I feel like dancing. (lifeinspanglish 2016)

In examples E (1), E (2), and E (3), code-switching is used as emphasis to underline the statement by repeating what has been said in Spanish. In example E (1), the code-switching is used to sum up what has been said about the girls' behaviour – in fact, it also implicitly indicates a topic shift because in the following paragraph the author is writing about another subject. This effect – summing up and making the statement clearer by doing so – can also be seen in E (8). In E (9), the switch is a mere repetition of the previous statement, so at first glance, it may be seen as a simple clarification. But against the contextual background, it seems to be a sort of emphasised way of topic shift; this is the reason for it being grouped in category E.

5.3 Discussion

The results suggest that the use of Spanglish in blogs can be defined as a deliberate strategy adopted to evoke shared knowledge and to create a virtual transcultural identity, different from Hispanic or American identity. Bloggers often tend to use each language consciously and strategically in order to construct a valid transcultural communication style.

The examples found in the data of the current study confirm the claim that bilingual speakers who use code-switching are highly proficient speakers of both Spanish and English (cf. Myers-Scotton 1997). This also supports the hypothesis that code-switching marks an intentional discursive practice because the bloggers seem to make use of this strategy in a very conscious way knowing exactly what effect their switching has. Each author applies code-switching in an individual way, which makes it difficult to generalise the findings. For example, an abundant use of code-switching with discourse markers was only found in one of the analysed blogs, but there it occurred regularly which might reflect the individual linguistic behaviour of this author. Possibly the blogger wishes to stress that she really lives on the border of two cultures, in a transcultural "zone". In contrast prefabs and idiomatic expressions were found in every blog. All authors though use code-switching at least in similar pragmatic functions.

Taking a more general perspective on the linguistic behaviour that bilingual bloggers are revealing, the individual choices can be perceived as "a way of saying that they belonged to both worlds, and should not be forced to give up one for another" (Zentella 1997, 112). Probably, the respective language choice even demonstrates the objective to create a new world – which suggests that the switches made by bilingual bloggers must be seen as discursive practices and as a deliberate and conscious choice of creating divergence.

In doing so, using code-switching becomes a purely emblematic strategy to demonstrate an allegiance to a shared cultural and epistemic knowledge – at least with regard to these written contexts. Language choice as intellectual decision in these cases can be considered as a conscious process of divergence. It is used by bloggers in spite of the social stigma that can be assigned to code-switching phenomena.[28] As well, their language choice is in line with the claim Gardt (2007) established concerning the construction of a discursive formation: *language as interaction*. Referring to the other elements, *expressing social thought patterns*, *acting as a stimulus for social change* and *intertextual interconnectedness*, almost all of them are present in the data. The use of Spanglish as a means of expressing social thought patterns can be found in the posts of the bilingual bloggers – especially in the posts of *elenamary* and *yonderliesit*, who can both be considered *blogeros de primera hora*.[29] They feel that there is a social and cultural need to define their identity as a new one that is different from a purely Hispanic or American identity. In their posts, the decision to switch between languages is often prompted by the bloggers' explicit raising of the issue of identity. The identity problem of Hispanics can often be found as a *leitmotiv* in their posts. Posts related to issues of transcultural identity seem to provoke the use of a specific language that reflects the blogger's feelings and attitude towards this problem, as described by the author of *yonderliesit*: "There is an almost blind belief that all Chicanos have Spanish as a second language or that they are at the very least influenced by it. The Chicano community is composed of a culture that is distinguished by its multicultural roots" (yonderliesit 2011). A similar passage is written by Elena Mary: "I am not a Pocha! I know my language, I know my culture. I don't need to take back a term for something that I am not" (elenamary 2012).

Both of them consider Spanglish to be a term that should be used for describing an attitude rather than the use of a specific language. As mentioned above, Elena Mary even denounces the label of incorrect language use – defined as using words from language A while speaking language B – with a specific term. For her, only highly proficient speakers of each language should code-switch, which she admits is an elitist view. Her opinion fits the distinction made by González Echevarría, who describes this attitude as typical for a more intellectual approach to the Spanglish phenomenon (González Echevarría 2008). The following passage shows a similar way of conceiving the identity problem: "We Xicanos need to put an end to the centennial bickering Mexicans and Americans have had since inception days. We the children can no longer take sides we are Mexican and we are American no matter what ye old blood feud says. Let Mexicans fear the Gringo; we Xicanos cannot do that. Let Gringos fear the Mexican; we Xicanos cannot do that" (yonderliesit 2009).

---

28 This also confirms the function Myers-Scotton is according to code-switching (cf. Myers-Scotton 1995; 1997).
29 As it has been stated, one cannot decide yet – and even less on the basis of a small database as the one of the current study – whether these discursive formations can influence society as a stimulus of social change.

Lifeinspanglish changes the languages in her blogging in a comparable way. The author wants to symbolise that her way of feeling, her identity, is something that cannot be reduced simply to biculturalism. This feeling of not belonging to either of one's two cultures and of not being able to make clear distinctions between the heritage and the target culture is also expressed by *elenamary* who goes so far as to describe this feeling as a "failure": "I've been watching a lot of Mexican stand-up comedy and joke telling as of late. I feel overwhelmed by a sense of disconnect and sadness. I am not really Mexican. I don't laugh at all and it makes me feel like a failure as a Mexican. I understand what is *supposed* to be funny but I don't find it funny" (elenamary 2011; italics as in the original).

Concerning the claim of intertextual interconnectedness, one has to assert that the bloggers are strongly connected – *elenamary*, *aislinnthealbinobean* and *yonderliesit* are linked by their "blogtítlan". Thus, given the fact that each of Gardt's four elements that define a discourse are found in the bloggers' writing, the initial question of whether language use in bilingual blogs is designed to construct a discursive formation that legitimises the requirement for a distinct and autonomous identity, can be affirmed.

6 Conclusion

As the present study demonstrates, bloggers perceive their ability to make conscious decisions about which language to use as part of "a superior expressive language repertoire" (Montes-Alcalá 2007, 169). This allows them to create a certain discourse formation that does not conceive transcultural identity as a simple mixture of elements taken from Hispanic or American culture, but as a complex, multifaceted, yet highly autonomous phenomenon.

The individual code-switching patterns of bilingual bloggers and their construction of a discursive formation as a way of legitimizing a Spanglish culture that is distinct from Hispanic or American culture may be taken as evidence of a gradual change in the perception of Spanglish by society. Bloggers using Spanglish do so deliberately in order to illustrate that this discursive practice reflects their transculturation process. Their behaviour likely refers to the social perception of their group and reflects the desire of creating divergence. As a consequence, the term "Spanglish" loses its negative connotation and social stigma, as Franco and Solorio underline in the following passage: "[...] the ever-increasing number of Spanglish speakers, as well as the raise in sensitivity, and understanding of bilingualism, has contributed to the fact that newer generations do not consider the word as a derogative one, but simply as the best label so far to describe the very interesting phenomenon of the long interaction between English and Spanish" (Franco/Solorio 2007, 82).

Going one step further, using certain linguistic patterns as a discursive formation, e.g. code-switching, may help second and third generation Hispanics to reserve the term "Spanglish" only for the complex cultural determination of their specific group, including, of course, the linguistic dimension (i.e., code-switching) which should perhaps be understood, in this special case, more as an expression of a particular discursive practice and a particular bilingual competence than as an expression of linguistic varieties. This is confirmed by the bloggers' definition of the function code-switching has within the process of creating a divergent identity – and it is a crucial one which expresses very clearly the desire of distinctiveness:

> "When for example, a white person, who studied in Spain for six months, describes their speaking in class as 'code-switching', it is a complete lack of understanding of who actually uses code switching. Having two items, two sets of ideas, two languages, two of anything and going back and forth doesn't mean you are code switching and it is insulting to those that use code switching as a radicalized form of survival" (*elenamary* 2017).

Possibly this perspective may contribute to the acceptance of Spanglish as a variety proper and as a concept of an autonomous transcultural identity – a concept that bloggers who use Spanglish help to distribute.

7 References

ACS = *American Community Survey*, 2010–2014, http://www.census.gov/programs-surveys/acs/ [last access: 13.07.2016].
Anzaldúa, Gloria, *Borderlands/La frontera. The new mestiza*, San Francisco, Aunt Lute Books, 1987.
Aparicio, Frances R., *From ethnicity to multiculturalism. The historical development of Puerto Rican literature in the United States*, in: Lomelí, Francisco (ed.), *Handbook of Hispanic cultures in the United States. Literature and art*, Houston, Arte Público, 1993, 19–39.
Appel, Rene/Muysken, Pieter, *Language contact and bilingualism*, London, Edward Arnold, 1987.
Betti, Silvia, *El Spanglish, ¿medio eficaz de comunicación?*, Bologna, Pitagora, 2008.
Betti, Silvia, *Español en/de los Estados Unidos. ¿Español estadounidense o spanglish?*, in: Betti, Silvia/Jorques, Daniel (edd.), *Visiones europeas del Spanglish*, Valencia, Uno y Cero, 2015, 12–25.
Betti, Silvia, *Con otro acento. El spanglish visto desde esta orilla. Spanglish*: <we speak both because we are both>, in: Betti, Silvia/Alegre, Enrique S. (edd.), *Nuevas voces sobre el spanglish. Una investigación polifónica*, New York/Valencia, Academia Norteamericana

de la Lengua Española (ANLE)/Universitat de València-Estudi General (UVEG), 2016, 7–10 (= 2016a).
Betti, Silvia, *Una cuestión de identidad... español y spanglish en los Estados Unidos*, Camino Real 8 (2016), 61–76 (= 2016b).
Betti, Silvia, *Spanglish imaginativo y sugerente. Entre práctica lingüística e identidad*, in: Betti, Silvia/Alegre, Enrique S. (edd.), *Nuevas voces sobre el spanglish. Una investigación polifónica*, New York/Valencia, Academia Norteamericana de la Lengua Española (ANLE)/ Universitat de València-Estudi General (UVEG), 2016, 17–42 (= 2016c).
Betti, Silvia, *Encuentros y desencuentros lingüísticos en los Estados Unidos. La práctica del Spanglish*, in: Cestero Mancera, Ana M./Paredes García, Florentino/Molina Marto, Isabel (edd.), *Investigaciones actuales en Lingüística*, vol. 5: *Sobre variación dialectal y sociolingüística*, Alcalá de Henares, Universidad de Alcalá, Servicio de Publicaciones, 2017, 177–196 (= 2017a).
Betti, Silvia, *Lenguas, culturas y sensibilidades en los Estados Unidos. Español y Spanglish en un mundo inglés*, Hispania 100:5 (2017), 35–40 (= 2017b).
Bybee, Joan L./Torres Cacoullos, Rena, *The role of prefabs in grammaticization. How the particular and the general interact in language change*, in: Corrigan, Roberta L./ Moravcsik, Edith A./Quali, Hamid/Wheatly, Kathleen (edd.), *Formulaic language*, vol. 1: *Distribution and historical change*, Amsterdam, John Benjamins, 2009, 187–217.
Ducar, Cynthia, *The Sound of Silence. Spanish heritage textbooks' treatment of language variation*, in: Lacorte, Manel/Leeman, Jennifer (edd.), *Español en Estados Unidos y otros contextos de contacto. Sociolingüística, ideología y pedagogía*, Madrid, Iberoamericana, 2009, 347–368.
Dumitrescu, Domnita, *Spanglish and identity inside and outside the classroom*, Hispania 96:3 (2013), 436–437.
Ellis, Rod, *Understanding second language acquisition*, Oxford, Oxford University Press, 2015.
Erker, Daniel/Otheguy, Ricardo, *Contact and coherence. Dialectal leveling and structural convergence in NYC Spanish*, Lingua 172–173 (2016), 131–146.
Fairclough, Marta, *El (denominado) Spanglish en Estados Unidos. Polémicas y realidades*, Revista Internacional Lingüística Iberoamericana 2 (2013), 185–204.
Field, Fredric, *Bilingualism in the USA. The case of the Chicano-Latino community*, Amsterdam/ Philadelphia, Benjamins, 2011.
Fishman, Joshua A., *Bilingualism and biculturism as individual and as societal phenomena*, Journal of Multilingual and Multicultural Development 1:1 (1980), 3–15.
Foucault, Michel, *Les mots et les choses. Une archéologie des sciences humaines*, Paris, Gallimard, 1966.
Foucault, Michel, *L'archéologie du savoir*, Paris, Gallimard, 1969.
Franco, Juan C./Solorio, Thamar, *Baby-steps towards building a Spanglish language model*, in: Gelbukh, Alexander (ed.), *Computational linguistics and intelligent text processing. Proceedings of the 8th International Conference, CICLing 2007, Mexico City, Mexico, February 18–24*, Heidelberg, Springer, 2007, 75–84.
Fresneda, Carlos, *Livin' hablando spanglish*, La Revista de "El Mundo" 191 (1998), http://www.elmundo.es/larevista/num191/textos/livin.html [last access: 14.08.2018].
Gafaranga, Joseph, *Talk in two languages*, Houndmills, Palgrave Macmillan, 2007.
García, Ofelia, *Bilingual education in the 21st century. A global perspective*, Oxford, Wiley/ Blackwell, 2009.

Gardt, Andreas, *Diskursanalyse. Aktueller theoretischer Ort und methodische Möglichkeiten*, in: Warnke, Ingo (ed.), *Diskurslinguistik nach Foucault. Theorie und Gegenstände*, Berlin/ New York, De Gruyter, 2007, 28–52.

Garrido, Joaquin, *El español en los Estados Unidos*, in: Palacios, Azucena (ed.), *El español en América. Contactos lingüísticos en Hispanoamérica*, Barcelona, Ariel, 2008, 17–32.

González Echevarría, Roberto, *Is Spanglish a language?*, in: Stavans, Ilan (ed.), *Spanglish*, Westport, Greenwood, 2008, 116–117.

Hall, Stuart, *The West and the rest. Discourse and power*, in: Hall, Stuart/Gieben, Bram (edd.). *Formations of Modernity*, Cambridge, Polity Press, 1992, 185–227.

Hurtado, Aida/Vega, Luis, *Shift happens. Spanish and English transmission between parents and their children*, Journal of Social Issue 60:1 (2004), 137–55.

Jiang, Nan, *Lexical representation and development in a second language*, Applied Linguistics 21:1 (2000), 47–77.

Koch, Peter/Oesterreicher, Wulf, *Lengua hablada en la Romania. Español, francés, italiano*, Madrid, Gredos, 2007.

León Jiménez, Raquel, *Identidad multilingüe. El cambio de código como símbolo de la identidad en la literatura chicana*, Logroño, Servicio de Publicaciones Universidad de la Rioja, 2003.

Lipski, John M., *Varieties of Spanish in the United States*, Washington, DC, Georgetown UP, 2008.

Lopez, Mark H., *Is speaking Spanish necessary to be Hispanic? Most Hispanics say no*, Pew Research Center, 2016, https://www.pewresearch.org/fact-tank/2016/02/19/is-speaking-spanish-necessary-to-be-hispanic-most-hispanics-say-no/ [last access: 24.07.2016].

López García-Molins, Ángel, *Teoría del Spanglish*, Valencia, Tirant Humanidades, 2015.

MacSwan, Jeff, *Codeswitching and generative grammar. A critique of the MLF model and some remarks on "modified minimalism"*, Bilingualism. Language and Cognition 8:1 (2005), 1–22.

Montes-Alcalá, Cecilia, *Blogging in two languages. Code-switching in bilingual blogs*, in: Holmquvist, Jonathan/Lorenzino, Augusto/Sayahi, Lofti (edd.), *Proceedings of the Third Workshop on Spanish Sociolinguistics*, Somerville, Cascadilla Proceedings Project, 2007, 162–170.

Montes-Alcalá, Cecilia, *Hispanics in the United States. More than Spanglish*, Camino Real 1:0 (2009), 97–115.

Montes-Alcalá, Cecilia, *Writing on the border. English y español también*, in: Junquera Martín, Imelda (ed.), *Landscapes of writing in Chicano literature*, New York, Palgrave Macmillan, 2013, 213–230.

Morales, Ed, *Living in Spanglish. The search for Latino identity in America*, New York, St, Martin's Press, 2002.

Myers-Scotton, Carol, *Social motivations for codeswitching. Evidence from Africa*, Oxford, Clarendon Press, 1995.

Myers-Scotton, Carol, *Code-switching*, in: Coulmas, Florian (ed.), *The handbook of sociolinguistics*, Oxford, Blackwell, 1997, 217–237.

Negrón, Rosalyn, *Spanish as a heritage language and the negotiation of race and intra-Latino hierarchies in the U.S.*, in: Potowski, Kim (ed.), *The Routledge handbook of Spanish as heritage language*, New York, Routledge, 2018, 107–123.

Otheguy, Ricardo, *El llamado espanglish*, in: López Morales, Humberto (ed.), *Enciclopedia del español en Estados Unidos*, Madrid, Instituto Cervantes/Editorial Santillana, 2009, 222–247.
Otheguy, Ricardo/Zentella, Ana C., *Apuntes preliminarios sobre nivelación y contacto en el uso pronominal del español en Nueva York*, in: Montrul, Silvana/Potowski, Kim/Cameron, Richard (edd.), *Spanish in contact. Educational, linguistic, and social perspectives*, Amsterdam, Benjamins, 2007, 273–293.
Otheguy, Ricardo/Stern, Nancy, *On so-called Spanglish*, International Journal of Bilingualism 15:1 (2010), 85–100.
Otheguy, Ricardo/García, Ofelia/Reid, Wallis, *Clarifying translanguaging and deconstructing named languages. A perspective from linguistics*, Applied Linguistics Review 6:3 (2015), 281–307.
Poplack, Shana, *"Sometimes I'll start a sentence in Spanish Y TERMINO EN ESPAÑOL." Toward a typology of code-switching*, Linguistics 18:7–8 (1980), 581–618.
Poplack, Shana, *Syntactic structure and social function of code-switching*, in: Duran, Richard P. (ed.), *Latino language and communicative behavior*, New Jersey, Ablex Publishing Corp, 1981, 169–184.
Postma, Regan L., *"Por qué leemos esto en la clase de español?" The politics of teaching literature in Spanglish*, Hispania 96:3 (2013), 442–443.
Potowski, Kim, *Identity and heritage learners. Moving beyond essentializations*, in: Beaudrie, Sara/Fairclough, Marta (edd.), *Spanish as a heritage language in the US. State of the science*, Georgetown, University Press, 2012, 283–304.
Potowski, Kim, *Language maintenance and shift*, in: Bayley, Robert/Cameron, Richard/Lucas, Ceil (edd.), *The Oxford handbook of sociolinguistics*, Oxford, Oxford University Press, 2013, 321–339.
Potowski, Kim, *Bilingual youth. Spanish-speakers at the beginning of the 21st century*, Language and Linguistics Compass 10:6 (2016), 272–283.
Prieto Osorno, Alexander, *Spanglish. Una patria, una identidad*, Centro Virtual Cervantes, 2004, https://cvc.cervantes.es/el_rinconete/anteriores/mayo_04/25052004_01.htm [last access: 11.07.2018].
Rodríguez González, Eva/Parafita-Couto, María Carmen (2012), *Calling for interdisciplinary approaches to the study of Spanglish and its linguistic manifestations*, Hispania 95:3 (2012), 461–480.
Romaine, Suzanne, *Bilingualism*, Oxford, Basil Blackwell, 1989.
Rothman, Jason/Rell, Amy B., *A linguistic analysis of Spanglish. Relating language to identity*, Linguistics and the Human Sciences 1:3 (2007), 515–536.
Salaberry, Rafael, *¿Qué es el Espanglish?*, Hispánica 12 (2002), 3–4.
Sánchez-Muñoz, Ana, *Who soy yo? The creative use of "Spanglish" to express a hybrid identity in chicana/o heritage language learners of Spanish*, Hispania 96:3 (2013), 440–441.
Sayer, Peter, *Demystifying language mixing. Spanglish in school*, Journal of Latinos and Education 7:2 (2008), 94–112.
Schiffrin, Deborah (2001), *Discourse markers. Language meaning and context*, in: Schiffrin, Deborah/Tannen, Deborah/Hamilton, Heidi (edd.), *Handbook of discourse analysis*, Oxford, Basil Blackwell, 2001, 54–75.
Sebba Mark/Mahootian, Sharzahd/Jonsson, Carla (edd.), *Language mixing and code-switching in writing. Approaches to mixed-language written discourse*, New York/London, Routledge, 2012.

Stavans, Ilan, *Spanglish. The making of a new American language*, New York, Rayo, 2003.
Taylor, Paul/Lopez, Mark H./Martinez, Jessica/Velasco, Gabriel, *When labels don't fit. Hispanics and their views of identity*, Pew Research Center, 2012, http://www.pewhispanic.org/2012/04/04/when-labels-dont-fit-hispanics-and-their-views-of-identity/#language-use-english-and-spanish [last access: 24.07.2016].
United States Census Bureau, http://www.census.gov/en.html [last access: 13.07.2016].
Villa, Daniel, *¿¡Cómo que Spanglish!? Creating a service learning component for a Spanish heritage language program*, in: Rivera-Mills, Susana/Trujillo, Juan Antonio (edd.), *Building communities and making connections*, Newcastle upon Tyne, Cambridge Scholars, 2010, 120–134.
Zentella, Ana C., *Growing up bilingual. Puerto Rican children in New York*, New York, Blackwell, 1997.
Zentella, Ana C., *Latin@ languages and identities. Latinos! An agenda for the 21st century*, in: Suárez-Orozco, Marcelo/Páez, Mariela (edd.), *Latinos. Remaking America*, Berkeley, University of California Press, 2002, 321–338.
Zentella, Ana C., *"Dime con quién hablas y te diré quién eres". Linguistic (in)security and Latino unity*, in: Flores, Juan/Rosaldo, Renato (edd.), *The Blackwell companion to Latino studies*, Malden, MA, Blackwell, 2007, 25–39.
Ziem, Alexander/Wengeler, Martin, *Wie über Krisen geredet wird. Einige Ergebnisse eines diskursgeschichtlichen Forschungsprojektes*, Zeitschrift für Literatur und Linguistik 173 (2014), 52–74.

Eugenia Mangialavori Rasia
Building locations from directional prepositions
Divergent uses of *estar hasta* in Spanish varieties

Abstract: This paper discusses divergent distributional patterns drawn by spatial prepositions in Spanish. We focus on constructions in Mexican Spanish (MS) where the copula *estar* 'be' and a prepositional phrase predicate headed by a directional boundary preposition (*hasta* 'until') are productively combined in a distinct, complex spatial predicate with additional semantic implications. This combination is (i) not found in standard Spanish; (ii) unpredicted according to general (cross-language) principles on spatial prepositions and stative verbs. Yet, we observe that these instances – along with a putative semantic conflict between a stative verb and a directional preposition – are readily accommodated under a general condition on directional prepositions bearing on endpoint interpretation. We argue that important distributional divergences are due to the fact that, in varieties like MS, the grammar systematically allows for non-trivial preposition alternations (*estar en/hasta* 'be at/be at [from here]') which produce sufficiently different constructions with consequent asymmetries in semantic complexity (e.g., location vs perspectival location). This leads to a contrast in the possibility to encode simple vs relative location with respect to a reference object, potentially involving distance/route.

Keywords: copula, *estar*, location, preposition, directional, stative, no-trivial alternation

1 Introduction

Puzzling patterns in a regional or national variety may not only point to contrasts with respect to the *standard* (so to speak) variety in productivity and distribution, but also raises questions about traditional assumptions and

---

Note: We would like to thank the participants of IberoCon (Ghent, 2015) for interesting discussions on a previous version of this paper as well as to anonymous reviewers for their insightful comments. Most of all, we want to thank Rafa Marin for his valuable contribution.

Eugenia Mangialavori Rasia, National Scientific and Technical Research Council-Argentina

https://doi.org/10.1515/9783110736250-008

major cross-linguistic principles. This paper focuses on occurrences of the locative copula *estar* 'be at' with the preposition (P) *hasta* 'until, up to' which are surprising considering the general syntactic and semantic rules of stative verbs and spatial Ps.

Particular varieties of Spanish display non-standard uses of directional Ps like *hasta* 'up to'. In Mexican Spanish (MS) in particular, this P is productively combined with the copula *estar* 'be' to locate an entity in space. The examples in (1) are adapted from naturally occurring data.[1]

(1) a. *La casa está hasta la punta del pueblo.*
      the house is$_{ESTAR}$ up to the tip of-the village
      'The house is at the end of the village.' (Mexican Spanish)
  b. *El puente está hasta el límite oeste de la ciudad.*
      the bridge is$_{ESTAR}$ up to the limit West of the city
      'The bridge is at the West border of the city.'
  c. *El salón estaba hasta arriba.*
      the room was$_{ESTAR}$ up to up.
      'The room was upstairs.'
  d. *En la lista de Fortune, Carlos Slim está hasta adelante.*
      in the list of Fortune Carlos Slim is$_{ESTAR}$ up to in front
      'In Fortune's list, Carlos Slim is ahead.'
  e. *El salón comedor estaba hasta el último piso.*
      the dining room was$_{ESTAR}$ up to the last floor
      'The dining room was on the top floor.'

Occurrences of this type – briefly reported in Dominicy (1982), Lope Blanch (2008), Bosque/Bravo (2011) – have largely remained unnoticed in the literature, although they imply relevant theoretical considerations.[2]

In particular, data like in example (1) contrast sharply with the standard distribution of locative constructions with *estar* (2). In the latter, a non-directional boundary P *a* 'at' alternates with either the *non*-bounded locative P *en* or with

---

[1] These data are quantitatively and qualitatively significant as can be seen in corpus searches (Davies 2016, CREA, CORDE). The present data were double-checked by a control group of 50 native MS informants via online surveys specifically designed for this study (e.g. https://www.surveymonkey.com/r/XKBDMLX). The examples directly taken from corpus search (unmodified) are provided with the relevant extraction data in footnotes (e.g. (3)b below).

[2] Corpus data show that these patterns are highly productive across different registers (oral/written).

non-bounded directional Ps like *hacia* 'towards', *adelante* 'in front of' (2)b-d, etc. The direct combination of *estar* with boundary directional Ps like *hasta* simply does not occur, or, in other words the MS construction is unavailable.

Moreover, examples like (1)c-d show that MS further diverges from standard Spanish (SS)[3] by freely combining *hasta* with other directional Ps and adverbs like *adelante* 'ahead' and *arriba* 'up'. These Ps/Advs are not rare with *estar* in general, but the difference is that, in SS, *hasta* is not required, nor allowed, between both elements *estar* and *hasta* ((2)c-d). In MS, by contrast, co-occurrence is optional but not trivial. In principle, the presence of *hasta* correlates with a perspectival flavour which is absent from the standard (*hasta*-less) combination. As will be shown below (Sections 1.3.2 and 4.1), (1)c-e could be translated (roughly) as 'upwards/ahead/on (from here)'.

(2) a. *La casa está {en/a/*hasta} la punta del pueblo.*
 the house is$_{ESTAR}$ in at until the tip of-the town
 'The house is at the end of the village.'   (Standard Spanish)
 b. *El puente está {hacia/en} el límite oeste de la ciudad.*
 the bridge is$_{ESTAR}$ towards in the limit West of the city
 'The bridge is towards/on the West border of the city.'
 c. *El salón estaba arriba.*
 the room was$_{ESTAR}$ up.
 'The room was upstairs.'
 d. *En la lista de Fortune, Carlos Slim está adelante.*
 in the list of Fortune Carlos Slim is$_{ESTAR}$ in front
 'In the Fortune list, Carlos Slim is ahead.'
 e. *El salón comedor estaba en el último piso.*
 the room dining was$_{ESTAR}$ in the last floor.
 'The dining room was on the top floor.'

In other Spanish varieties, like Colombian Spanish (CS), divergence from SS involves the temporal use of *hasta* with punctual verbs (4).[4] In MS, temporal *hasta* is

---

[3] We use "standard" sensu lato (e.g., not constrained to European vs American standards), etc. (see Paffey 2012 amongst others).
[4] Thus in the distribution of *estar* and temporal adverbials and quantifiers in stative predications (cf. *es temprano; somos pocos/menos* (lit. be$_{SER}$ early/few/less) in the standard distribution) (Mangialavori Rasia 2020).

(i) a. *Está temprano.*
 be$_{ESTAR}$ early
 'It's early [now].'

also non-standardly combined with *estar* to situate states in time, as illustrated in (3). What is striking about these cases is the (rather unexpected) semantic contribution of the P, as *hasta* 'until' does not mark the endpoint but rather the onset of the state – i.e., it acquires and an ingressive meaning –, as shown by the gloss (cf. also English: 'be ready up to/until').[5]

(3) a. *La tarea   estará   terminada hasta el   final del   día.*
        the homework be_ESTAR·FUT finished   up to the end of-the day
        'The homework will be finished by the end of the day.'
        (Mexican Spanish)
     b. *El estudio estará   listo hasta el final de la actual*
        the study be_ESTAR·FUT ready up to the end of the current
        Administración.[6]
        Administration
        'The study will be ready by the time the current administration finishes.'
     c. *La normativa recién estará   lista hasta julio de este año.*
        the regulation only be_ESTAR.FUT ready up to July of this year
        'The regulation will be ready by July of this year.'

(4) *Se fue   hasta las 12 pm.* (Colombian Spanish)
     ERG went until the 12 pm
     '(He) left at 12 pm.'

The patterns found in (3) significantly diverge from SS in two respects. First, a semantically equivalent predication reflects a divergent distributional pattern of the P selection, as (5) shows. Second, *hasta* can be admitted in SS in similar contexts; yet, when allowed, it gives a crucially different reading, in line with the basic semantics of the P ('until'), and contrasting with the particular ('from') reading in MS (6).[7] Finally, although we will not concentrate on (4), it is interesting to note

---

   b. *Estamos pocos/menos/muchos.*
      be_ESTAR .2PL few/less/many.
      'We are few/less/too many now'(= 'There's few/less/a lot of us [right now]).'
[5] Note, in particular, the 'after' reading of 'by' in the glosses, essentially related to the onset (left boundary) of the state, rather than to a finishing (end)point (right boundary), as expected given the basic meaning of the P (*until*).
[6] Extracted from http://asa.gob.mx/es/ASA/Noticias/2286/sintesis-informativa-20-04-2016 [last access: 8.6.2017].
[7] This issue with not be further discussed here (see Mangialavori Rasia 2018). Nevertheless, the semantic entailment is possible for SS cases where *estar* is also associated – although with

that in such contexts the P is possible in SS only under negation in SS, as in (7), following the general (cross-language) behavior expected from non-stative verbs.[8]

(5) a. *La tarea   estará   terminada a/hacia   el final del   día.*
       the homework be$_{\text{ESTAR-FUT}}$ finished at toward the end of-the day
       'The homework will be finished at/by the end of the day.'
   b. *El estudio estará   listo a/para el final de la actual*
       the study be$_{\text{ESTAR-FUT}}$ ready at for the end of the current
       Administración.
       Administration
       'The study will be ready by the time the current administration closes.'
   c. *La normativa recién estará   lista en/a/sobre julio de este año.*
       the regulation only be$_{\text{ESTAR-FUT}}$ ready in at over July of this year
       'The regulation will be ready in/by July this year.'

(6) *La Selección Nacional estará   completa hasta el lunes.*
     the National Team   be$_{\text{ESTAR-FUT}}$ complete up to the Monday
     'The National Team will be complete <u>until</u> Monday.'   (Standard Spanish)
     'The National Team will be complete <u>by</u> Monday.'   (Mexican Spanish)

(7) ***(No) se fue hasta las   12.*
     not   SE went up to the 12 (Standard Spanish)
     'He did *(not) leave until 12.'

In sum, the data addressed here are interesting not only because they point to a significant contrast with the syntax and semantics of SS, but they are unexpected from a wider (cross-linguistic) perspective, as shown in Section 1.1.

1.1 The point of divergence

As argued before, the problem posed by constructions like (1) is that a P standardly defined as a *dynamic boundary preposition* is found in a context (namely a locative construction) where a different type of P is expected. In principle, the

---

using a crucially different P – with the endpoint of an entailed *preparatory phase* concomitant with the establishment of the designated (result) state (e.g. *Estuvo lista en media hora* 'She was ready in half an hour', Brucart 2012, 23). If correct, the distinctive semantic flavour yielded by *hasta* in MS constitutes a relevant point of divergence with the 'standard' variety yet untapped, as far as our knowledge goes.
8 On the use of eventive (punctual) verbs and *hasta*, see Dominicy (1982) and Rico (2015).

boundary component of *hasta* is in itself not a problem. The P *a* 'at', which is the P standardly combined with *estar* in locative constructions (recall (2)a above), is also generally defined as a boundary P. Besides, boundedness is particularly relevant to copular distribution, as illustrated in (8), considering the affinity of *estar* with bounded predicates, especially in contrast with *ser*.[9]

(8) La casa {está/*es} hasta la punta del pueblo.
 The house is$_{at}$/is up to the tip of the village
 'The house is at the end of the village.' (Mexican Spanish)

Rather, what is important here is the classification of *hasta* as a *directional* or *dynamic* (boundary) P[10], as this kind of P is generally seen with dynamic verbs but not with stative ones – especially not with a copula – and is certainly not expected to yield locative predicates like (1), according to both SS and general (cross-linguistic) standards.

1.2 Analysis and alternatives

A question that arises is whether the *anomalous* (Lope Blanch 2008, 58) constructions – namely, the divergences shown by MS from SS – are to be dismissed as trivial (progressive) uses of either the copula or the P. An alternative approach, defended in this paper, is that the combination of *estar* and a directional boundary P instantiates a legitimate, non-trivial, and fully productive grammatical option in MS. An important issue motivating this line of inquiry is whether the use of *hasta* illustrated in (1) is part of a more general phenomenon which challenges the idea that directional Ps are not to be expected with stative verbs, and especially not with locative predicates.

A formal account of the problem must take several elements into consideration. First, we need to establish whether the combination of a directional P and a copula in locative constructions is possible in general (that is, outside the specific

---

9 See Marín (2010) and Husband (2012, 7) for a summary; Mangialavori Rasia (2013; 2018) on locative *estar*.
10 For the moment, we preserve both terms, since they are both frequently used in the literature. A basic opposition has been proposed between location/stativity on the one hand, and direction/dynamicity on the other one, where dynamicity and directionality are indistinguishably related (Winter 2005). Whereas the definition of *hasta* as a *dynamic boundary P* is not rare (Saldanya/Rigau 2005,17), we will note facts supporting its classification as *directional P* is also justified, especially given the clash between dynamicity and the stativity of these constructions see Section (0).

frame of SS grammar) under any circumstances. Secondly, we need to consider if *estar hasta* is somehow allowed in SS. If the answer is positive, we shall further analyse which (semantic) conditions allow this. As a next step, we consider whether *estar* is the only stative verb in MS with a directional boundary P or whether other verbs (possibly other types) are used productively in this pattern. This should cast some light on how MS converges with SS, but also how they diverge.

The standard use of *estar hasta* shows a construction in which the directional P also contributes to a stative predicate, as exemplified by (9). These constructions are important in two respects. First, the analysis of (9) will allow us to detect a semantic entailment central to a general constraint on the combination of copulas and directional Ps. Furthermore, these cases may help us to identify relevant ways in which the standard *estar hasta* constructions differ from comparable predicates formed by adjectival predicates (AP) and non-directional Ps. This, in turn, could allow us to pinpoint structural semantic properties of *hasta* which contribute to a semantically and syntactically distinct construction.

(9) Estar   hasta {el moño/el borde/la coronilla} (de problemas/trabajo/quejas)
     be$_{ESTAR}$ up to the bun/the seam/the crown   of problems/work/complaints
     'To be saturated with problems/work/complaints.'

By initial hypothesis, we assume here that: (i) *hasta* is freely available in MS for a spatial predicate with distinct semantic implications, which are somehow linked to the denotational properties of the P; (ii) the selection of *hasta* in MS responds to the possibility to construe a sufficiently different predicate from 'standard' locative constructions with *estar*, shown in (2). As a consequence, the standard constructions and the MS patterns with *hasta* show into significant variability.

Hasta being non-trivial to the construction (and its distinct denotation) is key to narrowing down the range of possible analytic options. For example, a coercion-like solution to the putative conflict between a stative verb and a dynamic P is naturally avoided if (1) is the result of a motivated grammatical alternative. A non-trivial contrast with the locative in (2) would discourage simplifications along these lines. Whatever the correct analysis is, it is clear that any successful approach cannot overlook the empirical fact that, for some reason, (2) coexists, and alternates non-trivially with (1) in MS.[11]

---

[11] An alternative approach to the alleged conflict between the stative V and the dynamic P would be to assume that at least one member of the predicate allows a reading amenable to

Finally, we also want to avoid an analysis carried out under the assumption that the P is ambiguous between a locative and a dynamic reading (a discussion that goes back to Dowty 1979, 263 amongst others), and this for two reasons. First, there are good arguments to assume that there are no lexically ambiguous Ps, but rather that these Ps are either locative or dynamic/directional. Second, it has been shown that the denotation of a relation different from the one lexically encoded by the P is the result of a composition (cf. Gehrke 2006 for a summary). For instance, examples of locative readings of directional Ps, such as (10)a-b (cf. Zwarts 2008, building on Cresswell 1978), are not rare in most languages. Importantly, they all seem to involve stative verbs.

(10) a. *The train is ahead/through the tunnel* (Jackendoff 1983, 167).
 b. *Alex lives over the hill/around the corner/across the road/past the railroad station.*

Consequently, it is not unreasonable to assume that the stativity[12] of the locative construction produced by *hasta* in (1) is also the result of a specific construction –

---

the semantic type of the other. In principle, if *hasta* is reinterpreted as a *locative* boundary P, the combination with *estar* would not be a problem but rather a natural choice, especially because this copula is the one normally used for stative location in Spanish. Moreover, locative boundary Ps also commonly combine with *estar* in non-spatial situations (e.g., *El billete está a 3€*. 'The ticket costs €3'), providing a prepositional alternative to the widely-analysed adjectival predication (e.g., *Juan está* ($_{AP}$gustoso/$_{PP}$a gusto) *con las reformas* 'Juan is pleased/at ease with the restoration'). Such a potential for the delivery of both locative and more abstract situations (states in general) is a hallmark of *estar* and is central to the facts under discussion herez (starting from the lack of productivity of V$_{stative}$+*hasta* with *ser* and the consequent lack of free copular alternation). Nevertheless, given that MS also features *estar a/en* constructions against which *hasta* is selected non-trivially, and the resulting predications are clearly different, the problem is not solved by simply analysing the locative situation produced with *hasta* as a result of a coerced interpretation of the P. As will be argued later, this is a compositional effect, clearly due to the semantic (locative) contribution of *estar*.

12 The *estar hasta* constructions show the expected behaviour for states: they do not form imperatives (unlike the eventive form *estarse*) and cannot be combined with culminative verbs like *terminar* 'finish' (Dowty 1979), as shown by (i). As (ii) indicates, they do not allow progressive inflection nor adjuncts.

(i) a. *¡{está/estate} hasta el tope! vs. ¡estate quieto!
 be$_{IMP}$ be$_{IMP.REFL}$ up to the top! 'Be up to the top.' be$_{IMP.REFL}$ still 'Stay still!'
 b. *? *Terminó de estar hasta el tope*
 finished of be$_{ESTAR}$ up to the top 'It finished being completely full.'

crucially, headed by the locative copula.[13] Nevertheless, the relevant observation here is that this constructional stativity does not neutralise the specific contribution of the directional P, which is relevant for various reasons. It will be shown that the denotational properties of *hasta* explain the particular semantic properties of this locative use, providing a natural explanation for the non-trivial prepositional alternation displayed by MS. Crucially, these semantic properties concur with a general (cross-linguistic) condition constraining the combination of directional Ps and stative verbs drawing on cases like (10) (see (13) below).

1.3 Hypothesis and proposal

The current approach rests on two assumptions. First, we need to allow for the possibility that *hasta* somehow instantiates a directional boundary P involved in circumstances other than merely expressing the goal and/or endpoint of a *dynamic* relation. What is crucial here is the classification of *hasta* as a *directional* rather than as a *dynamic* P (see footnote 10).

The second key to the problem will be provided by a cross-linguistic condition constraining the combination of a copula with a directional P (introduced in Section 1.4). This condition is supported by more contexts in which stative verbs productively combine with *hasta* in MS. This condition, applied to both locative and temporal MS constructions, supports the idea that the combination creates a specific circumstance where the Prepositional Phrase (PP) realizes a path boundary compatible with endpoint interpretation. The data would thus be consistent with the idea that *hasta* introduces either a quantitative or spatial *terminus*, which produces specific consequences compatible with the facts observed in MS.

The analytical alternative results from crossing the traditional definition of the P, reproduced in (11)a, with the two main semantic flavours adopted by *estar* (temporally bounded situations and locations), as summarised in (11)b. While the general approach is compatible with important definitions of the

---

(ii)   a.   *El salón estaba (*estando) hasta el tope (de gente).*
          the room was being.$_{ESTAR}$ up to the top of people 'The room was being bursting at the seams with people.'
     b.   *El salón estuvo hasta el tope *(gradualmente/progresivamente).*
          the room was$_{ESTAR}$ up to the top gradually progressively 'The room was bursting at the seams gradually.'

[13] For a detailed discussion and additional evidence, see Mangialavori Rasia/Marín (2018) and Mangialavori Rasia (2013; 2018) for a unified structural account of standard Spanish data.

Spanish P such as Talmy's (12), the specific analysis proposed here – presented in detail in Section (0) – is drawn from studies where the aspectual contribution of spatial Ps is laid out in terms of Vector Space Semantics (Winter 2001 amongst others).

(11) a. *Hasta*: prep. Conveys a terminus on time, places, actions o quantities (Real academia Española 2020 [DRAE]; translation is ours).
b. *estar hasta*: spatial/quantitative terminus.

(12) The Spanish P *hasta* appears to capture exactly the (g) notion (for both space and time) of motion or temporal continuation along an extent bounded at only one end, so that *hasta Chicago* means 'as far as/up to Chicago' and *hasta las 3:00* means 'until 3:00'.
(g)Notion: A point MOVE ALONG-TO an extent bounded at a terminating point, at a point of time/in a bounded extent of time (*The car reached the house at 3:05*) (Talmy 2000, 254).

If correct, there is a systematic way in which locative constructions with consistent structural characteristics can be produced from a directional P. This, in turn, explains a more general problem, involving its productive combination with stative/locative verbs other than *estar* in MS (see (25)–(27) below). To this end, however, we first need to take a look at the general problem posed by the stative reading of *hasta*, as well as the relevant condition under which its occurrence with a copula is expected.

1.4 The condition

It is widely assumed that locative Ps can always be used in combination with copulas like 'be' to form a locative predication, whereas directional Ps are somewhat unexpected – unless under certain circumstances. Various works on spatial Ps show that directional or dynamic Ps may be used in those cases where the location is understood as the endpoint of a *hypothetical journey*, described by the P, from an implicit *point of view* (Cresswell 1978; Zwarts 2005, 742), as in (13) a. Otherwise, dynamic Ps are allowed if accompanied by Measure Phrases (MPs), as in (13)b. The first condition – which we will call here End Point Condition (EPC) – provides us with a key to the problem of MS locatives, as argued below, and point to an important contrast between *hasta* and other PPs frequently combined with *estar*.

(13) a. *The house is {behind/outside/across} the woods (from here)* (Zwarts 2005, 3).
 b. *The house is* one mile *{from here/to the east/outside the town/behind the church}.*

The second condition – called the Measure Phrase Condition (MPC) – reveals, an interesting contrast. In Spanish, MPs occur with directional Ps; however, unlike in English, this circumstance also involves a locative boundary P, which is required (cf. (13)b vs. (14)a), independent of the directional PP (cf. the English gloss in (14)b).[14]

(14) a. *La casa está *(a) una milla (desde aquí/hacia el este/fuera de la ciudad).*
 the house is$_{ESTAR}$ (*at) one mile from here toward the East outside of the city
 'The house is one mile from here/to the East/outside the city.'
 b. *La casa está a una milla.*
 *the house is at one mile
 'The house is one mile away.'

Note, nonetheless, that, whereas MS differs from English ((15)a) in this respect, for a significant portion of natives *hasta* can be freely used to head the MP, as in (15)b.[15] Interestingly, this does not affect its interpretation in line with the one of (14)a. In SS, by contrast, comparable occurrences are allowed, but only with an 'up to' reading, as in (15)b.

(15) a. *La casa está* ??*(una milla) hasta { la punta del pueblo/el bosque/el este}.*
 the house is$_{ESTAR}$ one mile up to the end of-the town the woods the East
 'The house is (one mile) from the end of the town/the woods/the East.'

---

14 Interestingly, the English gloss suggests that a sense of distance is also involved in *estar a*. This issue will be taken up later and fully explained in Section (0). For the moment, it is important to stress that there are important grammatical differences involved.
15 More specific surveys showed mixed results (50% of the answers mark the construction as good, 30% as odd, while the remaining 20% rejects it. Apparently, informants feel more comfortable with an unspecified difference value (distance) calculated relatively (in relation to the location of the woods, the town, etc.). This latter sense of unspecific/relative distance is unanimously accepted. This problem is specifically addressed in Section (0).1.

b. *La casa está hasta una milla {fuera/detrás} del pueblo.*
   the house is up to one mile outside behind of-the town
   'The house is (one mile) outside/behind the town.' (MS reading)
   'The house is up to one mile outside/behind the town.' (SS reading)

Thus, the location yielded by *estar hasta* involves an important contrast with the one produced by *estar a*. Experimental surveys on natives show that 100% of the respondents report a clear difference in meaning between these alternatives in contexts like (1).[16] According to preliminary data, while the specific entailment of *estar hasta* is defined in terms of *lejanía* 'remoteness' (50%), *distancia* 'distance' (30%), *recorrido* 'route' (10%) and *dirección* 'direction' (10%), *estar a* is unanimously interpreted as a simple location. We will elaborate on this later Section (0); for the moment, it is important to bear in mind that the distinctive semantic flavour observed – and thus, the relevant difference behind the non-trivial P choice in MS – is intuitively related to some sort of *perspectival location* and *distance* (in the standard sense, e.g., Talmy 2000). Significantly, the additional semantic nuance in *estar hasta* is crucially amenable to the one introduced by 'from here' in (13)a. In fact, Cresswell (1978) argues that this possibility depends directly on the denotational properties of the directional P, which introduces a contextually determined *point of view* from which the object location is defined or identified. In sum, the relevant semantic component that we see in the 'journey' sense of spatial (directional) Ps above – crucial to locative use of the directional P with a copula, as shown in (16) –, is the same as the one that motivates the choice of P in MS. Moreover, this entailment is strong enough to make the 'from here' PP redundant in MS, as in (17).

(16) *The Post Office is through the hill *(from here)* (Cresswell 1978, 112).

(17) *La   casa   está   hasta   (detrás de) el lote (?desde aquí).*
     the house is$_{ESTAR}$ up to (behind) the lot   from here
     'The house is (at/behind of) the lot (from here).'   (Mexican Spanish)

Now, to show how the EPC explains the availability of *estar hasta*, we first need to complete the general frame by considering the standard uses, that is, cases aligned with the EPC in which MS and SS converge. This will provide a preliminary idea about the contribution made systematically by the P in stative predicates.

---

[16] See https://www.surveymonkey.com/r/XKBDMLX for the surveys.

2 *Estar*, states, and boundaries: the alternative available in Standard Spanish

2.1 Scalar boundaries and prepositional phrase predicates

As stated before, *estar hasta* is productive in SS. It is, nonetheless, restricted to more abstract (non-locative) uses with very specific properties. These characteristics contrast with the alternative presented by adjectival (AP) predicates which are frequently combined with *estar* in the denotation of states.

A simple corpus search shows that an array of *estar hasta* constructions like (18) is generally available for describing a state of affairs in (Standard) Spanish.

(18) a. *El artículo está hasta el borde de spoilers.*
the article be$_{ESTAR}$ filled up to the brim with spoilers
'The article is flooded with spoilers.'
Cf. *El artículo está (lleno) hasta el borde de spoilers.*
the article is$_{ESTAR}$ up to the brim of with spoilers
b. *El local estaba hasta los topes y no cabía ni un alma.*
the room was.$_{ESTAR.IMP}$ up to the tops and not fit not a soul
'The place was packed and there was no room for a[nother] soul.'
c. *Si el radiador está hasta el borde con agua, se tiene que drenar.*
if the radiator is$_{ESTAR}$ up to the brim with water SE has that drain
'If the radiator is saturated with water, it has to be drained.'
d. *El cortado no está hasta el borde.*
the latte not is$_{ESTAR}$ up to the brim
'The [cup of] latte is not to the brim.'

The construction diverges from regular state *estar* predicates as it involves a sense of saturation or maximal capacity in which an upper boundary is a relevant part of the denotation. A similar construction, exemplified by (19), is often used to convey a comparable sense of maximal capacity (in the sense of Hay/ Kennedy/Levin 1999, amongst others).

(19) *Juan está   hasta el   moño.*
    Juan is_ESTAR up to the bun
    'Juan is up to his crown'
    ['Juan has too much on his plate']
    cf. *Juan está   hasta el   moño [de trabajo]*
    Juan   is_ESTAR up to the bun   [of work]
    'Juan is really fed up.' 'Juan is burned out.'

Even if the defective interpretation of this type of constructions is associated with emotional saturation, note that any extreme degree can be implied. So the construction can be used if Juan is extremely busy, tired, depressed, etc. Even if we consider regional (lexical) variations, as in (20), we see that a significant number of PP predicates headed by *hasta* are used productively to express saturation applied to any state/condition, paralleling spatial saturation (21).

(20) *Estar hasta el moño* 'the bow', *las narices* 'the nose', *la coronilla* 'the crown', *el copete* 'the tuft' (Mexico), *las cejas* 'the eyebrows', *el gorro* 'the hat', *los pelos* 'the hair' (Spain), *las manos* 'the hands' (Argentina), *la tusa* 'the mane' (Chile).

(21) a. *El   tranvía a menudo está   hasta la bandera de gente.*
        the tram   often   is_ESTAR up to the flag   of people
        'The tram is often crammed with people.'
    b. *El   sitio   está   hasta la   gorra de vendedores   ambulantes.*
        the place is_ESTAR up to the hat   of street   vendors.
        'The place is saturated with street vendors.'

Now, a characteristic of states/situations yielded by *hasta* PPs is that boundedness is interpreted as a maximal point on a path/interval (e.g. an incremental scale). Initially, this sense of maximal degree or saturation seems comparable to the one yielded by AP predicates, especially when combined with maximality adjuncts, as in (22). There are, however, interesting differences.

(22) *El profesor   está   (completamente/totalmente/absolutamente)*
                        {cansado/triste/feliz}.
    the teacher is_ESTAR completely/totally/absolutely tired/sad/happy
    'The teacher is (completely/totally/absolutely) {tired/sad/happy}.'

Interestingly, the relevant scalar structure in *estar hasta* constructions (as MP/endpoint constructions) is crucially independent of further (e.g., AP/participial) predicates. In this sense, it might appear that an important part of the examples in (18) respond to some sort of elided (e.g., participial) form of a *filling*-type verb (e.g., *lleno* 'full') selecting for the boundary phrase (*hasta* + DP). This would involve a natural explanation at different levels. Namely, a predicate of the type of *lleno* (i.e., a participial form) could supply the eventive component on which dynamic Ps, along with a sense of perfectivity/telicity/resultativity[17] are expected. Furthermore, this predicate, associated with a property scale bounded at an upper/maximal value (McNally 2011 amongst others), would provide the desired scalar structure – i.e., one in which the scalar boundary coincides with maximal degree. Nonetheless, the presence of a participial or adjectival form is at least dubious in the construction exemplified by (19) (cf. *Juan está (*lleno/saturado) hasta el moño* 'Juan is filled/saturated to the bun'). The relevant sense of saturation is also independent of adjuncts normally contributing to the determination of a maximal scalar degree:[18] both *lleno* and *completamente* in (23)b can be left out without affecting the sense of maximal degree.

(23) a. *El   vaso   está   [completamente] lleno de agua.*
       the   glass is$_{ESTAR}$ completely   full   of water
       'The glass is [completely] filled with water.'
    b. *El   vaso   está   [#completamente] (lleno) hasta el   borde*
       the   glass is$_{ESTAR}$ completely   full   up to   the   brim
       de agua.
       of water
       'The glass is [completely] to the brim with water.'

Significantly, the SS construction is odd when either component – i.e., either the AP predicate or the maximality modifier – co-occurs with the prepositional predicate introduced by *hasta* (24). While the problem with the AP predicate can be explained on the basis of grammatical reasons – the copular predicate is already realised by the PP –;the combination with the maximality modifier is redundant.

(24) a. *El   profesor está   [?completamente] (*cansado/lleno/saturado)*
       the   teacher   is$_{ESTAR}$ completely   tired   full   saturated
       (hasta las cejas).
       up to the eyebrows
       'The teacher is [completely] saturated/filled/fed up.'

---

[17] These aspectual properties figure prominently in the discussion on *estar*, as for instance in Bosque (1990).
[18] Open-scaled APs like *feliz/triste* in (22) have been included to highlight the role of the adjunct, accordingly.

b. *El   profesor   está   [*?completamente] hasta las cejas*
   the teacher is$_{ESTAR}$ completely   up to the eyebrows
   (de trabajo/quejas).
   of work complaints
   'The teacher is [completely] saturated (with work/complaints).'

In sum, in *estar hasta* the distinctive scalar boundary does not depend (semantically nor syntactically) on an adjectival predicate nor on adjuncts contributing to the expression of a maximal degree situation. Instead, the sense of maximality seems to naturally follow from the structural properties of *hasta* and the EPC. To the extent that this state is understood as the endpoint of an incremental scalar structure, and that incremental scales can be safely related to scalar paths for states (see Hay et al. 1999 amongst others), the entailment of a corresponding scalar boundary and a maximal state in the data discussed here follows straightforwardly. Yet, it is important to bear in mind that the apparent stativity of these constructions contrasts sharply with the cases in which an incremental path involves change-of-state predications ultimately licensed by specific (e.g., participial) AP predicates of *estar* (23)a. Even if the situation is interpreted as the endpoint of an incremental scale in both cases, there is no dynamicity or process (event) entailed in *estar hasta*. This means that the path is not interpreted as a *journey*, strictly speaking, but merely as an incremental scalar structure mapped to property degrees.[19] Consequently, there is no resultative entailment, but only an upper boundary that produces the sense of *maximality* (see McNally 2011 amongst others) in question. How this scalar boundary is supplied is discussed in Section 2.2.

2.2 *Hasta* as a quantitative terminus

Notions on scale structures are useful to argue how a *quantitative terminus* (recall the definition of *hasta* in (11)) operates in the examples seen above, independently of constituents that typically introduce scales in stative predicates (e.g., AP).

---

[19] Note that, even if the *hypothetical journey* entailment would presumably licence a reading comparable to *incremental paths*, dynamicity is crucially not involved. Setting aside the fact that quantitative/qualitative scales are not exclusive to events, and that states may feature maximal points in a property scale without involving a process (the typical case made by adjectives, Hay et al. 1999, amongst others), it is widely accepted that magnitude can be involved independently of motion/eventivity. We do this by appealing to a non-temporal conception of Paths (see Section 4.2).

The general assumption is that degree expressions act on a degree variable, and that this variable corresponds to a *qualitative* scale for adjectives, and to a *quantitative* scale for nouns (Kennedy/McNally 2008, 140 amongst others).[20] This distinction is important and relates to how the crucial endpoint for EPC is estimated. On a *qualitative* magnitude what basically counts is how close the state yielded is to a scalar point or prototype for the designated property. By contrast, on a quantitative scale, the relevant scalar degree is calculated by how much of the entity is affected. In our case, what matters is that, first, the criterial boundary in (19)–(21) is amenable to quantitative maximality – i.e., the point at which the subject is maximally affected and second, the copular (PP) predicate marks this scalar boundary, in a sense that basically involves physical extension (even in abstract senses). The third point takes us back to the qualitative-adjective vs. quantitative-DP opposition discussed above, as the boundary at work is not of the type supplied by adjectives (property gradience), but rather, by a participant in the event(uality) which is consequently modelled in terms of its mereology or part structure (total affectation = event endpoint). The quantitative terminus explains the fact that a bounded scalar structure is available to the denotation of a maximal degree state even if no AP is there to contribute a relevant (i.e., property) scale.

Quantitative scalarity that bears on the nominal domain follows from the idea that the relevant scale is modelled on a quantised (part) structure supplied by an (affected) argument (Krifka 1998; Wechsler 2005 amongst others) that, arguably, provides the parameter with which maximal affectedness is estimated. This notion has many points in common with the way in which incremental themes measure out events, in the sense that the relevant magnitude is calculated against more and more *parts* of the entity being affected.[21] To this end, the DP must provide a scalar structure with an identifiable maximal point, which, in our case, is related to the extensional boundary defined by *hasta*. An important observation to make is that the scalar degree marked by the PP is interpreted as the *endpoint* of an incremental scale. Under the standard assumption,

---

[20] Experimental studies nonetheless suggest that both variables operate in AP predicates (Hansen/Chemla 2015).

[21] At this point, we should recall the caveat that maximality does not necessarily involve progression/eventivity. Quantitative maximal degrees have been studied extensively, even experimentally, in non-eventive predicates such as adjectival predicates and attributive constructions (see Hansen/Chemla 2017 for a summary and discussion). The quantitative/qualitative distinction allows us to differentiate between the *maximality* requirement holding for maximally-bounded scales, in contrast to *predominance* required for non-maximally closed scales (e.g., cases where the object only needs to be affected by 50% to be properly regarded as bearing the property in question; and, hence, for an attributive predication to hold, see also McNally 2011).

this structure is represented as a path (Kennedy/McNally 2005, 33, amongst others). In this sense, the situation is consistent enough with the EPC.

This said, consider examples (18)–(20) again. What calls our attention is that *estar hasta* constructions resemble maximal states in the form of a degree that amounts to reaching the filling line of a container (e.g., *The glass is full*) – i.e., maximal capacity – (cf. (21)). In stative predications in general, a comparable semantic structure can be formalised by analysing predicates like *full* as a function from container types to measure functions whose co-domains have different specific maximal values (Kennedy/McNally 2008; McNally 2011). For instance, while in maximal degree constructions like (18) saturation may vary among alternatives supplied by different choices of containers (*a room, a cup*), the regional variations in (20) involve arguably a same container (the experiencer) on which different boundaries are targeted, as different (lexical) ways to instantiate maximality. Again, the type of state experienced in each case is irrelevant and remains unspecified. What is important is the scalar (quantitative) endpoint instantiated by the PP, which, in combination with *estar*, produces the distinctive maximal degree entailment associated with these states.[22]

Finally, it has been argued that the relevant scalar structure is supplied by a participant, which is interpreted as the affected entity. In the specific case of psychological states, the participant would serve as a *fictive* container (Marín/Sánchez Marco 2012), which is then seen as bearing incremental degrees of any undefined emotion (e.g., tiredness, boredom, etc.). This accommodates the productive use of physical extensionality in general (e.g., *estar hasta los topes* lit. 'be up to the top(s)' 'to be fed up'). More importantly, abstract uses explain the combination of a stative/locative verb (*estar*) and a dynamic boundary (*hasta*) along the lines just described. If the assumptions discussed above are correct, the maximal degree corresponds to a situation in which the container (i.e., the experiencer) is *filled* with the emotion up to a maximal degree, with maximality determined by the *capacity* of the affected entity to accommodate incremental amounts of material, emotion, substance. Crucially, this is done in a way in which

---

[22] Notice that the *of-phrase* (*de agua/quejas/gente/vendedores* 'of water/complaints/people/vendors') in (21)–(23)b–(24)b) reflects the *Holistic Effect* seen in *of/with-phrases*. This (since Anderson 1971) accounts for a well-known semantic effect in the locative alternation, whereby the location (container) is interpreted as completely full if realised as the affected object, but not if realised as a goal. In both cases, the crucial implication is that the extent of a container coincides with the relevant endpoint on a quantitative scale that models the predicate's *Aktionsart*. Note that the *of-phrase* does not contribute the relevant scalar magnitude, but rather the medium of saturation: quantised (e.g. *complaints*) and cumulative (*water, tiredness*) mediums equally yield saturation.

it is unnecessary to appeal to telicity, dynamicity, or to a scalar boundary marked by a constituent other than the one contributed by the PP – nor to a scalar structure other than the one provided by the DP subject, what is important in the case in (24) and the independence of AP predicates.

We are now in a position to complete the general picture by specifying how MS' use of *hasta* displays important divergences as well as points in common with the SS use outlined above. In order to provide further support for these observations, but also to integrate the MS use of *hasta* in the analysis, we will introduce an analytic option bearing on spatial Ps in the frame of Vector Space Semantics. Notions like *located vectors* are a particularly useful device for dealing with both SS and MS constructions in a way that fits well with the relevant condition at work (EPC).

3 Mexican Spanish: the bigger picture

In this section, we briefly consider data that indicate that *estar hasta* constructions are part of a more general phenomenon in MS. A productive, systematic, progressive pattern (stative verb + *hasta*) would outweigh analytical alternatives in terms of *anomalies* (cf. Lope Blanch 2008 above), coercion or lexicalisation, and would contribute to a legitimate grammatical option with a principled and transparent structural semantics.

As mentioned above, the essential stativity of MS locative constructions involves not only an empirical divergence from SS but also a more general one, at theoretical levels. Recall that, in principle, static verbs equivalent to *be*, *stay* and *remain* can be freely combined with locative PPs, as in (25)a, but not with directional (dynamic) ones, as (25)b suggests. This assumption holds not only for SS but also for various other languages, including English and Romance (cf. Gehrke 2006, amongst others, for a summary). Nonetheless, in MS this use of *hasta* extends significantly, often appearing with the Spanish equivalent of *remain* (*quedar*) (26) and several other verbs such as *ubicar* 'place', *delimitar*[23] 'limit', *vivir* 'live', etc., as exemplified in (27). All these verbs are stative and productively alternate in the construction of locative predications with a similar semantic specification.

---

[23] For a specific analysis of *estar* and surround-verbs in stative predicates, cf. García Pardo (2016), but also Mangialavori Rasia (2013; 2016).

(25) a. *La casa   queda {en / sobre / bajo / tras}   el puente.*
the house stays   in / on / under / behind the bridge
'The house is located in/over/under/behind the bridge.'
b. *La casa   queda *{para / hacia / desde / a través (de)/hasta}   el puente.*
the house stays   to / toward / from / through / up to   the bridge
'The house is located to/toward/from/through/up to the bridge.'

(26) *Los terrenos están sobre esta misma calle, pero la casa queda hasta el final.*
'The lands are on this same road, but the house stands at the end [of the road].'

(27) a. *Fue ubicado hasta el final de la hilera de mandatarios, al extremo opuesto de Chávez.*
was located up to the end of the line of premiers at-the extreme opposite of Chávez
'[He] was located at the end of the row, at the opposite end from Chávez.'[24]
b. *En un link con   letra   pequeña   ubicado hasta   el   final de la*
in a   link with   letter   small   placed   up to   the end   of the
página.
page
'In a link in small font located at the end of the page.'
c. *Pero el   casco   histórico se   delimita hasta Limacpampa.*
but   the   historic quarter   SE delimits up to Limacpampa
'But the historic center is delimited at Limacpampa.'
d. *Vive hasta las afueras* (Lope Blanch 2008, 78).
live.3S up to the outskirts
'[He] lives at the outskirts.'
e. *Se sentó hasta adelante* (Lope Blanch 2008, 58).
ERG seated up to in front
'[He] seated in the front.'

The key point here is that the systematic combination with static (locative) verbs does not affect the structural properties of the P: *hasta* keeps licensing a grammatically explicit boundary DP, which is consequently interpreted, not as

---

24 Examples returned by corpus searches in the following sources (a) the Mexican newspaper La Jornada (http://www.jornada.unam.mx/); (b) a specialised website (technology) (http://conectica.com), and (c) the blog kokocusco.blogspot.com.

a simple location, but rather as the terminus of a directed line or linear arrange (the end of a row, of an avenue, or even the lower section of a sheet, as in (27) b). This is important not only as (non-dynamic) directionality is consistently involved, but also because the situation described (endpoint of linear arrangement) crucially concurs with Cresswell's definition of the EPC, presented above. Example (28) shows that the case at stake here, that is locative *estar hasta*, conforms to such patterns. In fact, in MS an expression, unavailable in SS, and in principle odd (if considered outside the compositional meaning) is productively used to express an indefinitely remote point in space, as in (29).[25]

(28) a. *El casco histórico está   hasta el límite   con   San Sebastián.*
the historic center is$_{ESTAR}$ up to the border with San Sebastián
'The historic center is on the border with San Sebastian.'
b. *Aquí la Puerta-Espejo está   hasta el fin   del   camino.*
Here the door-mirror   is$_{ESTAR}$ up to the end of-the road
'Here the Mirror Door is at the end of the road.'

(29) a. *Correos   está   hasta el fin   del   mundo.*
Post Office is$_{ESTAR}$ up to the end of-the world
'The Post Office is at the end of the world [at the end of nowhere].'
b. *Japón está   hasta el fin   del   mundo, dice Baldabiou.*
Japan is$_{ESTAR}$ up to the end of-the world says Baldabiou
'Japan is at the end of nowhere, says Baldabiou.'
c. *Preparar el   plano para la   obra del   cerro*
prepare the map for   the work of-the hill
cerro (que está hasta el fin del mundo).
that is$_{ESTAR}$ up to the end of-the world
'Set up the map for works on the hill (which is at the end of nowhere).'
d. *Fui   a   visitarla a   su   escuela, esa   que   está   hasta el*
went to visit   at her school that which is$_{ESTAR}$ up to the
fin   del   mundo.
end of-the world
'I came to visit her at the school, the one that is at the end of nowhere.'

---

25 Also here, advanced corpus searches show that the expression is found across different registers and contexts. The examples include tokens from oral production (29)a, literary texts (b), school papers (c), and blogs (d).

In sum, such patterns suggest that the principles behind the locative use of *hasta* are more general than expected, inasmuch as *estar hasta* represents a productive instance of a larger set of locative constructions obtained from the free combination of a significant array of static verbs with the directional boundary P.

As pointed out above, stativity[26] is crucial for both the verb and the interpretation of the PP. The general meaning conveyed by the P is important, as the structure obtained is not a dynamic but a locative one; and, at the same time, there is a non-trivial difference with the one produced by locative Ps.

Since this will play an important role in the discussion, it needs to be analysed in more detail. A fact that becomes evident from comparing divergent and standard locative constructions is that the selection of the directional (boundary) P in MS allows for a specific semantic entailment. It was argued above (Section 4) that this distinctive flavour is intuitively associated to remoteness and distance. This observation can be further refined. According to both descriptive studies (e.g., Lope Blanch 2008, 78) and judgments from native speakers of MS,[27] this distinctive trait is related to a sense of *distance* or relative situation *from a certain position*. Crucially, this position is unspecified enough to be potentially interpreted as set from the point of view of the speaker. This is central to the analysis in at least two ways: first, it draws a parallel with the '*from here*' entailment associated with the EPC; second, it lines up with the contextually determined point that is central to Cresswell's (1978) original formulation on how the hypothetical journey and the endpoint in question are established in stative + directional P constructions. Consequently, the key to the problem lies in the fact that the directional boundary P introduces an additional variable with which this sense of distance is calculated in a way close to (13)a –the prototypical example of EPC –, and which, at the same time, is different from the conditions enabling directional Ps via measure phrases in (13)b.

Crucially also, the DP introduced by *hasta* provides a boundary which is also different from endpoints normally yielded by directional PPs (e.g., the endpoint of a motion event). In this respect, a formal difference arises between non-standard and standard P choices (see the cases in (1) and (2) above). which anyhow conform to the definition of locative Ps "used to indicate where something is" as a result of the combination with a stative verb but also to other

---

[26] Which should be carefully distinguished from stativity insofar as not al stative predicates (e.g. Davisonian (event-like) states) are necessarily static.

[27] Obtained from a pool of 50 native Mexican Spanish speakers (see footnote 1). Here, for reasons of space and also of scope, we will concentrate on analytic data. For details and the specific experimental study, cf. Mangialavori Rasia/Marín (2018).

spatial relations yielded by dynamic/directional PPs, generally "used to indicate where something is going" (Zwarts 2005, 741). We will elaborate on these observations below. For the moment, let us anticipate that a clear distinction between dynamicity and directionality is necessary if we want to capture the non-trivial stativity of these constructions.

4 Two ways of producing boundedness from *estar hasta*

This section introduces an account for MS locative constructions based on Vector Space Semantics. This approach allows us to determine important ways in which MS converges and diverges with respect to SS and even other languages (e.g., in contrast to English).

4.1 Proposal: Vector Space Semantics

Vector Space Semantics (VSS) (Zwarts 1997; 2005; Zwarts/Winter 2000; Winter 2001) offers a natural account of spatial PPs and locative constructions using vectors and paths in its basic representation.[28]

The approach is compelling for different reasons. In our case, the insights offered are critical to develop an account of MS that captures the condition at work (EPC) and also retains the locative (non-dynamic) semantics in a way amenable to the sense of magnitude introduced by *hasta* in SS (i.e., non-spatial) constructions. In this respect, it is important to note that VSS allows for an account of attributive constructions which are comparable to the Spanish predicates under discussion (see Winter 2001) while it remains, at the same time,

---

28 Within the present framework, vectors – standardly conceived of as *directed* lines between points in space – are seen as the main ontological primitive in the compositional analysis of both locative and directional PP structures. Paths, on the other hand, are defined as the result of a composition (i.e., sets of vectors). However, we will not discuss the potential links between the account under consideration and alternative definitions of *path* offered in the literature (e.g. as nested sets of sequences of places, in Verkuyl/Zwart's 1992 view; as functions from some ordered domain to places in Cresswell 1978, amongst others), etc. Still, directionality is considered to be crucially involved, especially for the inconvenience of a filmstrip view pointed out by Jackendoff (i.e., the idea that event progression is not recorded as an event or as an ordered series of successive snapshots of the objects involved, at points along a timeline, see Jackendoff 1996, 306).

highly compatible with findings of semantic studies on scalar structures and maximal degrees also mentioned in this paper (e.g., Kennedy/McNally 2005).

Two basic assumptions are central to the discussion. First, under this framework, location and other spatial properties instantiate *relative* positions modelled by vectors (Zwarts 1997; 2003; Zwarts/Winter 2000). This is important to capture the fact that even simple locative predications (e.g., *La casa está detrás del bosque* 'The house is behind the woods') take a secondary located object as its main reference, rather than as a sequence of positions in an *absolute* space. Second, paths are analysed as *atemporal stretches of space*, which, in turn, require a fixed reference object (Zwarts 2005, 283). Even if such a reference object also figures, as just mentioned, in simple locative constructions, when applied to directional Ps this essential relativity provides the possibility to accommodate the sense of distance underlying *hasta* as a non-trivial choice in MS in terms of path structure. The careful separation of extension in space and time is crucial to account for the use of directional Ps and paths in stative constructions.

4.1.1 Locative prepositions

By definition, locative structures denote the situation of an object (the Located Object, henceforth LO) in the spatial frame provided by another object (the Reference Object, henceforth RO), as just mentioned. In the VSS framework, a fundamental property of locative Ps is that they denote a function that applies to the set of points where the RO is located and returns a set of vectors starting at potential zero-points to locate the LO (Zwarts/Winter 2000, 296).[29] These vectors all belong to one vector space with a zero element that describes the location of the RO. This means that in standard locative constructions like (30)a-b, where the relative location of the house (LO) is described in relation to the park (RO), all the vectors belong to one vector space with a zero-point set at (the location of) the RO, grammatically realised as a PP headed by a locative P. It follows that, for instance, in the case of the PP headed by *detrás* 'behind' (30)a, the location of the house is established by a set of *located vectors* extending backward from the park, thus determining the region within which the location of the house is framed.[30] In this located vector u <w_0, w_1>, illustrated in (31),

---

[29] The original proposal involves the assumption of a systematic mapping that shifts a *pointal* function into the corresponding P function in terms of vectors. For reasons of space, we leave this discussion for another paper.

[30] Of course, this type of relation can be compositionally used to deliver more complex situations involving multiple ROs (e.g. *La casa está detrás del parque y sobre la colina* 'The house is

which belongs to the set of vectors ($V \times V$) extending backward from the RO, the point w_O describes the location of the RO *park* (the zero vector <w, 0>) and w_1 describes the relative location of the LO *house* (Winter 2001).

(30) a. *La casa está detrás del (final del) parque.* (Mexican Spanish)
   'The house is behind the end of the park.'
   b. *La casa está en/a el (final del) parque.*
   'The house is at the end of the park.'
   c. *La casa está hasta el (final del) parque.*
   'The house is at the end of the park [from here].'

(31) $Vu <w_0, w_1> \in V \times V$

Measure phrases, which are relevant especially because of the MPC (recall (13) above), operate on these vectors. The essential claim behind this approach is that modifiers like *5 metros* '5 meters' in (32) predicate over distance, while the function denoted by locative Ps returns entities with measurable distance and direction (Zwarts/Winter 2000, 296). It follows that a composition like (32)a yields a measured difference as a product of intersection, as it returns the set of vectors pointing backward from the (end of the) park that are also five meters long.

Nonetheless, this may not be a general property of locative Ps. As (32)b-c show, at least in Spanish, not all locative PP constructions fit well with measure phrases. Even if this incompatibility may seem to hold equally for the standard locative construction (e.g., (32)b) and the combination characteristically seen in MS (32)c, these two instances actually relate to different problems. Whereas the impracticality of (32)b is predicted by the divergence between Spanish and English described above (recall (14)), and can be accounted for by virtue of established principles of the framework assumed here (see Winter 2001(1)),[31]

---

behind the park and over the hill'), where different (sets of) vectors, each with corresponding (disjoint) starting points at each RO (park/hill), are combined in the relative situation of the LO. However, this is not the type of complexity we are concerned with here. For a specific account of this possibility, see Winter (2001).

31 Winter (2001) explains this as the Modification Condition (MC). Basically, measure phrases are possible only if the modified set of vectors guarantees that for any measure phrase that denotes a non-empty set of vectors, the modification process (= intersection of the two sets) would not lead to an empty set. Nonetheless, and although we will not discuss this further, we believe that the observed cross-linguistic variation should figure in a discussion of these specific examples.

the case illustrated in (32)c is more complex and depends on structural properties of directional Ps, as we will see next.

(32) a. *La casa está (5 metros) detrás del (final del) parque.* (SS/MS)
    'The house is five meters behind the end of the park.'
  b. *La casa está (*5 metros) al (final del) parque.* (SS/MS)
    'The house is 5 meters at the end of the park.'
  c. *La casa está (*5 metros) hasta el (final del) parque.* (MS)
    'The house is at the end of the park [from here].'

4.1.2 Directional prepositions

Let's consider now the non-standard MS locatives with *hasta*. Initially, we can adhere to Zwarts/Winter's (2000, 28) proposal to use vectors directly in the semantics of directional Ps. In the original conception, the relevant path is analysed by representing the movement of an object along a spatial stretch (i.e., a vector) that connects the starting point and the endpoint of the movement. The interpretation of characteristic MS constructions like (30)c and (32)c, for instance, would therefore involve a path that starts at an arbitrary point and ends at the park. At first sight, this naturally accommodates the two semantic entailments central to the EPC: the contextually fixed starting point (the 'from here' entailment) and the interpretation of the location introduced by the directional P as a path endpoint.

There are, however, some problematic aspects of the specific definition behind this explanation. First, we are dealing with a locative (stative) construction, for which an analysis based on *movement* may not necessarily apply.[32] In fact, there are many constructions with a directional P that do not describe a *change in position* of the LO with respect to the RO (i.e., paths, as defined in Zwarts/Winter 2000, 27) – including Cresswell's original examples presented above –, and in which the RO is not interpreted as the endpoint of a displacement (motion) event. Secondly, constraining the use of directional PPs and paths to movement would prevent us from developing a unified approach to locative

---

32 The purported contrast between locative (a) and directional Ps (b) is the following:

(i) a. 'X is located at the endpoint of a vector pointing backward from the RO' (Zwarts/Winter 2000, 57).
  b. 'X (the LO) was first located at the beginning point and finally at the endpoint of a vector pointing to the RO.'

constructions yielded by locative and directional PPs, but also from offering a natural explanation for the relevant differences shown by languages in which these two alternatives coexist non-trivially, as in MS. Finally, and especially in view of the relevant contrast with other locative constructions available (paired in (30) above), *estar hasta* shows the need to set aside the unified role played by the RO as initially assumed for locative constructions in general.

Recall that locative Ps denote, by definition, a function that applies to the set of points where the RO is located and returns a set of vectors *starting at* potential zero-points to locate this object. So far, we have assumed, following Zwarts/Winter (2000), that for locative PP structures the RO is always the origin (the zero-point) of the set of vectors in the P's denotation. However, a unified definition of the role of the RO for locative predicates cannot be maintained to the extent that both MS locatives and standard (non-spatial) *estar hasta* denote states in which the RO is crucially interpreted as a path endpoint. Therefore, if we consider the contrasting semantics produced by *estar hasta*, together with its compatibility with an endpoint interpretation of the RO in line with the EPC (13)a, we need to allow for the possibility that different locative PP structures may supply ROs with different semantic functions. Specifically, we need to leave open the possibility that at least MS locative *estar hasta* constructions like (30)c involve a (set of) directed (located) vector(s) – that is, a path – ending at (i.e., extending *forward* to) the RO rather than *starting* at it. Alternatively, the problem would be solved by distinguishing locative *prepositional constructions* (arguably produced by locative and directional Ps in MS) from locative *Ps* (e.g. *a* 'at', *detrás* 'behind'; that is, the case where MS and SS converge in the construction of locatives with *estar*). Therefore, the contrast motivating the non-trivial P alternation in MS locatives would be precisely the one drawn by an opposition, internal to locative *constructions*, between those yielded by locative vs directional *prepositions*, insofar as this means that only for the former, the located vector *starts* at the RO. Consequently, a locative construction produced by a directional P, such as (30)c, would also denote a set of vectors, as seen with locative PPs (30)b, but the difference would lie in the way the grammatical subject of the sentence (that is, the LO) relates to these vectors.

A fundamental premise of the account adopted here is that paths are seen as directed stretches of space composed of *a sequence of vectors* with a starting point, an endpoint, and points in between, on which the path imposes an ordering (Zwarts 2005, 744). If our proposal is correct, this means that the path introduced by *hasta* would have an endpoint (or rather, its final vector) set at the RO and a starting point (or zero-point) set at an unspecified location, which, again, crucially lines up with the 'from-here flavour' involved in the formulation of the EPC. Now, given the assumption that atemporal usages of directional Ps determine that the path merely preserves a linear ordering (Zwarts/Winter 2000, 29), this means that *hasta* would impose the relevant ordering on the set of vector(s), which may be a line of sight, a walking distance or the route for the *hypothetical* journey described above in Cresswell's observations. Crucially, this aligns with the distinctive entailment described by natives, as shown above.

Recall that, as anticipated, in the VSS framework temporal and spatial stretches are carefully separated. The analysis of paths proposed by Zwarts/Winter (2000) follows Jackendoff (1983) (but see also Jackendoff 1996) in treating paths as functions from a non-temporal interval into space. In our case, this is important to keep paths (and incremental scalarity) within the realm of stative (i.e., non-eventive) predicates. In a semantic analysis along the lines proposed here, locative MS constructions would fall together with constructions like (33), in the wider class of stative predicates yielded by directional Ps in their *atemporal* guise. Arguably, in all these cases, the path structure is used for "locating plural or elongated objects expressing the direction of someone's line of sight" (Zwarts/Winter 2000, 29), which is also the specific semantic entailment described as the 'journey' senses of directional Ps in Cresswell's analysis of comparable stative (locative) constructions (1978, 97). This leads to two important consequences. First, the general situation fits well with the semantics observed, which is further supported by surveys with natives who consistently report a sense of distance or relative situation from a certain position – potentially determined along someone's eye of sight as well. Second, the idea retains the fact that there is an order-preserving mapping (a linear arrangement) to which the selection of the directional boundary P is central.

(33) Atemporal usages of directional Ps (Zwarts/Winter 2000, 29 (59))
    a. *The road leads to the city.*
    b. *John looked through the window.*

In sum, MS constructions like (30)c would be significantly different to the extent that they involve: (i) *an ordered sequence of vectors* (i.e., a non-temporal path) with an endpoint set at the RO; (ii) an underspecified starting point accommodating the additional ('from here') entailment involved in the EPC; and (iii) points in between on which *hasta* imposes an ordering. While the endpoint is grammatically realised as a PP, the zero-point is not syntactically explicit, just as in Zwarts/Winter's examples (33). Moreover, the determination of a measure function with two values other than the LO (i.e., the RO and the non-overt zero-point) establishes a non-trivial difference with the simpler locative structure yielded by locative Ps – that is, the point of convergence with SS – which does not feature such an additional variable.

The structural difference is grammatically visible, among other things, in the incompatibility with measure phrases (32)c that leaves MS constructions out of the MPC. Recall that, at least in principle, directional Ps should return entities with measurable distance and direction accommodating measure functions such as *5 metros*. However, if our analysis is correct, in the locative yielded by *hasta*, the magnitude of this distance is already established by the difference returned by the two points crucially involved (i.e., the RO, mapped as endpoint, and the implied, contextually fixed starting point). From here, the infelicity[33] of measure phrase modification over this pre-set difference value follows naturally.

If we adopt Winter's (2001) analysis of complex spatial situations, the location produced by *hasta* would involve, as any locative construction, a *located set of* vectors. The pair of vectors *w* and *v* in (34) represents the located vector *u*, where *w* determines the zero-point (*p*) of *u*, and *v* determines both its endpoint (i.e., *q*) and, in consequence, the order of the vectors in it (i.e., in *u*). In contrast to the structures yielded by locative Ps – where the LO and the RO represent the two main variables –, an important property of the construction produced by the directional P is that the endpoint *q* (the RO) and the LO crucially coincide, leaving the additional (starting point) as a relevant variable which, on its turn, delivers the characteristic sense of distance.

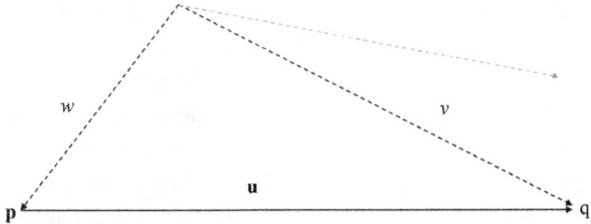

Figure 1: Vectors and located vectors.

(34) Vectors and located vectors (adapted from Winter 2001, 610)

In sum, we adhere to the definition of locative Ps as grammatical elements that map an LO to a set of vectors starting at potential zero-points (RO) to locate the object. In this sense, locative PP structures are relational, as location is defined within the spatial frame provided by the RO. However, a more general description of the use of vectors in locative constructions – especially given the problem presented by MS locatives – needs a less restricted view for two reasons.

---

33 Or, at least, oddity.

First, directional Ps are not necessarily used to denote changes in location of the RO; second, vectors are used to represent locations relative to an RO, but neither the orientation nor the route are default. Instead, these examples show that the RO may serve different roles in semantic representation of location. If this is defined by P (by its denotational properties), the non-trivial P alternation seen in MS is sufficiently motivated.

In general, this does not seem unreasonable, especially given that Zwarts/Winter (2000) admit that the role of the RO needs to be widened to embrace different relations posed by directional Ps. Just to give one example, it is clear that a directional P like *desde* 'from' (e.g. (15)) sets the RO not as the endpoint (as seen with *hasta*), but as the starting point. By contrast, a directional P like *através* 'through' presents a vector which does not set either its starting point nor its endpoint at the RO, but rather at its medial point. Finally, if the proposed account is correct, a directional P like *hasta* would have the RO serving as an endpoint, as argued above.

With this proviso, it seems safe to assume that directional PPs, at least in locative uses, all denote a set of located vectors. The difference is that their specific lexical semantics determines that the LO – grammatically represented as the subject in *estar* constructions – relates to these vectors in different ways. The variable role of the RO is essential to explain the fact that different Ps of the same class (e.g., directional Ps) alternate non-trivially. Moreover, the representation of the path either as the trajectory along which an object moves, or as an ordering-preserving function (e.g., a linear arrange), would hinge on the (lexical) semantics properties of the verb, in agreement with a general phenomenon attested in several languages (see Zwarts/Winter 2000, 27; Gehrke 2006). Applied to MS, this means that arguably *hasta* denotes the final vector of a path, with a zero-point set at the viewpoint from which the relative position is contextually established. The involvement of the copula or of other stative verbs in MS, guarantees that this path is interpreted in a non-temporal sense; that is, as a stretch of space. For the purpose of this paper, it is sufficient to keep in mind that in both MS and SS this path is interpreted as a measure function with its maximal value set at the point realised by the PP. In fact, we will see that something in this situation is extendable to non-spatial constructions where MS converges with SS. In these cases, the interpretation of the state as the endpoint of an ordered set of vectors is just as crucial to the sense of maximal degree yielded, as the atemporal use of the path.

4.1.3 From vectors to saturation of a container

Although this paper is concerned with the divergent use of *hasta* in MS, the proposal would not be complete without some indication of how the analysis can be extended to the standard use.

SS *estar hasta* can be naturally explained along the lines described above (i.e., VSS) assuming that a directed set of vectors is crucially involved in non-spatial predications as well.[34] Such a sequence of vectors would also include an underspecified starting point, an endpoint (supplied by the PP), and points in between, ordered accordingly. The difference resides in that these intermediate points would correspond to different degrees on an incremental scale, in a way that is broadly consistent with the analysis of paths followed in specific semantic accounts of maximal degrees and adjectival predicates (e.g., Hay et al. 1999). Therefore, an important difference with the locative constructions (i.e., the productive use of *estar hasta* seen in MS) is that in more abstract (non-spatial) uses, the located (set of) vector(s) can be mapped as a *quantised* scalar structure and interpreted as an incremental scale, while the endpoint marked by the PP is interpreted as the point of saturation of the container. Quantitative scalarity, together with the non-temporal use of paths, is nonetheless crucial. As shown above, the non-holistic reading of the subject is important to explain the fact that incremental scalarity figures relevantly in the semantic makeup of the construction even if no proper event (i.e., process) or qualitative measure function (e.g., AP predicate) is involved in the denotation of a maximal degree state. Nevertheless, there is an important sense of incrementality – supplied, as we argue, by the located set of vectors which preserve the linear order imposed by *hasta* for scalar progression – that accommodates the possibility of describing a maximal degree which is anyhow independent of further constituents. Hence, the endpoint interpretation that is crucial to the EPC can be ultimately seen as supported by a scalar function supplied by the subject of the predicate, although it is determined by the PP structure yielded by the directional boundary P.

---

[34] The fact that this non-spatial use is somewhat metaphorical, in contrast to the transparent (locative) use in divergent MS occurrences, can be ultimately related to the working assumption that the behavior displayed by MS relates to the availability of *hasta* as a legitimate and significant grammatical choice.

5 Final remarks

Given that this is a first analysis of the problem, much work remains to be done. Nonetheless, for stative predicates in general – e.g., including resulting states such as those exemplified by (3) –, MS data demonstrates clearly that scalar boundaries need not be the endpoints of a *motion* event to line up with the definition of paths and the denotational properties of directional Ps.[35]

Still, if we want to preserve the claim that MS constructions are best analysed as a particular way of structuring a stative predication via the directional boundary P, a final proviso is needed for Zwarts' (2000) definition of directional (bounded) Ps. Whereas Zwarts' (2005) analysis also involves the classification of Ps themselves as *telic*, we instead assume, more standardly, that telicity is not a property of P *per se*, but of *constructions* (e.g., Dowty 1991). MS shows that a directional boundary P can provide a legitimate grammatical device to express not only states of affairs, but also to convey locations crucially involving endpoints, without involving telicity.

However, we retain the distinction between 'bounded' and 'unbounded' denotations applied to Ps, in line with a considerable number of works on the general topic (e.g., Jackendoff 1991; Verkuyl/Zwarts 1992; Piñon 1993; among many others). This refinement is important in at least three respects: first, because an analysis in terms of *boundedness* is consistent with traditional descriptions of the characteristic flavour of *estar* (see Mangialavori Rasia 2018 for discussion); second, because *boundedness* is relevant to formalise the contrast with other types of directional Ps; and, third, because it allows a more refined analysis of aspectual boundaries, while it preserves a principled differentiation between (un)boundedness and (a)telicity, following a contrast that goes back to Depraetere (1995).

An interesting aspect of Zwarts' (2005) analysis is that paths are carefully differentiated from events. This is done by a demarcation of the domain on which they operate, spatial and temporal, respectively. In our case, a proper division between dynamicity/telicity (i.e., eventivity) and mere directionality,

---

[35] The divergent use introduced in (3) can be explained in similar terms, as *hasta* marks the endpoint of an incremental relation leading to a resulting state. Importantly, a preliminary investigation shows that natives report a specific stress not on the state established as a result, but rather on the preparatory phase the endpoint of which is marked by *hasta*. This is important, first, because it supports the alignment with the EPC over an inchoative analysis; second, this entailment fits well with the non-standard reading of the P seen in these cases, in contrast to the 'until' reading seen in clear stative cases. Significantly, this non-standard use of *hasta* is only possible with predicates allowing a process-like reading (see Mangialavori Rasia/Marín 2018). For a specific analysis and discussion of these constructions in SS, see Mangialavori Rasia (2016, 2018).

applied to locative structures (paths), is essential to account for the *Aktionsart* properties of the productive (and non-eventive) MS use of *estar hasta*, but also for the standard use of directional Ps which yield maximal degree or saturation in stative constructions without involving telicity or event progression.

Finally, an important consequence of recruiting a directional P in locative constructions lies on the semantic complexity defended here as a structural difference with locative (non-directional) Ps. The relative complexity of directional Ps is also expressed in configurational terms (internal PP structural configuration) correlating with the noted semantic asymmetry. In general, structural asymmetries of this sort are necessary to account for the non-trivial coexistence of *estar hasta* and *estar a/en* in MS and the richer content of the former.[36]

6 Conclusions

This paper provides evidence that MS *estar hasta* constructions are instances of a more general phenomenon of productive combination of stative (locative) verbs and directional Ps. It is argued that in MS a directional boundary P can be productively combined with the copula to yield locative constructions with consistently distinct semantic properties. Yet, while the locative (non-dynamic) denotation of the directional P arguably bears on composition (i.e., guaranteed by the stative verb), this restriction does not affect the structural properties of *hasta*, which are crucially preserved, and which determine important contrasts with non-directional Ps combined with *estar*. The alternation between a locative boundary P (*a*) and the directional boundary P (*hasta*) in MS could hence be predicted and explained as the possibility to grammatically realise either simple boundary location or a complex locative, including distance along a vector with two key variables: one realised as a PP (headed by *hasta*), and one which is not grammatically explicit, but which is consistently reported as main semantic contrast with the location yielded by non-directional Ps. Importantly, the latter observation agrees with the 'from here' entailment constraining the occurrence of directional Ps in locative predications with copulas at a more general level

---

36 Directional/dynamic Ps are commonly seen as a more complex structure than locative Ps. For instance, it is argued that the former yield a directional configuration (*Path*) embedding the simpler structure of the latter (see Koopman 1997; den Dikken 2003; Svenonius 2004; amongst others for different proposals and implementations). Under a slightly different terminology, directionality would involve a birelational (*Terminal Coincidence*) P embedding the simpler (*Central Coincidence*) P (Hale/Keyser 2002). Even if this needs to be carefully analysed, the general situation would pose a transparent relation between semantic and syntactic structure.

(Cresswell 1978 amongst others), making it compatible with the relevant condition at work. The analysis thus provides a natural answer to previously unnoticed facts concerning the semantics and syntax of spatial Ps in Spanish, including non-trivial divergences across varieties.

What is clear is that we are not dealing with an *anomalous* (Lope Blanch 2008) use of either the verb nor the P, but rather with a legitimate, productive syntactic and semantic alternative. As the divergent selection of *hasta* in MS is correctly regarded as a legitimate grammatical device, and at the same time, as a semantically relevant (non-trivial) P choice, MS patterns may be crucial in gaining a better understanding of how directional Ps may participate in the setup of complex stative predicates by simply drawing on data from less-studied languages and varieties.

7 References

Anderson, Stephen, *On the role of deep structure in semantic interpretation*, Foundations of Language 7:3 (1971), 387–396.
Bosque, Ignacio/Bravo, Ana, *Preposiciones e intervalos temporales*, talk held at Universitat Autònoma de Barcelona, December 2011. Non published Ms.
Brucart, Joan M., *Copular alternation in Spanish and Catalan attributive sentences*, Revista de Estudos Linguísticos da Universidade do Porto 7 (2012), 9–43.
Cresswell, Max, *Prepositions and points of view*, Linguistics and Philosophy 2 (1978), 1–41.
Davies, Mark. Corpus del Español. http://www.corpusdelespanol.org/ [last access: 2016].
den Dikken, Marcel, *On the syntax of locative and directional adpositional phrases*, Ms. Dissertation, City University of New York, 2003.
Depraetere, Ilse, *On the necessity of distinguishing between (un)boundedness and (a)telicity*, Linguistics and Philosophy 18 (1995), 1–19.
Dominicy, Marc, *La evolución del español "hasta" en Hispanoamérica*, Anuario de Letras 20:1 (1982), 41–90.
Dowty, David, *Word meaning and Montague grammar*, Dordrecht, Reidel, 1979.
Dowty, David, *Thematic proto-roles and argument selection*, Language 67 (1991), 547–619.
DRAE = Real Academia Española. *Diccionario de la lengua Española*. https://dle.rae.es/diccionario [last access: 8.5.2020].
García Pardo, Alfredo, *Argument structure in adjectival passives*, talk held at 3rd Workshop on Aspect and Argument Structure of Adjectives and Participles, Université Lille 3, June 2016. https://doi.org/10.7557/1.6.1.4095
Gehrke, Berit, *Putting path in place*, Proceedings of Sinn und Bedeutung 11 (2006), 244–260. https://doi.org/10.18148/sub/2007.v11i0.643
Hale, Ken. L./Keyser, Samuel. J, *Prolegomenon to a theory of argument structure*, Cambridge, MIT Press, 2002.
Hansen, Nat/Chemla, Emmanuel, *Color adjectives, standards, and thresholds. An experimental investigation*, Linguistics and Philosophy 40 (2017), 239–278.

Hay, Jen/Kennedy, Chris/Levin, Beth, *Scalar structure underlies telicity in "Degree Achievements"*, in: Matthews, Tanya/Strolovitch, Devon (edd.), *Proceedings of SALT IX*, Ithaca, CLC, 1999, 127–144.

Husband, E. Matthew, *On the compositional nature of states*, Amsterdam, John Benjamins, 2012.

Jackendoff, Ray, *Semantics and Cognition*, Cambridge, MIT Press, 1983.

Jackendoff, Ray, *Parts and boundaries*, Cognition 41 (1991), 9–45.

Jackendoff, Ray, *The proper treatment of measuring out, telicity, and perhaps even quantification in English*, Natural Language and Linguistic Theory 14 (1996), 305–354.

Kennedy, Chris/McNally, Louise, *Scale structure, degree modification, and the semantics of gradable predicates*, Language 81:2 (2005), 345–381.

Kennedy, Chris/McNally, Louise, *Adjectives and adverbs. Syntax, semantics, and discourse*, Oxford, Oxford University Press, 2008.

Koopman, Hilda, *Prepositions, postpositions circumpositions, and particles. The structure of Dutch PPs*, Ms., UCLA, 1997.

Krifka, Manfred, *The origins of telicity*, in: Susan Rothstein (ed.), *Events and grammar*, Dordrecht, Kluwer, 1998, 197–235.

Lope Blanch, José M., *El español americano*, México, Colegio de México, 2008.

Mangialavori Rasia, M. Eugenia, *Conciliating states and locations. Towards a more comprehensive and in-depth account of the Spanish copula "estar"*, Studies in Hispanic and Lusophone Linguistics 6:1 (2013), 37–78.

Mangialavori Rasia, M. Eugenia, *Semántica léxica y estructuración aspectual/eventiva. Telicidad, perfectividad y delimitación en el análisis de las cópulas españolas*, Lexis 40:2 (2016), 375–417.

Mangialavori Rasia, M. Eugenia, *(And yet) another proposal for ser/estar*, in: Berns, Janine/Jacobs, Haike/Nouveau, Dominique (edd.), *Romance Languages and Linguistic Theory 13*, Amsterdam, John Benjamins, 2018, 177–207.

Mangialavori Rasia, M. Eugenia, *Unexpected uses and occurrences of "estar" across times and varieties*, talk held at Universidad Complutense de Madrid, 2020. Non published Ms.

Mangialavori Rasia, M. Eugenia/Marín, Rafael, *Endpoints, location and stativity. A boundary directional P as a key to richer locatives*, talk held at Workshop on Endpoints and Scales, Humboldt Universität zu Berlin, 2018. Non published Ms.

Marín, Rafael, *Spanish adjectives within bounds*, in: Cabredo, Patricia/Matushansky, Ora (edd.), *Adjectives. Formal analyses in syntax and semantic*, Amsterdam, John Benjamins, 2010, 307–332.

Marín Rafael/Sánchez Marco, Cristina, *Verbos y nombres psicológicos*, Borealis 1:2 (2012), 91–108.

McNally, Louise, *The relative role of property type and scale structure in explaining the behavior of gradable adjectives*, in: Nouwen, Rick/van Rooij, Robert/Sauerland, Uli/Schmitz, Hans-Christian (edd.), *Papers from the ESSLLI 2009*, Heidelberg, Springer, 2011, 151–168.

Paffey, Darren, *Language ideologies and the globalization of "standard" Spanish*, London, Bloomsbury, 2012.

Piñon, Christopher, *Paths and their names*, in: Beals, Katharine/Cooke, Gina/Kathman, David/Kita, Sotaro/McCullough, Karl-Erik/Testen, David (edd.), *What we think, what we mean, and how we say it. Papers from the parasession on the correspondence of conceptual,*

semantic and grammatical representations, Chicago, Chicago Linguistic Society, 1993, 287–303.
CORDE = Real Academia Española. *Corpus diacrónico del español*. http://www.rae.es [last access: 1.2.2020].
CREA = Real Academia Española. *Corpus de referencia del español actual*. http://www.rae.es [last access: 1.2.2020].
Rico, Pablo, *Intensividad y preposiciones de trayectoria. La sintaxis dialectal de hasta y desde*, Talk held at XIX CILG, Pamplona, 2015.
Saldanya, Manuel/Rigau, Gemma, *"Cuesta arriba e por llano." The development of "postpositions" in Spanish and Catalan*, Journal of Portuguese Linguistics 4:1 (2005), 69–91.
Svenonius, Peter, *Spatial P in English*, Ms., University of Tromsø, 2004.
Talmy, Leonard, *Toward a cognitive semantics*, Cambridge, MIT Press, 2000.
Verkuyl, Henk/Zwarts, Joost, *Time and space in conceptual and logical semantics. The notion of path*, Linguistics 30 (1992), 483–511.
Winter, Yoad, *Measure phrase modification in vector space semantics*, in: Megerdoomian, Karine/Bar-el, Leora (edd.), *WCCFLXX Proceedings*, Somerville, Cascadilla Press, 2001, 607–620.
Winter, Yoad, *Cross-categorial restrictions on measure phrase modification*, Linguistics and Philosophy 28 (2005), 233–267.
Zwarts, Joost, *Vectors as relative positions*, Journal of Semantics 14 (1997), 1–57.
Zwarts, Joost, *Vectors across spatial domains. From place to size, orientation, shape, and parts*, in: van der Zee, Emile/Slack, Jon (edd.), *Representing direction in language and space*, Oxford, Oxford University Press, 2003, 39–68.
Zwarts, Joost, *Prepositional aspect and the algebra of paths*, Linguistics and Philosophy 28 (2005), 739–779.
Zwarts, Joost, *Aspects of a typology of direction*, in: Rothstein, Susan (ed.), *Theoretical and crosslinguistic approaches to the semantics of aspect*, Amsterdam, John Benjamins, 2008, 79–106.
Zwarts, Joost/Winter, Yoad, *Vector space semantics. A model-theoretic analysis of locative prepositions*, Journal of Logic, Language, and Information 9 (2000), 169–211.

Pedro Gras and María Sol Sansiñena
Discourse structure, constructions and regional variation
Non-embedded indicative *que*-clauses in three regional varieties of Spanish

Abstract: This paper presents a corpus-based interactional analysis of non-embedded indicative *que*-clauses (IQCs) in three regional varieties of Spanish (Madrid, Spain; Santiago, Chile; and Buenos Aires, Argentina), using data from the corpus COLA (*Corpus Oral del Lenguaje Adolescente*). On the one hand, we show that IQCs exhibit regional variation regarding the discourse contexts in which they appear: not all contexts are equally available for each regional variety. Moreover, we argue that this variation can be placed on a cline, which ranges from high discourse dependency to low discourse dependency, which might, in turn, suggest a divergent evolution of IQCs in the dialectal spectrum of Spanish. On the other hand, our analysis complements generativist typologies of IQCs in two respects: (i) it describes the discourse contexts in which different formal types of IQCs are used and (ii) it shows specific contexts and interpretations that had not been explicitly acknowledged in generativist studies.

Keywords: interactional linguistics, dialect syntax, divergence, complement clauses, quotative constructions

1 Introduction

Since the origin of modern dialectology in the 19th century, the study of geographical variation has been a valuable tool to understand general language mechanisms. In particular, traditional dialectological work – adopting a structuralist perspective – analysed phonetic, morphological and lexical variation in order to understand how paradigms were organised and how languages changed through space and time. Later, the study of language variation extended to account for syntactic phenomena as well. A good example of this interest in the area of Spanish linguistics can be found in the vast amount of

Pedro Gras, Universiteit Antwerpen
María Sol Sansiñena, KU Leuven

https://doi.org/10.1515/9783110736250-009

detailed regional variation contained in the most comprehensive reference grammars of Spanish published in the last twenty years: the *Gramática descriptiva de la lengua española* [GDLE, 'Descriptive grammar of the Spanish language'] (Bosque/Demonte 1999) and the *Nueva gramática de la lengua española* [NGLE, 'New grammar of the Spanish language'] (RAE-ASALE 2009).

However, there is an aspect of linguistic variation that has been understudied: the regional variation of the lexicogrammatical constructions that express *interpersonal and textual* meanings, often referred to as discourse markers or discourse particles.[1] This may be due to the fact that the systematic analysis of these elements is relatively recent in the history of linguistics (cf. Fraser 1988), when compared to the study of other areas such as phonology, morphology, syntax and lexicon. The reference works devoted to the analysis of Spanish discourse particles have mostly appeared in the course of the last two decades (Martín Zorraquino/Montolío 1998; Martín Zorraquino/Portolés 1999; Santos 2003; Briz/Pons/Portolés 2008; Fuentes 2010; Loureda/Acín 2010) and are based almost exclusively on European Standard Spanish. In spite of the existence of particular analyses of discourse particles in varieties other than European Spanish, the research devoted to the intralinguistic variation of discourse particles in Spanish is still very limited (cf. García Negroni/Marcovecchio 2014).[2]

The interest in the study of intralinguistic variation of discourse particles is two-fold. On the one hand, since discourse particles are extra-sentential elements, it is expected that their variation operates at a discourse-contextual level, i.e. they may appear in different discourse contexts in different varieties of a single language. Thus, an appropriate framework to account for the intralinguistic variation of discourse particles should include discourse-contextual features as analytical tools. On the other hand, it is widely recognised that discourse particles exhibit high levels of polyfunctionality, so that their concrete interpretation heavily depends on the specific (morphosyntactic and discursive) context in which they occur. The contrastive analysis of the same particle in different

---

[1] The research network *Discourse-Pragmatic Variation & Change* (DiPVaC) gathers researchers that investigate the variation and change of discourse particles, though not specifically in terms of regional variation within a single language. More information can be found on their website: http://www.dipvac.org/. We are using the term *discourse particle* as a cover term that includes extra-propositional elements that express interpersonal and/or textual meanings.

[2] Though originally based on European Spanish, the *Diccionario de partículas discursivas del español* ['Dictionary of Spanish discourse particles'] (Briz/Pons/Portolés 2008) is currently incorporating regional variation in two respects: (i) adding discourse particles only found in Latin American varieties of Spanish (e.g. *capaz que* 'maybe' in *Rioplatense* Spanish) and (ii) adding dialectal information (specific formal or functional properties) in the description of discourse particles shared by European and Latin American varieties of Spanish.

varieties of the same language may add supplementary evidence on how to model polyfunctionality by showing the shared contexts and, especially, those which are not shared. This comparison may be understood in terms of a divergent evolution of the same particle in different dialects of the language.³

An interesting case study is the use of initial complementiser *que* 'that' introducing non-embedded clauses in Spanish, either in subjunctive or indicative mood, as in (1).

(1)   a. *Que venga   María.*
          COMP come-PRS.SBJV.3SG María
   b. *Que viene   María.*
          COMP come-PRS.IND.3SG María

Non-embedded subjunctive *que*-clauses (abbreviated henceforth as SQCs) (1a) can receive a limited array of interpretations: an imperative-desiderative⁴ reading ('May María come!') or an exclamative-evaluative reading ('[It´s unbelievable] that María comes!'), depending on formal features such as intonation and tense selection (see Sánchez López 2015; Gras/Sansiñena 2017). On the other hand, non-embedded indicative *que*-clauses (abbreviated henceforth as IQCs) can receive multiple interpretations that depend not only on formal features, but also on the discourse context in which they appear (Gras/Sansiñena 2015), e.g. justification of a previous speech act (1'a), reported speech (1'b), correction of addressee's assumptions (1'c) or warning (1'd), amongst many others.

(1') a. *Date prisa, que viene María.*
        'Hurry up, [because] María is coming'
    b. *He hablado con Ana. Que viene María.*
        'I spoke to Ana. [She said] María is coming'
    c.   – *No conocemos a nadie en esa cena.*
          'We don't know anybody at that dinner'
       – *¡Que viene María!*
        '[But] María is coming!'
    d. [Looking through the window] *¡Que viene María!*
        'María is coming!'

---

3 We understand *divergence* in a broad sense, as a diachronic process by which two or more language varieties become structurally more dissimilar (Harnisch 2010, 275).
4 There is no agreement on whether imperative and optative interpretations can be subsumed under a single form-meaning pairing. For a discussion on this issue, see Garrido Medina 1999; Gras 2011; 2016; Sánchez López 2015; Sansiñena 2015; Sansiñena et al. 2015b; Pérez/Gras/Brisard 2021.

There is no agreement in the literature as to whether the contexts illustrated in (1') should be treated as a single polysemous construction or as different constructions with their specific formal features responsible for the attested interpretations. Moreover, since IQCs have been studied almost exclusively using data coming from Peninsular Spanish (cf. Sansiñena 2015), it is not known whether all the contexts in (1') are equally available in Latin American varieties of Spanish.

This paper presents a corpus-based interactional analysis of IQCs in three regional varieties of Spanish (Madrid, Spain; Santiago, Chile; and Buenos Aires, Argentina). On the one hand, we show that IQCs exhibit regional variation regarding the discourse contexts in which they appear: not all contexts are equally available for each regional variety. Moreover, we suggest that this variation can be placed on a cline, which ranges from high discourse dependency to low discourse dependency. On the other hand, our analysis complements formal typologies of IQCs in two respects: (i) it describes the discourse contexts in which different formal types of IQCs are used and (ii) it shows specific contexts and interpretations that had not been explicitly acknowledged in generativist studies.

The outline of this paper is as follows. Section 2 presents a panoramic view of the most representative studies on non-embedded *que*-clauses, focusing on types of IQCs. Section 3 describes the theoretical and methodological bases of the analysis. Section 4 describes the discourse contexts in which IQCs are used in the varieties under study, and Section 5 discusses the relevance of these results, both for the understanding of the regional variation of IQCs in Spanish and for the formal typology of IQCs. Section 6 presents our conclusions.

2 Non embedded *que*-clauses in Spanish: an overview

The use of complement clauses in non-embedding contexts has since long been acknowledged in Spanish Linguistics. Literature has identified several unrelated meanings, such as imperative/desiderative (see Bello 1847; Gili Gaya 1943; Moliner 1966–67; Garrido Medina 1998; Porroche Ballesteros 2000; Pons 2003; Sirbu-Dumitrescu 2004; RAE-ASALE 2009; Demonte/Fernández Soriano 2009; 2013a; Gras 2011; 2016; Villa García 2015; Sansiñena 2015;; 2017), exclamative/evaluative (see Garrido Medina 1999; Santos Río 2003; Biezma 2007; Gras/Sansiñena 2017) and various types of discourse/contextual meanings, such as reiteration, contrast, topic (re)introduction and echo, amongst others (see Spitzer 1942; Gili Gaya 1943; Alcina/Blecua 1975; Sirbu-Dumitrescu 1992; 1994a; 1994b;

1998; Cascón Martín 1995; Escandell-Vidal 1999; Porroche Ballesteros 2000; Pons 2003; Demonte/Fernández Soriano 2007; 2009; 2013a; 2013b; 2014; Etxepare 2008; 2010; 2013; Rodríguez Ramalle 2008a; 2008b; Gras 2011; 2013; Gras/Sansiñena 2015; Sansiñena 2015). However, two aspects remain unsolved. On the one hand, authors such as Gras and Sansiñena do not agree on how many different types of *que* should be posited. On the other, it has been barely studied whether there exists intralinguistic variation in this aspect of Spanish lexicogrammar. In this section, we review the different types of non-embedded *que*-clauses proposed in the literature, with a special focus on indicative clauses, and the existing works that study their geographical variation.

Non-embedded *que*-clauses started to be mentioned in early 19th century grammars (Bello 1847). They were treated as cases of ellipsis of a main predicate: their meaning was explained on the basis of the semantics of the elided predicate (*quiero* 'want', *digo* 'say', *espero* 'hope', etc.) and some of their contexts of use were listed (e.g. in Gili Gaya 1943; Alcina/Blecua 1975). In the last decades of the 20th century, due to an increase in the interest on spoken language, *que* began to be treated as a discourse marker. From a pragmatic approach, it was analysed either as a marker of background information (Porroche Ballesteros 2000) or as a modality marker (Pons 2003). However, these analyses failed to answer how specific formal properties (mood selection or clause type compatibility, for instance) were related to the interpretation of *que*-clauses (imperative, optative, evaluative, and so on). By contrast, more recent studies coincide in recognizing that non-embedded *que*-clauses do not constitute a single linguistic object and, therefore, different types of non-embedded *que*-clauses should be posited, being interpreted either as different form-meaning pairings (Gras 2011; 2013; 2016; Gras/Sansiñena 2015; 2017; Sansiñena 2015; Sansiñena et al. 2015a; 2015b) or as the lexicalisation of different functional categories placed in the left periphery of the sentence (Demonte/Fernández Soriano 2007; 2009; 2013a; 2013b; 2014; Rodríguez Ramalle 2008a; 2008b; Etxepare 2008; 2010; 2013; Corr 2016).

Regarding their mood selection, two types of *que*-clauses can be set apart: subjunctive *que*-clauses (SQCs) and indicative *que*-clauses (IQCs).[5] SQCs allow for a limited array of semantic interpretations: (i) imperative-optative, as in (2),

---

[5] Non-embedded *que*-clauses with a quotative interpretation select both indicative and subjunctive verb forms depending on the clause type being reported: indicative for declarative, interrogative and exclamative sentences, and subjunctive for imperative and optative sentences. The specific mood selection of quotative *que*-clauses can be taken as evidence for considering them a specific constructional type (Gras/Pérez/Brisard in press).

which expresses the speaker's interest towards the realisation of the propositional content or (ii) exclamative-evaluative, as in (3), which expresses the speaker's negative evaluation of a propositional content.

(2) *está gilipollas tía* [.]
    <u>que</u>   le   d-en   por   el   culo
    COMP DAT.3SG give-SUBJ.PR.3PL by   the   ass
    'She's silly, girl.
    Fuck her.'
    (MABPE2-01C, COLA M)[6]

(3) *en el día de mañana/ puedo tener hijos/ y*
    <u>que</u>   se   teng-a   que   ir   mi   hija
    COMP PRO have-SUBJ.PR.3SG COMP go.INF my   daughter
    sola   a   abort-ar/
    alone to   abort.INF
    pues no/
    'In the future I can have children, and
    that my daughter should have to go
    alone to have an abortion...
    well, no.'
    (MadSex, T17_V_M292_AC17_DEF)

There is sufficient formal evidence (such as intonation and tense selection) to consider these two interpretations as two different constructions or formal types (Sánchez López 2015; Gras/Sansiñena 2017). Interestingly, these same constructional types have been proposed for Germanic languages as well (see Verstraete/D'Hertefelt/Van Linden 2012; D'Hertefelt/Verstraete 2014; D'Hertefelt 2018).

As for the indicative clauses, the situation is less clear. As we already pointed out, the interpretation of IQCs heavily depends on the discourse context in which they are used (Gras 2013; 2016; Gras/Sansiñena 2015). Example (1'), reproduced below as (4), shows how the same *que*-clause (*Que viene María* Lit. 'That María is coming') receives different interpretations when used in different discourse contexts: it introduces a justification of a speech act when placed right after

---

[6] Corpus examples are identified by the conversation code and a letter indicating the subcorpora: M (Madrid), S (Santiago de Chile) and BS (Buenos Aires). For reasons of space, glosses will only be provided for the structures under analysis, and whenever the excerpt is short. A functional translation in English will be included below each example in Spanish. The corpus is described in Section 3.

that speech act (4a), it receives a quotative interpretation when an alternative speech situation is made available in the preceding co(n)text (4b), it corrects the addressee's assumptions when introducing a response (4c) and it expresses a warning to the addressee when reacting to an extralinguistic stimulus, perceived in or inferred from the situational context (4d).

(4) a. *Date prisa, que viene María.*
 'Hurry up, [because] María is coming.'
 b. *He hablado con Ana. Que viene María.*
 'I spoke to Ana. [She said] María is coming.'
 c. – *No conocemos a nadie en esa cena.*
 'We don't know anybody at that dinner.'
 – *¡Que viene María!*
 '[But] María is coming!'
 d. [Looking at the window] *¡Que viene María!*
 'María is coming!'

The question arises as to whether these contexts are instances of a single construction – a single form with different interpretations – or whether the differences in interpretation correlate with formal differences. Adopting an interactional approach, Gras and Sansiñena (Gras/Sansiñena 2015; Gras 2016) analyse contexts like (4) as contextually dependent interpretations of a single construction with an abstract indexical meaning: it points to the need to retrieve some semantic element that is accessible from the context, either from previous discourse (4a, b), shared knowledge (4c) or the physical context itself (4d). This indexical meaning can be realised in diverse, more concrete, situated meanings or interpretations, in terms of interactions of the abstract indexical meaning and certain aspects of the contexts in which these constructions are used.

By contrast, focusing on formal properties, generative cartographic approaches have suggested that cases like (4) should not be analysed altogether, given that they constitute different formal types, conceived as different projections in the (extended) left periphery of the sentence (Demonte/Fernández Soriano 2013a; 2013b; 2014; Corr 2016), though there is not an agreement regarding what specific types should be distinguished. Considering data coming from standard and non-standard Ibero-Romance varieties, Corr (2016) coins the term "illocutionary *que*" to refer to discourse-oriented functions of *que* in utterance-initial position, and distinguishes three distinct formal types, with their own formal and interpretive features: conjunctive (5), quotative (6) and exclamative (7).

(5) G01: *cuidado [.] que se cae*
 'G01: be careful, [QUE] it will fall'
 (MAESB2-01C, COLA M)

(6) [A girl tells about a date she had last week]
 G01: *joder Ana eres una cerda*
 eres una putilla con patas eh/
 J01: *eee/*
 G01: *que   eres   una putilla con patas*
            COMP be-PRS.IND.2SG   a   whore   with legs
 'G01: damn Ana you're a pig
 you're a little slut eh/
 J01: eh/
 G01: QUE you're a little slut'
 (MABPE2-01A, COLA M)

(7) [Two boys talk while playing with a turtle, which is approaching the mini-disk they are using to record the conversation]
 G05: *se lo digo a la tortuga*
 G01: *guuus ja ja* <laughter>
 G05: *groooooo*
 <u>*que*</u>   *se   lo   com-eee*   <laughter>
 COMP   you.DAT.SG it   eat-PRS.IND.3SG
 G01: *se va a comer el micrófono este tío coño mira mira*
 'G05: I tell it to the turtle
 G01: guuus ha ha <laughter>
 G05: grooooooo
 [QUE] he eats it\ <laughter>
 G01: this guy is going to eat the microphone damn look look'
 (MAESB2-01C, COLA M)

The first formal type is conjunctive *que*, whose "function is to contextualise utterance information for the benefit of the addressee" (Corr 2016, 199), as in (5), where the *que*-clause explains why the addressee needs to be careful. Secondly, quotative *que*-clauses[7] are "reported speech clauses introduced by the item *que*

---

7 Demonte/Fernández Soriano (2013a; 2014) distinguish between reportative *que* (a reportative hearsay evidential) and echoic *que* (a complementiser that reproduces previous discourse). By contrast, Etxepare (2010; 2013) and Corr (2016) consider echoic *que* a single formal type.

which, crucially, do not rely on a retrievable verbum *dicendi* to be felicitous" (Corr 2016, 155), as in (6), where no verb of saying is found in the previous turns. Finally, exclamative *que* is described as "an indicative clause [...] which has the illocutionary force of an exclamation" (Corr 2016, 84). According to Corr, exclamative *que* adds to the propositional content an expressive attitudinal value, whose precise interpretation depends on the specific communicative situation (Corr 2016, §3.3). In (7) *que* adds an expressive value of surprise and counterexpectation: speaker G05 is amazed at the fact that the turtle is trying to bite the minidisk and he warns the addressee about it.

As for the regional variation of non-embedded *que*-clauses, it has received little attention in the Hispanic Linguistic literature. Previous corpus studies show some variation between Peninsular and Latin American Spanish regarding SQCs, both imperative-optative (Sansiñena et al. 2015b; 2017), quotatives (Gras/Pérez/Brisard in press) and evaluative-exclamative (Gras/Sansiñena 2017). As for IQCs, even though there are no systematic dialectal studies, it has been suggested that some of the 'illocutionary' types are characteristic of European varieties – as opposed to Latin American – (Corr 2016, 24) and, conversely, that Latin American varieties show specific formal types not found in Peninsular Spanish, such as Chilean exclamative indicative *que*-clauses (8) (Gras/Sansiñena 2017).

(8) que   so-n   pelador-es
     COMP   be.PRS.IND-2PL   faultfinder-PL
     'How hypercritical you are!'
     (SCCCM4-04, COLA S, Chile)

This paper is a contribution to the study of the dialectal variation of IQCs in two respects. On the one hand, it aims to determine whether IQCs are used by speakers of different varieties in the same interactional contexts or whether some contexts are not available in some of the varieties under study, which might suggest a divergent evolution of IQCs in the dialectal spectrum of Spanish. On the other hand, it also aims to complement the typology of 'illocutionary' *que*, by showing in which interactional contexts each type is found and whether all contexts correspond to the formal types proposed, namely conjunctive, quotative and exclamative.

3 Methodology

This paper is theoretically and methodologically informed by Interactional Linguistics, a multidisciplinary approach to language that combines insights from (Functional) Linguistics, Conversation Analysis and Linguistic Anthropology (Ford 1993; Ochs/Schegloff/Thompson 1996; Selting/Couper-Kuhlen 2001; Ford/Fox/Thompson 2002). Interactional Linguistics is interested in the analysis of linguistic forms as tools employed by conversationalists to perform actions in interaction.

The study presented here is based on the analysis of three components of the *Corpus Oral del Lenguaje Adolescente* (COLA), which contains naturally occurring conversations among adolescents who are native speakers of different varieties of Spanish. The three subcorpora used correspond to the cities of Madrid (120,000 words), Santiago de Chile (150,000 words) and Buenos Aires (70,000 words). Even though the corpus is limited and the sizes of the three subcorpora are different, COLA is currently the only corpus which meets the requested criteria for this study: (i) it represents spoken informal interactions –non-embedded *que*-clauses are characteristic of spoken informal registers – and contains material representing different varieties of Spanish.[8] We are aware that differences in size could potentially affect the results, e.g. the fact that a specific context is not attested in the corpus might be due to size limitations. In order to prevent this, we corroborated with native speakers of the varieties under study whether IQCs were acceptable in contexts not attested for a certain variety.

A semi-automatic selection of occurrences was carried out, taking into account two basic criteria: (i) the presence of an initial *que* in a non-subordinate context (no ellipsis), i.e. contexts in which there is no element that can be considered as a main predicate, either in the intervention of the speaker or in the immediately previous intervention by an interlocutor, and (ii) a verb in one of the forms of the indicative mood. Following these criteria, we decided to exclude cases like (9), since speaker J01's answer may be taken to depend on an elided matrix clause, recoverable from the preceding question uttered by an interlocutor,[9] but we included instances of the so-called *causal que*,

---

[8] Another corpus of colloquial Spanish is being collected, the Ameresco corpus (*América Español Coloquial*): http://esvaratenuacion.es/corpus-discursivo-propio/.
[9] This phenomenon has been labelled as *dyadic dependency*. See Sansiñena et al. (2015a) for a detailed analysis.

such as (10), due to the fact that the *que*-clause is not embedded under a main predicate.¹⁰

(9) [A group of friends talking about their plans for a long weekend]
G03: *qué pasa el puente de mayo/*
J01: *que me mudo*
'G03: what will happen during the long weekend in May/
J01: [QUE] I'm moving'
(MAESB2-02, COLA M)

(10) G01: *cuidado [.] que se cae*
'G01: be careful, [QUE] it will fall'
(MAESB2-01C, COLA M)

The analysis has been carried out in three phases. The first phase consisted in analysing the relation of the IQC to the sequential organisation of the conversation: "the occurrence of any utterance in conversation can be related to its prior context in terms of how it fills its sequential slot" (Ford 1993, 10). We took into account two parameters: turn position and type of turn. According to its position in the turn, each token is classified as initial or non-initial. According to the type of turn, each token is classified as an initiation, a (preferred/dispreferred) response, or a response-initiation. Initiations are first parts in adjacency pairs, while responses are second parts. *Que*-constructions that form the first parts of adjacency pairs, i.e. turns that are not predicted by a previous turn, can be classified into *direct* and *indirect* initiations. Direct initiations, such as questions, invitations, offers or requests, require the presence of a following, predicted turn, such as an immediate answer or acceptance. Conversely, indirect initiations, such as comments or assessments, do not predict a subsequent turn. Additionally, responses are further classified according to the preference patterns as *preferred* – or structurally simple – and *dispreferred* – or structurally complex – responses (Levinson 1983, 307). Finally, response-initiations are reactions to previous turns which, at the same time, demand a response from the interlocutor (Gras/Sansiñena 2015). Due to space limitations, these concepts will be further exemplified in the results section (4).

---

10 The relation linking the two component clauses has been referred to as either "subordination" (see NGLE 2009, §46.6) or "parataxis" and "sociation" (see Aliaga García/Bustos Guadaño 1997; Iglesias Recuero 2000; Sansiñena 2015).

Second, we determined the situated meaning or interpretation of the construction. In order to do so, we have taken into account two types of evidence: (i) the cotext of the IQC (sequential organisation, rhetorical relation between the *que*-construction and its preceding context, and the co-occurrence of other linguistic forms that express pragmatic or interactional meanings, such as discourse markers, interjections and vocatives) and (ii) participants' reactions – "as each turn is responded by a second, we find displayed in that second an *analysis* of the first by its recipient" (Levinson 1983, 321, emphasis in the original). We have captured every situated meaning as a discourse pattern: "a recurrent interactional practice which has not become sedimented as a *grammatical* format, but is instead a *pragmatic* routine" (Couper-Kuhlen/Thompson 2008, 445).

Finally, once we have identified these situated meanings, in the third phase of analysis we checked the availability of each of these meanings in each of the varieties of Spanish studied. Moreover, we contrasted the relative frequency of use of the identified situated meanings per variety.

The total amount of IQCs obtained for each subcorpora of the COLA corpus (per city) can be observed in Table 1. The relative frequency of IQCs, taking into account the total amount of words per variety, shows that these structures are more frequent in the Madrilenian variety, relatively less frequent in the *Rioplatense* variety from Buenos Aires, and even more infrequent in the variety of Santiago de Chile.

Table 1: IQCs in the COLA.

Component	Total words	Discourse-connective *que*-constructions	Relative frequency in the corpus
Madrid	120,000 (selection)	158	0,13%
Santiago de Chile	150,000	36	0,024%
Buenos Aires	70,000	50	0,071%

4 Results

4.1 General distribution

In this subsection, we present the general distribution of initial and non-initial positions of these structures. On the one hand, we consider as 'initial' not only the cases in which *que* is the first word in the turn, but also the cases in which the *que*-construction is preceded only by a discourse particle, such as a discourse marker proper, a conjunction, an interjection or a vocative. In (11), for instance, the *que*-clause is preceded by *ah*, an interjection that could be glossed as 'I've just remembered'.

(11) [A group of friends chatting, when one of them receives a phone call]
J03: *si es para mí que no estoy vale/ que me he ido de vacaciones*
G02: *ah [.] que por cierto dijo [.] ah bueno ya te lo habrá dicho*
'J03: if it's for me, tell them I'm not here ok/ tell them that I've gone on vacation
G02: oh [.] [QUE] by the way [s]he said [.] oh well [s]he must have already told you'
(MABPE2-01C, COLA M)

On the other hand, we consider 'non-initial' those cases in which the *que*-clause is a turn increment, i.e. "any non-main-clause continuation of a speaker's turn after that speaker has come to what could have been a completion point, or a 'transition-relevance place,' based on prosody, syntax and sequential action" (Ford/Fox/Thompson 2002, 16). In (12), for example, the *que*-clause is an incremental construction that adds support to the previous directive speech act *calla* 'be quiet/shut up'.

(12) [An adolescent is listening to the radio but one of his friends keeps on talking]
J01: *calla* [.] *que   est-oy   escuch-ando*
               COMP be-PRS.IND.1SG listen-GER[11]
G01: *no me da la gana*
'J01: shut up [.] [QUE] I'm listening
G01: I don't want to'
(MABPE2-01B, COLA M)

---

[11] The abbreviation GER stands for 'gerund'. Note that this abbreviation is not found in the Leipzig Glossing Rules.

Table 2 below shows the distribution of IQCs in the three varieties of Spanish according to the position of the construction in the turn. Two opposite tendencies can be observed here. While in the corpus from Buenos Aires the non-initial position is much more frequent (92%) than the initial position (8%), the opposite tendency is observed – although it is not so pronounced – in the data from Madrid, where the majority of tokens are in initial position (64%), while fewer tokens appear in non-initial position (36%). In the corpus from Santiago de Chile there is a preference for the initial position, but it is not as marked as in the Madrilenian variety, which means there is a slightly more balanced distribution between initial (59%) and non-initial (41%) tokens.

Table 2: Distribution of IQCs according to the position in the turn.

Position in the turn	Occurrences (%) Madrid	Occurrences (%) Santiago de Chile	Occurrences (%) Buenos Aires
Initial	101 (64%)	33 (59%)	4 (8%)
Non-initial	57 (36%)	23 (41%)	**46 (92%)**
Total	158 (100%)	56 (100%)	50 (100%)

4.2 Results: non-initial position

In the analysis of constructions in non-initial positions we identified two types of situated meanings: 'support of a prior claim' and 'projection of a larger turn'. Both situated meanings are available and have been documented in the three varieties of Spanish.

The situated meaning of support of a prior claim occurs in conversational contexts in which an incremental *que*-construction justifies or adds support to a previous turn-constructional unit[12] (abbreviated henceforth as TCU) that is either a directive speech act, as in (12) above and (13), a dispreferred response to a directive speech act, or a previous *que*-construction with a deontic or volitional modal value. By using the *que*-construction the speaker justifies his/her own position to have carried out the previous speech act. There is a relation of pragmatic dependence between the *que*-construction and the previous statement in the turn, in that the *que*-construction introduces an assumption that justifies the adequacy of the previous act.

---

[12] A turn-constructional unit (TCU) is the smallest unit which can form a turn at talk (see Sacks/Schegloff/Jefferson 1974; Ford/Thompson 1996; Schegloff 1996).

(13) G02: *no faltes*
que   vos   so-s[13]   *el   el   la   mente   creadora*
COMP you   be.PRS.IND-3SG the the the mind   creative
de   nuestro grupo
of   our   group
'G02: don't be absent [QUE] you are the the the creative mind in our team'
(BABS2-08, COLA BA)

Table 3: Co(n)text and interactional meaning corresponding to 'support of a prior claim'.

Situated meaning: support of a prior claim	
Co(n)text	– non-initial position in the turn: speech act (e.g. directive, rejection) + *que*-clause – incremental *que*-construction
Interactional meaning	Justification or support of a previous speech act to point to some evidence that can be observed or inferred from the situational context

The second situated meaning identified is that of projection of a larger turn, which occurs in a different type of discourse context. Most turn projections occur within long interventions by one speaker, which are usually narrations in which a referent is introduced and the speaker not only offers additional information to characterise the referent, but also reports what this referent has said, i.e. (s)he reports a previous speech event. This information is usually presented by means of one or more incremental *que*-constructions, which means that, from the perspective of the conversational discourse, these are extensions in a multi-unit turn (Ford et al. 1996; Ford/Thompson 1996; Ford et al. 2002), as in (14). In this example, one student explains to his friends how a professor from Norway visited their school to introduce the project COLA and asked them to participate in it. Speaker G01 introduces the referent – *una noruega* 'a Norwegian woman' – and then reports her discourse by means of *que*-constructions.

(14) G01: *os cuento/ una movida rara yo*
sabéis lo de inglés de ayer
G03: *el qué/ ah sí*

---

13 As illustrated by the corpus data, both pronominal and verbal *voseo*, such as in *vos sabés* 'you know', are characteristic of the variety of Spanish spoken in and around the Río de la Plata basin.

G01: *lo de la noruega*
G02: *qué de inglés*
G01: *que vino una noruega y y y* [.]
<u>queee *de la Universidad de Bergen o no sé qué leches*</u>
<u>*que es la mejor universidad de Noruega y tal*</u>
<u>*que por lo visto el español es el segundo idioma de Noruega y tal*</u>
más importante y y y bueno el caso es que están estudiando
la evolución del español en plan palabras nuevas tú sabes
yyy eso lo estudian en los jóvenes entonces
<u>*que habían hecho ya unnn uno de esos estudios en Oslo*</u>
otro en Helsinki y otros en Estocolmo otro
eeen en Londres y no sé qué [.] *a ver cómo iban evolucionando las lenguas* [.]
no sé qué
'G01: shall I tell you/ a weird thing I\
do you know what happened in the English class yesterday\
G03: what/ oh yes
G01: the thing about the Norwegian
G02: what happened in the English class\
G01: [QUE] a Norwegian woman came and [.]
<u>[QUE] from the University of Bergen or I don't know what freaking thing</u>
<u>that is the best university in Norway and such</u>
<u>[QUE] apparently Spanish is the second language in Norway and such</u>
<u>most important</u> and and and well the thing is that they are studying
the evolution of Spanish like new words you know\
and they study that in youngsters so
<u>[QUE] they had already done oone one of those studies in Oslo</u>
another one in Helsinki and another one in Stockholm another one
in in London and I don't know what [.] to see how languages were evolving [.]
I don't know what'
(MAESB2-01B, COLA M)

The *que*-construction here is not interpreted as a justification of the previous speech act, but rather receives a quotative interpretation, given that the speaker reproduces an utterance from a previous communicative situation. In (14) the speaker indicates who the quoted person is (a Norwegian professor) and in what communicative situation the utterances were produced (in their last English lesson).

Some of these *que*-clauses could be analysed as relative clauses, although the structure is not as simple as that of relative clauses, e.g. between *que vino una noruega* and *queee de la Universidad de Bergen o no sé qué leches* we find and extension with *y* 'and', so it cannot be classified as a classic relative clause with a nominal antecedent positioned immediately before the *que*-clause. This means that, although some of these cases apparently look like relative clauses, they function differently (i.e. they receive a quotative interpretation) and occur in different positions.

Table 4: Co(n)text and interactional meaning corresponding to 'projection of a larger turn'.

Situated meaning: projection of a larger turn	
Co(n)text	– non-initial position in the turn (internal in a complex turn) – incremental *que*-construction
Interactional meaning	Speaker projects textual sequences within a turn and reports a previous speech event.

4.3 Results: initial position

Each *que*-construction attested in the data in turn-initial position has been classified as an initiation or as a response. As mentioned in the methodology section, an initiation is the first-pair part of an adjacency pair and is not projected by a previous turn, which very often implies a topic change. A response is a second-pair part of an adjacency pair and is projected by the previous turn. Interestingly enough, we documented constructions that simultaneously act as both a response and an initiation, i.e. which are projected by the previous turn *and* require a response. We refer to this special case as 'response-initiation'. Altogether, we took into account three contexts: initiation, response and response-initiation.

The distribution of *que*-constructions in initial position is very marked in the three varieties for initiations and responses. As Table 5 shows, if we consider the cases of responses and response-initiations simultaneously, given that they are both interventions that react to a previous one, these constitute the immense majority of tokens, especially for the subcorpora from Madrid and Santiago de Chile, in which they are quite productive. In the case of Buenos Aires, although we observe the same tendency as in the other varieties, given that there are very few tokens, no generalisations can be made.

Table 5: Distribution of IQCs in initial position.

Turn	Occurrences (%) Madrid	Occurrences (%) Santiago de Chile	Occurrences (%) Buenos Aires
Initiation	38 (37,6%)	12 (32,4%)	0 (0%)
Response	48 (47,5%)	20 (54,1%)	3 (75%)
Response-initiation	15 (14,9%)	5 (13,5%)	1 (25%)
Total	101 (100%)	37 (100%)	4 (100%)

In what follows we discuss the results for different types of turn, i.e. initiations, responses and response-initiations in more detail.

4.3.1 Results: initiation

Initiations were documented in two types of discourse context. In the first type of context, the *que*-construction does not constitute a reaction to a previous intervention, but to the situational context, as in (15–17). In the second type of context, the *que*-construction is in non-initial position, but resumes a topic previously discussed in the conversation, as in (18) below, or even a topic discussed in a previous interaction. The situated meanings identified in initiations are, respectively, warning and topic reintroduction.

Warning can be defined as an attention call about a circumstance that is accessible from the situational context and which implies an exhortation to act. This means that it can be classified as an indirect directive strategy. This situated meaning is clearly recognised in the varieties of Madrid and Santiago de Chile. The *que*-clause functions as an initiation, as it is the first-pair part of an adjacency pair, and it can be preceded by discourse markers and interjections that usually call the interlocutor's attention or make the position of the speaker explicit, as in (15–16).

(15) G01: eh [.] *que*   no   est-á   abierto
                  COMP   NEG   be-PRS.IND.3SG   open
[.] *esperar aquí*
'G01: eh [QUE] it's not open wait here'
(MAESB2-02, COLA M)

(16) J03: *ay*
<background noise>
J03: *ay* [.] *que*   me   est-ás   cuarte-ándo-me
             oh   COMP I.DAT be-PRS.IND.2SG cut.up-GER-me
el   dedo
the finger
J01: *ah ya*
'J03: oh
<background noise>
J03: oh [QUE] you are cutting my finger
J01: oh ok'
(SCEAB8-11, COLA S)

Table 6: Co(n)text and interactional meaning corresponding to 'warning'.

Situated meaning: warning	
Co(n)text	– turn-initial position – optionally preceded by an attention-gatherer: (marker) + *que*-construction – initiation (first-pair part of an adjacency pair)
Interactional Meaning	Speaker directs the addressee's attention to stimuli that can be directly observed or inferred from the situational context.

The warning situated meaning can be considered ambiguous, as two interpretations are plausible. From the point of view of the conversational sequence, they can be interpreted as clearly initiative interventions, but it is also possible to consider that the *que*-construction does not occur in an initial position, but that the discourse marker or interjection is the element that occupies the initial position in the intervention and by means of which the speech act is carried out. In (15) the interjection *eh* 'hey' gathers the attention of the interlocutor, and in (16) *ay* 'oh' expresses the pain that the speaker feels. The *que*-clause justifies the position of the speaker at the moment of performing the speech act. Both analyses are plausible but, the fact that it is possible, at least for the Madrilenian variety, to express this meaning without the presence of an interjection, as in (17), advances the idea that this situated meaning exists independently of that of support of a prior claim. In (17) speaker G01 is talking about a researcher who works in the COLA project and speaker G02 thinks that it is not polite to talk about her and points to the fact that the researcher may eventually listen to the recording.

(17) [A group of classmates talking about a researcher who visited their school]
G01: *es que se llama Ulla tío*
G02: *que te va a escu[char]*[14]
G01: *[me da igual] que se escuche*
ya lo sé que se lo lo va a escuchar tío pero yo soy como soy
'G01: her name is Ulla dude
G02: [QUE] she will he[ar you]
G01: [I don't care] that they can hear me
I know that that they are going to hear it dude, but that's just how I am'
(MABPE2-02, COLA M)

Topic reintroduction can be defined as the resumption of a topic in the conversation, i.e. the speaker resumes a topic which was introduced in a previous intervention within the conversation or in a previous conversation. This situated meaning has only been documented in the corpus from Madrid. In (18) a group of friends are chatting in a public square while babysitting a child and they are arranging to meet later on to go out. After they change the topic to talk about the baby and the baby's pacifier, speaker J01 reintroduces the topic, i.e. goes back to talking about meeting later on that day.

(18) J01: *bueno pues cuando vengáis del ciber venir porque dice la Tere que no vais a ir a su qu% porque cuando vengáis del cine*
J03: *no vais a ir a su casa/*
<cars passing by>
J03: *yo tengo que ir a bajar a por mi hermana*
[...]
J02: *joder a ver si le compramos un chupete que se lleva todo a la boca*
J03: *claro pero que si lo acaba de perder*
es que tenemos en casa perooo no tenía las llaves
J04: *a ver si se lo ha tragado je je je je*
J01: *se lo he lavado y se lo he puesto en la boca y todo pero no sé dónde ha podido soltar el niño [este XXX]*
J03: *[es mío]*
J02: *dámelo un poquito*
J04: *eh/*
<background noise>

---

14 Square brackets represent an overlap.

J02: *dámelo no/ dámelo [.] cuánto te lo quieres quedar/*
J04: *[pa ti]*
J01: *[que] cuando vengáis no sé si estaré yo en la calle sino estoy [.] pues [.] mañana [...] entiendes/*
J02: *venga toma*
'J01: ok well when you come from the cybercafé come because Tere says that you are not going to her % because when you come back from the cinema
J03: you are not going to her house/
<cars passing by>
J03: I have to go down to pick up my sister
[...]
J02: damn let's see if we buy a pacifier for him he is putting everything in his
mouth
J03: sure but he has just lost it
It's just that we have them at home but I didn't have the keys
J04: let's see if he has swallowed it he he he
J01: 1 [I've washed it for him and I've put it in his mouth and such but I don't know where this kid has lost it XXX]
J03: 1[it's mine]
J02: give it to me a little bit
J04: eh/
<background noise>
J02: give it to me right/ give it to me [.] how long do you want to keep it/
J04: 1[for you]
J01: 1[[QUE] when you come back I don't know if I will be in the street] if I'm not [.] well [.] tomorrow [...] do you understand/
J02: ok here you are'
(MABPE2-11A, COLA M)

Table 7: Co(n)text and interactional meaning corresponding to 'topic reintroduction'.

Situated meaning: topic reintroduction	
Co(n)text	– turn-initial position – (marker) + *que*-construction – initiation (first-pair part in an adjacency pair)
Interactional meaning	Speaker reintroduces a topic that has been previously discussed

4.3.2 Results: response

As has been said earlier, responses are the most frequent type of turn in the corpus and we classified them into *preferred* and *dispreferred* (Levinson 1983). Preferred responses are usually unmarked and culturally expected and they tend to be relatively brief and delivered promptly. On the contrary, dispreferred responses are marked – given that they are not expected –, structurally more complex, and tend to include hesitations. They are usually delayed second-pair parts of adjacency pairs.

There is a clear tendency for *que*-responses to be dispreferred turns. This tendency is more marked in the Madrilenian variety than in the variety from Santiago de Chile, while in the variety of Buenos Aires all instances count as dispreferred responses. The three situated meanings available for responses are emphatic contrast, elaboration and exclamative-evaluative. On the one hand, emphatic contrast is closely associated to a dispreferred response, and it is indeed the most frequent situated interpretation for responses in the Madrilenian variety, while in the Spanish from Santiago de Chile and Buenos Aires it is possible, but much less frequent. On the other hand, elaborative and exclamative-evaluative constructions have only been documented in the variety from Santiago de Chile. The elaborative construction is a preferred response, a type of collaborative intervention, while the exclamative-evaluative construction functions as an evaluative reaction to either the previous intervention by the interlocutor or an external, non-linguistic stimulus. Table 8 illustrates the distribution of preferred and dispreferred responses across the three varieties of Spanish.

Table 8: Distribution of que-constructions as preferred and dispreferred responses.

Response	Occurrences (%) Madrid	Occurrences (%) Santiago de Chile	Occurrences (%) Buenos Aires
Preferred	2 (4,2%)	6 (30%)	0 (0%)
Dispreferred	**46 (95,8%)**	14 (70%)	3 (100%)
Total	48 (100%)	20 (100%)	3 (100%)

Emphatic contrast can be defined as the dispreferred second part in an adjacency pair in which an interlocutor expresses some type of disagreement or rejection towards what has been said by the interlocutor, usually in the immediate previous intervention. The speaker shows an assumption that the interlocutor has not taken into account and which can be considered to be part of their shared knowledge. In (19) a group of friends discusses about religion and what God looks like.

While some participants in the conversation affirm that nobody knows what God looks like, speaker G33, who disagrees with the other interlocutors, makes explicit – even if she does so ironically – that God made us in his own image, i.e. what the other participants had not taken into account and what belongs to their shared knowledge, in this case, as part of their religious education.

(19) G32: *como que no hay fotos de dios*
  [...]
  G01: *nadie sabe que como es dios*
  G33: <u>que</u>   la   biblia dic-e   que   dios
     COMP the   bible   say-PRS.IND.3SG   COMP   God
     nos hiz-o   a   su   semejanza
     us   do-PST.IND.3SG   to   his resemblance
  'G32: like there's no photos of God
  [...]
  G01: nobody knows what God looks like
  G33: [QUE] the bible says that God made us in his own image'
  (SCAWM4-07, COLA S)

The emphatic contrast situated meaning is a dispreferred response, given that it expresses either total or partial disagreement with what has just been said by an interlocutor. Clear examples were found in the subcorpora of Madrid and Santiago de Chile (19), and only one dubious example was found in the subcorpus of Buenos Aires.

Table 9: Co(n)text and interactional meaning corresponding to 'emphatic contrast'.

Situated meaning: emphatic contrast	
Co(n)text	– turn-initial position – response (second-pair part in an adjacency pair) – dispreferred intervention
Interactional meaning	Speaker refuses a request or negatively assesses a prior intervention by the addressee

The situated meaning of elaboration has been defined for Germanic languages (D'Hertefelt/Verstraete 2014) as a type of turn in which the speaker completes his/her own intervention or an intervention by the interlocutor by drawing a conclusion or reformulating (Wide 2014; D'Hertefelt 2018). This situated meaning has only been documented in the subcorpus of Santiago de Chile, in which two examples were found. In (20) two friends are discussing the content of a vocational training course. Speaker G28 explains what the course consists in and after speaker G01 asks the clarification question *qué huevada/* 'what silly thing?', G28 extracts a conclusion about the scope of the course and expresses her assessment of it: the content of the course is not applied and bears no relation whatsoever with the practice.

(20) G28: *si mi hermano estudió electrónica y le enseñaron así a arreglar teles y todas esas voladas [.] después tenía que andar a en la práctica en los palo-postes de la huevada telefónica*
G01: *qué huevada/*
G28: <u>que</u>   nada   que   ver   lo   que
      COMP nothing COMP see.INF the COMP
vien-e   en   la   práctica
come.PRS.IND-3SG in   the   practice
'G28: yes, my brother studied electronics and they taught him to fix TVs and all
those silly things [.] then he had to practice on the silly phone electricity poles
G01: *what silly thing/*
G28: [QUE] it has nothing to do with what comes with practice'
(SCAWM4-07, COLA S)

Table 10: Co(n)text and interactional meaning corresponding to 'elaboration'.

Situated meaning: elaboration	
Co(n)text	– turn-initial position – response (second-pair part in an adjacency pair)
Interactional Meaning	Speaker draws a conclusion or reformulates a previous statement

Finally, the exclamative-evaluative situated meaning is found in constructions that present a degree evaluation of a property of the subject, typically an animate entity (see Gras/Sansiñena 2017). In (21), for instance, speaker J02 evaluates speaker G08's sentimentality as excessive by means of a *que*-construction that reacts to G08's immediately previous turn. The construction in (21) could be paraphrased as 'How sentimental you are!'.

(21) G08: *el lunes ibas a faltar* [.] *a mí qué me importa*
　　 J02: *ay que　　 eres　　　　　 sentimental*
　　　　　 oh COMP be.IND.PRS.2SG sentimental
　　 'G08: on Monday you were going to skip the class [.] what do I care?
　　 J02: oh, you are so sentimental'
　　 (SCEAB8-10, COLAS, Chile)

From a discourse-interactional point of view, the exclamative-evaluative *que*-construction usually occurs as a dispreferred response, but it can also occur within the intervention of the speaker, when (s)he evaluates an entity mentioned or alluded to in his/her own discourse. This situated meaning is also observed in contexts in which the speaker reacts to a non-verbal stimulus. In (22), retrieved from Google, the speaker reacts to a picture of a person posted online and the meaning of the utterance can be paraphrased along the lines 'How ugly and silly you are, Miley Cyrus!'.

(22) [Comment on a picture of Miley Cyrus on Facebook]
　　 Que　 eris[15]　　　　 *fe-a　　　y　　tont-a*
　　 COMP be.IND.PRS.2SG ugly-F.SG and silly-F.SG
　　 'You are so ugly and silly!'
　　 (Google)

Table 11: Form and interactional meaning corresponding to 'exclamative-evaluative'.

Situated meaning: exclamative-evaluative	
Co(n)text	– turn-initial position – response (second-pair part in an adjacency pair)
Interactional Meaning	Speaker presents an evaluative reaction to either the previous turn by the interlocutor or an external, non-linguistic stimulus

---

15 Depending of the formality of the speech event and the relation between interlocutors, Chilean Spanish speakers use different forms of address for the second person singular: *tú*, *vos* and *usted*, each with different verb conjugations. Verbal *voseo*, in which the standard conjugation for the present indicative *tú cantas/comes/escribes* 'you sing/eat/write' is replaced by *tú cantái/comí(s)/viví(s)* and the conjugation for the present subjunctive *que tú cantes/comas/escribas* 'that you sing/eat/write' is replaced by *que tú cantí(s)/comái/escribái*, is very frequent, mostly among young speakers.

4.3.3 Results: response-initiation

A response-initiation is a turn that is predicted by the previous turn and simultaneously predicts a subsequent turn. On the one hand, it constitutes a response, given that it has been planned and foreseen by a previous intervention but, on the other hand, it requires an intervention by the next speaker. There are two possible situated meanings for response-initiations: echo and self-repetition. These meanings have been clearly documented in the subcorpora of Madrid and Santiago de Chile, but there is only one example of a self-repetition use in the subcorpus of Buenos Aires.

In (23) speaker J01 uses a *que*-construction to partially reproduce the previous intervention of her interlocutor given that she could not hear the final word well. Her intervention represents a reaction to the previous turn but, at the same time, it demands a response from J06. *Que*-constructions which appear in initial position of response-initiation turns have been referred to as echoic questions (Escandell-Vidal 1999) and are always context dependent.

(23)　J06: *yo pensé que era más difícil*
　　　　J01:　*que*　　*er-a*　　　　　　　　*qué/*
　　　　　　　COMP be.PST.IPFV.IND-3SG what
　　　'J06: I thought it was more difficult
　　　J01: [QUE] it was what/'
　　　(SCCCM4-01, COLA S)

Table 12: Co(n)text and interactional meaning corresponding to 'echo question'.

Situated meaning: echo question	
Co(n)text	– turn-initial position – response-initiation
Interactional meaning	Speaker reacts to previous turn (usually with surprise) and demands clarification

A self-repetition is a turn in which the speaker repeats a previous intervention because the interlocutor (i) has not taken it into account, (ii) did not properly hear the speaker's intervention and therefore asked for clarification or (iii) does not agree with what the speaker said and expresses his/her disagreement by means of the clarification question *¿Qué?* 'What?'. The *que*-construction in (24) repeats speaker JX4's previous initiative intervention completely, given that it has not been successful. The initial *que* signals represented discourse.

(24) [A group of classmates are working together on a classroom project]
  J02: *qué te pasó Martín*
  G04: *nada*
  G05: *nada [.] es un falso [.] no hay vuelta*
  JX4: *no querías hacer nada*
  <pause>
  G04: *qué/*
  JX4: <u>que</u>   no   quer-ía-s   hac-er   nada
        COMP no   want-PST.IPFV.IND-2SG   do-INF   nothing
  'J02: what happened to you Martín\
  G04: nothing
  05: nothing [.] he's a liar [.] there's no way around it
  JX4: you didn't want to do anything
  <pause>
  G04: what/
  JX4: [QUE] you didn't want to do anything'
  (BABS2-06, COLA BA)

Interestingly enough, speakers from Buenos Aires can also reintroduce an initiative intervention without introducing it by means of *que*. In Peninsular Spanish the idiomatic formulation in such context is *que por qué* [...], but this is not the case for *Rioplatense* Spanish, as we observe in (25). In this example speaker G01 simply repeats his exact previous intervention without marking it as reported speech.

(25) [Students talking about a classmate]
  G01: *por qué la odiás tanto*
  G02: *ay*
  J01: *qué/*
  G01: <u>*por qué la odias tanto*</u>\
  'G01: why do you hate her so much\
  G02: oh
  J01: what/
  G01: why do you hate her so much\'
  (BABS2-08, COLA BA)

Table 13: Co(n)text and interactional meaning corresponding to 'self-repetition'.

Situated meaning: self-repetition	
Co(n)text	– turn-initial position – response-initiation
Interactional meaning	Speaker (partially) repeats their previous intervention for clarification purposes

5 Discussion

In this section we will discuss the relevance of the results of the present work in relation to its aim. The first objective of the present work is to confirm whether there are differences in the discourse contexts in which non-embedded indicative *que*-constructions are used across regional varieties of Spanish (Madrid, Spain, Santiago de Chile, Chile and Buenos Aires, Argentina). The second objective of this work is to prove whether there is a correspondence between the situated meanings identified in the conversational analysis and the types of constructions identified in previous generativist studies.

Regarding the regional distribution of discourse contexts, we observed that in all three varieties, non-embedded indicative *que*-constructions occur more frequently in non-initial position, where they give rise to the same types of interpretation across varieties, namely meanings mainly associated to the support of a prior claim and reproduced discourse. However, there is variation amongst the three varieties of Spanish in relation to the *que*-constructions that occur in *initial* position. *Rioplatense* Spanish is the most restrictive variety, given that there are only 4 occurrences in initial position in our corpus, 3 of which are instances of emphatic contrast and only one of which is a self-repetition. Chilean Spanish is located in an intermediate position, given that *que*-constructions occur in different types of reactive interventions (preferred and dispreferred responses and response-initiations), as well as in initiations that call the interlocutor's attention to the communicative situation itself. Finally, Madrilenian Spanish is the least restrictive variety. Initial occurrences of *que*-constructions are in general more frequent in Madrilenian Spanish than in the other two varieties, and they are (mostly) reactive, but they can also be initiative interventions that call the interlocutor's attention to an element of the communicative situation, and they even allow to resume a topic that has already been introduced in the ongoing conversation or in a previous communicative situation.

Table 14 summarises the availability and relative frequency of all situated meanings documented in the corpus, per variety.

Table 14: Distribution of situated meanings per variety.

Position/Type of turn	Situated meaning	Madrid	Santiago de Chile	Buenos Aires
Non-initial	Support of a prior claim	**X**	**X**	**X**
Non-initial	Projection of a larger turn	**X**	**X**	**X**
Initial: initiation	Warning	**X**	**X**	
Initial: initiation	Topic reintroduction	**X**		
Initial: response	Emphatic contrast	**X**	X	X
Initial: response	Elaboration		X	
Initial: response	Exclamative-evaluative		X	
Initial: response-initiation	Echo question	**X**	**X**	(x)
Initial: response-initiation	Self-repetition	**X**	**X**	x

X = documented with high frequency
X = documented with relative frequency
x = documented infrequently
(x) = Not documented but possible, according to native informants

If we take into account the relation between the *que*-construction and the discourse context that the construction is associated to, the observed variation amongst varieties can be represented on a cline ranging from high to low *discourse dependency*. Such cline includes the following stages: the speaker's intervention > the immediately previous intervention > the immediate communicative situation > a previous communicative situation. Each of the varieties analysed can then be located in a different stage on this cline:
- Spanish from Buenos Aires: the speaker's intervention > *previous intervention*
- Spanish from Santiago de Chile: the speaker's intervention itself > the previous intervention > *the immediate communicative situation*
- Spanish from Madrid: the intervention itself > the previous intervention > the immediate communicative situation > *a previous communicative situation*

This cline can also be understood in terms of a divergence process, by which the same element – an IQC – extends its scope and can therefore begin to occur in new discourse contexts that are not available in other regional varieties of the same language. In turn, this divergence process could receive a diachronic interpretation, in that the regional varieties under examination are situated at different stages of the cline, being Peninsular Spanish the variety that has further evolved on the cline and *Rioplantense* Spanish the most restrictive variety in terms of discourse dependency.

Regarding the second objective of the present work, we argue that there exists a partial correspondence between the situated meanings in our corpus and the formal types of constructions identified in the generativist literature. Table 16 shows the relation between the situated meanings identified in the conversational analysis and such formal types.

As can be observed in Table 15, some situated meanings correspond to certain formal construction types. The so-called conjunctive *que* has a stable discourse position: it appears in non-initial position in the turn and it is directly associated to the situated meaning of support of a prior claim by the same speaker within the turn. As for the so-called quotative *que*, it can have two types of discourse position: it can be an initiative intervention when it reproduces discourse from a different communicative situation, or a reinitiative intervention when it reproduces previous discourse by one of the interlocutors in the current communicative situation. Finally, the so-called exclamative *que* also has two types of discourse position: it can function as an initiative intervention, with the situated meaning of warning, or as a reactive intervention, with the situated meaning of emphatic contrast.

Table 15: Situated meanings found in our corpus study and their correspondence to formal types of initial que-clauses identified in the generativist literature.

Situated meanings	Position/turn type	Example	Formal types of initial que-clauses
Support of a prior claim	Non-initial	10; 12; 13	Conjunctive
Projection of a larger turn	Non-initial	14	Quotative
Warning	Initial: initiation	15; 16; 17	Exclamative
Topic reintroduction	Initial: initiation	18	Quotative?
Emphatic contrast	Initial: response	19	Exclamative

Table 15 (continued)

Situated meanings	Position/turn type	Example	Formal types of initial que-clauses
Elaboration	Initial: response	20	---
Exclamative-evaluative	Initial: response	21; 22	---
Echo question	Initial: response-initiation	23	Quotative
Self-repetition	Initial: response-initiation	24	Quotative

Other attested contexts in our corpus do not correspond to the formal types previously identified in the generativist literature. The exclamative-evaluative construction (21–22), which appears in initial position of the turn and presents an evaluative reaction, and the elaboration construction (20), which also appears in initial position of the turn and presents a conclusion or reformulation of a previous statement, are specific Chilean types. Finally, topic reintroduction, which counts as the resumption of a topic in the conversation (18), has only been documented in the subcorpus of Madrilenian Spanish. Interestingly enough, its meaning is *similar* to that of quotative constructions, and we argue that they maintain relations of family resemblance among each other. There is a set of meanings relatively associated to echoed or reproduced discourse, such as the situated meanings of echo, self-repetition, emphatic contrast and topic reintroduction.

6 Conclusions

The interactional analysis carried out here complements the syntactic-semantic explanations of generativist approaches. Our study has made it possible to identify the discourse contexts in which previously recognised formal types – conjunctive, quotative and exclamative – occur. Moreover, it has also enabled us to understand the reasons why speakers choose to use these constructions, as well as the discourse positions in which they use them.

Our interactional analysis also let us describe one particular level of variation, which is the variation in the contexts in which a construction is usually used. Although the three formal types mentioned above are documented in all three varieties, it is possible to identify differences at the level of contexts of use. The conjunctive type is stable, whereas the quotative one is infrequent in Buenos Aires and, according to our informants, it is not the idiomatic form in this variety. As for the exclamative type, it is not available equally in the three varieties of Spanish studied here: the context of emphatic contrast is present in the three subcorpus, while the context of warning is not present in the variety of Spanish spoken in Buenos Aires. Therefore, we believe that the interactional analysis nicely complements the syntactic-semantic one.

Finally, as our analysis took into account data from different varieties, it has allowed us to identify interpretations and contexts that do not correspond to the typical interpretations identified in the literature and that, in addition, only occur in one of the varieties studied here. Exclamative-evaluative and elaboration interpretations are exclusive of Chilean Spanish, and topic reintroduction only occurs in Madrilenian Spanish.

It remains to be discussed whether the contexts that only occur in some of the dialects are distinct constructional types (with their own formal and interpretative properties) or instances of any of the constructions analysed (conjunctive, quotative, exclamative). In the case of Chilean exclamative-evaluative constructions, it seems clear that differentiated formal and interpretative traits can be identified (Gras/Sansiñena 2017). However, this is not so clear for the contexts that correspond to elaboration and topic reintroduction.

Regarding the limitations of this work, given the relatively small amount of data available for the three varieties, there is a need to broaden the corpus or to use experimental methods, including assessments of contexts and situated meanings by native speakers that might help confirm the usage differences observed in this study. Finally, this paper also opens up new lines of research that we hope to undertake in the future. It would be interesting to look into the implications that the proposed cline – reflecting variation amongst varieties – from high to low discourse dependency might have for the explanation of the diachronic development of non-embedded indicative *que*-clauses, in order to answer whether the current variation reflects diverse processes of development.

7 References

Alcina, Juan/Blecua, José Manuel, *Gramática española*, Barcelona, Ariel, 1975.
Aliaga García, Francisco/de Bustos Guadaño, Eduardo, *Acerca de los límites entre gramática y pragmática. De nuevo sobre las oraciones causales*, paper presented at I International symposium of semantics, University of La Laguna, 1997. Non published Ms.
Bello, Andrés, *Gramática de la lengua castellana destinada al uso de los americanos*, Santiago de Chile, Imprenta del Progreso, 1847.

Biezma, Maria, *An expressive analysis of exclamatives in Spanish*, in: *Proceedings from Going Romance 2007. Twenty-First Symposium on Romance Linguistics*, Amsterdam, Universiteit van Amsterdam, 2007. https://mariabiezma.files.wordpress.com/2012/10/gr21.pdf [last access: 2016].

Bosque, Ignacio/Demonte, Violeta (edd.), *Gramática descriptiva de la lengua española*, Madrid, Espasa Calpe, 1999.

Briz, Antonio/Pons, Salvador/Portolés, José (edd.), *Diccionario de partículas discursivas del español*, Valencia, Servei de Publicacions de la Universitat de València, 2008, www.dpde.es [last access: 2016].

Cascón Martín, Eugenio, *Español coloquial. Rasgos, formas y fraseología de la lengua diaria*, Madrid, Edinumen, 1995.

Corr, Alice Victoria, *Ibero-Romance and the syntax of the utterance*, PhD dissertation, University of Cambridge, 2016.

Couper-Kuhlen, Elizabeth/Thompson, Sandra, *On assessing situations and events in conversation. "Extraposition" and its relatives*, Discourse Studies 10:4 (2008), 443–467.

D'Hertefelt, Sarah, *Insubordination in Germanic. A typology of complement and conditional constructions*, Berlin/Boston, De Gruyter Mouton, 2018.

Demonte, Violeta/Fernández Soriano, Olga, *La periferia izquierda oracional y los complementantes del español*, in: Cuartero, Juan/Emsel, Martine (edd.), *Vernetzungen. Kognition, Bedeutung, (kontrastive) Pragmatik*, Frankfurt, Peter Lang, 2007, 133–147.

Demonte, Violeta/Fernández Soriano, Olga, *Force and finiteness in the Spanish complementizer system*, Probus 21:1 (2009), 23–49.

Demonte, Violeta/Fernández Soriano, Olga, *El "que" citativo, otros elementos de la periferia izquierda oracional y la recomplementación. Variación inter e intralingüística*, in: Jacob, Daniel/Ploog, Katja (edd.), *Autour de "que"/El entorno de "que"*, Frankfurt am Main, Peter Lang, 2013, 47–69 (= 2013a).

Demonte, Violeta/Fernández Soriano, Olga, *Evidentials "dizque" and "que" in Spanish. Grammaticalization, parameters and the (fine) structure of Comp*, Linguística. Revista de Estudos linguísticos da Universidade do Porto 8 (2013), 211–234 (= 2013b).

Demonte, Violeta/Fernández Soriano, Olga, *Evidentiality and illocutionary force. Spanish matrix "que" at the syntax-pragmatics interface*, in: Dufter, Andreas/Octavio de Toledo, Álvaro S. (edd.), *Left sentence peripheries in Spanish. Diachronic, variationist, and typological perspectives*, Amsterdam, John Benjamins, 2014, 217–252.

D'Hertefelt, Sarah/Verstraete, Jean-Christophe, *Independent complement constructions in Swedish and Danish. Insubordination or dependency shift?*, Journal of Pragmatics 60 (2014), 89–102.

Escandell-Vidal, Victoria, *Los enunciados interrogativos. Aspectos semánticos y pragmáticos*, in: Bosque, Ignacio/Demonte, Violeta (edd.), *Gramática descriptiva de la lengua española*, vol. 3, Madrid, Espasa, 1999, 3929–3991.

Etxepare, Ricardo, *On quotative constructions in Iberian Spanish*, in: Laury, Ritva (ed.), *Crosslinguistic studies of clause combining. The multifunctionality of conjuctions*, Amsterdam, John Benjamins, 2008, 35–78.

Etxepare, Ricardo, *From hearsay evidentiality to samesaying relations*, Lingua 120:3 (2010), 604–627.

Etxepare, Ricardo, *Quotative expansions*, in: Baauw, Sergio/Drijkondingen, Frank/Meroni, Luisa/Pinta, Manuela (edd.), *Romance Languages and Linguistic Theory 2011. Selected papers from Going Romance Utrecht 2011*, Amsterdam, John Benjamins, 2013, 93–124.

Ford, Cecilia, *Grammar in interaction. Adverbial clauses in American English conversations*, Cambridge, Cambridge University Press, 1993.

Ford, Cecilia/Thompson, Sandra, *Interactional units in conversation. Syntactic, intonational, and pragmatic resources for the management of turns*, in: Ochs, Elionor/Schegloff, Emanuel/Thompson, Sandra (edd.), *Interaction and grammar*, Cambridge, Cambridge University Press, 1996, 134–184.

Ford, Cecilia, Fox, Barbara/Thompson, Sandra, *Practices in the construction of turns. The "TCU" revisited*, Pragmatics 6 (1996), 427–454.

Ford, Cecilia, Fox, Barbara/Thompson, Sandra, *The language of turn and sequence*, Oxford, Oxford University Press, 2002.

Fraser, Bruce, *Types of English discourse markers*, Acta Linguistica Hungarica 38:1–4 (1988), 19–33.

Fuentes, Catalina, *Diccionario de conectores y operadores del español*, Madrid, Arco, 2010.

García Negroni, María Marta/Marcovecchio, Ana María, *Igual a un lado y otro del Atlántico. Un origen común para dos valores argumentativos*, in: García Negroni, María Marta (ed.), *Marcadores del discurso. Perspectivas y contrastes*, Buenos Aires, Santiago Arcos, 2014, 141–158.

Garrido Medina, Joaquín, *Discourse structure in grammar*, Estudios ingleses de la Universidad Complutense 6 (1998), 49–63.

Garrido Medina, Joaquín, *Los actos de habla. Las oraciones imperativas*, in: Bosque, Ignacio/Demonte, Violeta (edd.), *Gramática descriptiva de la lengua española*, vol. 3, Madrid, Espasa Calpe, 1999, 3879–3928.

Gili Gaya, Samuel, *Curso superior de sintaxis española*, México, Minerva, 1943.

Gras, Pedro, *Gramática de construcciones en interacción. Propuesta de un modelo y aplicación al análisis de estructuras independientes con marcas de subordinación en español*, PhD dissertation, University of Barcelona, 2011.

Gras, Pedro, *Entre la gramática y el discurso. Valores conectivos de "que" inicial átono en español*, in: Jacob, Daniel/Ploog, Katja (edd.), *Autour de "que"/El entorno de "que"*, Frankfurt am Main, Peter Lang, 2013, 89–112.

Gras, Pedro, *Revisiting the functional typology of insubordination. Insubordinate "que"-constructions in Spanish*, in: Evans, Nicholas/Watanabe, Honoré (edd.), *Insubordination*, Amsterdam, John Benjamins, 2016, 113–144.

Gras, Pedro/Pérez, Sofía/Brisard, Frank, *1. Quotative "que" constructions in Spanish: a corpusbased constructional approach*, in: Hennecke, Inga/Wiesinger, Evelyn (edd.), *Constructions in Spanish*, Amsterdam, John Benjamins, in press.

Gras, Pedro/Sansiñena, María Sol, *An interactional account of discourse-connective "que"-constructions in Spanish*, Text & Talk 35:4 (2015), 505–529.

Gras, Pedro/Sansiñena, María Sol, *Exclamatives in the functional typology of insubordination. Evidence from complement insubordinate constructions in Spanish*, Journal of Pragmatics 115 (2017), 21–36.

Harnisch, Rüdiger, *Divergence of linguistic varieties in a language space*, in: Auer, Peter/Schmidt, Jürgen (edd.), *Language and space. An international handbook of linguistic variation*, vol. 1: *Theories and methods*, Berlin/New York, De Gruyter Mouton, 2010, 275–295.

Iglesias Recuero, Silvia, *Gramática de la oración frente a gramática del discurso. De nuevo sobre el llamado "que" causal*, in: de Bustos Tovar, José Jesús (ed.), *Lengua, discurso,* texto. *I simposio internacional de análisis del discurso*, vol. 1, Madrid, Visor, 2000, 333–344.

Loureda, Óscar/Acín, Esperanza (edd.), *Los estudios sobre marcadores del discurso, hoy*, Madrid, Arco, 2010.

Martín Zorraquino, María Antonia/Montolío Durán, Estrella (edd.), *Los marcadores del discurso. Teoría y análisis*, Madrid, Arco, 1998.

Martín Zorraquino, María Antonia/Portolés, José, *Los marcadores del discurso*, in: Bosque, Ignacio/Demonte, Violeta (edd.), *Gramática descriptiva de la lengua española*, vol. 3, Madrid, Espasa, 1999, 4051–4213.

Moliner, María, *Diccionario de uso del español*, Madrid, Gredos, 1966–1967.

Ochs, Elionor/Schegloff, Emanuel/Thompson, Sandra, *Interaction and grammar*, Cambridge, Cambridge University Press, 1996.

Pérez, Sofía/Gras, Pedro/Brisard, Frank, Semantic polyfunctionality and constructional networks. On insubordinate subjunctive complement clauses in Spanish, *Constructions & Frames* 13:1 (2021), 82–126.

Pons, Salvador, *"Que" inicial átono como marca de modalidad*, Estudios de Lingüística de la Universidad de Alicante (ELUA) 17 (2003), 531–545.

Porroche Ballesteros, Margarita, *Algunos aspectos del uso de "que" en el español conversacional. "Que" como introductor de oraciones "independientes"*, Círculo de Lingüística Aplicada a la Comunicación (CLAC) 3 (2000), 100–116.

Real Academia Española/Asociación de Academias de la Lengua Española, *Nueva gramática de la lengua española*, Madrid, Espasa, 2009.

Rodríguez Ramalle, Teresa María, *Estudio sintáctico y discursivo de algunas estructuras enunciativas y citativas del español*, Revista española de lingüística aplicada 21 (2008), 269–288 (= 2008a).

Rodríguez Ramalle, Teresa María, *Marcas enunciativas y evidenciales en el discurso periodístico*, in: Olza, Inés/Casado Velarde, Manuel/Ramón González Ruiz, Ramón (edd.), *Actas del XXXVII Simposio de la Sociedad Española de Lingüística (SEL)*, Pamplona, Servicio de Publicaciones de la Universidad de Navarra, 2008, 735–744 (= 2008b).

Sacks, Harvey/Schegloff, Emanuel/Jefferson, Gail, *A simplest systematics for the organization of turn-taking for conversation*, Language 50 (1974), 696–735.

Sánchez López, Cristina, *The mapping between semantics and prosody. Evidence from Spanish main sentences with the form <que + Vsubj>*, paper presented at the 48th Annual Meeting of the Societas Linguistica Europaea, 2015. Non published Ms.

Sansiñena, María Sol/De Smet, Hendrik/Cornillie, Bert, *Between subordinate and insubordinate. Paths towards complementizer-initial main clauses*, Journal of Pragmatics 77 (2015), 3–19 (= 2015a).

Sansiñena, María Sol/De Smet, Hendrik/Cornillie, Bert, *Displaced directives. Subjunctive free-standing "que"-clauses vs. imperatives in Spanish*, Folia Linguistica 49:1 (2015b), 257–285 (= 2015b).

Sansiñena, María Sol, *The multiple functional load of "que". An interactional approach to insubordinate complement clauses in Spanish*, PhD dissertation, University of Leuven, 2015.

Sansiñena, María Sol, *Eliciting evidence of functional differences. The imperative vs. free-standing "que"-clauses in Spanish*, in: Heinold, Simone/Van Olmen, Daniel (edd.), *Imperatives and other directive strategies*, Amsterdam, John Benjamins, 2017, 265–289.

Santos Río, Luis, *Diccionario de partículas*, Salamanca, Luso-Española de ediciones, 2003.

Schegloff, Emanuel, *Turn organization. One intersection of grammar and interaction*, in: Elinor Ochs/Thompson, Sandra/Schegloff, Emanuel (edd.), *Interaction and grammar*, Cambridge, Cambridge University Press, 1996, 52–133.

Selting, Margret/Couper-Kuhlen, Elizabeth, *Studies in interactional linguistics*, Amsterdam, John Benjamins, 2001.

Sirbu-Dumitrescu, Domnita, *Sintaxis y pragmática de las preguntas cuasi-eco en español*, in: Vilanova, Antonio (ed.), *Actas del X Congreso de la Asociación Internacional de Hispanistas*, Barcelona, University of Barcelona, 1992, 1323–1338.

Sirbu-Dumitrescu, Domnita, *Estructura y función de las preguntas retóricas repetitivas en español*, in: Villegas, Juan (ed.), *Actas del XI Congreso de la Asociación Internacional de Hispanistas*, vol. 1, California, University of California, 1994, 139–147 (= 1994a).

Sirbu-Dumitrescu, Domnita, *Función pragma-discursiva de la interrogación ecoica usada como respuesta en español*, in: Haverkate, Henk/Hengeveld, Kees/Mulder, Gijs (edd.), *Aproximaciones pragmalingüísticas al español*, Amsterdam, Rodopi, 1994, 51–85 (= 1994b).

Sirbu-Dumitrescu, Domnita, *Subordinación y recursividad en la conversación. Las secuencias integradas por intercambios ecoicos*, in: Haverkate, Henk/Mulder, Gijs/Fraile Maldonado, Carolina (edd.), *La pragmática lingüística del español. Recientes desarrollos*, Amsterdam, Rodopi, 1998, 277–314.

Sirbu-Dumitrescu, Domnita, *La expresión de buenos deseos hacia nuestro prójimo. ¿Un acto de habla cortés automático?*, in: Bravo, Diana/Briz, Antonio (edd.), *Pragmática sociocultural. Estudios sobre el discurso de cortesía en Español*, Barcelona, Ariel, 2004, 265–284.

Spitzer, Leo, *Notas sintáctico-estilísticas a propósito del español "que"*, Revista de Filología Hispánica 4:2 (1942), 105–126.

Verstraete, Jean-Christophe/D'Hertefelt, Sarah/Van linden, An, *A typology of complement insubordination in Dutch*, Studies in Language 36:1 (2012), 123–153.

Villa-García, Julio, *The syntax of multiple-"que" sentences in Spanish. Along the left periphery*, Amsterdam/Philadelphia, John Benjamins, 2015.

Susana Afonso
Impersonal *se* constructions in the Portuguese of East Timor
Notes on the relation between language contact and second language acquisition

Abstract: This chapter presents a preliminary discussion on impersonal *se* constructions produced by East Timorese speakers of Portuguese L2 taking into consideration the interplay between contact and general tendencies of second language acquisition. Data collection comprised the recording of a semi-guided interview with 21 informants living in Portugal and East Timor. Impersonal *se* constructions were extracted from this corpus. Innovations in the impersonal construction are observed, namely, deletion of the clitic and the rise of the double subject construction in which the actor is encoded both by an overt nominal subject and by the clitic *se*. The deletion of the clitic corresponds to a simplification of a morphological pattern which matches the morphological make-up of East Timorese languages. The double subject construction, however, corresponds to the emergence of a more complex pattern. Considering that both types of innovations are observed in other vernacular varieties of Portuguese that emerged in very different contact scenarios, this chapter discusses the relation between contact-induced changes and general processes of second language acquisition.

Keywords: varieties of Portuguese, Portuguese in East Timor, language contact, second language acquisition

1 Introduction

Contact plays a major role in the formation of new varieties of a language, particularly those that emerge in (post-)colonial contexts. The outcomes of contact vary according to a complex interrelation between both internal and external factors which are, to a certain extent, specific to each contact situation.

In the literature on vernacular varieties, two main perspectives, usually not complementary, persist: a retentionist one (Harris 1984), which advocates the

---

Dr Susana Afonso, University of Exeter Department of Modern Languages and Cultures, College of Humanities, Queen's Drive Exeter EX4 4QH United Kingdom

https://doi.org/10.1515/9783110736250-010

continuation of a vernacular brought overseas, and a contact perspective (Mufwene 2008; Kerswill 2010). The concept of vernacular universals (Chambers 2004) is based on the observation that vernaculars across the world show many similarities, due to universals of innate language development. Portuguese vernaculars also exhibit similarities, despite the very different contact scenarios in which they emerged and continuously develop a comprehensive analysis of a particular phenomenon must draw on both internal and external evidence. Rather than gathering evidence for the existence of vernacular universals, on the one hand, and for contact-induced changes, on the other, an interplay between contact and general tendencies of second language acquisition should be taken into account.

Using the impersonal *se* constructions as a case study, a polysemous construction, canonically marked by the clitic *se*, whose function is to demote the actor from an event (Kemmer 1993; Afonso 2008a; Malchukov/Siewierska 2011), this qualitative study aims at presenting a preliminary discussion of the hypotheses of contact and of second language acquisition in Portuguese L2 spoken by East Timorese speakers. Portuguese in East Timor is at the initial stages of partial restructuring (Afonso/Goglia 2015) and, as such, represents a unique opportunity to observe the interplay between internal and contact-induced patterns as they emerge in discourse. Some of these patterns may be adopted more widely and might be used more frequently also in other vernacular varieties of Portuguese.

The chapter is organised as follows: first it will present the socio-historical overview of Portuguese in East Timor (Section 2), followed by the presentation of impersonal *se* constructions in vernacular varieties of Portuguese (Section 3). After some methodological considerations (Section 4), the impersonal *se* constructions in the Portuguese spoken by East Timorese will be discussed (Sections 5 and 6). In the light of the similarities between the impersonal *se* constructions in the East Timorese data and in other varieties of Portuguese, the chapter discusses to what extent general tendencies of second language acquisition can be relevant to explain the emerging patterns in contact settings.

2 Portuguese in East Timor: socio-historical background

One of the legacies of the Portuguese colonial enterprise is the presence of Portuguese in all fomer colonised territories as official language and as semi restructured varieties. Contact between Portuguese and local languages, as well as processes of second language acquisition led to the emergence of innovative patterns. In some cases these became features of nativised varieties of Portuguese, as is the case of Brazilian Portuguese (Mello 2014). In other cases, such as Portuguese in Lusophone Africa and East Timor, the varieties are still undergoing a process of nativisation (Gonçalves 2004).[1]

In East Timor, Portuguese is largely an L2 and exhibits very wide variation partly due to historical circumstances. The presence of Portuguese in East Timor was always very limited since the beginning of colonisation in the 16th century until 1975 when the Indonesian regime took over. There has never been a significant influx of native speakers of any variety of Portuguese (Boxer 1947).[2] Portuguese was initially spoken by the local elite. During the Indonesian period, Bahasa Indonesia became the official language, and Portuguese was banned, hardly surviving the 25 years of Indonesian regime until East Timor's independence in 2002.[3] Portuguese was then chosen as one of the official languages together with Tetun Dili, a local lingua franca.

The ban on Portuguese during the Indonesian regime meant that the acquisition of Portuguese as an L2 variety, which could eventually lead to its partial restructuring (Holm 2004), was interrupted. The change in language policy had dramatic effects with regard to the linguistic repertoire of the several East Timorese generations. The majority of adults in active employment at the time of independence had been educated in Indonesian and had no or very little knowledge of Portuguese.[4] Even though Portuguese is one of the official languages now and has been taught in schools since independence, Portuguese is still part of the linguistic repertoire of mostly the social elite in East Timor.

Linguistically speaking, East Timor is a highly complex multilingual country comprising 15 to 20 local languages from two language families: Austronesian and Papuan (Lewis 2009).[5] Tetun Dili, an Austronesian language, developed from contact with Mambae, the second largest language in Timor, and with other local languages, especially at the morphosyntactic level. Tetun Dili became the lingua franca in East Timor and was heavily influenced by Portuguese at the lexical level with just a minor degree of contact-induced features at the morphosyntactic level (Hajek 2006, 164).

---

1 According to Hagemeijer (2018), Portuguese in São Tomé has fully nativised.
2 See also De Matos (2016) for a demographic overview of the Portuguese empire.
3 It should be noted that some (although few) religious schools were allowed to teach Portuguese as a foreign language.
4 See Taylor-Leech (2009) for a discussion on language policy.
5 There are different criteria to establish the number of local languages. The number of languages, therefore, varies according to the criteria (see Hajek 2002).

After independence, Portuguese has continued to influence Tetun Dili not only at the lexical level but also at the morphosyntactic level. For instance, a passive construction, inexistent in Tetun Dili, is currently emerging in the written media (Williams-van Klinken 2010). The other regional languages of East Timor gained the status of national languages in the 2002 Constitution, but little has been done to codify them and to actively promote their use. Consequently, a shift towards Tetun Dili as the dominant language is well under way (Williams-van Klinken/Williams 2015). Thus, the specific social and historical background of East Timor has important linguistic consequences allowing the rare opportunity to observe the development of Portuguese as an L2.

3 Impersonalisation, *se* constructions and innovations in vernacular varieties of Portuguese

Impersonalisation is considered here to be a functional category through which the highest ranked speech-act participant or "the principal semantic participant of the event denoted by the predicate (regardless of the semantic role by which it is identified)" (Kibort 2004, 241) undergoes different levels of demotion. When the participant is demoted, it moves down the hierarchy of syntactic roles to be encoded by a relatively more peripheral syntactic role (including suppression). The demotion of a highly ranked participant is related to its degree of cognitive saliency in the event, which may be real or construed by the speaker (Siewierska 1984; Kemmer 1993).

In Portuguese, impersonalisation is expressed by different constructions (Afonso 2008a), e.g. the passive construction, several types of the *se* constructions, impersonal uses of personal pronouns as well as existential constructions (Afonso 2008b). The present article will mainly focus on the impersonal *se* construction.

Canonical *se* constructions are overtly-coded, highly polysemous constructions which perform a range of functions. These constructions are placed on a transitivity continuum between two-participant and one-participant events, exhibiting detransitivisation or valency-reducing properties (Klaiman 1991). The types of *se* constructions in Portuguese are: reflexive and reciprocal (closer to two-participant events), middle (a vast category including body posture, emotional and cognitive events), anticausative, passive and impersonal (closer to one-participant events). The following examples are canonical impersonal *se* constructions.[6]

(1) Comia-   **se** azeitonas, figos e uma côdea de pão.
    eat.IMPF.3sg   IMP   olives   figs and a crust of bread
    'People ate olives, figs and a crust of bread.'

(2) Vive-   **se** bem aqui.
    live.PRES.3sg IMP   well here
    'One lives well here.'

In (1) and (2), the agent and experiencer are removed from the event, which is then construed as a generic event. As such, the highly ranked participant becomes cognitively less salient and the demotion is overtly marked by the clitic *se*. Impersonal constructions can be defined as transitive (1) or intransitive (2) events. With transitive events, there is no agreement between the verb and the following NP, distinguishing this impersonal construction formally from the passive *se* construction.

Variation in the use of these constructions is attested in non-standard varieties of Portuguese, both in L1 (Brazilian and European Portuguese varieties) and in L2 varieties. In some cases, the variation concerns the elision of the clitic, which is highly frequent in non-standard varieties of Brazilian Portuguese (Soares da Silva et al. 2021) and may suggest a tendency towards simplification of patterns. In the case of L2 varieties of Portuguese in Lusophone Africa, null *se* constructions as well as other innovations are also observed.

The following examples show some innovations in all types of *se* constructions attested in non-standard varieties of Portuguese.

As the examples (3)–(10) in Table 1 show, the innovations are of three kinds: generalisation of *se* to all grammatical persons (see (4), (7) and (9)), null clitic constructions (see (6), (8) and (10)) and double subject constructions in which an indefinite overt subject *a gente* 'we (the people)'[7] occurs in an overtly marked impersonal *se* construction (see (3)).

---

6 Unless stated otherwise, all examples from European Portuguese are taken from the *Museu da Pessoa* corpus (Almeida et al. 2000), a 313,929 word-corpus consisting of 109 transcribed and tagged interviews (personal narratives) conducted by the Portuguese part of the *Museu da Pessoa* project.
7 *Gente* and *a gente* mean 'people' but the latter, *a gente*, grammaticalised as a first person plural pronoun (Lopes 2003).

Table 1: Innovative *se* constructions.

Variety of Portuguese	Example	Type of SE construction
Vernacular European Portuguese	(3) *A gente chama-se rãs a isto.* we call.PRES.3sg.IMP toads to this 'We call these toads.' (Martins 2009)	Impersonal
	(4) *No mar ainda às vezes se orientamos.* At sea still sometimes IMP guide.PRES.1pl *pela vaga.* by.the wave 'At sea we still sometimes are guided by the waves.' (Martins 2009)	Reflexive
	(5) *as coisas desenvolveram Ø e estão* the things develop.PAST.3pl and be.PRES.3pl *juntos actualmente.* together now '[...] things developed and they are together now.' (Soares da Silva et al. 2018)	Anticausative
Vernacular Angolan Portuguese	(6) *começaram a complicar, o programa* begin.PAST.3pl to complicate the programme *alterou Ø.* altered 'they began to complicate, the schedule (was) altered.' (Bacelar do Nascimento et al. 2008)	Passive
	(7) *Nós conseguimos se entender.* We can.PRES.1pl RECIP.3sg understand 'We are able to understand each other.' (Inverno 2009)	Reciprocal
Vernacular Brazilian Portuguese	(8) *Ø Diz que na classificação de* say.PRES.3sg that in.the classification of *madeiras, essa madeira aqui é a segunda* wood, that wood here be.pres.3sg the second *melhor.* best 'They say that, according to categories of wood, this one here is the second best.' (Soares da Silva et al. 2021)	Impersonal
	(9) *Vou-se embora.* go.PRES.1sg REFL.3sg away 'I'm leaving.' (Narro/Sherre 2004)	Reflexive
Vernacular Mozambican Portuguese	(10) *O barco afundou ø.* the boat sink.PAST.3sg 'The boat sank.' (Gonçalves 2004)	Anticausative

In relation to (4), the innovation can be explained by the fact that in some of the European dialects in which (3) is attested, the 1pl *nós* has been replaced by *a gente* whose agreement patterns vary between singular and plural. Hence, Martins (2009) concludes that *se* might have replaced the 1pl clitic *nos* as well. As for the double subject construction in (3), the occurrence of *a gente* functions as a restrictor to the universal indefinite *se* construction.

With regard to the expression of impersonalisation in Brazilian Vernacular Portuguese, several studies (e.g. Duarte 1993; Cyrino/Duarte/Kato 2000; Duarte 2003) have shown that Brazilian Portuguese is at best a partial pro-drop language, with a clear tendency towards overt subjects. This tendency has been observed in syntactic contexts in which, in principle, in pro-drop languages the omission of the subject would be the preferred option because of direct access to the referent (Duarte 2003; Cavalcante/Duarte 2009). One of the consequences of the generalised tendency to include overt subjects is the increased impersonal use of personal pronouns (particularly, *você* 'you (2sg)' and *a gente* (Duarte 2003) and consequently, the decrease of the use of indefinite *se* in finite clauses. Cavalcante and Duarte (2009, 49) have also pointed out that, despite the tendency for overt referential pronouns, a 3sg null subject with arbitrary reference may occur in finite sentences albeit restricted to habitual actions in the present and past, as (8) shows. More recently, Soares da Silva et al. (2021) conducted a corpus-driven study, using multivariate statistical methods, and analysed the conceptual, structural and lectal factors that determine the choice of overt and null *se* constructions. The factor that is statistically correlated with most of the null *se* construction types, including the null impersonal construction, is the lack of focus on the moment of change, i.e. if the moment of change is profiled, the canonical impersonal *se* construction is produced, if the moment of change is not profiled, the null *se* impersonal construction occurs.

While the innovations in some dialects of European Portuguese and in non-standard varieties of Brazilian Portuguese are treated as a consequence of internal changes, in the case of the African varieties of Portuguese, innovations have generally been analysed as a consequence of contact with Bantu languages (Inverno 2009). Indeed, Bantu languages have only one marker to convey reflexivity and reciprocity, which might have influenced the pattern observed in (7). The omission of the clitic in unaccusative events, as in (10), has been attributed to an internal process of homogenisation of the transitive and unaccusative verbs which are treated in a similar way (Gonçalves 2004).

While in the above varieties of Portuguese these patterns seem to be rather stable, in the Portuguese spoken as an L2 in East Timor, divergent patterns emerging in all types of *se* constructions (Afonso/Goglia 2015) display a very high degree of variability.

4 Methodology

The data recorded for this research comprised informal semi-guided conversations between two or three East Timorese speakers. The data were recorded at two different moments. In 2010–2011, 16 informants from different generations were recorded. They were either students or professionals living in Portugal. The data collection with different generations is very relevant in the case of East Timorese, given that, due to the social history of the country (see Section 2), the linguistic repertoire varies according to the generation in question, i.e. the generation educated in Portuguese before 1975, the generation educated in Bahasa Indonesia between 1975 and 2002, and the younger generation educated in Portuguese and Tetun Dili after 2002. The second phase of data collection was in 2015 in Dili, the capital of East Timor where 5 informants were recorded.

The informants' data can be found in Table 2. The total recording time is 8 hours. All necessary ethical steps were taken in order to obtain consent of the participants and to preserve the informants' anonymity.

All overt impersonal *se* constructions as well as null impersonal *se* constructions in which the clitic is absent were extracted from the corpus of recorded interviews. As a way of comparison, other types of impersonal constructions, including the impersonal use of personal pronouns were also extracted.

5 Impersonal *se* constructions in the Portuguese spoken by East Timorese

There is a high level of variability in the Portuguese spoken by the informants. This is due to different factors, such as the duration of residence in Portugal, age, as well the exposure to Portuguese before arriving to Portugal, except for informant F who was born in Portugal and is a native speaker. One of the factors that correlate more strongly with the production of more innovative patterns is age. The Portuguese of the older informants, although L2 speakers of Portuguese, exhibit less innovations and is closer to standard Portuguese. These participants have also been living in Portugal for a longer time. The younger speakers, born in the late 80s and 90s are those who generally produce more innovative patterns, even though they have experienced education in Portuguese after independence. Although Portuguese became an official language and was implemented in education after the independence of East Timor, there were very few teachers who could teach Portuguese and use Portuguese as a vehicle language. Hence, exposure to Portuguese was limited.

Table 2: Information on informants (based on Afonso/Goglia 2015).

Conversation (Conv)	Informants (Inf) and date of birth	Place of residence and date of arrival in Portugal	Date of data collection
1	A: 1963 RA2[8]: 1981	Portugal (2009) Portugal (2003)	
2	B: 1989 C: 1987 RA2	Portugal (2009) Portugal (2009)	
3	D: 1942 E: 1975 F: 2002 RA1: 1970	Portugal (1976) Portugal (1976) Portugal (Born in Portugal) Portugal (1976)	
4	G: 1944 RA1	Portugal (1969)	2010–2011
5	H: 1961 RA2	Portugal (1994)	
6	I: 1985 RA2	Portugal (2007)	
7	J: 1975 RA2	Portugal (2005)	
8	K: 1961 RA2	Portugal (1976)	
9	L: 1981 M: 1983 RA1	Portugal (2010) Portugal (2010)	
10	N: 1980 RA1	Portugal (2000)	
11	O: 1992 P: 1993	Dili, East Timor Dili, East Timor	
12	Q: 1985 R: 1980	Dili, East Timor Dili, East Timor	2015
13	S: 1988 R: 1980	Dili, East Timor Dili, East Timor	
14	O: 1992 S: 1988	Dili, East Timor Dili, East Timor	

---

8 RA1 and RA2 stand for Research Assistant 1 and 2, who collected the data and who were also East Timorese living in Portugal.

The production of the canonical impersonal *se* constructions, in examples (11)–(15), is not very frequent overall. In some cases, they correspond to collocations, such as *como se diz?* (14), *logo se vê* (15). Canonical *se* constructions which are not frequent collocations are produced by speakers who have had some education in Portuguese and have lived in Portugal for a long time (e.g. Inf K, G) (see (11) and (13)). Speaker Q who is based in Dili and was educated in Portuguese after independence, produced a more collocational type of impersonal *se* constructions (see example (14)).

(11) *Como é que se paga   o búfalo   e   quem vai pagar?*
      how   FOC   IMP pay.PRES.3sg the buffalo and who pay.FUT.3sg
      'How will the buffalo be paid and who will pay for it?' (Conv 8, Inf K)

(12) *Então em Dare, no tempo da Indonésia   já   se ensinou*
      So   in Dare in.the time of.the Indonesia already IMP teach.PAST.3sg
      língua   portuguesa no   sexto ano.
      language Portuguese in.the sixth grade
      'So in Dare, during the Indonesian regime, Portuguese was already taught in the sixth grade.' (Conv 2, Inf RA2)

(13) *Geralmente em Timor utiliza-se   mais é ossos.*
      Generally   in Timor use.PRES.3sg IMP more FOC bones
      'Generally, in Timor what one uses more are bones.' (Conv 4, Inf G)

(14) *Imigrante, sempre, ah sempre, como se diz?*
      immigrant always ah always how IMP say.PRES.3sg?
      Sempre tentar para ganhar
      Always try.INF to earn.INF
      'The immigrants, always, always, how do you say? Always trying to earn.' (Conv 12, Inf Q)

(15) *Eu não sei   dizer,   logo se vê.*
      I not know.PRES.1sg say.INF later IMP see.PRES.3sg
      'I cannot say, we'll see what happens.' (Conv 7, Inf J)

Innovations observed in the data are of two kinds: deletion of the clitic, as (16) and (17) show, and the double subject construction (see Section 5.1).

(16) Quando nós falamos português,   ele vem
when we speak.PRES.1pl   Portuguese, he come.PRES.3sg
capturar e então,   por isso, meu pai   diz
arrest.INF and then therefore my father say.PRES.3sg
que não ø pode   falar   português, só falar   tétum.
that not ø can.PRES.3sg speak.INF Portuguese only speak.INF Tetun
'When we spoke Portuguese, he [the Indonesian military] comes to arrest [us] and so, because of that, my father says that we should not speak Portuguese, only Tetun.' (Conv 2, Inf B)

(17) RA2: *Dare?*
     'In Dare?'
  C: *Falamos mambae.*
     speak.PRES.1pl Mambae
     'We speak Mambae'
  RA2: *Mambae, né?   Também só ø   fala   em casa.*
       Mambae right? Also   only   speak.PRES.3sg at home
       'Mambae, right? It is only spoken at home.'
  C: *Também   se fala   em casa como tipo   desluto.*
     Also   IMP speak.PRES.3sg at home for example *desluto*
     'It is also spoken at home for example during the time of *desluto*.'[9]
     Fala   ø com os velhos   É   só
     speak.PRES.3sg ø with the old   be.PRES.3sg all
     'It is spoken with the elderly...That's all.'

Regarding the elision of the clitic seen in (16) and (17), the referent in the impersonal *se* construction is conceptualised as maximally unspecified, even though the referent is accessible through the immediate context - in (16) and (17) *nós* refers to the speaker and his/her family. Locatives can function as restrictors of the maximally unspecified subject, as *em casa* 'at home' in (17) shows, making the presence of the clitic redundant. With respect to non-standard Brazilian Portuguese, Avelar/Cyrino (2008), and Carvalho (2016) consider that prepositional locatives must be in subject position to render the null construction impersonal. Soares da Silva et al. (2021) show, however, that there is no quantitatively significant correlation between locatives and the instantiation of the impersonal null *se* construction. Our corpus, however, does not contain enough examples with locatives to make any generalisation. What can be observed is the alternation of the

---

9 *Desluto* is a ritual to shred the black clothes of mourning.

overt and null *se* construction by informant C. The deletion of the clitic is, to a certain extent, not surprising, considering that Austronesian languages are morphologically poor. In Tetun Dili, the language predominantly used by the informants, subjects may be readily omitted if the referent is accessible (Williams-van Klinken 2010). This pattern in observed in (16) and (17).

5.1 The double subject construction as complexification of the impersonal pattern

If the innovations which imply simplification of patterns may be contact-induced, the other innovation observed, namely the double subject construction shares no similarities with any Austronesian language. Examples (18)–(20) illustrate this phenomenon.

(18) *A minha infância   foi   muito feliz [laughs] e   assim*
     the my childhood   be.PAST.3sg very happy   and   like
     sei
     know.PRES.1sg not
     lá   brincar   com os meus amigos, como é óbvio,
     there   play.INF   with the my friends as be.PRES.3sg obvious
     como idem: a under uma   criança   e   a   estudar.
     as IMP do.PRES.3sg a   child   and   PRT   study.INF
     'My childhood was very happy [laughs] and like, I don't know, playing with my friends, obviously, as a child normally does, and studying.'
     (Conv 2, Inf B)

(19) *Foi com isso que saí err,   como se diz,*
     FOC with that FOC leave.PAST.1sg   what IMP say.PRES.3sg
     a testemunhar,   chamar a atenção internacional
     PRT testify.INF   call.INF the attention international
     e pedir   à comunidade internacional   para que se enviar
     and ask.INF   to.the community international so that IMP send.INF
     os grupos ou os ativistas ou os diplomatas, etc.,   para que
     the groups or the activists or the diplomats etc.   in order
     se possam   fazer alguma investigação em Timor.
     IMP can.IMPF.SUBJ.3pl   do.INF some investigation in Timor

'That was the reason why I testified, to attract international attention and to ask the international community to send groups or activists or diplomats, etc., so that they could investigate the matter in Timor.' (Conv 5, Inf H)

(20) <u>Eles foram</u>   <u>fazer- se</u>   um levantamento
     they go.PAST.3pl make.INF IMP a survey
     'They made a survey.' (Conv 5, Inf H)

The same innovation is produced by speakers with very different backgrounds: informant H has been in Portugal far longer than B; H was educated in Indonesian while B was educated in Portuguese and Tetun in post-independent Timor. Informant H's Portuguese, nonetheless, shows many innovations regarding the production of *se* constructions.

A similar construction occurs in non-standard dialects of European Portuguese. I concur partly with Martins' (2009) analysis according to which the presence of a lexically or strong pronoun-filled subject acts "as a restrictor on the denotative set of impersonal *se* and establish[es] its inclusive or exclusive reading" (Martins 2009, 186). This is what is observed in examples (18) to (20). Given the non-specific properties of the overt subjects – *uma criança* 'a child', *os grupos* 'the groups', *os ativistas* 'the activists', *os diplomatas* 'the diplomats' – the speaker is able to convey in an explicit way that s/he is excluded from the unspecified group of people mentioned. This restriction would not be available in the canonical impersonal *se* construction, although the linguistic context including adverbials, for instance, may impose a similar restriction.

Amongst the constructions performing the impersonalising function, the canonical impersonal *se* construction was posited on the specificity scale on the extreme end of a maximally unspecified actor. The variants of the impersonal *se* constructions (canonical, null, double subject construction) will also be posited on the continuum, with the null construction conceptualising the maximal degree of specificity.

Other impersonal constructions observed in the data are generic/impersonal use of personal pronouns, as well as indefinite pronouns. Lexical strategies are often preferred to express impersonalisation over impersonal *se* constructions, both canonical and innovative as illustrated by (21)–(24).

(21) E como   é   difícil, então, <u>gente</u> do departamento
And because be.PRES.3sg difficult then people from.the department
disse
say.PAST.3sg
'And because it's difficult, therefore people from the department said [...].'
(Conv 14, Inf O)

(22) <u>Alguém</u> em Europa, por <u>Ele</u> pode tentar, tentar, sozinha mesmo e exemplo.
Someone in Europe for He can.PRES.3sg try.INF try.INF alone.fem even instance   and
ele pode acompanhar   notícias em Timor através do serviço média.
he can   accompany.INF news   in Timor through the service media
'Someone in Europe, for instance. He can try by himself even and he can follow the news from Timor through the media.' (Conv 12, Inf Q)

(23) <u>Nós</u> temos que experimentar de tudo,   o mais difícil   e o mais
We have.PRES.1pl to try.INF of everything the most difficult and the most
fácil. Assim   é que se vive   a vida.
easy This.way FOC IMP live.INF the life
'We have to try everything, the most difficult and the easiest things. This is how one lives one's life.' (Conv 1, Inf A)

(24) Aquele que <u>a gente</u> chamamos   pela o segundo massacre.
That   which we   call.pres.1pl by the second massacre
'The one which we call the second massacre.' (Conv 5, Inf H)

Example (21) illustrates the use of a lexical item with generic reference, preferred over the use of the 3pl verb inflection, without the corresponding overt subject. This preference is also attested in the examples (22)–(24) with the choice of different lexical impersonalisation strategies: indefinite pronoun *alguém* co-referred by an overt 3sg *ele* in (22), and an indefinite use of the 1pl *nós* and *a gente* in (23) and (24).

5.2 The contact hypothesis

In theory, the hypothesis of contact between the native languages of our informants and Portuguese to explain the production of impersonal patterns in the Portuguese spoken by East Timorese is plausible, as Portuguese spoken by East Timorese is being produced in a setting where language contact is pervasive and multilingualism is the norm.

All informants are speakers of at least two Austronesian languages, one of them being Tetun Dili. Austronesian languages are morphologically poor languages, without verb inflection, gender or number agreement, and with very little productive affixes.[10] Impersonalising strategies are restricted to the use of personal (1pl pronoun) and indefinite pronouns as well as lexical strategies, e.g. *ema* 'person' in Tetun Dili (Williams-van Klinken et al. 2002, 51–53).

Therefore, it is not surprising that patterns such as clitic deletion and overall preference for personal pronouns as an impersonal strategy are observed in the data. However, the contact-induced hypothesis is not straightforward for two reasons. First, contact patterns cannot explain the emergence of innovative double subject constructions. Second, these constructions are found in other varieties of Portuguese and, therefore, cannot be solely the outcome of contact between East-Timorese languages and Portuguese, as the contexts of the other contact zones are very different (different languages in contact with Portuguese). The next section will discuss the interplay of contact, internal changes and general tendencies of second language acquisition in the impersonal patterns that emerged in the East Timorese data.

6 Internal changes and universal tendencies of second language acquisition in contact-induced changes

Given the sociolinguistic and historical context of East Timor, different stages of acquisition are observed with individual L2 varieties presenting relative degrees of divergence from the target language (TL). As Winford (2003) has pointed out, at the early stages of acquisition, speakers produce a simpler version of the TL, what Klein and Perdue's (1997) called "basic variety", ruled by principles of organisation and structure. These changes, however, decrease as speakers are exposed to more L1 input, and the L2 varieties converge towards the target language.

---

10 Note that Tetun Dili, for example has detransitiviser prefixes *nak-* and *-an*, a reflexive clitic (Williams-van Klinken et al. 2002, 528), a calque of the Portuguese reflexive pronoun *se* as well as the suffix *-dor* to express agentivity. The latter is borrowed from Portuguese (Hajek/Williams-van Klinken 2003).

When considering the emergence of indigenised varieties of a target language, in this case, Portuguese, the developmental stages and the constraints of the emerging variety are very relevant.

The configuration of L2 varieties has been discussed from at least three perspectives, which in some cases, have conflicted with one another. These L2 varieties have been treated as products of contact between languages, as products of internal changes of the interlanguages, and as products of universals of interlanguages (Chambers 2004).[11] These vernacular features are also observed not only in working-class and rural vernaculars, but also in child language, pidgins, and creoles. Therefore, Chambers (2004, 128) concludes that they are connected to the species-specific bio programme underlying the innate language faculty. These so-called vernacular universals are a small set of phonological and grammatical phenomena, e.g. conjugation, regularisation or levelling of irregular verbs, default singulars or subject-verb non-concord, multiple negation or negative concord and copula absence or deletion (Chambers 2004, 129).

Even though approaches to vernacular universals have not considered the role of contact-induced changes (and vice-versa), the field of contact linguistics recognises that the similarities observed in varieties emerging in different contact situations must consider general tendencies of second language acquisition (SLA, henceforth) (Winford 2003; 2009). These are general learning principles, i.e. "expectations about grammatical structure which help impose order in the intake data and which impose constraints on the kinds of creative restructuring in the building of [the interlanguage] grammar" (Winford 2003, 226). Other types of observed similarities have been formulated in terms of typological universals, easier to learn as they are more frequent and unmarked.

Thomason (2009) also argues against the dichotomy between general tendencies of SLA and contact-induced changes. The outcomes of SLA and contact can in fact be the same, as "ease of learning also informs many or most types of contact-induced change" (Thomason 2009, 249).

When considering the case of the individual L2 varieties of Portuguese spoken by East Timorese and the specific case of the impersonal constructions, the question as to how patterns observed in the data emerge immediately leads us to consider both approaches. On the one hand, considering the socio-history of East Timor and the intense contact between Timorese languages, also with Portuguese, the patterns observed in the data may well be contact-induced, as

---

11 Chambers' (2004,128) theory on vernacular universals was formulated for varieties of English, but he states that the features of vernaculars might as well be the same for varieties of other languages.

Timorese languages, especially Tetun Dili, continue to be influenced by Portuguese ever since it became an official language e.g. the emergence of a new passive construction in written registers. (Williams-van Klinken 2010). Likewise, some features of Timorese languages have also been transferred to Portuguese L2, e.g. the use of aspectual markers *ainda* 'still/yet' and *já* 'already' (Batoréo 2010; Albuquerque 2014).

In the case of the impersonal constructions, clitic deletion and the use of personal pronouns as a preferred strategy for impersonalisation are influenced by the morphological configuration of Timorese languages. However, the fact that many of the patterns are also observed in other vernacular varieties of Portuguese, which either emerged in rather different contact zones or in a context without any contact at all (e.g. double subject construction found in dialectal European Portuguese), may be a good indication that these patterns are examples of general tendencies of language acquisition. According to Winford (2009, 209), the likelihood of similar innovations being observed in contact languages would be higher if there were differences in just one or two of the variables involved. This might be the case of the similarities observed between Brazilian Vernacular Portuguese and some African varieties of Portuguese (most notably Angolan Portuguese), which, to a large extent, share the substrate languages as well as a continuing influx of Portuguese native speakers throughout history. Still, if similar innovations are found in quite different contact situations, "such innovations would be prime candidates for explanation in terms of universal principles" (Winford 2009, 209). In relation to the similarities observed in the L2 varieties of Portuguese spoken by East Timorese, Brazilian Vernacular Portuguese and in African varieties of Portuguese, the contact situation in East Timor is possibly the one exhibiting more different contact variables: a limited number of Portuguese native speakers over time, no or very limited influence of African languages, Indonesian as the superstrate language during the Indonesian regime which imposed a ban on Portuguese for 25 years.

The approach taken here will follow Winford (2009) and Thomason (2009) who consider general tendencies of SLA as those informing processes of contact-induced changes.

6.1 Influence of L1 in L2 varieties and the null impersonal construction

Determining the influence of Timorese languages (L1) on the acquisition of Portuguese (L2) is not an easy task since the vast majority of the population speak at least two languages: one or more regional language(s) and Tetun Dili, and possibly Indonesian and Portuguese. With the exception of Tetun Dili, the language for wider communication, many of the other Timorese regional languages are yet to be described. In the present chapter, Tetun Dili will be the only East-Timorese language used to discuss its influence on L2 varieties of Portuguese for the following reasons: (1) it is reported to be the language mostly used by all the informants in Dili (Timor) and in Portugal (Goglia/Afonso 2013); (2) the regional languages are used in quite specific contexts and are losing importance as compared to Tetun at a very fast pace; (3) most informants report Tetun Dili to be one of their native languages. As reported by Hajek (2006, 166), 65–80% of East Timorese speak Tetun Dili and "[a]lthough there is no doubt that for most East Timorese [Tetun Dili] is the preferred means of interethnic communication, there is some local bilingualism, especially at the boundaries of ethnic groups and in some mixed areas outside of Dili".

The clitic *se* is functionally non-transparent and not easily identified given the polysemic nature of the constructions in which the clitic occurs. The reanalysis of a superstrate morpheme according to the rule of the substrate has been shown to be a constraint, namely the "availability constraint" (Andersen 1983), to the acquisition of morphology by creoles. Given this constraint, simplification such as the reduction of morphology and the replacement with periphrastic constructions which are functionally similar to the morphemes in target language are observed. As we have seen, the reduction of morphology including the deletion of *se* as well as the use of personal pronouns, indefinite pronouns and lexical subjects with indefinite reference are the preferred strategies to convey impersonalisation. These are not only more transparent than the clitic *se*, but they also illustrate the accessibility constraint, as impersonalisation is primarily expressed in Tetun Dili by the use of personal pronouns, like *ema* ('person', 'people', 'someone') and *ita*, the indefinite use of the 1pl pronoun. This is an example of Thomason/Kaufman's (1988, 56) hypothesis that morphological means of expression are more likely to be replaced by syntactic ones, particularly if the two languages in contact are typologically distant: "If the source language expresses a given category syntactically and the recipient language expresses it morphologically, the recipient language is quite likely to adopt the syntactic means of expression".

In addition, these strategies also interact with the different stages of the formation of the individual L2 varieties of Portuguese. Structures produced by Different speakers, even from the same generation, and even by the same speaker, exhibit a lot of variability with canonical impersonal *se* constructions co-occurring with innovative constructions.

The same principles also apply to other contexts in which Portuguese is in contact with very different substrate languages. In Lusophone Africa, Portuguese is in contact with the Bantu substrate. In Brazil, Portuguese was in contact with Amerindian, Bantu and other African languages substrates (e.g. Yoruba), as well as Portuguese-based creoles. Vernacular Brazilian Portuguese and African varieties of Portuguese (mostly L2) exhibit similar processes of simplification of the morphological patterns, eliminating the clitic, or using indefinite personal pronouns and lexical items. These strategies are more transparent with regard to the form-function mapping, and easier to learn.

6.2 Internal changes to the L2 varieties system

Internal changes to the language systems are another general tendency in SLA which may play a role in contact-induced patterns. According to Winford (2003, 218), internal processes may be related to learners' need to systematise the L2 grammar guided by the need for more transparency in the developing grammar. This is what Meisel (1977) referred to as 'elaborative simplification'. This analysis was proposed for Brazilian Portuguese whose tendency for lexically-filled subjects is responsible for the reduction of the use of the clitic *se*.

Based on Duarte (2003), syntactic contexts were also investigated in order to determine to what extent internal changes might be in line with the preference for lexically-filled subjects with indefinite reference. According to Duarte (2003), the referent might be more difficult to be accessed syntactically if elements to the left of the subject (after relative and interrogative pronouns, subordinate conjunctions, adverbial adjuncts) are present, favouring, therefore, the occurrence of overt subjects. However, in the Brazilian data, there is a tendency, albeit not a very pronounced one, for overt subjects to occur in contexts in which the referent was syntactically accessible.

In the East Timorese data, the more divergent the idiolects are from the standard, the more frequent lexically-filled subjects are, not only in contexts where there are elements to the left of the subject but also in contexts in which the referent is syntactically accessible, as (25) and (26) show.

(25) <u>Neste momento</u>, <u>eu</u> *estudo*   *área de comunicação social*,
at.the moment   I study.PRES.1sg   area of communication
Faculdade de Ciências Sociais, Universidade
Faculty of   Social Sciences University
Nacional de Timor Lorosae e   <u>eu terminei</u>
National of Timor Lorosae and   I finish.PAST.1sg
o meu estudo de ensino secundário in Suai,
the my study of teaching secondary in Suai

'At the moment, I study in the area of social communication, at the Faculty of Social Sciences, National University of Timor Lorosae, and I concluded secondary school in Suai (Conv 11, Inf P)

(26) *Eu? Não, eu   moro   em Becoro eu perto de Carlos é*
     Me? No   I   live.PRES.1sg in Becoro I near of Carlos be.PRES.3sg
     meu vizinho.   Carlos é   aqui lado e eu ao lado.
     my neighbour.   Carlos be.PRES.3sg   here side and I to.the side
     Somos também Viqueque e   ele também Viqueque   mas ele viver
     be.PRES.1pl also Viqueque and he also Viqueque   but he live.INF
     aqui em Dili. Ele é   bom
     here in Dili.   He be.PRES.3sg   good.masc
     pessoa
     person.fem
     Ele fala   bem, fala francês,   fala   português,
     He speak.PRES.3sg   well speak.PRES.3sg French speak.PRES.3sg   Portuguese
     fala   inglês   e fala   também tétum terik.
     speak.PRES.3sg   English   and speak.PRES.3sg also   Tetun Terik.
     'Me? No, I live in Becoro, I live near Carlos, who is my neighbour. Carlos lives here and I live next door. We are also from Viqueque and he is also from Viqueque, but he lives here in Dili. He is a good person. He speaks languages well, he speaks French, he speaks Portuguese, he speaks English and he also speaks Tetun Terik.' (Conv 13, Inf R)

After an adverbial in (25) (*neste momento* 'at the moment' and *depois [d]isso* 'after that'), and in coordinated clauses where the referent is accessible (e.g. *eu* 'I'), the subject is lexically filled. In (26), all occurrences of lexically-filled pronoun subjects are functionally motivated by the presence of two human referents (*Carlos* and the speaker), except the last two (*Ele* 'he') as the referent is syntactically accessible. The pattern observed in (25) and (26) seems to emphasise the role of internal changes in the interlanguages to simplify and regularise the system rather than it provides a clear case for a contact-induced pattern.

In the cases in which the individual L2 varieties are closer to the target language, a more regular pattern of lexically-filled vs null-subjects is observed, according to the syntactic contexts (27).

(27) RA2: *Então quer   dizer   que quando tu*
         So   want.PRES.3sg say.INF that when   you
         estavas   em Timor tu não aprendeste
         be.IMPF.2sg in Timor you not learn.PAST.2sg
         a língua portuguesa?
         the language Portuguese
    J: *Não. Lá em Timor não. Foi   cá   que eu aprendi.*
       No. There in Timor no. Be.PAST.3sg here FOC I learn.PAST.1sg
       li   muitos jornais,   muitos livros e   vi
       read.PAST.1sg many newspapers, many books and watch.PAST.1sg
       televisão também para conseguir   apanhar
       television also   to try.INF   get.INF
       'RA2: So this means that when you were in Timor, you didn't learn Portuguese?
       J: No, not in Timor. It was here where I learnt it. I read many newspapers, books and also watched TV in order to try to be able to understand it.'
       (Conv 7)

The first lexically-filled subject produced by speaker J (*eu* 'I') is syntactically motivated as there are elements fronted to its left. In the remainder of the turn, there is only the presence of null subjects in syntactic contexts in which the referent is accessible. There seems to be a correlation between the use of lexically-filled subjects and the production of impersonal *se* constructions. At the early stages of the interlanguage, when there is a preference for lexically-filled subjects in syntactic contexts triggering the null-subject strategies other than the impersonal *se* constructions (with the indefinite use of personal pronouns) are produced, and vice-versa.

7 Conclusion

The study of vernaculars provides us with a wealth of knowledge about how particular structures emerge. For a language with such a global spread such as Portuguese, comparative studies between varieties at different stages of development can shed light on the dynamics behind the emergence of particular L2 varieties. In particular, they can help determine what role is played by contact or by general tendencies of second language acquisition and the interplay between the two.

This chapter has emphasised the importance of contact in the formation of varieties of Portuguese world wide, but has also presented evidence that general processes of SLA must necessarily be taken into account, given the similarities between different varieties of Portuguese emerging in different contact settings. Following Winford (2009) and Thomason (2009), this chapter took the position that different approaches to the same phenomenon should be explored and should complement each other.

The case study – a preliminary and qualitative study of impersonal *se* constructions in Portuguese spoken by East Timorese – was chosen because of its morphosyntactic and functional complexity in the developing vernacular Portuguese in East Timor. It is uncontroversial that, in contact scenarios in which L1 (s) are morphologically poor languages, some level of simplification would be expected. However, the results from the data analysis showed a more complex situation: (1) structures vary in their degree of innovation, diverging from the standard in different degrees; (2) the deletion of the clitic *se* is shared by other, more stable, varieties of Portuguese L2 or varieties which started as L2 (Brazilian Portuguese) with a very different history from the East Timorese one; and (3) the subject doubling construction shares a remarkable similarity with the subject doubling construction in some L1 dialects of European Portuguese, what puts the contact hypothesis into question.

Both contact and general tendencies of second language acquisition, such as simplification, as well as internal changes of the L2 varieties, play a role in the emergence of innovative constructions. While the phenomenon of clitic deletion corresponds to a formal simplification of the impersonal *se* construction, the subject doubling construction, used by speakers of different generations with different degrees of proficiency in Portuguese, on the contrary, shows a complexification of the pattern. This innovative impersonal *se* construction, which functionally corresponds to a restriction of the maximally unspecified actor, imposes a scalar property to the impersonal *se* construction.

8 References

Afonso, Susana, *The family of impersonal constructions in European Portuguese. An onomasiological constructional approach*, unpublished PhD dissertation, University of Manchester, 2008 (= 2008a).

Afonso, Susana, *Existential constructions as impersonalising devices. The case of European Portuguese*, Transactions of the Philological Society 106:2 (2008), 180–215 (= 2008b).

Afonso, Susana/Goglia, Francesco, *Linguistic innovations in the immigration context as initial stages of a partially restructured variety. Evidence from "se" constructions in the Portuguese of the East-Timorese diaspora in Portugal*, Studies in Hispanic and Lusophone Linguistics 8:1 (2015), 1–33.

Albuquerque, Davi, *Influência das L1 nativas no português de Timor-Leste. Um estudo de marcadores verbais*, Signótica 26 (2014), 111–121.

Almeida, João/Rocha, Jorge/Rangel Henriques, Pedro/Moreira, Sónia/Simões, Alberto, *Museu da Pessoa – arquitectura*, paper presented at the Encontro da associação portuguesa de bibliotecários e arquivistas (2000), http://alfarrabio.di.uminho.pt/~albie/publications/mpessoa.pdf [last access: 01.08.2020].

Andersen, Roger, *Transfer to somewhere*, in: Gass, Susan/Selinker, Larry (edd.), *Language transfer in language learning*, Rowley, Newbury House, 1983, 177–201.

Avelar, Juanito/Cyrino, Sonia, *Locativos preposicionados em posição de sujeito. Uma possível contribuição das línguas Bantu à sintaxe do português brasileiro*, Linguística : Revista de Estudos Linguísticos da Universidade do Porto 3 (2008), 55–75.

Batoréo, Hanna, *Funções do marcador polissémico "já" no Português de Timor-Leste. Importância do conhecimento da(s) línguas(s) materna(s) dos aprendentes do Português L2 no processo da aquisição/aprendizagem da língua não-materna*, in: *Textos seleccionados do 25th Encontro Nacional da APL*, Lisboa, Associação Portuguesa de Linguística, 2010, 211–224.

Boxer, Charles, *The Topasses of Timor*, Amsterdam, Indisch Instituut, 1947.

Cavalcante, Silvia/Duarte, Maria Eugénia, *Arbitrary subjects of infinitival clauses in European and Brazilian Portuguese*, in: Tsiplakou, Stavroula/Karyolemou, Marilena/Pavlou, Pavlos (edd.), *Language Variation. European Perspectives II. Selected papers from the 4th International Conference on Language Variation in Europe (ICLaVE 4)*, Amsterdam, John Benjamins, 2009, 47–58.

Chambers, Jack, *Dynamic typology and vernacular universals*, in: Kortmann, Bernd (ed.), *Dialectology meets typology*, Berlin/New York, Mouton de Gruyter, 2004, 127–145.

Cyrino, Sonia/Duarte, Maria Eugénia/Kato, Mary, *Visible subjects and invisible clitics in Brazilian Portuguese*, in: Kato, Mary/Negrão, Esmeralda (edd.), *Brazilian Portuguese and the null subject parameter*, Frankfurt/Madrid, Vervuert/Iberoamericana, 2000, 55–104.

De Matos, Paulo, *Counting Portuguese colonial populations, 1776–1875. A research note*, The History of the Family 21:2 (2016), 267–280.

Duarte, Maria Eugênia, *A evolução na representação do sujeito pronominal em dois tempos*, in: Paiva, Maria da Conceição/Duarte, Maria Eugênia (edd.), *Mudança lingüística em tempo real*, Rio de Janeiro, Contra Capa, 2003, 115–128.

Duarte, Maria Eugênia, *Do pronome nulo ao pronome pleno. A trajetória do sujeito no português do Brasil*, in: Roberts, Ian/Kato, Mary (edd.), *Português brasileiro. Uma viagem diacrônica*, Campinas, Edições da UNICAMP, 1993, 107–128.

Gonçalves, Perpétua. *Towards a unified vision of classes of language acquisition and change. Arguments from the genesis of Mozambican African Portuguese*, Journal of Pidgin and Creole Languages 19:2 (2004), 225–259.

Hagemeijer, Tjerk, *From creoles to Portuguese. Language shift in São Tomé and Príncipe*, in: Álvarez López, Laura/Gonçalves, Perpétua/Ornelas de Avelar, Juanito (edd.), *The Portuguese language continuum in Africa and Brazil*, Amsterdam, John Benjamins, 2018, 169–184.

Hajek, John, *Language maintenance and survival in East Timor. All change now? Winners and losers*, in: Bradley, David/Bradley, Maya (edd.), *Language endangerment and language maintenance*, London, Routledge, 2002, 182–202.

Hajek, John, *Language contact and convergence in East Timor. The case of Tetun Dili*, in: Aikhenvald, Alecandra/Dixon, Robert (edd.), *Grammars in contact. A Cross-linguistic typology*, Amsterdam, John Benjamins, 2006, 163–178.

Hajek, John/Williams-van Klinken, Catharina, *Um sufixo românico numa língua austronésia. "-dor" em Tétum*, Revue de Linguistique Romane 67 (2003), 55–65.

Harris, John, *Syntactic variation and dialect divergence*, Journal of Linguistics 20 (1984), 303–327.

Holm, John, *Languages in contact. The partial restructuring of vernaculars*, Cambridge, Cambridge University Press, 2003.

Inverno, Liliana, *A transição de Angola para o português vernáculo. Estudo morfossintático do sintagma verbal*, in: Carvalho, Ana Maria (ed.), *Português em contacto*, Madrid/Frankfurt, Iberoamericana/Vervuert, 2009, 87–106.

Kemmer, Suzanne, *The middle voice*, Amsterdam, John Benjamins, 1993.

Kerswill, Paul, *Contact and new varieties*, in: Hickey, Raymond (ed.), *The handbook of language contact*, Oxford, Wiley-Blackwell, 2010, 230–251.

Kibort, Anna, *Passive and passive-like constructions in English and Polish*, PhD dissertation, University of Cambridge, 2004.

Klein, Wolfgang/Perdue, Clive, *The basic variety (or: couldn't natural languages be much simpler?)*, Second Language Research 13 (1997), 301–347.

Lewis, M. (ed.), *Ethnologue. Languages of the world*, Dallas, SIL, [26]2004, http://www.ethno logue.com [consulted: 12.2019].

Lopes, Célia, *A inserção de "a gente" no quadro pronominal do Português*, Madrid/Frankfurt, Iberoamericana/Vervuert, 1988.

Malchukov, Andrej/Siewierska, Anna (edd.), *Impersonal constructions. A cross-linguistic perspective*, Amsterdam, John Benjamins, 2011.

Martins, Ana Maria, *Subject doubling in European Portuguese dialects. The role of impersonal "se"*, in: Aboh, Enoch/van der Linden, Elisabeth/Quer, Josep/Sleeman, Petra (edd.), *Romance languages and linguistic theory*, Amsterdam, John Benjamins, 2009, 179–200.

Mello, Heliana, *African descendants' rural vernacular Portuguese and its contribution to understanding the development of Brazilian Portuguese*, in: Mufwene, Saliloko (ed.), *Iberian imperialism and language evolution in Latin America*, Chicago, University of Chicago Press, 2014, 168–185.

Nascimento, Maria Fernanda/Pereira, Luísa/Estrela, Antónia/Gonçalves, José, *Aspectos de unidade e diversidade do português. As variedades africanas face à variedade europeia*, Veredas. Revista da Associação Internacional de Lusitanistas 9 (2008), 35–59.

Siewierska, Anna, *The passive. A comparative linguistic analysis*, London, Croom Helm, 1984.

Soares da Silva, Augusto/Afonso, Susana/Palù, Dafne, *Null "se" constructions in Brazilian and European Portuguese. Morphosyntactic deletion or emergence of new constructions?*, paper presented at the SLE (Societas Linguistica Europea) 51, 2018.

Soares da Silva, Augusto/Afonso, Susana/Palù, Dafne/Franco, Karlien, *Null "se" constructions in Brazilian Portuguese. Morphosyntactic deletion or emergence of new constructions?*, Cognitive Linguistics 32:1 (2021), 159–193.

Taylor-Leech, Kerry, *The language situation in Timor-Leste*, Language Issues in Language Planning 10:1 (2009), 1–68.

Thomason, Sarah, *Why universals VERSUS contact-induced change?*, in: Filppula, Markku/Klemola, Juhani/Paulasto, Heli (edd.), *Vernacular universals and language contacts. Evidence from varieties of English and beyond*, Oxford, Routledge, 2009, 349–364.

Thomason, Sarah/Kaufman, Terrence, *Language contact, creolization, and genetic linguistics*, Berkeley, University of California Press, 1988.

Williams-van Klinken, Catharina/Williams, Robert, *Language shift or language landslide? Changes in the home language in Timor Leste from 2004 to 2010*, paper presented at the Second Workshop of the *Shifting Sociolinguistic Realities in the Nation of East Timor and its Diasporas* international network, 2015.

Williams-van Klinken, Catharina, *Voice and valency in Tetun Dili*, in: Ewing, Michael/Klamer, Marian (edd.), *East Nusantara. Typological and areal analyses*, Canberra, Pacific Linguistics, 2010, 167–184.

Williams-van Klinken, Catharina/Hajek, John, Nordlinger, Rachel, *Tetun Dili. A grammar of an East Timorese language*, Canberra, Pacific Linguistics, 2002.

Winford, Donald, *Introduction to contact linguistics*, London, Wiley, 2003.

Winford, Donald, *The interplay of "universals" and contact-induced change in the emergence of new Englishes*, in: Filppula, Markku/Klemola, Juhani/Paulasto, Heli (edd.), *Vernacular universals and language contacts. Evidence from varieties of English and beyond*, Oxford, Routledge, 2009, 207–230.

Index

accentuation 132, 140
actor 18, 120, 123, 129–130, 281–282, 293, 302
address (forms of) 7, 74–75, 269
adstrate 3, 8, 91–92
agent 50, 285, 295
agreement 5–10, 31–35, 41–42, 75, 82, 101–102, 118–119, 285, 287, 295
– gender agreement 8, 31, 75, 102, 295
– number agreement. 8, 102, 295
Aktionsart 226, 241
allomorphy 9, 103–104, 109
Amerindian languages 28, 44, 48–51, 66, 299
animacy 63–64, 67
– Animacy Hierarchy 6, 34, 65, 70
– animate 4, 6, 31, 33, 34 39, 44, 51, 63, 65–66, 68, 70–72, 82
– human (parameter) 29, 33, 35, 40
– inanimate 4, 6, 31, 34, 39, 45, 47, 51, 63, 65–68, 70–72
anticausative 284, 286
Arabic 96, 98, 116, 139
Aragonese 90–91, 103
Argentina 16, 45–46, 49, 222, 245, 248, 272
Atlas Linguarum Europae (ALE) 150
Atlas Lingüístico y Etnográfico de Aragón, Navarra y La Rioja (ALEANR) 27, 37
attitude 3, 6, 8, 11, 59, 91, 118, 166, 202
Austronesian language 18, 283, 292, 295

Bantu (languages) 287, 299
Basque
– Basque Country 4–5, 25–52, 55–82
– Basque (language) 3–7, 25–52, 55–82, 106
– Basque Spanish 4, 7–8, 25–52, 55–82
bilingual (bilingualism) 4–7, 14, 27–28, 36–39, 43–52, 55–61, 66–82, 87–91, 93, 96, 102–104, 108, 116, 121, 127, 130–134, 137–140, 143, 179, 181–185, 187, 190–196, 200–204, 298
Bolivia 5, 44, 46
border (borderland) 5, 9–11, 46, 115, 117–120, 124–125, 127, 130–132, 134, 136–137, 139–140, 142–145, 148–150, 156, 192, 201
borrowing 89, 95–99, 106, 108–109, 115, 180, 190–191, 195
boundedness 15, 214, 222, 231, 240

calque 99, 101, 108, 180, 295
cartography (cartographic approach) 251
case 5–6, 25–26, 28–35, 40–41, 49–51, 57, 59, 64, 71, 75–76, 106
– accusative 3, 5–7, 25–26, 29–36, 38, 40–47, 49–51, 63, 65, 66, 70–73, 75, 81–82, 105–106
– dative 3, 5–6, 25–26, 28–34, 38, 40, 44, 46, 48–52, 55, 60, 63, 66–70, 72–73, 75, 82, 105–106
– ergative 57, 70–71, 82
– absolutive 70–71, 82
Cantabria (Cantabrian) 30–33
Castellón 89, 107, 109
Castilianism 12, 95, 161, 164, 167
Catalan 87–110, 123
– Eastern Catalan 88, 94
– Western Catalan 88
– Majorcan Catalan 8
– Medieval Valencian 104
– Standard Catalan 96–98, 103–106, 109
– Valencian Catalan 8–9, 87–110, 161
(language / linguistic) change 2, 4, 59, 88 148, 184, 186
Chaves 9–11, 115, 124–125, 130–131, 135–137, 142–144
clitic 3–8, 18–19, 25–27, 29–30, 33–36, 38, 40–52, 56, 62–73, 75, 82, 87, 103–104, 107, 281, 282, 285, 287, 288, 290–292, 295–302
– accusative (direct object) clitic 3, 5–6, 25–52, 65–76
– adverbial clitic (pronoun) 8, 107
– clitic doubling 4, 34, 41, 52, 70
– clitic placement (position) 8, 103
– dative clitic (pronoun) 3, 5–6, 25–26, 29, 33, 44, 46, 49–51, 63, 66–70, 72–73, 75, 82

- enclitic 8, 103–104
- proclitic 8, 103–104
- (clitic) *se* 18–19, 30, 281–282, 284–293, 298–299, 301–302
code-switching 14, 61, 87, 92, 179, 195, 196, 204, 180–183, 186–198, 200–204
coercion 15, 215, 216, 227
colonisation 152, 154, 192, 281–283
colloquial 87, 89, 92–93, 95–102, 104–107, 128, 161, 254
communication 6, 59, 62, 72, 77, 92, 100, 132, 153, 156, 170, 181–182, 186–187, 201, 298, 300
compositional (meaning) 216, 229, 231
conjunction (conjunctive) 17, 123, 141, 251–253, 257, 274–276, 299
consonant 132, 162, 165–166
- apical 162
- apico-alveolar 150, 162, 165
- fricative 61, 98, 101, 141, 150, 155, 165–166
- nasal 165–167
- postalveolar 150, 162, 165–166
- sibilant 150, 162, 165
- velar 165–167
convergence 1–10, 13, 16–17, 25–26, 35, 41, 48–49, 51–52, 55, 58–60, 71, 76, 81, 87–89, 95, 99, 101–103, 106–108, 110, 115–116, 143, 147, 152, 154, 161, 169, 179, 180, 183, 184, 188, 190, 236
- non-convergence 2, 9–10, 13, 115, 143
- structural convergence 8, 88–89, 101, 107, 183
contact 5, 91, 94–96, 117, 149, 151–152, 167, 170, 179, 189, 195, 281–283, 287, 296–302
- contact hypothesis 19, 294–295, 302
- contact-induced changes 6–8, 25–26, 57–60, 75, 81, 89, 102, 109, 183, 281–282, 292, 296–297, 299
- intense contact 4, 9, 11, 37, 41, 70, 117, 296
- language contact 1–3, 6, 9, 11, 13, 18, 26–28, 40, 46, 51, 56, 59, 66, 70, 72, 77, 87–89, 99, 108–109, 115, 143, 147, 148, 158, 161, 297
Corpus Oral del Lenguaje Adolescente (COLA) 246, 254, 256, 259, 263

Corpus Oral y Sonoro del Español Rural (COSER) 3, 27, 37–39, 43
(un)countable (noun) 30–33

Definiteness Hierarchy 65, 70
diachronic (diachrony) 2, 35, 123, 247, 276
dialect 1, 11, 16, 19, 32, 43, 51, 62, 88, 91, 94, 148, 151, 162, 183, 245, 247, 276, 287, 293, 302
dialectology (dialectological) 245
diastratic 4, 43, 88
diatopic (diatopy) 4–5, 102
Differential Object Marking (DOM) 41, 107
diglossia (diglossic) 7, 57, 87, 91, 93, 108, 184
discourse 12, 14, 16–17, 41, 63, 80, 108, 118, 154, 156–157, 163, 168, 170–171, 179, 187, 189–192, 195, 198, 200–201, 203, 245, 247–248, 250, 256, 257, 259, 262–263, 269–270, 272, 274–276, 282
- discourse link 7, 78–80
- discourse marker 100, 191, 199, 201, 246, 249, 256, 257, 262, 263, 265, 287
- discourse prominence 78
- discourse-structuring element 101
- parliamentary discourse 147, 167
- political discourse 147, 167
- public discourse 11, 147, 149, 164
divergence 1–3, 8–9, 11, 13–14, 16–18, 103, 107, 116, 147, 149, 179, 180, 184–185, 194, 201, 203, 211, 213, 227, 233, 246, 274, 295
double subject construction 281, 285, 287, 290, 292, 293, 295, 297
dynamicity 214, 224, 227, 231, 240

Ecuador 44, 46
ellipsis 249, 254
episteme 179, 189
event (eventive / eventivity) 18, 66, 72, 102, 103, 120, 213, 216, 223, 224, 225, 230, 231, 234, 236, 240, 241
Eurocity 9–10, 125, 135–136, 138, 142–143
exclamation (exclamative) 17, 247–253, 266–269, 273–276
experiencer 226, 285

Feces de Abaixo 9, 11, 124–125, 134–138, 144
focalisation 7, 76, 78
formulaic language 196
Fuentes de Oñoro 9, 11, 115, 124–125, 134–140, 144

Galician 8, 11–13, 99, 102, 124, 138, 142–143, 147–171
Galicianist movement 153, 156, 168
gender 5–7, 25, 29–30, 32–33, 41–42, 47, 49, 52, 63–64, 68, 71, 73, 76, 82
– gender agreement 8, 31, 33, 75, 102, 295
– gender loss (elimination) 5–6, 25–26, 33, 35, 40–41, 43–46, 49–52
– gender marking (marker) 4–5, 7, 25, 42, 46, 50–52, 72, 75–76
Generalitat Valenciana 94
Guaraní 5, 28, 41, 44, 46, 50
Guatemala 47, 49
grammar 4–5, 12, 16, 34, 42, 51–52, 59–60, 81–82, 147, 148, 155, 194, 209, 215, 296, 299
grammaticalisation (grammaticalised) 62, 74, 101, 103, 285

heritage
– culture 180, 185, 189, 194, 203
– language 179–181, 183–187, 200
Hispanic 3, 14, 179–190, 192, 194, 201–204, 253
Historical Corpus of the Basque Country (HiCoBasCo) 27

Iberian Peninsula 1, 3, 13, 62, 96
identity (construction) 2, 9, 11, 13–15, 66, 108, 115, 117, 148, 152, 158, 159, 169, 170, 179–204
ideology 11–13, 147, 159, 167–168, 170
idioms 120, 191, 196, 200, 201, 271, 276
impersonal *se* construction 18–19, 281–285, 288–290, 293, 301–302
information structure (information structural) 77
– new information 78
incremental (incrementality) 222, 224–226, 236–240, 257–261

Indexicality 11–12, 147, 149, 159, 167, 170, 251
indexing features 13, 147
indicative 17, 20, 61, 245, 247, 249, 250, 253–254, 269, 272, 276
idiolect 97, 299
idiom (idiomatic) 120, 127, 134, 191, 196, 200–201, 271, 276
inflected infinitive 12–13, 160, 163, 167
Instituto da Lingua Galega (ILG) 152, 153
Interactional 16
– linguistics 245, 248, 251, 253–256, 259–270, 275, 276
– sociolinguistics 13, 170
interference 35, 93, 115–116, 118, 123, 132–133, 139–140, 140–142

laísmo 32
left–dislocation (left-dislocated) 4, 40, 62, 64, 66–70
leísmo 3–8, 2, 5, 25–40, 46–47, 50–51, 62–63, 71–72, 74–75, 81, 106
– feminine (female) *leísmo* 7, 25–26, 35, 37–38, 41–44, 51, 52, 55
– politeness *leísmo* (*leísmo de cortesía*) 7, 30, 74
– *leísmo aparente* 29
letter 6–7, 27, 36, 55, 57, 60–62, 72–73, 79–81, 132
lexicalisation 227, 249
lexicon 12, 95–96, 154–155, 159, 170, 200, 246
lingua franca 116, 283
linguistic
– Linguistic Atlas of the Iberian Peninsula (ALPI) 150–151
– linguistic continuum 88
– linguistic landscape 10–12, 115–121, 123–124, 127, 130, 134–135, 139–140, 143–144
– linguistic errors 122, 132, 139–140
– linguistic routine 13–14, 179, 196–200
– linguistic (in)stability 1–2, 9, 50, 60, 66
literacy 55, 58, 60
loans (loanwords) 87, 89, 96, 98–101, 108, 148, 158, 164, 167
loísmo 5, 32, 45, 49

language
- H–language (prestige language) 8–9, 91–95, 109–110
- language acquisition 2, 18, 49, 182–187, 190
- language loss 4–5, 8, 25, 40, 43–46, 50–52, 71, 81, 96, 102, 151, 180–181, 196
- language maintenance 33, 109, 180, 184
- language policy 115, 123, 283
- prestige language 91–94
- (non-)official language 10, 56, 92, 94, 119, 121, 126, 150, 154, 282–283, 288, 297
Lusism 12–13, 155, 160, 164, 167

Mayan languages 5, 28, 44, 47
Mexico 48–49, 194, 222
minority (minorities) 56, 60, 100, 147, 148, 155, 170, 180, 189, 195
migration (immigrant, immigration) 181, 185, 192
monolingual 4, 6–7, 28, 38–39, 43, 52, 55, 58, 60, 62, 66–68, 71–3, 77–81, 91, 93, 126–129, 134–135, 137–138, 180, 191, 196, 199
morphology (morphological) 6, 19, 28, 33, 40–42, 49–50, 72, 76, 98, 153–155, 159, 161, 163, 170, 183, 190, 245, 246, 281, 297–299
multilingualism (multilingual) 2, 10, 59, 116, 119–120, 122, 126, 131, 134, 138, 180, 187, 283, 285

nationalism (nationalist) 11, 13, 155, 157, 160, 168, 169, 170
Navarre 4, 26, 28, 30, 37, 43, 56, 71, 102, 129
(linguistic) norm (normalisation) 96, 99–101, 150–155, 159, 160, 168, 181, 295
null argument
- null object 7, 34, 70–71, 82
- null subject 287, 293, 300–301
number 5, 8, 29–30, 32, 36, 41–43, 46, 49–50, 63–64, 67–68, 71, 76, 102, 106, 109, 295

object
- direct object 3, 5–8, 26–30, 33–35, 38–42, 45, 50–52, 55, 58, 60, 62–67, 69–73, 75, 77, 79, 81–82, 102, 105–108
- indirect object 27, 29, 72, 105–108
- preverbal object 7, 77–82
- postverbal object 78
orthography 36, 61, 141, 153, 156, 162, 169 (also orthography)

Paraguay 46–47, 50
parenthetical 196
passive construction 284, 286, 297
Peru 44–46, 49
phraseology (phraseological) 89, 95–96, 99
polyfunctional(ity) 17, 246, 247
pragmatic(s) 3, 7, 14, 16–17, 59, 72, 77–78, 87, 89, 182, 190, 194, 196–198, 200, 201, 249, 256, 258
Portugal 9–10, 18, 116–117, 121, 124–127, 129, 132, 134–136, 138–139, 143–145, 148–152, 156, 288–290, 293, 298
Portuguese 3, 98–99
- Brazilian Portuguese 283–287, 291, 297, 299, 302
- European Portuguese 9–13, 19, 101–103, 117–125, 127–145, 147–156, 158–160, 162–171, 285–287, 293, 297, 302
- East Timorese Portuguese (East Timor) 18, 281–302
phonetics (phonology) 12–13, 147–151, 155, 157, 159, 161, 163, 165, 166, 167, 169, 170, 245, 246
preposition 15–16, 41, 51, 63, 98, 107, 159, 164, 209, 210, 213, 216, 217, 221, 223, 235, 291
proficiency 18–19, 47, 50, 58, 94, 180, 181, 185–187, 190–191, 195–196, 198, 200–202, 302
pronoun (pronominal) 4–6, 12, 25, 28–34, 40–42, 46–47, 49–52, 55, 62–65, 67, 73, 75, 82, 103–110, 128, 132, 141, 160, 190, 184, 285, 287–288, 293, 295, 297–301
- adverbial pronoun 9, 107, 110
- direct object pronoun 8, 29, 39, 51, 55, 66, 68, 100, 105–106
- indirect object pronoun 29, 32, 62, 72, 105–106, 108
- pronominal system / paradigm 5–6, 8, 26, 28, 30, 32–35, 30, 44, 47–50, 70–72, 75–76, 82, 103, 105–109

– unstressed pronoun 6, 28–29, 48–52, 103
prosody (intonation) 166, 247, 250, 257

Quechua 5, 28, 41, 44–46, 49–50
que-clauses 17, 245–276
quotation (quotative) 17, 196, 245, 249, 251, 252, 253, 260, 261, 274–276

Real Academia Española (RAE) 30, 218
Real Academia Galega (RAG) 152, 153
referential 34, 287
– referential discontinuity 80
– referential persistence 78, 80–82
– referential system 30, 32–33
referent (reference) 7, 26–27, 29, 31, 36, 62–63, 65, 69, 71, 75, 78, 259, 291, 299–300
– animate (referent) 4, 44, 65–66, 70–72, 82, 107
– female (feminine) referent 3, 5, 7, 42, 46, 55, 58, 63, 72–73, 75–76
– human (referent) 3, 40, 51, 68, 70, 73
– inanimate (referent) 4, 6, 65, 67–68, 70, 72
– male (masculine) referent 5, 46, 63, 71–72, 74–75
reflexive (clitic / pronoun) 12, 161, 284, 286, 295
Reintegracionismo (Reintegrationism / reintegrationist) 11–12, 148, 149, 154–157, 159, 160, 162, 168–170
Rexurdimento 153
rural (area) 4, 6, 9, 13, 27, 38–39, 43, 46, 52, 57, 60, 91–93, 109, 124, 150–151, 169–170, 296

scalar / scalarity 221–227, 232, 239, 240
second language acquisition (SLA) 18, 281–283, 295–298, 301–302
social class 13, 57, 92, 170
sociolinguistic(s) 4, 9–10, 13, 20, 30, 34, 42, 50, 90–91, 94, 109, 116, 147, 149, 151, 166, 169, 170, 295
Spain 9–11, 16, 26–27, 30–32, 37, 51, 56–58, 62, 91, 115, 117, 122, 124–126, 129, 134–135, 137, 139–140, 144–145, 148, 150, 155, 166, 222, 245, 248, 272
Spanglish 1, 13–14, 179–204

Spanish 1, 3–17, 25–31, 34–52, 55–58, 60–62, 65–67, 70–72, 75–78, 80–82, 87–110, 115–145, 147–171, 179–204, 209–242, 245–276
– Basque Spanish 4, 7–8, 25–52, 55–82
– Bolivian Highland Spanish 5
– Castilian Spanish 28, 51, 67, 92
– Colombian Spanish (CS) 211
– Chilean Spanish 17, 253, 269, 272, 275, 276
– Ecuadorian Highland Spanish 5, 44–46
– Latin American Spanish 5, 17, 25–26, 44, 48, 51, 246, 248, 253
– Madrilenian Spanish 16–17, 248, 256, 258, 263, 266, 272, 275, 276
– Mexican Spanish (MS) 15–16, 194, 202, 203, 209–242
– Peruvian Highland Spanish 5
– Rioplatense Spanish 17, 246, 256, 271, 272
– Standard Spanish (SS) 15–16, 38, 49, 51, 65, 70, 88, 93, 96, 105, 209, 211, 217, 211, 246
speech community 6, 59, 93, 95
spelling 12, 128, 131, 136, 141, 148, 155, 157, 163 (also spelling)
standardisation (process) 11–12, 56, 149, 150, 152, 169
stativity (state) 30, 39, 209–242, (also verb, stative verb)
subjunctive (future subjunctive) 12, 61, 154, 160, 167, 247, 249, 269
substrate 3, 50, 297–299
superstrate 297–298
suffix 13, 154, 159, 295
syntax 15, 95, 101, 103, 213, 242, 245, 246, 257

telic (telicity) 223, 227, 240, 241
tense 12, 59, 61, 66, 103, 160, 247, 250
– past tense 101–103, 10–109
– perfect tense 101–102, 109
Tetun Dili 283, 284, 288, 291–293, 295, 297, 298
text 4, 10–11, 122–123, 126–127, 129, 131, 136, 138, 143, 164
– borrowed text 120
– bottom–up text 10–11, 122–123, 126–127, 129, 131, 143–145

– guest text 120, 143
– mobile text 118
– private text 126, 131
– public text 126
– shared text 119–121
– stable text 118
– static text 118
– top–down text 10–11, 122–123, 126–127, 143–144
topicalisation 76

United States (U.S.) 1, 179, 181–185, 188–189
unit of analysis 119–120, 122
urban (area) 4, 11, 13, 27, 38–39, 43, 52, 92–93, 109, 125, 131, 152, 167, 169–170

Valencia 88, 90–93, 96
variety (varieties) 1, 3, 5, 7, 9–11, 13–15, 17–18, 26, 32, 34–35, 40–41, 43–44, 50–51, 58, 60, 61, 64, 72, 76–77, 88, 91–96, 102–104, 107, 109, 116, 123, 134, 148–149, 151, 157, 162–163, 165, 169–170, 180–181, 183, 187, 192, 195, 204, 209, 248, 254, 256, 258–259, 263, 266, 272–274, 276, 282–283, 295–302
– contact variety 5, 26–28, 41, 44, 47–49, 51
– diatopic variety 5
– high (or H–)variety 90–93
– hybrid variety 13, 164, 179, 183–184, 188, 192–193, 200
– low (or L–)variety 8, 93
– non-contact variety 55, 60, 76, 81–82
– social variety 88
– standard variety 51, 57, 64, 88, 90, 93, 209, 213, 287
vector space semantics 15, 218, 227, 231, 232–237, 241

vernacular (language / dialect) 18, 88–89, 93–94, 154, 160–162, 187–188, 281, 282, 284, 286, 287, 296, 297, 299, 302
(un)voicing 8, 96
verb 4–6, 9, 13, 15–16, 29, 34–35, 38–39, 41–42, 44, 57, 64, 71, 74, 76–77, 80, 98, 103, 105, 107, 133, 154, 163, 190, 211, 223, 238, 241–242, 249, 253–254, 259, 269, 285, 294–296
– auxiliary verb 42, 70, 82
– copular verb 15, 209, 210, 214–220, 223, 225, 238, 241, 296
– (non–)finite verb 8, 64, 103, 287
– intransitive verb 285
– stative verb 15, 66, 210, 213–218, 226–228, 230, 238, 241
– transitive verb 285, 287
– unaccusative verb 287
Verín 9–11, 115, 124, 135–138, 142–144
Vilar Formoso 9, 11, 115, 119, 124–125, 128–132, 136, 144
Vila Verde da Raia 9, 11, 124–125, 129, 132, 144
vocative 256, 257
vowel 8, 12, 95–96, 98, 151, 155, 161, 162, 165–167
– stressed position 95, 151, 161–162, 165
– unstressed position 95
– vowel reduction 95

word order (constituent order) 77, 81
– object–verb (OV) 5, 7, 64
– verb–object (VO) 64
– subject–object–verb (SOV) 7, 57
– subject–verb–object (SVO) 57

www.ingramcontent.com/pod-product-compliance
Lightning Source LLC
Chambersburg PA
CBHW050515170426
43201CB00013B/1964